INCOMPLETE CONQUESTS

D1594615

INCOMPLETE CONQUESTS

THE LIMITS OF SPANISH EMPIRE IN THE SEVENTEENTH-CENTURY PHILIPPINES

STEPHANIE JOY MAWSON

SOUTHEAST ASIA PROGRAM PUBLICATIONS
AN IMPRINT OF CORNELL UNIVERSITY PRESS
Ithaca and London

First published 2023 by Cornell University Press

Library of Congress Cataloging-in-Publication Data

Names: Mawson, Stephanie Joy, 1984– author.
Title: Incomplete conquests : the limits of Spanish empire in the seventeenth-century Philippines / Stephanie Joy Mawson.
Description: Ithaca : Southeast Asia Program Publications, an imprint of Cornell University Press, 2023. | Includes bibliographical references and index.
Identifiers: LCCN 2022040567 (print) | LCCN 2022040568 (ebook) | ISBN 9781501770265 (hardcover) | ISBN 9781501770272 (paperback) | ISBN 9781501770289 (epub) | ISBN 9781501770296 (pdf)
Subjects: LCSH: Indigenous peoples—Philippines. | Philippines—History—1521–1812. | Philippines—Colonization—History—17th century. | Spain—Colonies—Asia—History—17th century.
Classification: LCC DS674 .M397 2023 (print) | LCC DS674 (ebook) | DDC 959.9/02—dc23/eng /20220923
LC record available at https://lccn.loc.gov/2022040567
LC ebook record available at https://lccn.loc.gov /2022040568

Contents

ILLUSTRATIONS

ACKNOWLEDGMENTS

This book has taken shape over the course of many years, following a personal journey that began with a trip to archives in Mexico City while still an undergraduate and continued across many oceans and continents. Over the course of this journey, I have developed a debt of gratitude to many people whose conversations, assistance, and support shaped my ideas in many ways, large and small, and without whom this book would not exist.

My passion for early modern global history from below was first cultivated while at the University of Sydney, where I was surrounded by academics who encouraged me to develop my ideas and to pursue ambitious topics that took me beyond my comfort zone. Thanks particularly to Frances Clarke, Clare Corbould, Nick Eckstein, Andrew Fitzmaurice, John Gagné, Blanca Tovías, and especially to Mike McDonnell, who supervised both my honors and master's theses and remains a friend and mentor to this day. During my time at Sydney, I was able to travel to archives in Mexico, Spain, and Guam. Special thanks go to Omaira Brunal-Perry of the University of Guam who offered me a warm welcome and helped me navigate my way around the collections at the Micronesian Area Research Center, and to Kevin Atalig and his family for showing me around Rota, an experience that left a lasting impression and shaped my thinking on indigenous history in the Pacific.

Pursuing my doctoral dissertation at the University of Cambridge introduced me to many exciting new conversations about global history. During this time, I was lucky to be supported by several scholarships and grants from the Gates Cambridge Trust, the Royal Historical Society, the Cambridge History Faculty, the Hakluyt Society, and the Vatican Film Library at St. Louis University, which supported research in archives across Spain, the Philippines, and the United States. A four-year postdoctoral fellowship at St John's College, Cambridge following my PhD allowed me the space to write this book and also to travel to the Philippines to conduct nontraditional research in the Cagayan Valley. In Cagayan I was lucky to make a wonderful friend, Ramil Catral, who helped guide me around his home and introduced me to his lovely family; thanks also to Derlyn, Hanani, Romana, and baby Marlyn for sharing our adventures and inviting me into their home. Staff at various museums and libraries were also welcoming and generous with their time, including Lorie O. Malbog of the Cagayan Museum, Jeremy Godofredo Morales and Visitacion Maguddayao at St. Paul University, and Jeff Ordonez at the Isabela Museum and Library. In the Cordillera, Marlon Martin introduced me to the cultural heritage project, Save the Ifugao Rice Terrace movement, as well as the amazing archaeological work that he and Stephen Acabado have conducted on the Kiyyangan rice terraces. Joel Ognayon and Ariel Marc Hambon were excellent guides around the Banaue region, helping also to facilitate a ritual ceremony led by the Mumbaki of their community—an eye-opening experience that gave me rich insights into continued and evolving cultural practices in Ifugao. In Manila, Ricky Trota José and the staff at the Miguel de Benavides Library at the University of Santo Tomas provided friendly and helpful access to their early colonial archival collections.

I will forever be grateful to have found a wonderful doctoral supervisor at Cambridge, Sujit Sivasundaram, who provided careful and considerate feedback and inspired me to extend my intellectual horizons. His support really helped to make my time at Cambridge a manageable and enjoyable experience. Additionally, the regular reading group that he organized among his students and colleagues was immensely helpful. Thanks especially go to Alix Chartrand, Scott Connors, Tamara Fernando, Lachlan Fleetwood, Meg Foster, Emma Gattey, Taushif Kara, Seb Kroupa, Catie Peters, Tom Simpson, Charu Singh, Tom Smith, Kate Stevens, Callie Wilkinson, James Wilson, Adèle Wright, and Hatice Yildiz for their feedback on multiple chapter drafts. This book has also benefited from various conversations, exchanges, and feedback from numerous friends and colleagues, including Tara Alberts, Richard Allen, Andrew Arsan, Christopher Bahl, Isobelle Barrett-Meyering, Mark Philip Bradley, Melissa Calaresu, Natalie Cobo, Bronwen Douglas, Martin Dusinberre, Kristie Flannery, Annabel Teh Gallop, Hans Hägerdal, Tim Harper, Kris Lane, Mary Laven, Ruth Lawlor, Ruth MacKay, Eva Mehl, Christine Moll-Murata, Louise Moschetta, Linda Newson, Oona Paredes, Katie Parker, Irina Pawlowsky, Helen Pfeifer, Maarten Prak, Gabriela Ramos, Anthony Reid, Matthew Restall, Elly Robson, Ricardo Roque, Katherine Roscoe, Matthias van Rossum, Ulinka Rublack, Lynette Russell, Emma Teitelman, Yevan Terrien, Kathryn Ticehurst, Sonia Tycko, Alex Walsham, Birgit Tremml Werner, James Warren, and Chris Wilson.

The editorial staff at Cornell University Press have been exceptionally helpful and patient as I have developed this project; thanks especially to Sarah Grossman and Jacqulyn Teoh for their expert guidance and assistance. Robert Batchelor very generously created an updated version of his interpretation of the Selden

Map for publication in this book. Thanks to Philip Stickler for his expert design of the custom maps, and to Rhiannon Davis for compiling the index.

Writing a book would be a miserable existence were it not for the care of friends and family—especially those who travel across the world to visit homesick antipodeans. There are too many to list, but special thanks to my wonderful family support network of Christine (mum), Emily, Małgosia, Janusz, Cynthia, Gabby, Staszek, Betty, Suzanne, and Brian, and to my dear friend Emma Nicholls for always laughing with me about ridiculous Cambridge customs. The greatest thanks belong to Karol who, as always, read more than anyone, listened the longest, provided much-needed hugs, and took me hiking and camping in the forest when I most needed it. Without him, this journey would have been impossible.

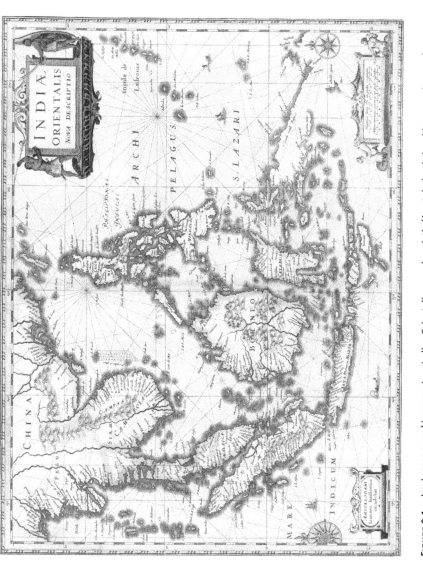

Figure 0.1. Jan Jansson, and Jansson, Jan, *Indiae Orientalis nova descriptio* (Amstelodami: Apud Joannem Janssonium, 1630), National Library of Australia MAP RM 4527.

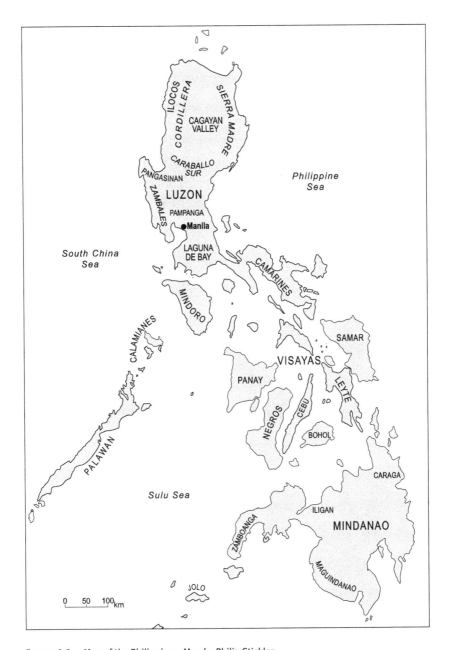

Figure 0.2. Map of the Philippines. Map by Philip Stickler.

INCOMPLETE CONQUESTS

Introduction

In the beginning, before the land was formed, there was just sky and water, and in the space in between, a kite flew continuously. With nowhere to rest, this bird became very tired. One day the kite flew up and told the sky that the sea was planning to rise up so high that it would fill the sky with water. Responding in anger, the sky threatened to throw rocks and islands down to punish the sea. When the kite told the sea of this, she too became very angry and began to throw herself upward with such energy and determination that she filled the sky with water. In fright, the sky retreated higher and began to place very large rocks in the sea, forming the first islands and causing the sea to subside. Finally, the kite had somewhere to land. As he was resting on one of the beaches, the kite noticed a cane being swept by the current of the sea until it knocked against his feet. The kite pecked at the reed, making two holes from which emerged a man and a woman. These were the first people ever to live in the world. The man was called Calaque and the woman Cabaye.[1]

This origin myth was recorded in the Boxer Codex—an anonymous manuscript dating from the late sixteenth century—and tells of the creation of the Visayan archipelago and of the Visayan people.[2] It is just one of many Philippine origin stories that were passed down through song and storytelling and recorded within Philippine folklore.[3] Landscape and the natural world are important features in many of these stories, reflecting the impact that local geographies and environments had on indigenous ontologies. In Mindanao, the Mandaya believed that their ancestors came from two eggs laid and hatched by the limokon bird.[4] They also believed that the anger of the sun caused him to chase the moon and scatter the stars across the sky—accounting for the turn of the months—while the tides were caused by the submarine shuffling of a bad-tempered crab.[5] The Igorot of the Cordillera Mountains in Northern Luzon believed that a Great Spirit named Lumawig fashioned the first people from many reeds, which he placed in pairs in different parts of the world.[6] Elsewhere, Philippine communities spoke of a God who created the earth.[7] In Samar, this God was called Badadum and was responsible for rewarding or punishing people, while another God, Macaobus, was responsible for the end of the world and would send a spirit called Tava as a harbinger of death.[8] Both Spanish chronicles and modern anthropology reveal that every community in the Philippines had their own mythologies and spirits, with their own unique names and narratives.[9] Although united by the common threads of animism and ancestor worship, the cosmology of the pre-Hispanic Philippines was exceedingly diverse. Communities believed that spirits inhabited the natural world that surrounded them, being present in trees and rocks, in birds and animals, and that these spirits could determine the fate of a community.

Colonial histories of the Philippines likewise continue to emphasize the importance of landscape and environment, focusing in particular on the role of the ocean as a conduit of peoples and goods, connecting the mangrove-lined shores of Manila Bay with the bustle of distant ports in Fujian and Acapulco. The crashing of waves amid violent tempests at sea upset these trade links, with broken crates and other debris from shipwrecks washing up on Philippine beaches, reminders of the power of the sea to disrupt as well as connect. Calms at sea were often as disruptive as storms, with the health of crews destroyed by the monotony of a stalled voyage, contributing to long-held colonial visions of the Pacific as "empty space" and the Philippines as a land that lay at the end of the earth. More locally, seas facilitated interisland trade, linking this archipelago of more than seven thousand islands to a larger maritime Southeast Asian world, rich with spices, sea raiders, and trade and migration pathways that extended across the Indian Ocean.

And yet, our perspective on Philippine history shifts if we begin not with the sea that crashed on island shores but within the rising lands that allowed the kite in the above origin myth to finally take his rest. We will begin, then, not in the streets of Intramuros Manila, as is customary, but in the center of the Cagayan Valley, some hundreds of miles to the north. If we stand on the Calvary Hills in the small Cagayan town of Iguig, the landscape unfurls around us in a sweeping panorama that stretches across the rice- and cornfields that dominate the valley. Foothills begin to peek along the western horizon, providing the first hints of the rugged Cordillera mountain range behind them. Much closer to the east lies another set of mountains, the Sierra Madre, now a protected landscape and home to seminomadic Aeta communities. In between these two mountain ranges extends the vast plains of the Cagayan Valley, stretching for over three hundred miles from north to south and connected to the Luzon Strait by the slow meanderings of the Cagayan River, the longest river in all the Philippines.

From this vantage point, it is possible to see these geographies as intimately connected, flowing seamlessly into each other from mountain to valley to river to sea, along the line of sight. Despite this, these places are often disconnected within historical imaginings, as if they were located on two sides of a profound ravine. The mountains of Northern Luzon are the indigenous heartlands of the Philippines, spaces where Igorots, Ifugao, Ilongots, Aeta, and many others brazenly and successfully resisted Spanish colonization for more than three hundred years. They remain places where indigenous peoples continue to assert autonomy from their lowland neighbors, as uplands never colonized, where sovereignty was never ceded.[10] The Cagayan Valley, by contrast, is located within a familiar Spanish colonial story that began in the Visayas in 1565 and ultimately saw the transformation of Philippine lowlands into colonized spaces.[11] The Cagayan River was the conduit for this transformation, bringing missionaries, soldiers, settlers, and trade, while valley plains were devoted to productive rice agriculture and, later on, to extensive tobacco plantations.[12]

This divide between the indigenous uplands and the colonized lowlands has defined Philippine history and preoccupied Philippine historians for more than a century. The rapid and dramatic colonization of the lowlands led the nineteenth-century nationalist revolutionary José Rizal to lament that Filipinos had been transformed by centuries of war, rebellion, and subjugation into mere shadows of their former prosperous and industrious selves.[13] More than a century later, the anthropologist Fenella Cannell has argued that such historical perceptions have influenced how Filipinos view themselves, their history, and their culture. Colonization is seen as having destroyed all that was authentic and distinctive about lowland Filipino culture. She writes that "the recognition that the history of the lowland Philippines has been forcefully shaped by colonialism has been elided with something quite different; an anxious and discouraging notion in both the academic and non-academic literature, that the lowlands was perhaps nothing but the sum of its colonial parts, a culture without authenticity, or else was only to be defined in a series of negatives, by what it had failed to be."[14]

Yet, returning to the Cagayan Valley, evidence for this all-pervasive colonization is surprisingly hard to find: etched into tiny plaques fixed to a small number of eighteenth-century church facades, retold in legends about the miraculous statue of Our Lady of Piat, found among a handful of undated ruins of Spanish-era brickworks and ovens, or, perhaps most evidently, found in the expansive cornfields that are the pride and economic backbone of Isabela Province. An enormous gulf of distance separates this history from the present-day realities of the Cagayan Valley; almost as if this history happened to other people, elsewhere.

And perhaps this is because it was a history that happened to other people. For the Cagayan Valley never fit into this neat divide between the subjugated lowlands and the independent mountains. The anthropologist Felix Keesing described the history of Cagayan as "rendered embarrassingly complex by the escapings of valley peoples" into upland spaces.[15] Time and time again over the course of the seventeenth century, communities of Ibanags, Gaddangs, Isnegs, Kalingas, Itawis, and many others led rebellions against colonization attempts, burning down churches, desecrating religious icons, abandoning Spanish villages, and fleeing into the fastness of the neighboring Cordillera and Sierra Madre mountain ranges. From the vantage point of these mountains, these fugitives, apostates, and rebels continued to attack Spanish settlements, frustrating colonization and evangelization attempts, and delaying the advance of soldiers and missionaries into the southern half of the Cagayan Valley for more than 150 years.[16] Cagayan has consequently often been left out of histories of the colonization of the Philippines: an anomalous place where communities resisted and evaded colonial rule, frustrating the aims of the colonial state and complicating an otherwise uncomplicated narrative of expanding colonial control. And what if Cagayan was not the only part of the archipelago with such a history?

This book starts from this premise: what happens if, rather than focusing on the processes that drove colonization—the ways the colonial state was formed and consolidated and the interests associated with this project—we instead focus on the limitations of the colonial state? How does this change our understanding of the story of colonization? The chapters that follow examine the myriad factors that placed limitations on the establishment and expansion of empire in this Southeast Asian environment. Histories of resistance, flight, evasion, conflict, and warfare are unearthed from across the breadth of this diverse archipelago. The limits of control were a result both of factors internal to the Spanish empire—including a lack of personnel, weak bureaucracies and financial crises, local corruption, imperial overreach, and the contingent accommodation of indigenous elites—as well as of factors that relate explicitly to the nature of Philippine society, including kinship-based social and economic structures, indigenous methods of warfare, and geographic and environmental factors. Crucially, what has sometimes been seen as the inherent weakness of Philippine precolonial society—intense social fragmentation and the lack of any established state-like structures—was in fact a real strength when confronting colonial expansion.

The narrative opens with an account of a rebellion: a moment of crisis that led, over the course of three years, to imperial contraction. Colonial rebellions such as these have at once been adopted as symbols of nationalist pride—often depicted within national monuments—while at the same time interpreted by historians as exceptional moments within an otherwise unbroken history of continuous colonization. Yet such moments also contain within them many of the signs of the quotidian nature of colonial rule: the strengths, the weaknesses, the breaking points that led to ruptures and crises. Chapter 1 challenges us to look beyond the exception to see within accounts of rebellion and resistance indications of the everyday unraveling of colonial authority.

At the same time, we need to be careful when using terms like "rebellion" and "resistance." The Spanish used words like *alzamiento, sublevación, rebelión, levantamiento*—among others—almost interchangeably to talk about very different events, actions, and responses by indigenous communities. Some of these instances—as with the rebellions outlined at the beginning of chapter 1—follow established patterns wherein once-loyal, once-pacified communities genuinely did rebel against colonial authority. But, in many other instances, these terms are less clear cut. The "Sangley revolts" of 1603, 1639, and 1662, for instance, were in reality state-sponsored pogroms of Chinese people. In this instance, the idea of a Chinese "rebellion" is used to justify the extraordinary, violent reaction by Spanish authorities that led to tens of thousands of deaths. Elsewhere, whole regions of the Philippines that were routinely described as "in rebellion"—as in the case of Cagayan—were parts of the archipelago where Spanish sovereignty had never been established or accepted. Spanish soldiers who attempted to collect tribute in such regions were often killed, while missionaries could not travel without armed escorts.

How useful then are terms like rebellion and resistance? Can we really describe the actions of communities who were never subjugated as "resistance?" Focusing on "flash points" like rebellions sometimes leads to overlooking far less dramatic and yet no less important processes, while a focus on the concept of resistance creates a binary between colonizer and colonized leaving little room for moments of cooperation or collaboration.[17] Equally, while granting agency to indigenous peoples, a resistance–dominance framework nevertheless frames all indigenous actions in relation to the actions of colonizers.[18] The archaeologist Lee Panich proposes a persistence framework instead, which "allows us to place colonialism in the long-term context of indigenous histories through the exploration of how native peoples drew on existing yet dynamic cultural values to negotiate the colonial period."[19] Refocusing on indigenous persistence also necessitates a shift away from colonial settlements and sites of colonial domination toward indigenous spaces, viewing the empire from the outside in. This means critically interrogating research agendas that place the colonial state at the center of historical action.

This book adds a further concept to understanding these dynamics: that of limitation. The factor that unites all these actions by disparate communities—whether they were integrated into colonial structures or wholly outside of them, whether they were "accommodating" or "oppositional"—is that they limited colonial rule. Thus, as we chart the limitations of early modern imperial sovereignty, it is important to remember that such limitations were not merely by-products of imperial overreach or weaknesses of the colonial state. They are also determinedly shaped by the actions of indigenous and other non-European actors. As Pekka Hämäläinen argues, indigenous histories of empire need to do more than show "how native peoples countered and coped with colonial expansion. . . . Such an approach reinforces the view of European powers as the principal driving force of history and tends to reduce indigenous actions to mere strategies of subversion and survival."[20] Hämäläinen contends that in many cases the actions of indigenous people mattered more in shaping the course of events than did the actions of Europeans. And so this history of empire's limits is determinedly a Southeast Asian history, driven squarely by fugitives, apostates, and rebels, by Chinese laborers, Moro slave raiders, native priestesses, Aeta headhunters, Pampangan woodcutters, and so many others.

Reexamining Empire in the Philippines

The story of the colonization of the Philippines is by now a familiar one. Europeans first crossed the Pacific in 1521, when Magellan landed in the Philippines after months of drifting across the vast and calm expanse of ocean. Magellan was famously slain by Visayan warriors led by the *datu* Lapulapu, in the Battle of Mactan in April of that year.[21] Despite this initial defeat, the archipelago remained within the sights of Spanish imperial ambitions, as a potential gateway for expansion into Southeast Asian waters with the promise of entry into the lucrative spice trade. After several transpacific voyages over the ensuing decades, eventually a conquering party was sent in 1565. Its leader Miguel López de Legazpi was instructed to establish a permanent Spanish settlement in the islands. In May 1571, Legazpi signed peace treaties with Rajahs

Soliman, Lakandula, and Matanda, establishing the port city of Manila as the center of Spanish power in the archipelago. Ever afterward, the history of the Spanish Philippines was defined by its orientation toward the Pacific.[22] Nearly nine thousand miles of ocean separated the islands from the nearest outpost of the Spanish empire, the Viceroyalty of New Spain. Yet, the Pacific crossing was enduring. Galleons plied Pacific waters between Manila and Acapulco for two and a half centuries, transporting cargoes of Chinese silks to New Spain and bringing back to Manila boatloads of soldiers, missionaries, silver, and much needed supplies to support the Spanish settlement.[23]

According to the standard colonial narrative, following this "relatively bloodless" conquest,[24] the real work of instituting colonial control began. This process was achieved through the combined efforts of missionaries, soldiers, and secular officials, who reduced the native population into *encomiendas*, founded new Spanish settlements, instituted new tribute and labor regimes, erected churches, and baptized and converted *indios* rapidly and efficiently. Within a few short years, reports sent back to Madrid by both religious and secular officials proclaimed the great and rapid success of the conquest. According to Bishop Fr. Domingo de Salazar, by 1588 Luzon boasted a tribute-paying population of 146,700, with hopes of incorporating a further 200,000 once Cagayan was properly pacified. Fr. Salazar believed that all these tribute payers had been converted to Christianity, although he conceded that in these early days few of them had regular access to a priest.[25] By 1593, the Augustinians claimed to have baptized the entire population of Pampanga and reached 55,000 out of 80,000 souls in Ilocos and Pangasinan and 60,000 out of 80,000 souls in Laguna de Bay. The same year, Franciscans had baptized 30,000 people, while the newly arrived Dominicans had reached 14,000 souls.[26] Similarly, by 1601 the Jesuits had baptized up to 12,000 souls in just four years in the Visayas, and they believed they could increase this number to 40,000 very quickly.[27] The conquest proceeded apace. By 1655, nearly half a million Philippine indios were divided into encomiendas and subject to colonial systems of labor and tribute.[28]

While this story is familiar, historians have remained divided over how best to interpret what came next. Following the influential work of John Leddy Phelan, twentieth-century historians took the claims of Spanish missionaries and royal officials at face value, interpreting the sheer numbers of tribute payers and converts to Christianity as evidence of a wholesale and rapid colonization that was largely completed—with minimal opposition—by the end of the seventeenth century.[29] Where some saw this as a benefit to Philippine communities—bringing the Philippines out of "her chaotic, primitive sociopolitical status into a modern, well-organized society"[30]—others argued that the Spanish conquest was "nothing short of catastrophic,"[31] ushering in "a comprehensive program of [Spanish] territorial expansion, economic exploitation, Christian conversion, and cultural change,"[32] and generating "a history of suffering, despair, anguish, and hopelessness of the Filipino people."[33] In this view, the Spanish colonization of the islands was a moment of rupture; ever afterward, the Spanish were the principal agents of change in the archipelago. Echoing Rizal, Nicholas Cushner argued that Filipinos were paralyzed by the wholesale changes wrought by colonization—a paralysis interpreted as laziness or indolence, but which was, in reality, a process of mourning or adaptation to colonial rule.[34]

Filipino historians played a key role in writing the agency of indigenous people back into this history of imperial conquest. Teodoro Agoncillo famously rejected the colonial period altogether, arguing that "Philippine history before 1872 [was] a lost history," since the historical record could only reflect the views and actions of Spanish colonial actors.[35] Agoncillo's words were provocative. His dismissal of the colonial period was a rejection of obviously biased, ideological colonial texts that were produced with the explicit purpose of overexaggerating Spanish claims to sovereignty. Yet his words also acted as a challenge to an emerging generation of historians wishing to reclaim the centuries that came before the rise of the nation state. Inspired by new trends in ethnohistory, Philippine historiography turned in search of what William Henry Scott famously called the "cracks in the parchment curtain" that allowed historians to recover indigenous voices and histories from within colonial archives and to trace cultural continuities as well as indigenous agency within the colonial era.[36]

Following Vicente Rafael's groundbreaking work on translation and Christian conversion, these new histories show the ways in which Philippine culture and knowledge were incorporated into diverse colonial domains, from religion to labor, warfare, and commerce.[37] Taken together, they have added a depth and complexity to our understanding of colonization in the Philippines, disrupting the view of colonization as a rupture by emphasizing the way in which indigenous actors interacted with and shaped the extent and nature of colonial power. At the same time, there is a growing body of literature focused on spaces that remained outside of colonial control, in particular the Cordillera Mountains of Northern Luzon and the Muslim-oriented southern archipelago.[38] It is no longer possible to talk of a completed conquest in the Philippines, as colonial power was diffuse and always mediated via indigenous actors.

And yet, even within this nuanced literature, the colonial state looms large. If no longer the only historical agent, it is nonetheless still the key driver of change, witnessed by the simple fact that most of this new ethnohistorical literature continues to focus on different colonial institutions: the military, the encomienda, religious conversion, the structures of colonial administration, the mechanisms of Spanish global trade and exchange. Some contributions to the discipline have sought to emphasize the strength of Spanish power, casting Philippine indios as either victims of empire—enslaved or killed by Spanish conquistadors—or collaborators with empire—willing participants in the conquest and conversion of other indigenous peoples—without regard for the widespread and ongoing nature of resistance, rebellion, and frontier violence in most parts of the archipelago.[39] Even the development of new theoretical trends that look at uncolonized spaces via the concept of "pericolonialism" expand the influence of the colonial state beyond its immediate spheres of control.[40] At the same time, another trend—reflected within the title of a series of essay collections, *More Hispanic Than We Admit*—has begun to embrace Spanish cultural heritage. Rather than something to be ashamed of, this literature reclaims Spain and Spanish history as the missing piece within Philippine historical identity, thus reversing Agoncillo's critique.[41] Historical interpretations of the colonial period have thus shifted over time from emphasizing rupture and conquest to foregrounding the importance of indigeneity and finally to reembracing Spanish colonial heritage.

Within the pages of this book, I argue that this focus on colonial institutions grants the colonial state a semblance of power, coverage, and scope that it simply did not have. Our view of early modern empires—and of the Spanish empire in particular—has changed substantially over the decades with historians now readily acknowledging limitations and weaknesses in imperial control. Matthew Restall has written about this as a dismantling of the "myth of a completed conquest," or the idea that the Spanish established control rapidly and often with only minimal resistance.[42] The steady dismantling of this myth has involved recovering indigenous voices in the history of empire, to show not just where empire was resisted but the way in which it was shaped by indigenous allies and intermediaries. At the same time, many of the historical sources used to study imperial expansion present an overexaggerated picture of colonial power and territorial control.[43] Maps are the most visually powerful of such sources.[44] Late seventeenth- and early eighteenth-century maps of Cagayan, for instance, depict oversized missionary outposts and garrison towns while eliding the expansive territories that were as yet uncolonized and the tens of thousands of people who lived outside of these neat Spanish settlements, many of which were themselves sites of regular rebellion.[45] Critical engagement with such sources has shifted our interpretation of empire's extent: colonial power operated in a much more nodal fashion. Colonial states had degrees of influence, ranging from areas of complete consolidation to sites of exchange, like trading outposts. Beyond this control were frontier zones where colonial power was contested and zones that remained entirely outside of colonial control.[46] As Lauren Benton has so eloquently put it, "empires did not cover space evenly but composed a fabric that was full of holes, stitched together out of pieces, a tangle of strings."[47]

While claims to territorial sovereignty are often most clearly inscribed into maps, in the Philippines this process of claiming sovereignty was much more frequently represented through the number of souls converted to Christianity and tributes added to an encomienda. As we have already seen, missionaries and colonial administrators claimed rapid and stunning successes, transforming hundreds of thousands of Philippine indios into Christian converts and tribute-paying subjects of the Crown in just a few short years. These claims have formed the backbone of the image of a rapid spread of colonial domination of Philippine lowlands. Yet, as with cartographic depictions of colonial control, such claims formed part of the process of constructing an imagined imperial sovereignty and were a common feature of Spanish colonial efforts across the empire.[48]

While church historians in the Philippines have been eager to accept the claims made by missionaries,[49] the archival record itself is full of evidence that casts doubt over the success of conversion and colonization. Throughout the seventeenth century, missionaries lamented the lack of constancy among Philippine indios, who would attend mass with varying degrees of willingness and cajoling but afterward return to their settlements and continue to practice traditional religious customs. In regions further outside of colonial control, communities would agree to convert, accepting missionaries and tribute collectors into their midst for a short time, before leading an often-violent rebellion and abandoning newly founded Spanish settlements in favor of their own autonomy. Missionaries and tribute collectors were regularly killed, churches were burnt down, and whole settlements abandoned as indios escaped into the mountains. In some instances, this reversal of colonial fortunes lasted for many decades or, in the case of places like Apayao, were more or less permanent. By the eighteenth century, substantial areas remained not only outside of Spanish control, but also beyond the limits of Spanish geographic knowledge. Exploration and encounter were still occurring well into the eighteenth century, particularly in regions like Nueva Ecija and Nueva Vizcaya.

To some extent, the problems of consolidating claims to colonial sovereignty may have been even greater in the Philippines than in other parts of the empire. The demographic imbalance between Spaniards and Philippine communities was stark. Although demographic data for the Spanish population is hard to find, for much of the seventeenth century the colonial population hovered around 2,000, by comparison to an estimated initial population of 1.4 million in Luzon and the Visayas.[50] Petitions and complaints about chronic shortages in soldiers, sailors, missionaries, and other critical personnel are among the most common documents within Philippine colonial archives.

Unlike other colonial frontiers, the Philippines also had the additional pressures of distance from the rest of the empire and a reliance on the vagaries of the transpacific galleon route, which rendered the Spanish colony extremely precarious in the seventeenth century. The Manila galleons are famous in the annals of global history for facilitating a globalized trade in silk and silver. Yet they were also the lifeline of the colony, bringing in all material and financial supplies as well as replenishing the numbers of soldiers, missionaries, merchants, and royal officials needed for the colony to function and survive. Just one shipwreck or another kind of disruption to the regular dispatch of the galleons could have dire consequences for these supply lines. At the same time, the dangers of the transpacific crossing and the perception among many Spaniards that the Philippines lay "at the ends of the earth"—a place from which many soldiers and missionaries never returned—meant that there were seldom sufficient volunteers to meet the needs of the colony.[51] Combined with crippling debts and a lack of silver to pay them, these limitations are extraordinarily relevant when critically evaluating claims to colonial control. Colonial rule in the seventeenth-century Philippines begins to look much more like Benton's description of early modern colonial settlements as "enclaves such as missions, trading posts, towns, and garrisons . . . strung like beads along interconnected corridors."[52]

Moreover, colonial order began to fray and recede within colonial outposts that were beyond the center of imperial or viceregal power. In such spaces "the ordinary rules of law, jurisprudence, and royal oversight collapsed in the entropy of decentralization."[53] Importantly, this fraying of order was not simply a by-product of a peripheral existence; rather, it was an essential part of colonial rule, resulting from diffuse forms of authority and power instituted by the largely private enterprise of the conquistador class, the intrinsic reliance of administrators on local political interests, and the competing corporate groups behind Christian conversion. In short, the actions of agents of empire within local settings were more often explained by individual concerns and interests than by imperial policy or ideology. In the pages that follow, we trace priests and military officers who pursued their own interests, often undermining the process of colonization within local communities and at times facilitating processes of evasion and resistance. For example, military officers in Cagayan were embroiled in illegal trading networks that funneled Spanish supplies into uncontrolled hinterlands, making these autonomous communities all the more viable while opening a channel for arms to be brought into the mountains and later used against Spanish soldiers. Similarly, priests exploited local communities—particularly engaging in largely nonconsensual sexual liaisons with indigenous women—directly undermining their conversion efforts. The most powerful example of this disparity between imperial objectives and legal frameworks and the on-the-ground political realities, however, is the debate over the abolition of indigenous slavery. In this example, imperial reformers found themselves undermined and even subject to persecution particularly by the religious orders who, by the second half of the century, were intent on upholding the status quo.

Acknowledging the inherent weaknesses of Europeans in imperial spaces, historians have pointed out that colonial power often rested on indigenous intermediaries and allies.[54] Where there were shortfalls in colonial power or authority, these were often made up through strategic alliances with indigenous elites or even whole communities like the Tlaxcalans, who allied themselves with Cortes and helped him conquer Tenochtitlán in Mexico.[55] In the Philippines this was also the case. The Spanish were reliant particularly on the Pampangans to help supplement their meager military forces.[56] Most of the labor of the colony was provided through levies of local communities. Indigenous guides led expeditions of exploration and conquest, often accompanied by large forces of indigenous soldiers. Beyond the role of indigenous allies and intermediaries, the Spanish colony in the Philippines relied on the participation of Chinese merchants and laborers. The city of Manila—the center of Spanish colonial authority—was only able to function with the labor, goods, and services supplied by the Chinese community, so much so that Chinese merchants and laborers came to control every aspect of the city's economy—including the domestic supply of silver. This was a consistent source of tension for colonial authorities, creating a paranoia that led to some of the most violent massacres in the history of the Spanish empire.

At the same time, reliance on indigenous allies as agents of empire should not be overstated. The terminology of indigenous allies itself may grant too much agency to the colonizers by suggesting that indigenous people allied themselves to the Spanish and not the other way around.[57] Equally, the corollary of indigenous participation in the construction and consolidation of empire was that the very same participants could easily subvert the rules of colonial society. In Jane Burbank and Frederick Cooper's words, "successful empires produced . . . neither consistent loyalty nor constant resistance: they produced contingent accommodation."[58] So contingent was this accommodation in the seventeenth-century Philippines, that the majority of rebellions against colonial rule were led by one-time allies of the Spanish, many of whom had been promoted into positions of colonial authority. The leader of the 1661 rebellion in Pangasinan, Don Andrés Malong, was even awarded an encomienda—a privilege reserved only for the most loyal of indigenous servants—by the Council of Indies in Madrid. Thanks to the tyranny of distance, the Council remained unaware that at the very moment they were approving this award, Malong's headless body was swinging from a hook after he was shot for treason by authorities in the Philippines.[59]

Empire was limited not merely because of the corrupt or floundering structures inherent to the colonial state; indigenous agency was vital in defining the limits of empire. A full appreciation of pre-Hispanic indigenous culture, social relations, and economies is therefore vital for understanding just how indigenous peoples shaped the scope of empire. Despite this, the characteristics of pre-Hispanic Philippine society have sometimes led Southeast Asian historians to make assumptions about the ease of colonization in the archipelago.[60] And yet, in the pages that follow, we will come to see that the social structure of the Philippines was in fact the single most defining factor that limited—rather than facilitated—Spanish colonization. Empire expanded in spaces with preexisting state structures, where colonial rule could interact with existing methods of tribute and labor extraction, and authority could operate via indigenous intermediaries who became allies of the new colonial regime. Where such structures did not exist—particularly among semi- and nonsedentary communities—the colonial project often floundered.[61]

The Limits of Colonial Control

Pre-Hispanic Philippine society was highly fragmented and dispersed. Philippine communities were typically organized as local kinship-based groups. Communities known as *barangays* normally encompassed around a hundred families, although some larger communities of up to a thousand people have been recorded.[62] In 1565, the population of Luzon and the Visayas is estimated at 1.4 million.[63] Pre-Hispanic barangays were thus numerous and occupied a diversity of geographies, from the rugged mountains of Northern Luzon to the fertile plains of Cagayan, Pampanga, and Laguna de Bay, from the maritime world of the Visayan archipelago to the estuaries, swamps, and mountains of Mindanao. It is thus unsurprising that Philippine animistic belief systems reflected a close connection to specific places and landscapes, creating a seemingly infinite panoply of spirits that was as diverse as the number of barangays in the archipelago. The spirit world was etched into the landscape that surrounded each community and formed a part of self-identity and a connection between the past and the present.

Most barangays subsisted on a mix of agriculture, hunting, and gathering, and settlements were often scattered into distant or isolated hamlets.[64] Early descriptions of Spanish explorations often described abandoned villages, suggesting that communities moved from place to place throughout the year.[65] In addition to subsistence patterns, a number of specific geographic factors contributed to the scattered nature of Philippine settlements. In 1575, the Franciscan missionary Juan de Plasencia noted that intergroup warfare had a major impact on where communities were willing to settle and which land they wished to farm. Periodic conflict compelled many to flee into the mountains to escape violence or warfare.[66] This situation was most pronounced in the Visayas, where annual incursions by slave raiders regularly drove communities into the hills to avoid being captured or slaughtered.[67]

In sum, communities were largely kinship based and bound together by bonds of mutual obligation that structured social hierarchies and underpinned local authority. Colonial authorities had to contend with this context when attempting to impose new colonial systems of tribute, labor, and religious conversion. Spanish missionaries and tribute collectors faced a very practical logistical problem: how to have regular and consistent interaction with large populations sparsely settled over vast tracts of territory. They developed two key strategies for overcoming this problem. The first was the reduction of indios into larger towns, where a church could be built and missionaries could better work on conversion and ministering to communities. The second was the introduction of a rice-based taxation system which compelled communities to produce surplus rice for the colonial state. Both strategies were unevenly applied and resulted in differing levels of success, reliant often on the numbers of missionaries and soldiers available, their ability to maintain a consistent presence in a particular location, and their willingness to resort to methods of coercion and violence. The unevenness of these colonization methods contributed toward the patchy and nodal presence of the colonial state: for every successful town established, there lay vast areas of land outside of colonial control, hosting populations of people who refused to shift into or actively abandoned newly established settlements.

Neither can we conclude that Spanish military prowess helped to overcome these problems.[68] The Spanish military presence was weak and heavily reliant on unfree labor—both in the form of convict and otherwise coerced recruits from New Spain and often forcibly recruited indigenous soldiers.[69] Spanish officials continually struggled to adequately garrison key military outposts that were essential for defending the islands against external threats such as Dutch or Moro raids, leaving few military resources for responding to the myriad problems experienced within the provinces. The seventeenth century therefore presents a history of constantly competing needs, where underresourced companies of soldiers were shunted around the archipelago from crisis to crisis, rarely staying long enough in one location and often, in the process, dying in significant numbers from local pathogens.[70] Supplies of munitions and armor were also meager; in one battle in Mindanao, Captain Juan Ronquillo was forced to withdraw because his soldiers ran out of gunpowder.[71] More often than not, Spanish soldiers were easily outmaneuvered by seminomadic communities who used their superior knowledge of local ecologies and geographies to their tactical advantage. In such contexts, the arquebus proved of limited use against the bow and arrow or the headhunter's *bolo*. Spanish naval defenses were similarly consistently outpaced by the light and quickly maneuverable *caracoas* used by Maguindanao and Sulu slave raiders. As the century wore on, military commanders began to recognize these limitations, objecting to the proposed military offensives so often advocated for by the religious orders within uncontrolled territories like the Cagayan Valley.

Violence is thus an enduring feature of the history that follows. As David Weber notes, the edges of empires—often described by colonizers as borderlands or frontiers—experienced greater episodes of violence than those areas already under control, thanks particularly to a more even balance of power between colonial forces and indigenous communities.[72] But it would be wrong to conclude that, just because contact between indigenous and European communities engendered violence, that violence was an essentialized part of pre-Hispanic Philippine society and culture, while Europeans somehow attained the status of peaceful and impartial arbiters.[73] For every account of a priest whose head was severed by a headhunter, we can equally furnish an example of Spanish violence in the form of whippings, beatings, rape, and slaughter. Where indigenous communities displayed heads as trophies, Spaniards scattered body parts along roads as a warning of future punishments.[74] During the 1639 massacre of the Chinese, royal officials paid rewards for every severed head that was delivered to them.[75]

Throughout this period, Europeans debated the appropriate use of violence, with notable tensions emerging between official imperial policy—which promoted peaceful conquest and conversion—and local, on-the-ground realities where violence was often the only resource available to Spaniards when confronted with their own limitations and weaknesses. At the same time, the oft-cited truism that missionaries were the defenders of peace and protectors of indigenous peoples falls away once we discover that missionaries were not only often the main perpetrators of violence within communities, but also the greatest advocates of military interventions, indigenous slavery, and retaliatory raids. If only European violence is interpreted as political and strategic, we risk relegating indigenous people to the role of victims, downplaying their capacity to assert their own forms of sovereignty in the face of colonial conquest. Indigenous communities used violence both defensively and strategically; where raids on colonial settlements were clearly designed as disruptive tactics, violent attacks on missionaries often preceded the preferred strategy of flight away from colonial authority.

Equally, we need to take seriously the widespread nature of evasion and abandonment as deliberate choices and actions.[76] The records relating to flight indicate that the porous boundaries of colonial control existed everywhere throughout the islands. James Scott has famously written about the phenomenon of what he calls "nonstate spaces" that formed in the uplands of mainland Southeast Asia. Communities wishing to evade the burden of the state—particularly in the form of grain-based taxation systems—would move into areas traditionally seen as harder to cultivate and where rugged geography frustrated the construction of state infrastructure like roads or shipping routes along navigable waterways.[77] The presence of nonstate spaces made them attractive for anyone wishing to flee or evade oppressive social relations. We see many of the same patterns in the seventeenth-century Philippines, with colonial archives filled with reports of *indios cimarrones*, apostates, and fugitives living in the *montes*—a vague term used to describe wooded and hilly terrain that lay outside of colonial control. Tribute numbers were depleted substantially in many core centers of Spanish control like Pampanga as people simply moved away to neighboring areas not subject to the colonial state. From these upland sites, communities used headhunting, raiding, rebellion, alliance building, and open warfare to frustrate, halt, and even reverse colonial expansion.[78]

Such actions have been documented across a wide expanse of the Spanish empire, suggesting that flight and evasion were common responses to colonization and that these limitations of colonial control over both peoples and territories are in fact prevailing features of Spanish imperial history.[79] Crucially, however, the geographic composition of the Philippines shows that while upland spaces were an important element to this story—and one that increased in importance in the centuries that followed—they were not the only places where it was possible to live beyond colonial control. The patchwork nature of Spanish sovereignty in the seventeenth-century Philippines meant that not all *montes* were mountains but could also refer to any region where Spanish geographic knowledge ceased to be reliable.

Responding to the polarization between Philippine upland and lowland spaces, the historian Oona Paredes and the archaeologist Stephen Acabado have put forward the concept of pericolonialism, which suggests that the impact of colonization could be felt even within areas that remained outside of colonial control.[80] While colonial sovereignty was limited, uneven, and patchy, colonization nevertheless had substantial impacts on the way societies functioned and the way Philippine communities interacted with each other.

Yet we might also turn this concept of pericolonialism on its head: just as colonization impacted uncolonized spaces, so too did the uncolonized have an impact on colonized spaces. By virtue of existing and even thriving outside colonial rule, such spaces fueled resistance to colonization elsewhere. The example of the Cagayan Valley is illustrative. From the late sixteenth century onward, Cagayan was the site of ongoing and extensive rebellion against colonial rule. Communities periodically set fire to churches and villages and fled into the mountains. Their actions successfully halted the advance of the colonial frontier at the foothills of the mountains. The territorial boundaries of Spanish sovereignty were thus defined by the agency of Philippine communities, who resisted incorporation into colonial settlements through evasion and flight, warfare, rebellion, raiding, and killing. Frontiers were rendered porous, intangible, uncontrolled. The Spanish found it virtually impossible to claim sovereignty over people they rarely saw and who refused to be reduced into larger settlements.

Spanish control was thus constantly contested, confined territorially, and much smaller than imperial claims suggest. Combined, the chapters that follow tell the complex story of how, after more than a century of Spanish claims to colonial sovereignty over the Philippines, by the end of the seventeenth century they maintained only a tenuous position in the archipelago, with their power restricted to very specific regions of influence. The actions of Philippine communities defined the limits of empire territorially, economically, spiritually, and militarily.

CHAPTER 1

A Moment of Crisis, 1660–1663

When Sabiniano Manrique de Lara disembarked in Cavite in July 1653 to take up his position as governor of the Philippines, he found the Spanish colony in a desperate way. Manila lay in ruins, still covered in dust and debris following the devastating earthquake of 1645. He wrote later that the city looked more like it was inhabited by wild animals than part of a republic of men. As he soon discovered, this ruin was more than just superficial; it extended into the heart of the military and political life of the colony. Manrique de Lara's predecessor, Don Diego Fajardo, was widely seen as a weak governor who had allowed control of the colony to pass to the military commander, Manuel Estacio Venegas, who used his position to seek out wealth and power. Venegas had set about imprisoning and exiling all of his opponents so that, by 1653, the city's jails were filled with Manila's wealthiest and most influential citizens—those who had refused to support Venegas's grab for power—leaving many of the vital offices of government vacant. At the same time, the royal treasury was in a dire state. The islands were ever reliant on yearly dispatches of money and other supplies from New Spain but, over the previous decade, these dispatches had fallen vastly short of what was needed. Some years the galleons had not arrived at all. By the time Manrique de Lara reached Manila, the royal treasury had more than a million pesos in debt, not including another half a million in unpaid wages owed to the soldiers stationed across the archipelago. A sizable amount of this debt was owed to indigenous communities who were tasked with provisioning the royal ware-houses and the presidios with rice and other supplies, but who had received nothing in return for these goods for nearly two decades. To make matters worse, the would-be governor Venegas had stolen money from the Crown and had illegally requisitioned the unfree labor of Pampangans and convicts to build himself a sumptuous palace while the real governor was housed in a small wooden shack amid the rubble of the struggling city.[1]

Taking stock of all of this, Manrique de Lara set to work. Although he com-plained of failing health, he took his new appointment as governor seriously and promised to quickly restore the colony to a state of order by balancing the finances of the royal treasury and repairing the Crown's relationships both with indigenous communities and the soldiers that served in the archipelago. Yet, in the space of a decade, these first signs of unsteady colonial governance had expanded into a full-scale crisis that extended into almost every corner of the Spanish colonial project in the Philippines, shaking the very foundations of imperial sovereignty in the archipelago. Over just a few short years—between 1660 and 1663—once-loyal indigenous allies mutinied and rebellion spread out across most of Luzon, the Chinese warlord Koxinga threatened Ma-nila with invasion, slave raiders attacked Visayan outposts, and the Spanish were forced to withdraw almost completely from the southern archipelago, marking the greatest contraction of territorial control that the Spanish ever experienced in the Philippines.

The multiple shocks that rocked the Philippines between 1660 and 1663 are widely regarded as an exceptional moment of crisis for Spanish colonization.[2] And yet, when read against a backdrop of weak and contested power, these events begin to seem more inevitable than exceptional. Buried within the course of events, we can begin to trace the limits of Spanish control from mul-tiple angles: By the 1660s, the colony was crippled by debt, unable to pay the wages of its soldiers or for the labor of its indigenous allies. The galleon trade had ground to a halt and supplies were not forthcoming. The military was weak and overstretched, reliant on convicts, underaged boys, and elderly or crippled men to fill the shortfalls in reinforcements. The rise of powerful Mus-lim sultanates—combined with Dutch advances in the neighboring Spice Islands—represented an almost unassailable challenge to these depleted forces. At the same time, alliances with indigenous communities began to disinte-grate, as once-loyal allies mutinied against unpaid wages and then took the opportunity to pursue a full-scale rebellion aimed at ejecting the Spanish alto-gether. In Manila, Spanish control was challenged by the economic power of the local Chinese community that boomed off the back of migrations from Fujian. In the 1660s, these multiple challenges came together all at once to bring the colony almost to breaking point. Yet, as the chapters that follow demonstrate, this moment of crisis is emblematic of the nature of colonial control throughout the seventeenth century.

Labor Rebellions in Pampanga

The first rumblings of this looming crisis were felt toward the end of 1660. In the logging camp near Mount Malasimbo, to the northwest of Manila, a contingent of more than 1,000 mostly Pampangan laborers were cutting wood to be used in the Cavite shipyards. At the start of October, 330 of these Pampangans mutinied. Downing their tools, they took up arms, set fire to the camp, and elected the indigenous *maestre de campo*, Don Francisco Maniago, as the leader of their rebellion. The mutineers then marched to the town of Lubao in Pampanga, where they gathered strength and support for their rebellion. A smaller contingent was stationed in Bacolor to blockade the main waterways into Pampanga. News of these events spread rapidly across the province and communications were dispatched to the neighboring provinces of Pangasinan and Ilocos to encourage communities there to join. Meanwhile, the mutineers set up blockades along all the major waterways of Pampanga to block trade from coming in or out of the province.[3]

This mutiny began as a labor dispute. In addition to paying annual tribute, indigenous communities that accepted Spanish sovereignty were expected to labor for the Crown. Colonial labor regimes fell broadly under two key systems—the *repartimiento* and *bandala*—both of which were designed by imperial authorities in Madrid as paid, free-waged labor systems, but that inevitably functioned much more like forced labor and were rarely ever paid. These two systems were essential for the survival of the Spanish colonial regime since they fulfilled the vast majority of Spanish labor needs in the archipelago. The repartimiento was essentially a labor draft, where indios were recruited to work on particular projects, primarily to support shipbuilding activities. Indios consequently worked as woodcutters, shipbuilders, dockyard workers, construction workers, as oarsmen and sailors in galleys and other ships, as ropemakers, foundry workers, carpenters, knife grinders, blacksmiths, stonemasons, tailors, and porters among many other things. Additionally, the repartimiento was used to recruit indigenous soldiers to participate in missions of pacification or defense. By contrast, the bandala was designed as a means of ensuring the Spanish population was adequately provisioned and allowed the Crown to requisition agricultural products, especially rice, to feed the population of Manila and the garrisons of soldiers stationed across the archipelago.[4] Investigations into the bandala conducted in the 1650s by the attorney Juan de Bolivar y Cruz indicate that communities were allocated quotas of particular supplies that they were obliged to provide each year.[5]

While all of this labor was supposedly freely contracted in exchange for wages, in reality indios were rarely paid. Decades of insufficient financial aid meant that by 1660 the royal treasury in Manila was experiencing crippling debt and indigenous laborers were just one of a number of groups who regularly went unpaid.[6] Fed up with harsh and exploitative conditions, many indios fled into uncolonized upland spaces, while others were forced to sell themselves into slavery to meet their labor obligations.[7]

The mutiny of woodcutters in 1660 was all the more serious for Spanish control because of the prominent place that the province of Pampanga occupied within the colonial landscape. The general nature of documents relating to colonial labor regimes gives the impression that these institutions were applied equally across all regions of the Philippines. Yet, if we attempt to sketch a geography of colonial labor, we find that particular provinces are overrepresented, while others are virtually never mentioned.[8] The provinces of Pampanga, Laguna de Bay, and Camarines all emerge as common sources of repartimiento and bandala labor.[9] Where financial debts were recorded as being owed by the Crown for the labor communities provided under the repartimiento and bandala, they were always highest in Pampanga.[10] In part, the reliance on the Pampangan region was environmental as well as geographic. Pampanga was extremely fertile and produced a large amount of rice each year that helped supply the royal warehouses, while interconnected river systems made transporting food and other products relatively easy. The province also contained forests of timber appropriate for shipbuilding.[11]

The relationship between Spanish society and Pampanga went deeper than this, however. The datus of Pampanga were among the first indigenous elites to welcome the Spanish into the islands in the 1570s, and their acceptance of the Spanish presence in Manila was so complete that, by 1574, they came out in force to help defend the Spanish settlement against the Chinese pirate, Limahong.[12] Early in the seventeenth century, Pampangans were praised for their support of the Spanish side during the Chinese uprising of 1603, with the castellan of Fort Santiago describing them as a "people of great spirit."[13] Above all other indigenous groups, Pampangan *principales* were frequently granted rewards for their service to the Spanish Crown, including encomiendas and land grants that recognized their position of local authority within the most important province in the Philippines.[14]

The loyalty of the Pampangan elites to the Spanish Crown nonetheless resulted in an overburdening of local Pampangan communities. Pampangans were overrepresented in every aspect of indigenous labor—they provided the most rice under the bandala system, they conducted the majority of wood-cutting and provided laborers for the shipyards in Cavite and elsewhere, and they enlisted in large numbers in the military with companies of Pampangan soldiers stationed across the majority of Spanish presidios in the archipelago, as well as in the Maluku Islands (1606–1663), Taiwan (1626–1642), and the Marianas Islands (from 1667).[15] That the Spanish authorities in Manila pushed the Pampangans to breaking point reflects the fact that many other provinces in the archipelago were much more volatile and could not be relied on to provide the labor needed to support the mercantile and defensive needs of the Spanish population. Indeed, the overburdening of Pampanga was long recognized by royal officials; but attempts to share the responsibility for the labor needs of the colony only resulted in resistance and rebellion from other communities. For example, in 1649, authorities attempted to draft labor from the Visayas for a major shipbuilding enterprise in the port of Cavite. The Visayans were outraged at being forcefully uprooted from their communities and a major rebellion emerged, starting in Samar and extending across the provinces of Camarines, Masbate, Cebu, Leyte, Caraga, and Iligan. This rebellion took a year to subdue.[16] Officials did not attempt labor levies on such a scale in the Visayas again.

The reliance of the Crown on Pampanga was thus as much a reflection of the weakness of their control in other parts of the archipelago. The Spanish did not have the control needed to impose labor drafts where the Spanish population was weak and largely reliant on missionaries for the imposition of colonial authority. Over the course of the century, the Spanish increasingly came to rely heavily on Pampangan elites and their vassals to fulfill the military and labor needs of the state. Outside of this region, loyalty among indigenous elites always remained less certain.

Many Spanish officials were well aware that without the Pampangans the Spanish settlement in the Philippines would surely falter. Yet this dependence also came at a price. When the Pampangan laborers mutinied in October 1660, their demands included a claim of nearly twenty years of unpaid wages totaling more than 300,000 pesos. Moreover, royal officials in Manila were well aware of the extent of this debt, but without further aid from New Spain they claimed to be powerless to do anything about it.[17] In 1658, the attorney Juan de Bolivar y Cruz attempted to warn the treasury about the consequences of these unpaid wages. In response, the treasury in Manila prevaricated for some time, claiming that it had not received Bolivar y Cruz's petitions and then later stating that the amount of debt owed was unknown.[18] The mutiny that started in the forests of Pampanga and turned into a widespread, armed rebellion was thus a mobilization of last resort by a desperate people. The injustice they struggled against was not only the beatings and abuses they experienced at the hands of the men overseeing the woodcutting, but also the fact that they were asked to labor relentlessly, year in and year out, as woodcutters, shipbuilders, dockyard workers, soldiers, and sailors with only the promise of an elusive future payment in wages.

The Pampanga rebellion represents a moment when the most loyal of indigenous allies turned to disobedience and for this brief time their integration with Spanish society became their most powerful weapon.[19] Their prominence within the Spanish military meant that they were experienced in and knowledgeable of Spanish methods of warfare. As the chronicler Casimiro Diaz noted, the Pampangans were known as "the most warlike and prominent people of these islands," and their rebellion "was all the worse because these people had been trained in the military art in our own schools, in the fortified posts of Ternate, Zamboanga, Jolo, Caraga and other places where their valor was well known."[20]

When word of the rebellion reached Manila, Governor Manrique de Lara looked for a quick and peaceful settlement to these events. He traveled with twelve military officers and three hundred soldiers to the province with the intention of issuing a general amnesty. Sailing up Pampanga's waterways, Manrique de Lara's soldiers removed the stakes that blocked their entrance into the territory one by one, arriving finally in Macabebe where the governor established a base for his army. From there, he sent word to a long-standing indigenous ally of the Spanish, Don Juan Macapagal, asking him to pledge allegiance to the Spanish cause and to establish another military outpost in his town of Arayat, further inland along the route to Pangasinan. Macapagal immediately responded by declaring his support for Manrique de Lara, thus providing the Spanish army with a secure base within the province.

Once this was done, Manrique de Lara prepared to negotiate with Maniago, the rebel leader, who remained in Bacolor surrounded by his armed supporters. The governor sent two generals with the terms of a settlement that included the payment of 14,000 pesos out of the 300,000 the Pampangans were owed, pardoning them from supplying rice to the Crown for that year, and publishing decrees that any indio engaged as a sailor, shipbuilder, woodcutter, or soldier should be paid for their labor. In addition, Manrique de Lara acknowledged the need to remedy the rampant exploitation that Pampangans suffered across these varied labors. Within the woodcutting expeditions, he agreed that overseers should be instructed that all work should cease at night and that those who were sick were to be allowed to leave the forest. The collection of tribute and the requisitioning of goods were to be conducted without

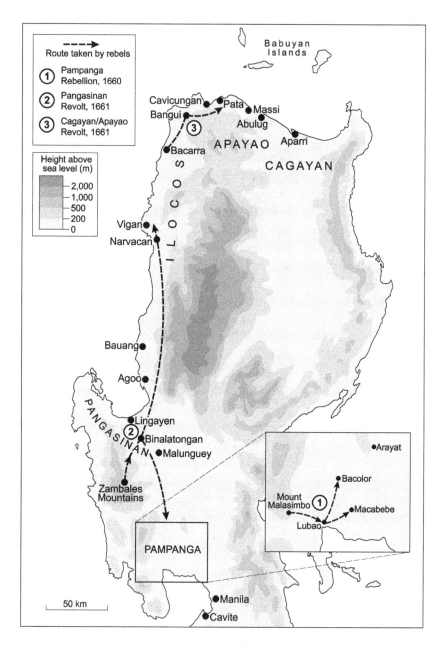

Figure 1.1. Sites of rebellion, 1660–1661. Map by Philip Stickler.

extortion by local officials and the treasury was to pay their debts for the use of indigenous labor on an annual basis. Finally, Manrique de Lara instructed that Pampangan soldiers should be treated as equals to their Spanish counterparts, "without being subject to vile occupations."[21]

The generosity of this proposed settlement reflected how seriously the governor took the threat posed by his once-loyal allies. Maniago agreed to Manrique de Lara's terms of settlement in full and for a moment it seemed as if the rebellion had ended. A celebration took place across Pampangan villages throughout the afternoon and evening following Maniago's concession, but by eleven o'clock that night the celebration turned suddenly into turmoil. The Pampangan rebels took Maniago prisoner as a traitor to their cause, elected themselves a new leader, Don Nicolás Manuit, and took up their weapons and returned to their posts, effectively locking down the town. Both the archival sources and the later chronicles of the rebellion concur that the reason for the continued rebellion was a misunderstanding by the rebels as to the contents of the governor's concession. Yet, Manuit also declared outright war against the Spanish and ordered the flight of his supporters into the mountains, suggesting that there was more to the rebels' intentions than the sources make clear.

Manrique de Lara responded quickly to this turn of events. According to Casimiro Diaz, the governor "knew that the most suitable means of securing an honorable peace is to make more formidable the preparations of war."[22] Calling his army together, he sent them to occupy three strategic locations across the province. One group marched into the nearby mountains, cutting off this handy retreat, while another traveled by boat to prevent any possible retreat upriver. At the same time, Don Juan Macapagal was called on to reinforce the town of Arayat, which was located on the road out of Pampanga to Pangasinan, thus preventing any rebels from leaving or other supplies from coming into the province. Undeterred, Manuit and his followers armed themselves and sailed in eighty vessels to the village of Macabebe at one in the morning to confront the governor in person. This renewed show of force unnerved the Spanish military officials; however, the meeting between the two sides also presented an opportunity for the governor to properly explain the terms of his amnesty. The rebels in turn asked the governor for a new pardon that exempted them from other burdens, including the payment of tribute. Manrique de Lara agreed to this new demand and the mutiny was finally brought to a conclusion. Spanish soldiers returned to Manila, the Pampangan mutineers dispersed back to their homes to tend their fields, and all remained quiet.

Yet, whispers of rebellion continued to echo in the provinces of Northern Luzon. It was not long before the second and more overtly anticolonial wave of uprisings broke out.

Escalation in Northern Luzon

The dissensions that broke out in response to Maniago's acceptance of Manrique de Lara's amnesty were representative of a deep-rooted unease among the communities of Luzon toward their alliance with Spain. Over the next two months, the whispers of rebellion spread quietly northward and into the neighboring provinces of Pangasinan and Ilocos "through the hidden passage of the intercourse between villages."[23] At first, this second wave of rebellion was limited to small and isolated outbursts in the towns of Pangasinan; however one such instance in Binalatonga on December 12, 1660 sparked the launch of widespread rebellion across Northern Luzon.[24] On this day the townspeople of Binalatonga seized arms and elected Don Andrés Malong as their leader. Proclaiming that they would no longer pay tribute or participate in Spanish labor regimes, the rebels marched on Lingayen and killed the local *alguacil mayor*, the *alcalde mayor* and his wife, and up to twenty other Spaniards, including some soldiers who were stationed in the region. They then sacked and burned the church. Very quickly many thousands of indios rallied to join Malong's rebellion, and he dispatched an army of two thousand to reignite the rebellion in Pampanga and another three thousand to head north into Ilocos, reserving two thousand for his own defense. Malong then took the radical step of declaring independence from Spain and crowned himself King of Pangasinan.[25]

Often seen as a radical extension of the Pampanga rebellion, the events in Pangasinan were made possible by the seditious space opened up by the Pampangan rebels. The porous borders of the provinces of Northern Luzon meant that any Pampangans who were dissatisfied with the outcome of the Pampanga mutiny could have traveled into Pangasinan to continue their rebellion against Spanish authority. At the same time, the spread of rebellion into Northern Luzon was a greater cause for concern to authorities in Manila, who were aware that the further away from Manila their settlements were, the less they could guarantee colonial control. Indeed, much of Northern Luzon remained uncolonized and even largely unexplored by the 1660s. Spanish settlements had been established in the province of Pangasinan and along the Ilocos coastline, a narrow strip of land that separated the sea from the steep slopes of the Cordillera Mountains. Indigenous communities in the Cordillera Mountains famously resisted Spanish colonization attempts for more than three centuries.[26] In the seventeenth century this resistance extended through the mountains and across most of the Cagayan Valley, into the Sierra Madre and Caraballo Sur mountain ranges, onward to the rugged and remote northeastern coastline, and even into the lowland regions adjacent to Pampanga and Pangasinan.[27]

Given the limits of colonial control in Northern Luzon, the outbreak of rebellion in the seemingly pacified regions of Pangasinan and Ilocos was therefore of considerable concern. More than this, Spanish officials were particularly worried that pacified and Christianized indigenous communities would find common cause with their upland neighbors who had repeatedly and violently rejected colonization attempts. Up to that point, Spanish authorities had successfully exploited divisions between lowland communities and uplanders in regions like Pangasinan, depicting their neighbors in the Zambales and Cordillera Mountains as violent, barbarous, and capable of waging war against peaceful lowland Christian settlements.[28] A break with that status quo and the forming of alliances between former enemies would make any rebellion in Northern Luzon very dangerous indeed.

This is in fact exactly what happened in 1661. After capturing Lingayen—the capital of Pangasinan—Malong appointed Don Pedro Gumapos as the leader of a contingent that would march northward into Ilocos, laying waste to Spanish settlements up and down the coast of Northern Luzon. Gumapos included in his company a group of Zambales indios from the nearby Zambales Mountains. Up to that point, the Zambales had been long-standing enemies of the lowland Pampangans and Pangasinanes, regularly raiding their villages—a tactic that only increased with the establishment of Christian settlements.[29] They were renowned for their use of headhunting as a method of resistance against Spanish colonization. A little more than a decade earlier, in 1648, the Dominican missionary Fr. Pedro de Valenzuela had been shot with arrows and had his head cut off while traveling through the Zambales Mountains.[30] The incorporation of these indios into Gumapos's army therefore marked a significant break in these animosities between lowlanders and uplanders. Over the course of January 1661, Gumapos and his army of Zambales rebels attacked Bauang, Agoo, Narvacan, and finally Vigan, the Spanish capital of Ilocos, which they sacked and burned along with the neighboring settlements of Santa Catalina and Bantay. In the process, Gumapos and his soldiers took all the Spanish missionaries stationed in Vigan hostage.[31]

At the same time that this was taking place, the rebellion continued to spread further north, led by the former *maestre de campo* of Bacarra, Don Juan Magsano. By early January, Magsano had climbed into the Apayao mountain range from the Ilocos coast to build an alliance with the Isnegs. Like most of the communities of the Cordillera Mountains, the Isnegs had thus far resisted Spanish colonization. Attempts made by Dominican missionaries over the preceding half century had resulted in the establishment of two Spanish settlements at the foot of the Apayao Mountains, in Pudtol and Capinatan, near the banks of the Abulug River. Despite persistent hopes among the Dominicans of converting the mountain communities higher up in the Apayao Mountains, both of these settlements experienced wave upon wave of violent rebellion.[32] Magsano made effective use of these animosities in January 1661.

Word of the approaching rebel army reached the Spanish in Cagayan only when a boat from the Babuyan Islands arrived in the quiet coastal village of Pata, on the northwestern Cagayan coast. These Babuyanes told the priest who was stationed there, Fr. Antonio Calderón, that Magsano and the Isnegs had burned down the church of Bangui, killed two priests, and were marching toward Cagayan. This news sparked panic among the priests stationed along the Cagayan coastline. All of the indigenous and Spanish soldiers stationed in the province had been sent to the port of Aparri, on the other side of the Cagayan River—along with all of their munitions—and were at that moment waiting for a ship to take them to Pangasinan to join the fight against Malong's rebel army. Cagayan was left defenseless against Magsano's army that marched across the Apayao Mountains.

Within a matter of days, Magsano and his forces reached the town of Cavicungan, sacking its church and cutting off the head of the local priest before dumping his body along the roadside. The priests stationed in nearby Pata were forced to flee for their lives. Fr. Calderón described a panicked journey through the black of night amid driving rain and wading knee-deep through swamps, always looking over their shoulders for signs of the rebels. Once they reached Massi, Fr. Calderón was able to send word to the general stationed in Aparri, who immediately began preparing his soldiers to march toward Cavicungan. This force was able to repel the rebels and drive them back toward Ilocos, but not before they sacked and desecrated the church at Pata, smashing everything they could find. Fr. Calderón wrote with dismay that it was clear that the rebels' sole intention was to kill or drive out the Spanish from the province. They meant no harm to the local indigenous communities; in fact, they were almost willingly embraced by the residents of Cavicungan and Pata who offered no resistance to the onslaught and failed to defend the priests or their churches from attack. Several townspeople from Pata and Cavicungan were later sentenced to death for their roles in the rebellion, while it was discovered that the governor of Cavicungan had fled alongside Magsano as he retreated to Ilocos. The provincial of the Dominican order recommended to the priests stationed in these towns that they abandon them as the residents had demonstrated clearly that they did not believe in God and did not care for His ministers.[33]

The Spanish response to these events in Northern Luzon was decidedly different from their actions in Pampanga. What had begun as a labor dispute had spiraled out of control into a generalized rebellion aimed at removing

Spanish rule over Northern Luzon. Previously pacified communities were joining forces with upland groups who had always resisted colonization. The response had to be swift and decisive. Armies were mustered to sail up the coast of Luzon, while other forces were sent overland. They began in Pangasinan and Pampanga. As with the previous rebellion in Pampanga, the rebels of Pangasinan had attempted to blockade the waterways around Lingayen, preventing entrance of the Spanish armies into the province. General Felipe de Ugalde spent four days attempting to enter the Agno River while being assaulted by bullets and arrows from hastily constructed fortifications on the shore. Although the resistance was fierce, Ugalde was able to rout the rebels by splitting his forces and sending some of them overland. As the Spanish soldiers began to march through the province, Malong and his followers were forced to retreat to the towns of Binalatonga and Malunguey before fleeing into the Zambales Mountains, setting fire to the towns as they went.[34]

Over the course of January and February 1661, Spanish forces pursued the remaining rebels across the length of Pangasinan and the Ilocos coastline. In the process, they captured more than 1,500 rebels and impaled dozens of heads on spikes across the villages that they defeated as an example to other rebels. Finally, Malong was captured and taken prisoner. He was condemned to be shot and his head was cut off and placed on a hook, while his headless body was hung from the feet in his hometown of Binalatonga. On his body hung a sign which read in Spanish and the Pangasinan language: "As a traitor to God and the King I have condemned him to the law."[35] Another 133 rebels were shot or garroted, with their heads and body parts scattered along the roads as a reminder of what befell rebels. A further 158 were sentenced to serve as forced laborers in the docks at Cavite or as servants to the religious orders, thus effectively ending this wave of rebellion in Northern Luzon.

Following these events Manrique de Lara wrote to the king to notify him of his success in putting down the rebellion. The islands were now at peace, he wrote, but the situation for the Spanish in the Philippines remained desperate. The colony was weak and exposed to risk. In particular, Manrique de Lara emphasized the lack of yearly financial and military aid sent from New Spain to support their efforts. The chronic debt that the treasury was experiencing had played a large part in prompting the outbreak of rebellions in Luzon in the first instance. At the same time, the number of soldiers sent to replenish their military defenses was so deficient that it caused "intense pain to the infantry and military chiefs." The uprising of once loyal indios in Pampanga had only heightened this situation, since they relied on companies of Pampangan soldiers to supplement the meager dispatches of soldiers sent onboard the galleons. Although they had managed to avert disaster this time,

Manrique de Lara was sending a strong indication to the king and the Council of Indies that the same may not be true the next time around unless more was done to support the Spanish outpost in the Philippines.[36]

The Threatened Invasion of Manila

Barely a year later, an even greater threat to Spanish sovereignty in the Philippines materialized. In May 1662, the Dominican Fr. Vittorio Ricci disembarked in Manila from a Chinese junk dressed in mandarin robes. He had arrived as the ambassador of Zheng Chenggong—otherwise known as Koxinga, the head of the famous Zheng clan—and bore a letter that inspired panic among the Spanish population of Manila.[37] In this letter Koxinga demanded that the Spanish pay him tribute, and threatened that if they did not do so, he would invade with "hundreds of thousands of able soldiers [and an] abundance of ships of war," with which he would "burn your forts, lakes, cities, warehouses, and all other things."[38] Spanish officials in Manila were well aware of Koxinga's recent successful invasion of Taiwan.[39] At the end of 1661, forty to fifty thousand Chinese soldiers reportedly besieged the Dutch Fort Zeelandia in Tainan where they burnt all of the Dutch ships and slaughtered most of the Dutch soldiers. In February 1662, the Dutch surrendered and evacuated the island.[40] Since 1650, Koxinga had been leading a resistance war against the newly emergent Qing dynasty. Over the course of those years, he had mustered thousands of supporters along the coastal regions of Fujian, but gradually his resistance was overpowered. His seizure of Taiwan marked his retreat from mainland China. Keen to bolster his resistance and continue fighting this war, Koxinga looked to the Fujianese population of Manila and, by extension, the port city itself.

Koxinga's threatened invasion escalated long-standing tensions between the Spanish and Chinese populations of the port city. Since its founding in 1571, Manila had expanded on the back of the galleon trade, which brought junks from Fujian laden with silks to exchange for silver arriving in the colony from New Spain. Chinese merchants and laborers began migrating to the city onboard Fujianese trading junks shortly after the trade with China opened in 1574. The Chinese population of Manila peaked at more than forty thousand in 1639, outnumbering Spaniards up to twenty times.[41] Because of this demographic imbalance, Chinese merchants and laborers soon controlled the domestic economy of Manila, occupying all of the laboring, artisanal, and commercial functions in the city and monopolizing the internal circulation of silver currency. While the Spanish attempted to control this community, particularly through rigid segregation of the city, they were confronted by the fact that Manila was as much a Chinese colony as it was Spanish. Distrust grew between the two communities, leading to a number of very violent interactions. In 1603 and 1639 the Spanish engaged in wholesale pogroms of the Chinese, slaughtering tens of thousands of Chinese people.[42]

Manila had thus remained under Spanish control by the threat of violence and its periodic enaction, but an external invasion coupled with an internal rebellion in the Parian would quickly topple Spanish power. After the arrival of Koxinga's ambassador, a council was called that determined that there should be a general expulsion of the Chinese from the islands. So as not to cause too much of a disturbance, the council delayed publishing this decree until they were able to muster cavalry and military units to defend the city.[43] Despite this, the Chinese community heard rumors of the preparations being made by the city and began to fear that another pogrom was being planned. Many feared that they would be slaughtered by the Spanish and some began to prepare to defend themselves. The governor was made aware that a revolt was brewing on May 24—however, a number of observers later wrote that the Chinese actually planned to flee rather than rebel and that this was motivated by their fear of slaughter.[44]

On May 25, Governor Manrique de Lara went into the Parian and promised to give the Chinese a contingent of soldiers to protect them, but this only created more fear. Eventually, a skirmish broke out at the city gate to the Parian and the soldiers on the ramparts fired into the crowd. In panic, a large number of people threw themselves into the river. Many of those unable to make use of rowing boats drowned. Those who survived boarded a larger ship and set sail away from the city. The rest of the crowd went to Santa Cruz, on the other side of the river, while about fifteen hundred people remained in the Parian, principally merchants who wanted nothing to do with the panicked crowd. The governor understood that these events largely resulted from fear and wanted to avoid a confrontation, not least because it would drain military resources from the defense of the city against Koxinga.[45]

When the body of a dead priest was discovered in the Parian later that night, many Spanish residents called for a bloodletting; however, Governor Manrique de Lara was more concerned with negotiating a peaceful expulsion. He met with the captains of the visiting trading vessels and negotiated that they would deport as many Chinese onboard these vessels as possible. The expulsion began on June 2, with Christian Chinese allowed to remain behind in the districts of Santa Cruz and Binondo. All of those who had fled the city and refused to return to the Parian were then hunted down by a contingent of Pampangan soldiers led by Juan Macapagal and Francisco Lacsamana. Over the next two weeks, fifteen hundred Chinese were slaughtered during skirmishes with the Pampangan infantry in the foothills of the Zambales Mountains, while a number of others were decapitated, including two leaders of the alleged rebellion, who had snuck back into the Parian to try to board the ships bound for China.[46] On June 10, a further fifteen hundred Chinese were expelled back to China, with only six hundred non-Christian Chinese being allowed to stay to help with the fortification of the city in preparation for Koxinga's invasion.[47]

In the meantime, Manrique de Lara convened a general council of the royal audiencia and the religious and military authorities in Manila. They conducted a serious assessment of their capacity to defend against Koxinga's forces, and, on finding that they had no money in the treasury to pay the tribute and insufficient infantry and munitions to defend the city, the council of war agreed that it was necessary to withdraw all of the Spanish forces from the presidios of Ternate, Zamboanga, Iligan, and the Calamianes, along with all of their artillery and munitions, to concentrate on the defense of Manila.[48] All of these presidios were located in the southern archipelago, on islands where Spanish sovereignty was both contested and violently resisted. Over the course of the century, these outposts had drained vast amounts of military power, with contingents of hundreds of soldiers stationed there in a desperate attempt to exert some control over the resolutely autonomous Muslim south. Throughout this period, the Spanish had suffered from chronic shortages of soldiers and were often forced to rely on convicts and other involuntary recruits to fill their ranks.[49] These shortages were intensified as the century wore on, leaving the colony in a desperate state when faced by the existential threat posed by Koxinga in 1662. In the wake of the rebellions in Northern Luzon, Manrique de Lara wrote an angry letter to the King noting that in 1661 he had only received forty-one soldiers in the dispatch from New Spain that year, consisting of eight volunteers, nineteen convicts with pay, and fourteen convicts without. The governor said that such a shortage of numbers forced the soldiers that he did have in his presidios to "resign themselves to death from a life of fatigue without resources."[50] Furthermore, he went on, in the past twenty years, the viceroys of New Spain had not contributed a tenth of the number of soldiers who had died in the various wars that they had been fighting, and the supply that arrived that year was not even a sixth of what they needed.[51]

Aware of the extent of Koxinga's forces, the council of war could see no other option than to withdraw some of their soldiers to fortify Manila. Over the course of the next year, twelve companies of soldiers were withdrawn from the southern archipelago—six from Ternate, four from Zamboanga, and one each from Iligan and the Calamianes. The majority of these soldiers were redeployed to Manila, while the remainder bolstered numbers in Cavite, Cebu,

Oton, Caraga, and Cagayan. The governor also commissioned major reforti-fication works in Manila and Cavite at this time, including the construction of a seawall and a new bastion to oversee the port and the shipyards.[52]

In July 1662, the Spanish sent Fr. Ricci back to Taiwan with their response to Koxinga's request. In this letter, Governor Manrique de Lara informed the Zheng warlord that under no circumstances would they pay him the tribute he requested. Furthermore, they had expelled many of his subjects, they would no longer accept trade with his agents, and they were preparing to defend Ma-nila for war.[53] By the time Ricci arrived in Taiwan with this defiant message, however, Koxinga had contracted malaria and died soon afterward. His son, who took over leadership of Taiwan and of the Zheng clan, never pursued his father's claim for sovereignty over the Philippines.[54]

Colonial Contraction, Imperial Retreat

The extensive contraction of territorial power that this military withdrawal entailed horrified officials in Madrid. While Koxinga's invasion was clearly the immediate threat that forced this unprecedented withdrawal of forces, it was not merely coincidental that the soldiers were withdrawn from presidios sta-tioned in the southern archipelago where tensions with various Moro polities had been increasing over the past decade. The Spanish had been in a protracted war with the polities of the southern archipelago for nearly a century. Despite early hopes of being able to spread Spanish control southward and seize the lucrative spice trade, the polities of Maguindanao and Jolo in particular re-sponded aggressively to the Spanish presence in their archipelago. Conquest attempts were countered with extensive slave raiding, eroding Spanish author-ity in the Visayas. Although an uneasy peace had been negotiated following two conquest attempts led by the Spanish in 1637 and 1638, this peace had be-gun to break down over the decade leading up to 1662. The powerful Moro leader, Cachil Kudarat, had begun building alliances with neighboring polities and the yearly slave raids had resumed by 1656.[55]

In recounting his decision to withdraw these soldiers, Governor Manrique de Lara emphasized the threat posed by the raiders of Mindanao and Jolo and ar-gued that the withdrawal of these soldiers was needed as much to establish peace with the bellicose Moro rulers as it was to prepare Manila against possible invasion. With new intimations of war particularly with Maguindanao, the con-tinued presence of Spanish forces in the southern archipelago was untenable. The consideration with regards to the forces of the Maluku Islands was slightly different—while these soldiers were not affected by ongoing raiding activities, they were situated on a frontier with the Dutch and surrounded by hostile populations allied to the Dutch-aligned King of Ternate. Many officials had long believed that the Maluku presidio served no purpose at all, while the soldiers themselves deserted in large numbers.[56]

For the next two decades, the king issued decree after decree ordering successive governors in Manila to reestablish the presidio at Zamboanga in Mindanao, saying that this retreat was not only an embarrassment for the Spanish Crown in the region but also opened up the opportunity for the Dutch to gain control over the southern provinces.[57] The withdrawal from Ternate had already effectively ceded control of the Indonesian archipelago to the Dutch and ended any influence the Spanish claimed over the Maluku Islands or Sulawesi. The Council of Indies knew that reestablishing a base in the Maluku Islands would be virtually impossible; the Zamboanga presidio on the southwestern tip of Mindanao was a good compromise as a strategic location that would prevent the Dutch from extending their influence further into the Philippines. Yet, royal officials in Manila were all in agreement that reestablishing the Zamboanga presidio would risk reigniting war with the Moros of Mindanao and Jolo. The withdrawal from Zamboanga had been accompanied by considerable violence. The Jesuits reported that many of the towns and churches that they had established in Mindanao had since been burned by the Sulus and Camucones, who had also killed two missionaries. Fr. Juan Bautista was stabbed to death when he refused to accompany a raiding mission, while Fr. Barrena died after having been taken captive. At the same time, the Maguindanao leader Cachil Kudarat saw the Spanish withdrawal from Mindanao as an opportunity to extend his authority over the islands and the Christianized Lutaos of the Zamboanga peninsula were all brought under his control.[58] Consequently, most officials were in favor of maintaining peace with the Moros, even if this meant forfeiting the right to the territories of the southern archipelago.[59]

In September 1663, Diego Salcedo arrived in Manila to take over the position of governor and Manrique de Lara left the islands after having served as governor for a decade. Despite his best efforts, he left the colony in a weaker position than when he arrived, having overseen a dramatic contraction of Spanish-controlled territory after the withdrawal of military units from the southern archipelago in 1662. Yet the multiple crises that Manrique de Lara had to contend with were not of his own making; rather they are emblematic of the long-term contradictions inherent in Spanish colonization of the Philippines. The imposition of imperial authority across the territory of the Philippines by soldiers and missionaries had its corollary in the long history of indigenous resistance against this authority. Throughout the seventeenth century, indigenous populations oscillated between integration and rebellion and sizable pockets of unconquered territory opened up possibilities for indigenous populations to simply leave the Spanish sphere of influence altogether. On top of this, the Spanish presence was numerically weak, crippled by financial debt, and was constantly undermined by the activities of Moro slave raiders.

The history of the Philippines in the seventeenth century is thus a rich history of conflict and confrontation. The limitations of the Spanish presence opened up spaces for indigenous people to operate and to influence the course of empire in their region. Cognizant of their numerical weaknesses, the Spanish relied from the start on indigenous elites to help institute colonial tribute and labor regimes. As with elsewhere in the empire, these labor regimes were modeled on preexisting social structures. At the same time, even with the aid of indigenous allies, the Spanish remained territorially overextended, while apparently unwilling to abandon their ambitions to extend control throughout the archipelago. They thus found themselves embroiled in ongoing military conflicts both in Northern Luzon and Mindanao. Despite common assertions regarding the inherent military superiority of Europeans, in both arenas indigenous communities used tactics of warfare that consistently overwhelmed Spanish efforts.

CHAPTER 2

Slavery, Debt, and Colonial Labor Regimes

The indigenous rebellions that began in Northern Luzon at the end of 1660 were destabilizing to the Spanish regime not just because they took place in the very heartlands of Spanish control. The leaders of these rebellions were also once loyal supporters of Spanish colonization, men that the royal officials in Manila had grown to trust and rely on. This was particularly the case with Don Andrés Malong. Prior to helping initiate the second wave of rebellion beginning in Pangasinan, Malong had been considered one of the most loyal supporters of the Spanish regime. He was educated from an early age by Dominican missionaries and served in a number of military and administrative positions before going on to be appointed as *maestre de campo* of the province of Pangasinan. In this role, he served as collector of tributes, waged war against raiding Igorots, and provisioned Manila through the mass requisitioning of rice from the provinces. Shortly before the outbreak of rebellion, he had even successfully petitioned to be granted an encomienda—a recognition of loyalty and service to the king that was rarely ever awarded to indigenous subjects.[1] Over the course of his life, Malong had helped to impose the very institutions that he and his followers later rebelled against. Thus, Malong's rebellion was truly an act of treason in the eyes of the Spanish.

But what caused Malong to undergo such a radical shift in loyalty? At the heart of this problem lie questions about the nature of power, authority, and labor relations within seventeenth-century Philippine communities. This chapter examines the role of indigenous labor in the colonial economy, showing how colonial extraction of labor and tribute was built on the foundations of pre-Hispanic systems of debt servitude.[2] Power within pre-Hispanic Philippine communities typically relied on control of local labor resources, with indigenous elites measuring their social status through the amount of labor power on which they could rely. Indigenous elites therefore played an essential part in integrating new colonial demands into existing labor systems. Because of this, they continued to wield significant power as brokers between the colonial state and local communities, while at the same time ensuring that new colonial labor regimes integrated existing methods of organizing labor.

In order to understand this situation, we need to first understand the power relations that existed within pre-Hispanic Philippine communities at the advent of Spanish colonization. This chapter thus begins by looking at pre-Hispanic social and economic structures in the Philippines and the relationship between debt servitude, class structures, and political authority and control. Doing so then allows us to understand how new colonial institutions adopted these preexisting forms of power, relying on debt to mobilize labor within the repartimiento, bandala, and tribute systems. The co-option of these systems by the Spanish had serious social consequences for Philippine communities, leading to famine and increased debt servitude. Part of what prompted leaders like Malong to rebel was a growing sense that the burdens imposed on local communities by the Spaniards broke the traditional bonds of mutual obligation on which the power of local indigenous elites relied. Indeed, many Philippine communities were overwhelmed by the burdens imposed on them by the Spanish, and instead turned to rebellion, fleeing Spanish villages, and living in fugitive communities that formed in the uplands of most islands. Throughout the century, numerous attempts were made to reform these labor regimes without success; the debates raised by these reformers further reveal fundamental tensions among secular and religious officials over the reliance of the colonial state on the slave-owning indigenous elites. Ultimately, this reliance on preexisting social and economic structures was a double-edged sword, both supporting the colonial project whilst also sowing the seeds of its ongoing disintegration and unmaking in the form of flight and rebellion.

Class Structure in the Pre-Hispanic Philippines

When the Spanish arrived in the Philippines in the late sixteenth century, they found a society which was characterized by geographic dispersion and intense fragmentation of power. Philippine communities tended to be small, clan-based units called barangays, which averaged around a hundred families, although some communities of up to a thousand people also existed.[3] Both early Spanish ethnographic accounts and Philippine folklore help to unravel the social relations that existed within baranganic society in the sixteenth century.[4] Origin myths such as that recorded in the Boxer Codex shortly after the Spanish arrived in the archipelago also tell of the beginnings of class society. Following this legend, the first Visayans, Calaque and Cabaye, produced many, many children who all turned out to be very lazy. Enraged at their idleness, their father threatened to beat them with a stick. The children fled and hid in different parts of the house. The children who fled to the bedroom became the datus, or rulers, and celebrated military leaders of the barangay; those who remained in the main room were the *timawas,* or free vassals, who often served as warriors but did not provide agricultural labor; and those who entered the walls were the debt servants, or *oripuns,* who provided all the agricultural and other labor within baranganic communities. The children who hid among the pots and chimneys of the kitchen were the Agtas who lived in the forests and mountains of many Visayan islands, while those who left the house disappeared completely, and so represented everyone else in the world who lived outside of Visayan culture.[5]

Such hierarchical divisions were common across baranganic societies in the Philippines and structured both social relations and local labor systems. In Tagalog, the free vassal warriors were known as *maharlikas* and the debt servants as *alipins.*[6] Debt played an essential role in determining the extent to which an individual owned their own labor time or was compelled to work for other members of the community.[7] This mirrored other social systems that extended across most of Southeast Asia in the early modern period, from China to Timor, Japan to Bangladesh, and exhibiting similar patterns of social organization in all these contexts.[8] Anthony Reid argues that Southeast Asian society was "held together by the vertical bonds of obligation between men," wherein power was derived from how much labor an individual could control.[9]

The functioning of these pre-Hispanic forms of labor and servitude was a source of great curiosity for many Spanish observers in the late sixteenth century.[10] They were particularly keen to understand the relationship between common debt servants and datus. Nevertheless, the use of the term slave (*esclavo*) and slavery (*esclavitud*) used within Spanish documents to refer to *alipins* or *oripuns* has left a lasting legacy of confusion and misconception in the historiography of the early colonial Philippines, with some historians seeking to make comparisons to the contemporaneous chattel slavery occurring in the Atlantic slave trade.[11] While there is evidence that slaves were bought and sold as commodities both by Spanish and indigenous owners,[12] the slavery that observers like Lavezaris witnessed within Philippine communities in fact represented complex relationships based on degrees of dependency and servitude. Most historians of the pre-Hispanic Philippines have concluded, therefore, that this type of slavery is better understood as debt servitude rather than chattel slavery.[13]

Historians of Southeast Asian slavery talk of gradients of servitude that extended from outright chattel slavery—usually entered into through capture or sale—through to debt bondage that itself had gradients of servitude and indebtedness. Writing about slaves in Timor, Hans Hägerdal noted that whereas debt bondsmen often existed in a situation very similar to European serfdom—indentured to a particular master and tied to a particular location—captives of war were treated much more like bounty that could be traded or sold.[14] Angela Schottenhammer argues that different Asian terminologies for "slave" reflect this division of different types of servitude, where "'slave' can, depending on the context, also mean 'debtor,' 'dependent' or 'subject.'"[15] Across Southeast Asia, debt servants vastly outnumbered slaves captured in raids or through warfare.[16] Debt servitude could also be voluntary, at least to an extent if individuals chose to indebt themselves, and theoretically impermanent—an indebted slave could labor to pay off their debt.[17] Sometimes individuals could find greater social security and stability within a dependent and paternal relationship of debt servitude to their master than as a free individual without the protections afforded by that relation of dependency.[18] However, debt servitude was also utilized as a form of criminal punishment for crimes ranging from sexual impropriety or adultery to other breaches of social norms.[19] In many locations—including the Philippines—milder and harsher forms of debt bondage were applied according to the nature and origin of the debt.

Social relationships formed around debt are thus integral to how pre-Hispanic Philippine communities operated, structuring relationships of power and authority as well as systems of labor organization.[20] Spanish ethnographic sources from the sixteenth century reflect the complexity of different types of servitude and dependence experienced within the archipelago at that moment in time.[21] To establish a simplified typology within this complex system, William Henry Scott distinguishes between those who were debt servants who nonetheless had some degree of freedom and those who were closer to chattel slaves and could be bought and sold. In the first category—known as *alipin namamahay* in Tagalog—debt servants typically occupied their own house and land and paid their debts through a designated amount of labor time. The amount of time owed to a master varied widely, and thus Spanish observers often talked of "half-slaves" and "quarter-slaves."[22] Some servants in this category could commute their labor into tribute in the form of agricultural products. Others were allowed to work in military service—either as oarsmen on raids or as foot soldiers—and even received rewards for their participation. Still others did not perform field labor, but provided other kinds of labor for their masters, such as construction work, and might pay tribute in the form of goods, usually rice or textiles. By contrast, the second category of slave—known as *alipin sa gigilid* in Tagalog—typically lived in their master's house in a state of dependency. They also performed differing degrees of labor—a combination of agricultural and domestic work—with some days off for themselves. While both categories of slave could technically work their way out of service, this second category included slaves who were captured in raids and those who could be sold or exchanged as chattel.[23] The relationships of dependency that existed between datus and *alipins* were also one of mutual obligation: a datu was obligated to provide a degree of protection and economic security in return for the tribute and labor provided by their debtors.[24]

An internal economy where debt and labor obligations reinforced the hierarchical bonds within baranganic communities was a key organizing principle across lowland Philippine communities. But by the late sixteenth century, it was also shaped by an external economy, one increasingly focused on trading networks and slave raiding as a means of extending power and control. Spanish colonial authorities stepped into this political economy with their own needs for tribute and labor and immediately began the process of establishing local networks of authority and control. Since they relied so heavily on the co-option and support of powerful *datus*, the Spanish assimilated these pre-existing structures of power and vassalage.

The service record of one of Malong's contemporaries exemplifies this relationship. In 1667, Don Juan Macapagal similarly petitioned to be granted an encomienda in recognition for his services to the Crown. At the time of writing this petition, Macapagal was the *maestre de campo* of the Pampangan infantry stationed within Fort Santiago in Manila and had fought on the opposite side to Malong and Maniago during the 1660 to 1661 rebellions, helping the Spanish to finally bring the region back under control. He had dedicated his entire life to the service of the Crown. Within the military, he had previously served as a soldier, squadron leader, sergeant, and captain of infantry. He had also taken up the civil offices of *gobernadorcillo*, *juez de sementeras*, and *principal* of the towns of Arayat, Candaba, Apalit, and the foothills of the Zambales Mountains.[25] Yet, more than this, Macapagal came from a line of esteemed and loyal indigenous supporters of the Spanish Crown. His great-grandfather was Don Carlos Lakandula, the native lord of Tondo, Bulacan, and surrounds who was among the first to recognize Spanish sovereignty over Luzon when Miguel López de Legazpi arrived in Manila in 1571. Lakandula instructed his vassals to build a house and a garrison for Legazpi and his men, and he and his children were baptized and received the holy sacrament. Later on, he accompanied the *maestre de campo* Martín de Goiti in his conquest of the province of Pampanga and used his authority to convince the Pampangans to give their obedience to the Crown.[26] While Lakandula and his descendants reaped rewards and recognition as key indigenous allies of the Spanish, their power was premised on their ability to assemble and supply a labor force to resource all of these projects.

The role that elites played in imposing these systems of labor has sometimes been taken as evidence that Philippine elites willingly supported colonial rule in exchange for rewards of status, authority, and noble title. In reality, the power that these elites held over the colonial project went deeper. Without their cooperation, the colonial project never would have extended beyond Manila's city walls. The Spanish had to either co-opt or confront the power of the indigenous elite. While individual leaders like Lakandula and his descendants were particularly noted for their allegiance to the new colonial power, this loyalty was by no means guaranteed among the majority of Philippine elites. Indeed, many colonial sources make clear that the enthusiasm of local elites for the colonial state waned as the distance from Manila grew.

Crucially, practices of debt servitude and their integration into new colonial labor regimes became a source of consternation among some colonial officials, leading to numerous attempts at reform throughout the seventeenth century. At the heart of these debates were competing visions over the nature of colonial rule and the duty of the colonial state to its subjects. Yet, every attempt at reform had to confront the fundamental reality that colonial power rested on the loyalty of indigenous elites, whose authority was in turn wedded to and reliant on maintaining the existing hierarchies within local communities.

Debt and the Colonial Labor Economy

Very early on in the history of the Spanish empire, restrictions were placed on the use of indio labor. The enslavement of indigenous peoples was formally abolished by a series of royal decrees beginning in 1526, decades before the Spanish took possession of any territory in the Philippines.[27] These decrees declared it unlawful to enslave any indio regardless of whether the Spanish had engaged in just war against their people. Following the famous interventions of theologians and missionaries such as Francisco de Vitoria and Bartolomé de las Casas, this imperial policy was intended as a means of curtailing the excesses of Spanish conquest. At the same time, debates around indigenous slavery also had wider consequences for the organization of indio labor. The New Laws of 1542 stipulated that all indigenous labor was to be freely contracted and all indios were to be paid for the work they performed. The aim was to curb the exploitation of indio vassals particularly by *encomenderos*.[28]

While these debates took place prior to the colonization of the Philippines and centered on experiences in New Spain—where the brutality of mass enslavement drove early colonial expansion—they nonetheless reverberated in the Philippines decades later. Royal decrees were issued early and frequently, emphasizing the inalienable freedom of indigenous subjects of the king, and establishing the legal precedents for new colonial labor regimes to operate as voluntary waged labor.[29] Yet, the widespread existence of indigenous forms of slavery and debt servitude made the implementation of these decrees problematic, if not impossible. In particular, it was unclear whether these laws also applied to indigenous people themselves. Were Philippine indios also prohibited from holding slaves according to their customs? Moreover, the existence of an established system of debt servitude made it possible for Spaniards to flaunt the specifics of the decree, particularly in the first decades of the Spanish presence. Many Spaniards were said to have received indigenous slaves from local elites as well as engaging in debt bondage themselves.[30]

At the heart of these debates was the role that the indigenous elites played in facilitating a transition to colonial rule within Philippine communities. To assert the fundamental liberty of indigenous subjects of the king would ultimately require breaking the established bonds of servitude that underpinned most Philippine communities. Some reformers—most notably missionaries in this early period—campaigned strongly in favor of abolishing all slavery in the Philippines.[31] In the 1580s, royal officials in Manila sought to clarify with the Crown whether the enslavement of Philippine indios by other indios was legal.[32] The gradual phasing out of indigenous forms of slavery was suggested in 1586, with all children born free and no new slaves accepted as legal. But this proposal was never implemented, largely because of the weight of evidence to suggest that indigenous elites would rebel heavily against the implementation of such a proposal and the Spanish presence in the islands would consequently be placed at risk.[33]

This same dynamic continued to characterize the new colonial labor systems established by the Spanish over the course of the next century—with royal decree after royal decree asserting the principles set out in the New Laws and royal officials in Manila—both secular and religious—continually arguing the exceptionalism of the Philippine case and the need for exemption from these royal provisions. Time and again, the practicalities of administering the colonial frontier outweighed the desires of even the most idealistic reformers to implement royal decrees. In practice, Spanish control at the community level was too weak, limited, and reliant on local elites to effect a wholesale reform of the political economy that relied on degrees of unfree labor. And so, new colonial labor and tribute regimes were modeled much more closely on pre-Hispanic regimes of debt servitude than on the free waged labor systems described in the New Laws.

Indeed, debt was written into the very core of the colonial economy. A definitive royal decree issued in 1609 established once and for all that no labor could be performed by indios under these systems unless it was of their own free will and adequately remunerated.[34] Despite this, throughout the century we witness a reluctance on behalf to the colonial authorities to pay the wages owed to the indios. This situation of chronic debt to indigenous laborers has often been explained as arising from the Spaniards' own shortages in currency.[35] However, it is also evident that containing the spread of currency into indigenous communities was deliberate, to keep debt at the forefront of local economies. To truly implement the royal decrees that regulated the use of indigenous labor would have required replacing a system based on debt servitude with one based on waged labor. However, flooding Philippine communities with silver would have the consequence of undermining the leadership of the datu elite and threatening the very power structures that the Spaniards relied on for labor mobilization in the first place. Therefore, for much of the century, Spanish officials attempted to deliberately restrict the supply of coins in circulation to prevent a transition to a currency-based economy within Philippine barangays. Several indigenous observers commented on this situation. For instance, in 1691, the *principales* of Cagayan Province reported that the flow of silver was always out of the province toward Manila, where the *alcaldes mayores*, religious orders, *vecinos*, and encomenderos sent their wealth to purchase goods and wares for their houses.[36] Even indio leaders were known to do this, rather than spending the money in their own province.[37]

The Spanish desire to control currency is evident when looking at the history of the tribute system. In theory, tribute should have helped to introduce a silver-based economy into the archipelago, since tribute payers were obliged to pay in a quantity of *reales*. Yet, the Spanish learnt early on that by introducing a silver-based economy into Philippine communities, they were directly challenging the established social order that had previously relied on debt as the means of organizing labor. Thus, tribute was almost always paid in-kind, reflecting the lack of circulation of currency.

Initially, the first governor of the Philippines, Miguel López de Legazpi, established tribute payments as eight reales per tribute per year,[38] which was later increased to ten reales.[39] Legazpi valued the eight reales as equivalent to one hundred *gantas* of rice as well as one piece of cotton measuring two *brazas* by one *braza*, one *maes* of gold, and one chicken each year.[40] Yet, very quickly, the substitution of monetary value for in-kind products led to great extortions in tribute collections, owing in part to the fact that gold was scarce and this part of the tribute needed to be substituted for alternative goods. Tribute collection resulted in wide variations in the quantities of goods that were considered a sufficient substitution for the eight reales. In 1581, Diego de Zárate reported that during the process of collecting tribute, the encomenderos would regularly extort more tribute from the indios than was legal.[41]

The response to this situation was to allow indios to pay half of the tribute in specie and the other half in-kind, in the hopes that this would lessen the extortionate ways in which tribute was being collected.[42] However, shortly after the introduction of this reform, the *vecinos* in Manila complained that this encouraged the indios not to labor so hard to produce an agricultural surplus for the Spanish to live off.[43] By 1593, the governor Gómez Perez Dasmariñas conceded that the new order for tribute to be paid in specie had not worked. The islands had suffered from great shortages in agricultural products since many indios preferred to wander for many months at a time away from their homes into the hills, abandoning their fields. The governor concluded that there was a need to control the labor time of the indios in order to keep them obedient to the Spanish Crown and the means by which they paid tribute was essential to this.[44] Echoing these sentiments, the Cabildo of Manila argued in 1603 that the change toward collecting tribute in specie had resulted in prices of goods escalating—doubling in just six years—as the indios refused to work. They preferred to purchase Chinese clothes and goods rather than make their own products.[45]

Undoubtedly, a return to the payment of tribute in-kind exacerbated widespread extortion and profiteering. In 1623, Fr. Juan de Valmaseda noted that there were great variances in how tribute was calculated and collected in different parts of the islands, resulting in what he believed was an overpayment of tribute by more than two hundred thousand *ducados* each year. Since the price of goods were variable, the collection of tribute was also subject to abuse. In some regions the indios were paying just eight reales each, while in other areas they were paying twelve or sixteen reales.[46] In 1627, the Dominican Fr. Melchor de Manzano reported that the indios of Bataan were paying much more tribute than the Pampangans, with greater quantities of rice being taken from them than elsewhere.[47] Meanwhile in Cagayan, the four reales that the indios were supposed to pay in specie was in fact worth sixteen because of the unjust prices applied to the rice that the indios sold to the Spanish.[48] Most of these extortionate measures also had the consequence of keeping indios in a situation of constant debt to the colonial state.[49]

This situation was similarly carried through to the repartimiento and bandala systems. While these were both systems of compulsory labor, they were at least in theory legally differentiated from slavery or serfdom in that the labor was remunerated.[50] Despite this, indigenous laborers rarely ever received payment.[51] The 300,000 peso debt owed to Pampangan laborers that sparked the 1660 mutiny was not the first of its kind. For instance, in 1620, Franciscan Fr. Pedro de San Pablo conducted a similar investigation into Franciscan provinces and found the Crown owed the indios of Laguna de Bay, Tayabas, Tondo, and Bulacan 524,789 pesos for seven years of service, while the indios of Camarines were owed 22,023 pesos for the same period.[52] Although some of the debt was paid to the Pampangans following the conclusion of the 1660 mutiny, the debt that the Crown owed the Pampangans remained vast twenty years later, as confirmed by a 1680 petition.[53]

Furthermore, the common practice of selling rice back to communities at inflated prices kept debt levels high while also compelling communities to keep producing more rice because they could not afford to purchase it at the market. This type of extortionate behavior was noted throughout the century.[54] For example, in 1683, Bishop Ginés Barrientos wrote that, under the bandala system, indios were obliged to sell what they did not have and were then forced to purchase rice for two or three times more than what they sold it for. In many cases, they were not paid, were paid late, or paid in-kind with goods that were of such poor quality they were not fit for use. Moreover, the repartimientos were not merely of rice, but also included all the fruits of the land, placing a great burden on the indios.[55]

Thus, although colonial labor regimes and economic structures were on paper "new" and less exploitative of indigenous people, in practice, they relied on both the continuation and intensification of old systems of labor and debt servitude. But, although the new colonial labor systems fit within Southeast Asian traditions of servitude and obligation, communities did not automatically accept these conditions, as has been suggested by some historians;[56] resistance to labor exploitation was endemic during this period and periodically spilled over into violent rebellion.

Possibly the greatest consequence of the new colonial labor regime was that it forced indios further into debt. Unable to meet their obligations to the state, many indios were forced to sell themselves into debt servitude.[57] The Augustinians commented on this as early as 1581, noting that the tribute levied on the indios was so great that many accrued debts to one another so that they might meet their payments. The debt regularly increased each month, and many indios found themselves unable to pay it back, resulting in enslavement for them and their children.[58] Meanwhile, in 1620 Fr. San Pablo reported that in the provinces of Laguna de Bay, Tayabas, and Bulacan, more than 473 indios had been forced into slavery as a result of their debts to the Crown, while

704 indios had died during the labor drafts. In Camarines Province, more than 271 had been forced into slavery, 438 had died. Significantly, even larger numbers of indios abandoned their villages altogether, with 1,322 and 2,665 fleeing into the mountains from each of these respective regions—a phenomenon that will be discussed in greater detail in chapter 5.[59]

Flight away from Spanish controlled areas was in fact the most cited response of indios to the burdens imposed on them by the colonial state.[60] Fleeing Spanish occupation, whether by displacement or by choice, thousands chose to live autonomously in independent mountain communities. In 1667, Fr. Rodríguez reported that in the surrounds of Manila there was a greater number of Pampangans than in Pampanga. Although they had been asked on different occasions to return to their towns, the Pampangans would refuse and would instead run away so that they could not be burdened as before.[61] In 1681, the Pampangan principales argued that the number of tributes in the province had fallen from eight thousand to three thousand in the space of just fifteen years, "because most have fled as they cannot suffer the continuous repartimientos and personal services in which we are occupied."[62]

That Philippine communities would turn to rebellion against the colonial state is in many ways unsurprising. Throughout the century, many observers commented on the disastrous social consequences of the labor regimes imposed by the new colonial state. As early as 1582, widespread famine was experienced in the Pampanga region as Pampangans struggled to feed themselves while also meeting the demands of the bandala, repartimiento, and tribute systems. The Bishop of Manila, Fr. Domingo de Salazar, reported that the labor levies had forced many indios away from their fields for months at a time. Some of the laborers died and those who returned to their fields were exhausted and unable to produce a sufficient harvest. Consequently, the region suffered a major shortage in rice that year and many indios died of starvation, with more than a thousand deaths in one encomienda alone.[63] Twenty years later, in 1602, Governor Francisco Tello reported that famine and death from starvation were still widespread in the Pampanga region.[64]

Widespread famine was a natural consequence arising from the Spanish imposition of taxation and forced requisitioning of food from communities while also recruiting able-bodied men into lengthy periods of labor away from their regular agricultural duties. Woodcutting, in particular, required thousands of men to work in forests at any one time. Labor was mostly sourced from the Tagalog and Pampangan regions, but levies also occurred in the Visayas and Camarines at particular points in time. Labor drafts were seasonal, and woodcutting occurred in mobile camps established within the forests. Severe conditions within the forests led to death, flight, desertion, and ultimately rebellion.[65]

In 1680, a group of Pampangan principales said that laborers in the forests often worked until they died and that the overseers "treat us worse than slaves, beating us without mercy so that we work more than we have the strength for."[66] The next largest areas of indio labor were shipbuilding and military service, both of which could result in terms of service lasting many months or even years. The main shipyards were established in Cavite as early as 1582, leading to the development of a vibrant port city with 1,400 laborers working in the docks at any given time.[67] Secondary shipyards were also established at Oton, Camarines, Balayan, Lampon, Marinduque, Ibalon, Mindoro, Masbate, and Leyte,[68] and ships were periodically constructed in response to shipwrecks or shortages in available vessels. Pampangan indios served in military companies stationed all over the archipelago, while indios from other parts of the Philippines were regularly recruited into supporting extraordinary military expeditions involving thousands of indigenous soldiers.[69]

With the men away for months at a time, the women of the communities had to assume responsibility for agricultural work. Fr. Salazar described the wives of laborers weeping at having been "left for dead."[70] In 1619, the Franciscan Fr. Pedro de San Pablo related a story of an *india* from the province of Camarines being driven to infanticide out of desperation and overwork. Eight days after having given birth, this woman put a poisonous substance on her breasts so that the baby could not feed and to make it appear as if the baby had died of hunger. Her husband had been away from his family for such a long time, and she did not want to have any more children because of the amount of work that it involved. She felt she was living in a worse condition than slaves who at least were given clothes and food.[71]

A further consequence of this situation was that indios also struggled to meet the requirements of the bandala. In 1658, the attorney Juan de Bolivar y Cruz conducted an investigation into the bandala in different provinces in the islands, finding that many communities could not meet their quotas for agricultural output due to a lack of laborers since many men were recruited to work in woodcutting or the shipyards.[72] Some petitions for reprieve were successful. For example, in August 1657, a delegation of a hundred Pampangan women from the town of Apalit arrived at Bolivar y Cruz's house in Manila to present a petition asking to be relieved from the bandala that they had been asked to provide, which consisted of 871 *cavanes* of rice.[73] They said they were unable to provide this amount because their harvests that year had been so lacking. In response, their *gobernadorcillo* had begun to harass them and to arrest and jail their husbands, brothers, and relatives, as well as widows and poor people. He also threatened to give fifty lashes to those who refused to contribute. They wanted to go to other towns to buy rice, but no one was available for this kind of journey because many of their husbands were already serving in woodcutting in the forests. Their poverty was so great that they were sustaining themselves and their children from tree roots and fruits of the forest because they had no rice. They humbly petitioned to be granted mercy and to be given a reprieve from the bandala. Having received this petition, the royal officials in Manila noted that the royal warehouses were very short on rice and that it was impossible not to requisition more to provision both Manila and Cavite. After the intervention of Bolivar y Cruz, a decree was issued saying that the indios needed to be paid for the goods they provided and that they should not be compelled into providing these services or subjected to any abuses. Additionally, the town of Apalit was excused from providing any more than three hundred *cavanes* of rice for the bandala that year.[74]

In 1691, the principales of Cagayan wrote about the combined impacts that Spanish tribute and labor regimes had on their communities. They noted first that there was no silver in the province with which to pay the tribute that was being asked of them. Tribute collections were consequently regularly accompanied by whippings and beatings and some indios were imprisoned in the forts as punishment for their inability to pay. The leaders protested that "even if they murdered us and tore us to pieces, it is impossible for most of us to pay [the tribute] because no one can give what they do not have."[75] The use of force in the collection of tribute caused many Cagayanes to flee into the mountains or to other provinces, some men leaving behind wives and children. Meanwhile, those who stayed were forced into labor for Spanish and indigenous officials for up to a year at a time in order to make up for the unpaid tribute. Families were torn apart by this situation, harvests were abandoned, and children were left without the means to provide for themselves. The Cagayanes concluded that many chose to abandon Spanish settlements altogether, fleeing into the mountains where they fought bitterly to maintain their liberty and independence.[76]

The Pampanga mutiny of 1660 is the most dramatic example of a rebellion against colonial labor regimes, demonstrating through the tactics of river blockades that Pampangans were intimately aware of their economic role and the power this granted to them. Yet, this was not the only or even the first example of such a rebellion against the repartimiento and bandala.[77] In 1649, rebellion spread across the Visayas in response to a particularly onerous labor draft that would have meant sending thousands of Visayan Indians to the shipyards of Cavite and the forests of Pampanga as part of a major shipbuilding project. The rebellion began in the island of Samar, one of the eastern-most islands in the Philippines. Like Malong, the leader—Sumoroy—was a prominent ally of the Spanish, serving as the castellan of the Spanish fort in Samar.

On hearing that he would be among those sent to serve in the shipyards at Cavite, Sumoroy mobilized the disaffection felt by other indios in Palapag and led a group of rebels to murder a Jesuit priest and sack and burn the church. His actions served as a signal for the uprising to spread and churches were put to flame across the province. The rebels retreated into the mountains, where they fortified themselves. Meanwhile, the rebellion extended across the Visayas to Camarines, Masbate, Cebu, Caraga, Iligan, Northern Mindanao, and Leyte.[78]

Sumoroy is memorialized as a heroic figure of Filipino resistance to Spanish imperialism. Yet he is also emblematic of the way in which Philippine elites could switch from cooperation to rebellion within one lifetime. For Spanish chroniclers, he was a figure that represented betrayal to the Spanish cause, and he was cast as debauched, unholy, crazed, and drunken. This need to discredit him personally must have come in large part from Sumoroy's prominent position as a local community leader, member of the Spanish military, and castellan of the Spanish fort. Men like Sumoroy held power in their communities, and their choice to rebel posed a great threat to Spanish authority. Nevertheless, the rebellion of once loyal indigenous leaders like Sumoroy reveals a precarious balance in which indigenous elites oscillated between loyalty and disobedience to the Spanish cause. When attempting to muster forces to crush Sumoroy's rebellion, the *alcalde mayor* of Samar confronted this reality. He tried to gather forces from among the "adventurers in the province, mestizos, and Indians; but, as the former were all collectors [of tribute] and the latter all relatives [of the insurgents], some were not accustomed to the hardships of campaigning, and the others could not use weapons against those of their own blood."[79]

Reform, Counter-Reform, and the Role of Indigenous Elites

Not all Spanish officials were comfortable with the reliance of colonial labor regimes on debt servitude. By the mid-century, following Sumoroy's rebellion, it was evident to some that colonial labor demands had imposed excessive burdens on local communities, creating chronic instability and resistance both in the form of widespread flight into the mountains as well as violent rebellion. In the 1650s, a group of secular reformers began to agitate against labor exploitation and its impact on increasing debt servitude among indigenous communities. They did this through publishing a series of pamphlets and engaging in interventions within the audiencia. These reformers argued in favor of the application of imperial laws that protected the fundamental rights of indigenous people as free subjects of the Crown. Yet, the interventions of these secular reformers prompted a backlash principally from the religious authorities, revealing that the dependence on unfree labor extended into every aspect of colonial rule. Crucially, these debates expose the key contradiction of the Spanish colonial project in the Philippines: the dependency of colonial order on pre-Hispanic labor relations and the need to maintain debt servitude in order to retain the loyalty of indigenous elites.

Calls for reform of colonial labor regimes coalesced around the senior *oidor* Don Salvador Gómez de Espinosa y Estrada and a tract that he wrote in 1657 called the *Discurso Parenético* that strongly condemned the widespread abuses occurring in Philippine communities.[80] The *Discurso Parenético* investigated the central role of unfree and illegal labor regimes within Philippine communities, which Gómez de Espinosa described as a form of "slavery, violence, and tyranny" that contravened the natural liberty of indigenous people.[81] The type of labor described by Gómez de Espinosa was typically labeled in colonial documents as *servicios personales*, or the forced requisitioning of indigenous labor for the personal advantage of encomenderos and other Spanish officials. As will be evident, the servicios personales described by Gómez de Espinosa were a natural extension of the debt servitude that underpinned colonial labor relations.

Servicios personales were roundly condemned by royal officials in Madrid as a gross violation of Spanish jurisprudence, which respected the personal liberty of all indigenous vassals of the king, and had been prohibited very early on in the history of the Spanish empire, first in 1536 and then again with the publication of the New Laws in 1542.[82] Philippine indios should have benefited from these early reforms; however, evidence from throughout the late sixteenth and seventeenth centuries demonstrates that these decrees were flaunted time and again.[83] Thus, decades after their prohibition, servicios personales were a persistent reality in many Philippine communities and missionaries, encomenderos, royal officials, and indigenous elites alike all relied on them for both the imposition and continued functioning of colonial rule at the barangay level.[84] Gómez de Espinosa's work exposed the tension between the theoretical liberty of indigenous subjects within Spanish jurisprudence and the realities within the Philippines. At the heart of this tension were the indigenous elite, who continued to operate within the same structures of kinship-based debt and obligation.

The *Discurso Parenético* describes clearly how preexisting structures underpinned the widespread exploitation of indio labor within Spanish settlements. According to Gómez de Espinosa, servicios personales would not be possible without the participation and sanction of indigenous elites and the existence of a highly structured community hierarchy reliant on debt servitude. *Cabezas de barangay* occupied the highest position within local communities and were, alongside their offspring, exempt from participating in the bandalas and repartimientos. Instead, they occupied political and military posts. Below the cabezas were the principales and their offspring, who typically participated in both the bandala and repartimiento systems but were also rewarded with public, political, and military positions. At the bottom were the commoners who not only served in woodcutting and other labor drafts but also as oarsmen, porters, and in all the other menial, low, and mechanical jobs.[85] Each cabeza had under his care thirty tributes, known as a *cabanza*. The cabeza was responsible for collecting tribute from the cabanza to pass on to the *alcalde mayor* and the encomendero. But Gómez de Espinosa notes that the cabanza was also the means by which missionaries and royal officials could secure direct access to indio labor. The cabezas and principales not only took advantage of the sweat and labor of these indios, but they also sold them and managed them "as if they were their masters and absolute lords."[86] If someone had the need to cut, cart, or carve wood to build a house, he would make a contract with the cabeza and they would agree on the price. The cabeza then provided his cabanza to do the labor and they participated despite never receiving a real of the agreed price, which the cabeza kept all for himself. Gómez de Espinosa said that the rule of the cabezas was one of "despotic domination over goods, body, and treasury."[87]

These structures within Philippine communities facilitated the extension of servicios personales, allowing Spaniards access to local labor via the cabeza and his cabanza. Missionaries feature prominently within the *Discurso Parenético*'s critique of this system. The religious orders routinely made demands on labor time, asking indios to labor in the construction and repair of church buildings without any limits or regulation.[88] Young, unmarried women were made to weed and sweep the patios of the churches, to sow seeds and water the vegetable patches, and gather flowers to adorn the churches, while also traveling from town to town carrying rice to be placed in the church granaries. All of this was done despite the fact that there were sacristans designated to assist in the churches.[89] Additionally, missionaries engaged in illegal requisitioning of goods, especially rice, which was seen as a kind of compulsory alms that in some provinces was called *Pasalamat*. Gómez de Espinosa described the missionaries as standing at the church door and asking all those who arrived for prayer or service to make a contribution of rice. On Fridays, Saturdays, and on holy days, indios were obliged to provide the missionaries with fish and eggs. Two houses were chosen in the town each week to pay two reales—one for fish and one for eggs—and if they did not pay then they were punished severely. They were also asked to provide chickens for ordinary and extraordinary expenses, including visits from guests and from superiors. Finally, some missionaries were implicated in extracting goods in order to engage in profiteering and trade. Indios were forced to contribute blankets, handkerchiefs, quilts, shawls, bolts of silk and cotton, wax, civet, safflower, rice, coconut oil, *lampotes* (Philippine cotton cloth), and other fabrics, among many other things.[90]

Although frequently accused of exploiting indigenous labor, missionaries were not the only ones engaged in these kinds of activities. Indios frequently labored as porters for *alcaldes mayores* and other travelers.[91] In 1580, two Franciscans pointed out that the Spaniards in the islands had become accustomed to using indios as oarsmen even in instances where they could navigate by sail. They behaved as cruel tyrants toward these indios, whipping them, calling them dogs and other insults, and taking them by force, paying them little or nothing.[92] Gómez de Espinosa reported that on journeys between the provinces and Manila, indios typically transported clothes, provisions, and other luggage. All the goods would be placed on hammocks and litters carried on their shoulders. These journeys put additional strain on the villages they passed through that had to provide the travelers with food. When a visit was made to inspect the provinces, the officials demanded provisions of wood, water, vegetables, lemons, tomatoes, chilies, onions, salt, vinegar, and other items.[93]

Those who refused these labors would be subjected to cruel whippings, forced to cut their hair, or placed in stocks and irons or in private jails built for the purpose of punishing indios.[94] The result was that indios lived in fear of the priests, alcaldes mayores, and encomenderos and, although they were asked frequently during inspections of the provinces if they were mistreated, none dared to speak up.[95] Gómez de Espinosa concluded that servicios personales could not "be free donations but compelled exactions, not voluntary alms but violent extortions."[96]

The involvement of indigenous elites in the orchestration of servicios personales may help to explain the unwillingness of indios to speak out to colonial authorities since this type of exploitation sat firmly within the logic of existing debt servitude relationships within communities. This was certainly the opinion of the attorney Juan de Quesada Hurtado de Mendoza who placed the blame on the Philippine elites rather than on the impositions of the Spanish. He recommended in 1630 that the audiencia organize an inspection to determine whether the repartimiento and bandala were taking place appropriately, with the aim of such an inspection to place at liberty some of the indios that were being held as slaves by principales. While some of these slaves were hereditary, others had been made into slaves through the loan of rice or other goods. Hurtado de Mendoza argued that by these means, parents, children, and an entire generation had been placed in servitude. He noted that even though he and his predecessors had put a lot of effort into tackling the injustice of slavery, they had not been able to free many. He believed that this was because when an owner heard that his slave wanted to go and plea for liberty, he would capture and imprison him and punish him in a thousand ways. Hurtado de Mendoza denounced the indios as "a cruel people" and believed that the king should step in to resolve the situation.[97]

Although reformers like Hurtado de Mendoza failed to tackle the underlying structures of slavery within Philippine communities, many royal officials both in Manila and Madrid attempted to control and restrict the abuses committed by Spanish missionaries and officials through servicios personales. Between 1575 and 1700 dozens of decrees were issued dealing with the treatment of indios by royal officials and missionaries.[98] In the 1650s, two royal officials—the oidor Don Salvador Gómez de Espinosa y Estrada and the attorney Don Juan de Bolivar y Cruz—made a concerted effort to abolish servicios personales in the archipelago. While Gómez de Espinosa's Discurso Parenético was the centerpiece of this effort, the majority of his findings were repeated by Bolivar y Cruz in supporting letters sent to the Crown in 1657 and 1658.[99] The two officials argued that indios were, by nature, free and that this freedom was protected by the Catholic faith and by their incorporation into the Spanish Crown. For this reason, they could not and should never be forced to perform any service against their will.[100] Toward the end of the Discurso Parenético, Gómez de Espinosa reasserted the provision in the New Laws that stated that all indigenous labor must be free and paid, and that payment should be made directly into the hands of the laborers themselves, and not into the hands of the cabezas or principales. He additionally advocated for strict regulation on the hours worked, the seasonal timing of labor drafts, and the conditions experienced by indios while laboring for the Crown.[101]

While the efforts of these two reformers were received well by the Council of Indies in Madrid, this was not the case in Manila, where the publishing of the Discurso provoked great outrage and protestation, particularly from the religious orders. The Bishop of Nueva Segovia, Fr. Rodrigo de Cardena, thought the book was dangerous and unfairly attacked the goodwill and aims of the missionary orders. The Franciscan Fr. Francisco Solier openly attacked the Discurso from the pulpit, warning that it could cause great damage to the project of conversion, and he suggested that Gómez de Espinosa was doing the devil's work.[102] An anonymous pamphlet argued that the Discurso was an example of "theological error" and was "intolerable and scandalous." The author of this pamphlet cautioned that Gómez de Espinosa could become the next Las Casas and that the information contained within the Discurso could fall into the hands of the enemies of Spain—particularly Makassar, China, and Siam—and be used against them.[103] Gómez de Espinosa was greatly disheartened by the reaction of the priests and he wrote to Madrid to say that he believed that their attacks had overshadowed the original intentions of the work. In the wake of the uproar, he agreed to gather up all of the copies of the *Discurso* and hand them to the prior of the convent of Santo Domingo, who organized for them to be burned on a pyre.[104] For good measure, the religious orders also made a formal complaint against the tract before the Inquisition in New Spain.[105] Unfortunately, by the time letters of support for the *Discurso* from the Council of Indies reached Manila,[106] Gómez de Espinosa had already left to take up a position in Guatemala where he died shortly afterward.[107] Although many of his efforts were carried on by Bolivar y Cruz, who succeeded him as *oidor* in the audiencia, there is very little evidence to suggest that any real reform was made to the servicios personales or to the ongoing practice of debt servitude within Philippine communities.

Nevertheless, the efforts of Gómez de Espinosa and Bolivar y Cruz undoubtedly contributed to the publication of a new royal decree abolishing all forms of indigenous slavery in the Philippines in 1679. This decree, issued on June 12, 1679 by King Charles II, stated that there was "no cause or any pretext to make slaves of the native indios of the Western Indies and the islands adjacent; but that [the indios] must be treated as vassals of His Majesty."[108] Building on more than 150 years of royal decrees regulating the use of native labor and sanctioning the exploitative behavior of Spanish officials,[109] the decree was devoted to abolishing the practice of enslaving indigenous captives of war—a practice that was common in frontier regions like Chile, as well as the Philippines.[110] Yet, in the case of the Philippines, it also targeted the pre-Hispanic institution of indigenous debt servitude.

Whereas in the case of the *Discurso Parenético* opponents of reform had been able to stifle the contents through political maneuvering and the use of the Inquisition, this time they had to answer directly to the king. Their justifications given for maintaining debt servitude in the Philippines provide us with the most coherent explanation for its importance both to the economic life of the archipelago and the ongoing survival of Spanish colonial rule. In making their reply to the king in 1682, the City of Manila and the religious orders argued that slavery was a part of the spiritual and temporal life of the indigenous people of the islands. They expressed grave concerns that if the slaves of the principales were liberated, there would be a shortage in farmworkers and a lack of hands to cultivate rice and other crops and to work on the livestock estates, which could result in severe shortages of food and other necessities. Prices would rise, placing pressure on local communities. The potential was for a generalized famine across the archipelago that, in turn, would weaken the Spanish defenses since many would die and they would be open to invasion from surrounding enemies, which could result in a total loss of the archipelago. They furthermore feared that the principales would simply abandon the Spanish territories to go and live in enemy kingdoms among the Borneans, Sulus, and Maguindanaos, and so it was necessary to abandon the royal decree to avoid a great revolt. A confederacy between native elites and surrounding enemies would be enough to completely defeat them and the Spanish would lose the Philippines altogether.[111]

It was the actions of figures like Sumoroy, Maniago, and Malong—all once-loyal indio leaders who led rebellions against the colonial state—that were at the forefront of the minds of colonial officials when responding to this decree. Although the audiencia initially agreed to abide by the decree, by September 1682 the royal courts had been inundated with petitions for freedom from indigenous debt servants, prompting concerns that indigenous elites would withdraw their support for the colonial state if the decree was fully enacted. The audiencia consequently decided to suspend the decree and reverse any decisions made to liberate indigenous slaves. In explaining their actions, they argued that "these islands should not be considered the same as the rest of the kingdoms and provinces of the Americas, where the slaves are negros and mulattos or pure indios: because in these islands there is such a diversity of nations that it is not easy to comprehend all of them and impossible to record them."[112] Although a new decree was issued in 1692 that opted for the gradual phase out of indigenous slavery by abolishing the right to trade slaves by loan, sale, or inheritance, it nevertheless upheld the right for indigenous communities to continue to practice debt servitude and thus opened up pathways for labor exploitation to continue.[113]

In closing this chapter, we might finally answer why the once-loyal Malong chose to rebel, and why his rebellion was furthermore so treacherous to the Spaniards. As we have seen, communities responded to the excessive and combined burdens of new colonial labor regimes through flight, abandoning their lands and in doing so abandoning their kinship networks. This was a response to a new regime which exceeded the traditional limits of mutual obligation that underpinned the economy of Philippine communities. Yet, it also meant that indigenous elites typically found their grip on authority slipping, as their bondspeople disappeared into the hills. Rebellion remained a final option for leaders like Malong, who sat at the intersection of colonial and precolonial systems of power and social organization. Malong's rebellion represents the tenuous nature of colonial control in the seventeenth century, where Spanish power was itself beholden to the continued loyalty of local elites and their capacity, in turn, to keep their own subjects in control.

CHAPTER 3

Contested Conversions

In 1622, Bancao, the datu of Carigara on the Visayan island of Leyte, decided to leave his village and the watchful gaze of Jesuit missionaries and set to work building a new temple to the local ancestor spirits. He was aided in this task by his son and another man named Pagali. Once the temple was finished, Bancao issued a declaration of rebellion against the Spanish and incited six villages across Leyte to rise up and join him. Like Malong, Bancao was intimately integrated into the new colonial order in the Visayas, having reportedly been one of the first datus to welcome Legazpi in 1565. Although he initially converted to Christianity, it appears that Bancao grew tired of the Spanish yoke over the course of the intervening decades and longed for a return to pre-Hispanic spiritual practices.

In response to Bancao's rebellion, Don Juan de Alcarazo commanded an armada of forty vessels containing both Spanish and indigenous soldiers, who joined the soldiers already stationed on the island. As the Spanish troops gathered, Bancao and his followers retreated, drawing the soldiers into the hills with the hopes that the rugged terrain would prove to their advantage. Despite this, many of the Visayans were injured and killed in the ensuing battles. Alcarazo seized and occupied Bancao's temple for ten days and then burnt it down. In one of the melees, Bancao was killed with a lance and his head was placed on a stake as a warning to the others. His son was also beheaded, and his daughter was taken captive. Several other rebels were shot and one of the native priests was burnt as a warning to the rest of the population of Leyte.[1] Notably, after these events, missionary activity in this part of Leyte remained limited throughout the seventeenth century.[2]

The religious dimensions of Bancao's revolt—played out within the grounds of his hilltop temple—were not unusual. Particularly in the Visayas, native priests, known in the Visayas as *babaylans*, led a number of major rebellions, resulting not only in the abandonment of Christian conversion but often also in the violent death of Spanish missionaries.[3] The babaylans who led these rebellions in the Visayas tell us something about the power of indigenous religion as a counteractive force to Spanish colonization.

This chapter considers the impact of native priests and their connection to local spiritual landscapes on the progression of Christianization in the seventeenth-century Philippines. Early conflicts over conversion—such as that which took place in Leyte in 1622—provide an important backdrop to the process of religious syncretism that anthropologists have long argued is a hallmark of modern Filipino folk Catholicism. In most pre-Hispanic communities, religious leadership was performed primarily by women and when men took on the role of priest they would typically dress in women's clothing.[4] A Spanish interrogation of idolatrous practices in the Zambales Mountains in 1686 uncovered 159 women who were either known priestesses or regularly engaged in ritual sacrifices.[5] Despite this, many Spanish chronicles mask the agency and power of these women.[6] At the same time, there is evidence that as religious leaders came to take on a more martial character—often leading rebellions—this role did pass to men. This transition occurred contemporaneously to the assimilation of many datus into new colonial leadership roles. For communities that rejected colonization, religious leaders thus became important symbols of community cohesion and resistance.[7] Native priests and priestesses formed a second pillar of power in Philippine communities, alongside that of the datus. Their power was derived from their ability to commune with the spirit world—especially with dead ancestors—and for their perceived abilities as healers and fortune tellers.

The academic literature on religion in the Philippines displays a strong tension between an assumption often articulated in historical accounts that the project of Catholic conversion was completed rapidly through most of the lowland and island regions,[8] and the abundance of modern anthropological evidence that pre-Hispanic belief systems are still prevalent across the breadth of the archipelago.[9] The first perspective was reflected in Phelan's account of the colonial era. While acknowledging many problems inherent within the process of conversion—including shortages of priests, abusive behavior among the missionaries, and the commercial interests of some missionaries—Phelan's conclusion that the project of Christianization was completed by the end of the seventeenth century has nonetheless endured within the wider historiography.[10] A generation of historians following Phelan underplayed the caveats that he highlighted, preferring instead to view the "expansive, prolific [and] glorious"[11] efforts of the missionaries as responsible for bringing the Philippines out of "her chaotic, primitive socio-political status into a modern, well-organized society."[12] For these historians, missionaries achieved more in the conquest of Philippine indios than any soldier. They depict the friars as engineers, sailors, architects, builders, physicists, naturalists, linguists, mathematicians, astronomers, cosmographers, artists, artisans, teachers and pedagogues, moralists, and champions of indigenous rights.[13] From within this view, the idea that conversion was partial or incomplete is difficult to contemplate. Missionary requirements that converts demonstrate a full and sincere understanding of the Catholic faith before they were baptized left no room for partial conversion.[14]

These conclusions contrast starkly with the findings of numerous twentieth-century anthropologists, who emphasize the persistence of pre-Hispanic animist religious beliefs and practices throughout the Philippines. Their studies show that nominally Christian communities continue to believe in the existence of a spirit world that needs to be acknowledged and placated through ritual observances. Rituals and ceremonies invoking these spirits take place especially during moments of crisis or illness or as part of social or economic activities like the beginning of the harvest or the construction of a road.[15] These arguments naturally raise questions regarding the completeness of Christian conversion centuries earlier during the colonial era—a question that a new generation of historians has also sought to address. Writing about the Western Visayas, the historical anthropologist Alfred McCoy concluded that "Visayan animism had not merely survived as some atavistic curiosity, but in fact remained the dominant spiritual force in the Western Visayas."[16] Indeed, he argues that "folk Catholicism" hardly accounts for the processes that have taken place in the Visayas, where Catholicism did not supplant animism but was merely—and only very partially—incorporated into the preexisting belief systems.[17] Vicente Rafael similarly shows how Philippine communities both adopted and transformed Christian beliefs through the process of translating them both linguistically and culturally.[18]

Missionaries across the Philippines only achieved conversion when they adapted their practices through a concerted engagement with existing cultures and belief patterns. In particular, missionaries needed to adopt many of the practices of native priests and priestesses in engaging with the spiritual landscape of local communities. At the same time, this adaptation was not merely a matter of cultural translation. The conversion process itself was widely contested and engendered violence on both sides. While Philippine communities at times rejected conversion through acts of rebellion, running away, or killing priests, missionaries were responsible for some of the most extreme cases of abuse and corruption witnessed in the archipelago. This history of abuse and violence has largely been written out of the historical record thanks in part to the dominant interest in church history by historians who themselves have missionary backgrounds.[19] The archival record demonstrates that peaceful conversion was by no means the favored strategy of religious orders. Throughout the century a tension is evident between those who believed that conversion could only be achieved through force and those who realized that the use of force provoked greater resistance to conversion. Ultimately, a nonviolent adaptation demonstrated by certain missionaries was a response to the strength of existing religious beliefs as well as the insistence of Philippine communities in maintaining a connection to their spiritual landscapes.

Spiritual Landscapes

The archival record is full of stories of missionary accounts of conversion activities. A typical example from 1601 depicts two Jesuit missionaries setting off to preach the Holy Gospel in Catubig, in the very northeast of the Visayan island of Samar. They struggled for many days through difficult terrain, wading through thigh-high water and knee-high mud. They climbed up rugged and dense mountains, sometimes scaling cliffs with their bare hands. They suffered both hunger and thirst and their clothes became ragged. The missionaries felt that the task was worth these temporal discomforts because they encountered many people interested in their Christian religion. Fr. Juan de Torres related how one night they gathered together the communities of three towns, who rejoiced at the priests' arrival. They told these Visayans of matters relating to the afterlife, of the immortality of the soul, of how God rewarded the Christians in heaven, and of the torments in hell for those who did not convert. In response to these teachings, Fr. Torres claimed that all the Visayans begged to be made Christian and to be allowed to build a bigger church.[20]

Appearing in chronicles, letters, and the regular annual reports produced by the Jesuit order, such accounts portray miraculous conversions achieved by a small group of religious men in formidable environments.[21] Yet, it was not just difficult terrain and the shortage of missionaries that encumbered the conversion process.[22] Missionaries also had to confront both temporal and spiritual cultures that made the process of conversion more challenging. Foremost among these was the way in which Philippine communities related to their local environments. The landscape was not only a place of economic productivity—a place to plant and harvest rice crops or to hunt or forage—but also a place deeply connected to their concept of the spirit world. Thus, for the Visayans of Catubig, the forests that Fr. Torres and his companion traversed were not only wild and rugged places but were also filled with the presence of both good and evil spirits whose humors could determine the fortune of those who passed through them.

Communities across the Philippines believed that their landscapes were inhabited by spirits and that signs within the natural environment needed to be closely observed and respected as portents for the health and well-being of the community.[23] Although the specific nature of these beliefs differed across the archipelago, all Philippine communities shared the common belief that the world was guided by invisible spirits who could either be good or evil. Some of these spirits belonged to ancestors who had died, while others were said to occupy particular sites—like a rock or a tree—and performed different spiritual functions.[24] In describing Philippine beliefs, Pedro Fernández del Pulgar wrote in the mid-seventeenth century that the different spirits that communities worshipped—known as *divatas* by the Visayans and *anitos* by the Tagalogs—were intimately connected to place. Some spirits had ownership over the mountains and the countryside and community members would ask them for permission to travel through these regions. Others looked after crops and ritual sacrifices were made to ensure the success of the harvest. There was an *anito* for the sea and for fishing and navigation, and an *anito* for the house, who looked after the person who was born there.[25] Fr. Pedro Chirino noted that many of the spirits were thought to take the form of animals or birds. Particular animals, like the crocodile, were held in reverence and offered sacrifices in order to keep them happy. Spirits also occupied specific locations like trees, stones, rocks, reefs, and cliffs.[26] In reality, the pantheon of spirits and the functions they served differed from community to community. In the 1680s, the Zambales reported the names of a hundred different spirits, all with different purposes.[27] The Tagalogs of Santo Tomás in Laguna de Bay in 1686 gave some examples of these purposes. For instance, there was a spirit for childbirth, another for midwives, others responsible for highways, hunting, farming, pathways, merchants, winds, harvests, cripples, navigation, marriage, plants, for the dead and sick, and two that were considered to be guardians of the temple where they believed the souls gathered after death.[28]

Perhaps as a consequence of these variations across communities, the worship of these spirits was also specific to particular locations. The chronicler Antonio de Morga suggested that Philippine communities did not have any temples or other places of worship outside the home, where most ritual observances took place.[29] But what Morga and others may have missed is that this worship often took place in locations in the natural world that had designated spiritual importance. His contemporary, Chirino mentions a famous site in Mindanao where warriors would shoot a volley of arrows into a cliff-face each time they set out on a slave raiding mission. Another known site of worship was a rock at the mouth of the Pasig River in Manila.[30] For communities across Laguna de Bay, these sites were typically caves or gullies found in the mountains. The Tagalogs described gatherings in these sites that often involved more than a hundred people who would eat, drink, sing, and make offerings to the spirits.[31] Other locations attained spiritual importance after they became the burial site of an important ancestor. Chirino relates the story of a warrior in Leyte who had a hut constructed on a part of the coast where his body was placed after he died and this site became a place of worship by all those voyagers who passed by.[32] Fields, where communities harvested their crops, were also common sites of ritual observance, where the spirits were called on to ensure the success of the harvest or in times of plague or pestilence.[33] Other parts of the countryside could not be cultivated as they were considered to be inhabited by ancestor spirits.[34]

Thus, the Philippine landscape was heavily imbued with spiritual meaning. Native priestesses presided over religious ceremonies in Philippine communities. In the Visayas, these women were known as babaylans, while in Tagalog they were called catalonans. Pedro Fernández del Pulgar said that the role of priest was often inherited, although others were chosen for their natural aptitude for communing with the spirits.[35] The Zambales described a hierarchy among priests that the Dominican missionaries interpreted as being equivalent to the hierarchy of the Catholic Church. In this region, some were like bishops who said the equivalent of mass that they called *mamagat*, others were priests called *mogatao*, and those who delivered the gospel were called *mibaniac*. Apostles were called *mibuaya*, acolytes were called *sumanga*. The priestesses were called *baliang*, and they occupied the highest offices. During ceremonies, a sacrifice was usually made involving a pig or another animal and offerings were made to the spirits in the form of silver, pigs, deer, chicken, fish, eggs, tamales, cooked rice, wine, oil, vinegar, grapes, and other types of food. These celebrations were typically performed as a way of communing with the dead, in times of illness, to mark the start of the harvest, or before hunting, fishing, or commencing a long journey.[36] Spanish observers described the behavior of the native priestesses as akin to being possessed by the devil.[37] Yet, for community members, the theater of the sacrifice was an essential part of communing with the spirit world.

A former native priest from Zambales reported that each priestess had their own methods of performing ceremonies. His usual practice was to prepare the food and drink and then to sit beneath an awning and invoke the spirit with certain sung words. He conveyed with signs that the spirit sat on his shoulder where all of those present could venerate it, crossing their arms and asking the spirit to help them. They would give the *anito* offerings of food and drink while the priest sang praises to the spirit. Everyone then ate and drank, including the priest, in the name of the spirit, which showed signs when it was satisfied and ready to go.[38] Other Zambales described seeing the priestess urinate in front of the gathering as a way of expelling the spirit. In Laguna de Bay sacrifices often involved the symbolism of a large serpent, which they called Sava. One woman said she had seen this serpent in the mouth of a cave and that the priestess spoke to it saying—"move aside, grandpa, allow your grandchildren to come and visit with you"[39]—after which the serpent disappeared, causing the woman to be very afraid. She had also seen the priestess with eyes as if they were on fire, talking unintelligibly in a manner that terrified all that were present. Priestesses in this region were believed to be capable of miracles, such as causing water to spring from rocks.[40]

Missionaries were forced to confront these spiritual beliefs when convincing indios to join newly founded Spanish settlements and convert to Christianity. Despite this, the number of missionaries engaged in this work was relatively limited compared to the extensiveness of their claims to the rapid and complete conversion of hundreds of thousands of souls in just a few short years. Over the course of the seventeenth century, the missionary population of the Philippines averaged around 350 priests, about a quarter of whom were stationed in Manila. These numbers fluctuated throughout the century, reaching a high of 490 in 1610 and falling to just 211 in 1691 (see tables 1 and 2). Requests for more missionaries to be sent to the islands were among some of the most common petitions sent back to Spain throughout the century.[41]

As a way of overcoming these numerical shortcomings, royal officials and missionaries alike advocated the reduction of indios into towns where they could be congregated into populations of several thousand people, following similar settlement patterns utilized by missionaries in Latin America.[42] Doing so would aid the process of conversion, especially in the context of great shortages in the number of priests for such a dispersed population.[43] Yet, the process of founding new towns was severely curtailed by the preexisting settlement patterns of Philippine communities. Throughout the islands, community members preferred to live in small, scattered, and isolated hamlets or villages, where they could be close to their fields.[44] The idea of living congregated into a town made little economic sense to the majority of communities who lived off a combination of subsistence farming and hunting and gathering. Since most rice crops did not produce a surplus that lasted for the entire year, com-

Table 1   Missionaries serving in the Philippines, 1588–1691

RELIGIOUS ORDER	1588[1]	1591[2]	1593[3]	1598[4]	1601[5]	1610[6]	1656[7]	1691[8]
Augustinians	63			158	162	169	84	60
Franciscans	72			120	126	139	64	48
Dominicans	1			71	51	80	43	38
Jesuits	4			43	30	86	64	16
Recollects						16	26	14
Secular clergy	7			Unknown	Unknown	Unknown	59	35
TOTAL	147	142	103	392	369	490	340	211

[1] Archivo Histórico Nacional, Colección Documentos de Indias, leg. 26, núm. 10.
[2] Archivo General de Indias (hereafter AGI), Patronato, leg. 25, ramo 38. This document only records the total number of missionaries and not the breakdown by individual religious order.
[3] AGI, Audiencia de Filipinas (hereafter Filipinas), leg. 79, núm. 22. This document only records the total number of missionaries and not the breakdown by individual religious order.
[4] AGI, Filipinas, leg. 18B, ramo 8, núm. 106; see also AGI, Filipinas, leg. 6, ramo 9, núm. 167.
[5] AGI, Filipinas, leg. 19, ramo 2, núm. 29.
[6] AGI, Filipinas, leg. 20, ramo 4, núm. 34.
[7] AGI, Filipinas, leg. 9, ramo 3, núm. 45. Note that the figures here do not include missionaries stationed in Manila and Cavite.
[8] AGI, Filipinas, leg. 32, núm. 100.

Table 2   Distribution of missionaries in the Philippines, 1588–1691

PROVINCE	1588[1]	1591[2]	1610[3]	1691[4]
Manila	43	12	128	48
Pampanga (including Bataan and Tondo)	18	28	30	22
Pangasinan	0	8	11	7
Ilocos	5	20	32	11
Cagayan	2	0	27	22
Laguna (including Batangas and Balayan)	37	34	46	22
Camarines	25	15	139[5]	33
Visayas	16	20	77	32
Mindoro, Calamianes, and Marinduque	1	1	0	6
Mindanao	0	0	0	8
TOTAL	147	138	490	211

[1] Archivo Histórico Nacional, Colección Documentos de Indias, leg. 26, núm. 10. Copy in AGI, Audiencia de Filipinas (hereafter Filipinas), leg. 74, núm. 31.
[2] AGI, Patronato, leg. 25, ramo 38. Note that there are significant discrepancies with the numbers recorded within this document, with totals for each province often not matching the number of priests recorded at individual locations. The final total of missionaries present in the islands was recorded as 142, which does not match the number of priests recorded within individual provinces (138).
[3] AGI, Filipinas, leg. 20, ramo 4, núm. 34.
[4] AGI, Filipinas, leg. 32, núm. 100.
[5] In this instance the Franciscans did not differentiate between provinces, so this number also includes missionaries stationed in Manila and Laguna de Bay.

munity members supplemented their harvests with fishing, hunting game, or the gathering of root vegetables and fruits from the forests. Especially in highland areas, communities were often seminomadic, and it was not uncommon for tribute collectors or missionaries to find previously occupied towns abandoned.[45] The Jesuit Fr. Mateo Sanchez noted that Philippine communities had very little need for the towns that the Spanish created. The great amount of labor that went into cultivation and hunting and gathering meant that community members were fully occupied in the countryside, whereas in the towns they had nothing to do. Moreover, he wrote, since most indios preferred to work barefooted and wore little clothing, there was not even a need for towns as centers of artisanal production.[46]

The choice to live in scattered hamlets was largely shaped by a subsistence economy, yet this pattern of land use also had a clear spiritual dimension. Communities were connected to particular locations both for the worship of important and powerful spirits that could determine the success or failure of a harvest and for the ritual remembrance of ancestors. The process of removing populations into towns disrupted these connections and required missionaries to sever the ties that indios felt with the land and with their own ancestors. Thus, the work of missionaries could lead to violent confrontations. In 1600, two Jesuit friars, Fr. Valerio de Ledesma and Brother Dionisio, traveled to the island of Bohol to try to reduce the population into small towns. After working for some months and founding several settlements where the Boholanos could be baptized and hear mass, the two friars were attacked by forty men armed with spears and shields who intended to take them by force. The friars were forced to flee. On their way back to Cebu, they visited the newly founded settlement of Tubigon where they were again attacked by another group of forty-eight men who set fire to the church and assaulted the newly converted Christians. The Jesuits established a sentinel and a watch fire to be lit at night to ward off anyone trying to enter the town. Nonetheless, the attackers besieged the town, attacking anyone who tried to enter or leave.[47]

At times, priests were killed for their work in newly converted communities. In 1645, the Jesuit Fr. Juan Domingo de Arezu was praying in the church of Carigara in Leyte when he was stabbed in the back by three Visayans, who left him to die in a pool of his own blood. One source says that this was a revenge attack by a Visayan who the priest had reprimanded severely for not informing the church that his mother was dying, and so denying her the last rites.[48] In 1659, the Jesuit Fr. Jaime Esteban attempted to convince a particular man from the mountains of Negros to cease cohabiting with a woman and to instead come to live within the Spanish town where he could convert to Christianity. When the friar sent the woman away to another town, the man became so enraged that he plotted along with two others to murder the priest, eventually stabbing him to death.[49]

The common response of communities was simply to retreat further away from missionaries and to continue to practice their own religious observances. In 1682, the Augustinian Recollect Tomás de San Jerónimo wrote that the Caragans of Eastern Mindanao regularly fled from Spanish settlements to resettle back into the mountains, dissolving into small family units and living at a great distance from one another. Despite every effort of the missionaries, they were unable to consolidate any major settlements in this region. He said that, at best, the Caragans would spend a night in the towns established by the Spanish but, at daybreak, they would disperse once again into the surrounding countryside.[50] On the island of Mindoro, the Recollects were similarly frustrated by their inability to form permanent settlements. In this instance, Fr. San Jerónimo wrote that it was the work of some ancient and superstitious principales who were able to convince the majority of those living in the Spanish towns to retreat into the interior of the island and renounce the Catholic faith. By 1682, the Recollects in Mindoro barely controlled two hundred baptized indios.[51] While flight was an opportunity for communities to continue their pre-Hispanic religious practices, it was also a means of escaping the exploitation and abuses that indigenous people experienced in Spanish settlements, often at the hands of the missionaries themselves.

Missionaries and Local Communities

Many missionaries were reluctant to admit that their orders were involved in widespread exploitation or abuse as doing so would undermine their requests for ongoing aid and increased authority over indigenous communities. Nonetheless, ample evidence exists to implicate missionaries in exploitative behavior. The dispersed and isolated nature of missionary work meant that priests operated without much day-to-day scrutiny, leading some to adopt immoral or corrupt ways. In 1690, the audiencia accused the missionary orders in general of having largely abandoned their apostolic aims and of being "those that most afflict the natives and inhabitants."[52] In 1683, the Bishop of Nueva Cáceres gave a damning description of the secular clergy serving in Camarines at that time. His main complaint was that the priests had failed to administer to their flock, did not teach the religious doctrine to their communities, and left many indios to die without having received the Holy Sacraments. Some clerics were accused of abandoning their parishes for months at a time, gathering to gamble by night and by day. They were also addicted greatly to buyo—betel nut and lime—and González claimed that many of them felt that it was a mar-tyrdom to have to abandon chewing this highly addictive substance for more than a quarter of an hour. Additionally, the bishop accused the priests of be-ing principally interested in despoiling and robbing their flock and enslaving them and putting them to work in their service instead of teaching them the benefits of the Catholic religion.[53] In 1670, in the town of Sampaloc, just out-side Manila, the Franciscan Fr. Francisco Solier was accused of punishing four Tagalogs—a man, two women, and a young boy—for a theft that they did not commit. The man and boy were whipped and chained to stocks by the friar, while the women were imprisoned and tortured in the priest's bedchamber for a period of eight days. All four were then forced to leave town. A similar case took place the same year in the town of Dilao, Tondo, where four *cabe-zas de barangay* were tied up and whipped by a priest for refusing to pay alms. The document suggests that the friar was attempting to run his parish like an encomienda, extracting money and goods as "alms" for the church.[54]

Missionaries were regularly accused of being more interested in commercial gain than conversion.[55] In Mauban, Tayabas, an indigenous alcalde mayor[56] was beaten black and blue by Fr. Andrés de Talavera in 1670 for having uncovered the fact that the priest was engaged in stockpiling food and rice while demanding more from the indios in his communities. In a fit of rage, Fr. Talavera ripped all the clothes off the indio and treated him so badly that he returned to his house near naked and covered in bruises. This created a great scandal among the indios of the town, who were scared and astonished by the behavior of the priest. Shortly afterward, many of the indios fled from the town into the mountains.[57] In 1686, the Zambales reported that the Augustinian Recollects were "great friends of silver" and would extort money from them as punishment for sins that they committed, including cohabiting outside marriage or polygamy—both of which were common in newly converted communities. Other Zambales were forced to leave aside their own harvests in order to go in search of wax in the mountains for the fathers. Idolatries remained strong within these mountain communities.[58] One cleric in Laguna de Bay, Don Miguel de la Cueva, was said to have been entirely occupied with a horse and cattle ranch and rarely ever came to town to preach. The Tagalogs of this region generally despised him.[59]

Sexual exploitation by priests was even more prevalent. The illicit involve-ment of priests with indigenous women was widely acknowledged and tac-itly accepted within the Philippines throughout the century. Some of these affairs were clearly consensual and involved long-term relationships that led some priests to have many children with their india partners. This was the case with the priest Cristóbal del Castillo Tamayo, who was reportedly suspended by the archbishop in Manila in the 1680s for living with his illegitimate children in the province of Laguna de Bay.[60] In 1683, the bishop of Nueva Cáceres told a story of a Franciscan priest who fled his post after a group of soldiers were dispatched to take him from the arms of his lover, an india servant of a Spanish captain.[61] In 1608, the Bornean woman Inés Mena reported that Fr. Alonso de Quiñones was so in love with her that when he returned to New Spain he wept in her arms, took a lock of her hair, and then wrote her name down on a piece of paper so that he would have it with him as he crossed the sea.[62] Some missionaries blamed the beguiling ways of the indias for their situation. In 1601, the Jesuit Fr. Ledesma commented that many indias had very loose morals around sexual relations, believing that it was fine to copulate with the friars or other men so long as it took place outside of mass.[63] Another Jesuit, Fr. Mateo Sanchez commented in 1603 that the women of the Visayas were very provocative and attractive and it took a great strength of character for the priests to resist them.[64]

Yet, not all liaisons between missionaries and indigenous women were consensual; there is also evidence of widespread sexual violence committed by friars. In the Zambales Mountains in the 1680s, one Augustinian Recollect was accused of systematically deflowering all of the young girls in the towns where he preached. One witness reported that he had seen this friar fondling a young girl and afterward saw the same girl covered in blood and on the point of death after having been raped.[65] In 1615, the Jesuit Fr. Pedro de Velasco was accused of climbing through the window of a house one night in the town of Palapag wearing a pillow for a nightcap and a blanket in place of a cloak. However, instead of encountering the india of his desires, he came face to face with her family who were all very shocked to see him in such a state. The Jesuit hierarchy appeared to take such crimes seriously. For this and other offences, Fr. Velasco was whipped severely and placed in the stocks for two months before finally being convinced to leave the order.[66]

The solicitation of sex from women and girls during confession was acknowledged as widespread and condemned by church authorities.[67] A sample of inquisition records from 1607 to 1627 documents thirty-nine individual cases of solicitation during confession in Manila and the provinces.[68] Most of these demonstrate a fairly common pattern of events, where the priest would approach a woman and either invite her to have sex with him—which was usually refused—or rape her, sometimes during the confession itself and sometimes afterward in his chamber. Although women were almost exclusively the subjects of these assaults, one inquisition record suggests that men could also be subjected to sexual abuse. In 1618, Isabel Bini, the *principala* of the town of Mexico in Pampanga, reported that she had witnessed the Augustinian Fr. Augustin Mexia engaging in mutual masturbation with a group of men. She went to confront some of those who were involved, telling them that they were unclean, and they responded that they always washed their hands afterward. They also told her that the priest had said that it was only a sin if it involved women, that everyone did it in Spain, and that it could be absolved through confession.[69]

Some priests publicly whipped indias who refused their advances, as happened to Juana Limin in 1605.[70] In 1608, María Sanayin was threatened with public flogging after she violently resisted the advances of Fr. Augustin de Peralta, but she defiantly declared that even if he flayed her she would not do as he wished.[71] The same year, in the town of Pila, Laguna de Bay, the fifteen-year-old Inés Singo was raped and assaulted by three Franciscan priests—including two priests she went to for help after the first rape—before a Dominican friar finally encouraged her to report these crimes to the inquisition.[72] Another india, Antonia Silicia, was abducted in 1615 and kept prisoner by Andrés Manuel, a cleric who had been expelled from the Company of Jesus. Fr. Manuel enlisted the help of bailiffs to capture her and drag her before him; he then whipped her before sending her to a house where she remained a prisoner for many months. He kept her there and would visit every few days to rape her.[73]

That these various activities had an impact on the efficacy of conversion is hardly surprising. Some communities responded by rejecting particular missionary orders rather than abandoning the Christian faith entirely. In 1679, the indios of Mindoro wrote several formal petitions, complaining about the abuse they had received by the Recollects and saying that they instead wished to be administered by the Jesuits. These indios threatened to apostatize and flee into the mountains, abandoning the faith and abandoning the Spanish yoke.[74] Very similar cases can also be found in Panay in the 1660s and the Zambales Mountains in the 1680s, where indio communities threatened to abandon Spanish towns and the Christian faith if they were not administered by Jesuit missionaries.[75] While these examples involve intervention from the Jesuits, who were motivated by their own desire to be allowed into new missionary fields,[76] they nonetheless demonstrate that communities experienced exploitation and injury by the missionaries that came to convert them, and would act on this.

Rebellions of the Babaylans

In the most extreme cases, indios responded to the abuses they received by priests through wide-scale rebellion. In 1621, four of the six towns on the Visayan island of Bohol rebelled and their residents fled into the hills, joining an existing community of fugitives who were living outside of Spanish control. The rebellion was led by four babaylans, or native priests, who encouraged the indios to burn down their villages and churches and desecrate any Christian religious items that they could find. The babaylans had been instructed to do this by a *divata*—or ancestor spirit—who appeared before them in the forest and told them to abandon the Jesuit missionaries and seek a life of freedom and abundance in the hills and forests. The priests told their followers that the *divata* would protect them in their encounter with the Spanish, causing the mountains to shake and the bullets of the Spanish muskets to misfire.[77]

The rebellion of the Boholanos caught the Jesuits by surprise. Bohol was long regarded as one of the most quiescent of all the Jesuit missions in the Visayas. Yet, this rebellion must have taken considerable planning as it was executed when the majority of Jesuit missionaries had left the island to celebrate the beatification of San Xavier in Cebu. In the mountains, the babaylans had constructed a series of clever fortifications. It took six months for a Spanish military force of fifty Spanish and a thousand indigenous soldiers led by Don Juan de Alcarazo to overcome the rebels. Using the rugged and swampy terrain of the interior of the island, fifteen hundred rebels brazenly attacked Alcarazo's vanguard but were repelled by the superior firepower of the Spanish. After Alcarazo sacked one of the key settlements in the mountains, killing large numbers, the rebels retreated to a rugged hill fort where they were protected by thick and thorny vegetation. Along the roads to their fort, they placed sharp stakes driven into the ground and positioned men armed with crossbows and stones in the trees ready to hurl at the Spanish soldiers. After six months, Alcarazo eventually mustered sufficient strength to assault this hill fort. The battle was fierce and bloody. Alcarazo's forces tore through the rebel stronghold, killing many and effectively ending this episode of rebellion, although many of the Boholanos escaped punishment by fleeing into the mountains.[78]

Jesuit annual reports continued to mention the existence of active communities of rebels and apostates in the hills of Bohol over the next few decades. In 1627, one of the babaylans who led the original rebellion sent a message into the Spanish settlements urging all of the indios to rebel and join him in the mountains, promising to wage war if they did not. In response, the Jesuits organized a manhunt which lasted twenty days and resulted in the death of another captain of the rebellion but without successfully discovering the whereabouts of the babaylan leader or convincing any of the rebels to return to the coastal lowlands.[79] In 1639, a fire that destroyed the church in Loboc was blamed on these apostates living lawlessly in the mountains.[80]

In 1631, four Augustinian Recollects were killed during a major rebellion in the province of Caraga.[81] This rebellion has often been considered a response to abusive behavior by the soldiers stationed in the province and also had strong connections to the political divide between the Spanish and the neighboring

Maguindanaos. Yet the Recollects themselves saw the events as an anticolonial rebellion where the Caragans specifically rejected Christianity. An internal investigation that the order conducted into the rebellion suggested that the indios saw the priests as much as instruments of colonization as the soldiers. The symbolism used by the rebels during the rebellion supports these assessments. On entering the town of Tandag, the rebels laid siege to the church and the convent, killing the prior, his companion, and two other priests and robbing and sacking the buildings, destroying any religious artifacts that they could find. They desecrated religious images, broke and smashed crucifixes, and took their axes to statues of Christ. After this, they held a mock mass in the church, where a woman called Maria Campan dressed herself in the priest's robes and then threw holy water around the church, declaring "I am Father Jacinto." Following this mass, the rebels continued their sacking of the town, and the church in Tago was also burnt to the ground.

Despite these devastating events, the Recollects continued to return to Caraga, refusing to give up their mission. The death of the four missionaries in 1631 was considered a type of martyrdom by the order. Nevertheless, the events in Caraga were severely concerning for many other missionaries, with the Jesuits worrying about the possibility of a "general uprising" that could spread across the rest of the islands.[82] Just three years later, in 1634, news arrived that more than three thousand indios had risen up in the islands of Leyte, Samar, Ibabao, and Caraga, although we have no further record of these events or how they were dealt with.[83]

The story of the murder of Augustinian Fr. Francisco de Mesa in the mountains of Panay in 1663 suggests that some communities utilized Christian symbolism in order to assert their own religious autonomy in times of rebellion. The chronicler Diaz notes that at this time a number of Visayans were living in the dense forests of the mountains of Panay where they continued with their indigenous religious practices. One of their leaders was a priest called Tapar, a babaylan who dressed in women's clothing and practiced ceremonial sacrifices in caves and among the trees of the forests. Tapar was revered as a prophet by his followers, and he led many of them in customary practices of ancestor worship. At the same time, Tapar appointed those among his followers as the Son, the Holy Ghost, the Virgin Mary, apostles, popes, and bishops. It is unclear from Diaz's account whether this was done as a way of convincing converted Christians to return to indigenous religion; however, he implies that it aided Tapar in solidifying his following. The Spanish viewed the ritual celebrations that took place in these caves as akin to devil worship, involving unspeakable debaucheries, sex acts, excessive drinking, and sacrifices to demons.[84]

When word of these activities in the mountain reached the lowland Spanish villages the Augustinian Fr. Francisco de Mesa asked for assistance from the alcalde mayor Pedro Durán de Monforte, who began to muster a force of Spanish, Pampangan, and Merdica soldiers. In the meantime, Fr. Mesa traveled by himself into the mountains to attempt to talk to the apostates. The Visayans refused to come and meet with the friar, saying that "they had taken refuge for the sake of their safety—not, however, for fear of the Spaniards, whom they esteemed but lightly, for they themselves were accompanied by all the Holy Trinity, the Blessed Virgin Mary, and all the apostles, who would defend them by working miracles."[85] They declared that they no longer needed the services of the missionaries because they had their own bishops and priests and asked the friar to leave them alone as they did not intend to do any harm to any Christians.[86]

Despite making these promises, Tapar and his followers hatched a plot to kill Fr. Mesa. At midnight one night, a mob descended from the mountains and entered the village of Malonor where the friar was sleeping. They surrounded his house and with great shouts they thrust their lances through the bamboo walls and floor, wounding the friar. In desperation, Fr. Mesa attempted to jump out of the window, but he leapt straight into the crowd and was attacked again. He struggled across the road to the cemetery and died with his arms around the cross, as the crowd continued to lance him. The rebels then set fire to the church and the house. When the force mustered by the alcalde mayor arrived, they found the body of the slain father, but the insurgents were nowhere to be seen. They began to scour the hills for them and eventually found them and engaged them in battle. Several rebels were brought to Iloilo where they were killed and tied to stakes in the river. The woman who had been given the role of Virgin Mary was impaled on a stake and placed at the mouth of the river.[87]

Religious Adaptation

In 1677, the king issued a royal decree chastising the different missionary orders for their inability to prevent apostasy and failure to convert pagan communities living outside Spanish control.[88] Although the decree ordered each of the missionary orders to devote four or five friars to the conversion of these populations, the missionaries responded with strong evidence that they were already engaged in this work—indeed, that they were overwhelmed by the task of converting mountain communities made up of apostates and those who refused to recognize the Christian God.[89] Missionaries confronted great difficulties in traveling to these remote and dispersed communities. In some instances, such as in Santa Ines in Antipolo, missionaries established towns close to mountainous regions and attempted to create incentives for communities to voluntarily join the settlement. This approach met with very limited success.[90] Even in successful cases, as the Jesuit Fr. Ignacio Alcina noted, it was common for the indios to leave their faith at the church door.[91]

Faced with the combined problems of flight, apostasy, and rebellion throughout much of the archipelago, missionary orders in the late seventeenth century were forced to confront the reality that, for some communities, conversion had simply failed, and new strategies had to be considered. Some missionaries believed that conversion had to be forced on unwilling communities by fire and sword. As early as 1585, Franciscan and Augustinian missionaries had argued that unconverted heathen communities should be severely punished for their persistent idolatries. In response, the senior *oidor* drafted thirty-six proposed ordinances that stipulated the kinds of punishment that could be meted out to indios for specific crimes committed against God or the Crown, including imprisonment, public whipping, sentences to serve in public works, or even execution.[92] Nearly a century later, the Augustinian Fr. Diego de Jesús argued that no inhabitant of the archipelago would ever hear the word of God "if they had not first heard the thunderclap of the arquebuses."[93] Furthermore, he believed that a constant military presence was needed to ensure against apostasy. He cited the long-standing resistance of the Igorots in the highlands of Luzon, who had shown some interest in converting while soldiers occupied their towns, but as soon as the military retreated, the Igorots abandoned the faith.[94] The Augustinian Recollect Fr. Jesús de San Jerónimo was inclined to agree, saying that there were all too many communities who were fierce and bloodthirsty and hated with a passion the idea of being subjected to the Spanish yoke. Particularly in regions like Caraga, Fr. San Jerónimo argued, conversion relied on the exercise of His Majesty's arms.[95]

The Zambales Mountains were one region where this policy of conversion by arquebus was attempted. In 1680, a campaign of blood and fire was waged throughout these mountains. For four months, a band of soldiers tore through the region, setting fire to the crops and houses in an attempt to force the Zambales to move into lowland areas. The military commander of this expedition, Ayudante Alonso Martín, spoke of it as a form of cleansing in the service of God. He believed that through the actions of his soldiers, they had convinced a thousand Zambales to join the Dominican settlements on the coast where they could attend mass and be taught the Holy Gospel.[96] Yet, just five years later, the Dominicans reported that despite all of their efforts, there was still a substantial population that willingly lived outside of Spanish control in the mountains. These communities were afraid of the coastal villagers and chose to live separately from them. The Dominicans reported that it was almost impossible to convert these communities. After any religious observance, they would scatter back into the mountains and continue to practice their native religion. In 1685, Doctor Nicolas de la Vega Carvallo conducted an investigation into continued idolatries in Zambales, involving the interrogation of hundreds of witnesses and the confiscation of thousands of different religious items used in sacrifices and other ceremonies. This investigation revealed that Christianity was almost completely absent from the day-to-day lives of the communities that lived in these mountains.[97]

By comparison, the strategy of the Dominican priest Fr. Juan Ibáñez among communities of Laguna de Bay was very different. In May 1686, an investigation into the religious customs in this region found that many of the people living in the towns of Santo Tomás, San Pablo, Tiaong, Batangas, Lobo, Gulacan, Lipa, Sala, and Tanauan would frequently gather in great numbers to worship their own spirits and demons, including a type of serpent. Typically, these celebrations would take place in particular caves or gullies hidden in the nearby mountains of Makiling, Malarayat, and Daguldol, where community members would gather for days at a time in numbers that often exceeded two hundred people.[98] The persistence of these idolatries had been noted previously by the alcalde mayor of the province, Captain Miguel Sanchez. However, it was not until August 1685, when Fr. Ibáñez traveled to the town, that a real investigation was undertaken. Fr. Ibáñez began by visiting the house of a particular *mestiza de sangley* where he witnessed a sacrifice invoking the spirit of a sister who had died some days before.[99] On witnessing this ceremony, the friar seized the food and offerings that were prepared and threw them into the river. Shortly after this, he did the same for another sacrifice that was prepared in a different house for a child who had been cured of smallpox.[100]

In September 1685, the friar was led into the mountains to be shown some of the caves that were used by the townspeople in their ceremonies. Some were in gullies with wide caverns, others were in the hills. The friar performed exorcisms in all these places, covering over the entrances and placing a cross in front. In some of the caves, he found evidence of the ceremonies that had taken place, including incense and braziers with ashes and coals and preparations of buyo and tobacco. In one cave near the town of San Pablo de los Montes, the friar found a stone table that had holes that were like drawers where he discovered bowls and other vessels that were used to drink from. After each of his sojourns into the mountains, the townspeople went back to the town and the friar preached to them and exhorted them to repent and give grace to God. Throughout the months of September and October, he continued these activities, finding resistance in some villages but eventually convincing the villagers to confess and repent. Fr. Ibáñez was successful in these activities because the villagers believed that he was imbued with extraordinary spiritual power. One witness told a story of how some villagers were worried because it had not rained even though it was time for the monsoon. Fr. Ibáñez told them not to worry but to pray to God and after they had done this, the rains began. In another town, one of the native priests resisted Fr. Ibáñez's call to convert and, in response, the friar told him that he should worry about God's punishment. Three days later, one of his daughters died and this tragedy reportedly prompted the entire town to convert. Other witnesses spoke of how some of the caves that Fr. Ibáñez exorcised had collapsed, which created a great fear within the community.[101]

An engagement with the spiritual landscape was essential for successful conversion, and priests like Fr. Ibáñez found a way to integrate existing belief structures into their practice of Christianity. Fr. Ibáñez' exorcism and closure of more than a dozen caves—followed by the miraculous collapse of at least one—convinced the indios of Laguna de Bay that the priest had more power than their own spirits who dwelled in the caves. Writing about Christian conversion in Eastern Central Luzon in the eighteenth century, Mark Dizon similarly concluded that indigenous people saw conversion to Christianity as a way to potentially escape the evil effects of ancestor spirits. This was especially so for young children who were baptized very early and were thus taken out of the traditional spiritual family and could be rescued from the illness and misfortune that a community might feel these spirits were visiting on them. Dizon argues, ultimately, that "the arrival of the new religion did not eliminate spirit beliefs; it simply gave converts in Southeast Asia access to more powerful spiritual forces to tame the traditional spirits."[102]

Yet, in order for this to work, priests had to be able to prove that Christianity did indeed have superior power over local spirits. This was often achieved through symbolic acts or miraculous events. For instance, when the Jesuit missionaries in Dulac, Leyte built a pyre out of pagan religious artifacts in 1601, they did so to prove that such items contained no special spiritual powers.[103] Fr. Ibáñez's miraculous exorcisms in caves were similarly mirrored elsewhere. Alfred McCoy tells the story of a Recollect missionary who used a Latin invocation to cast out the evil spirit from a thicket, greatly impressing the locals who believed that anyone who touched this thicket would be killed.[104] In 1601, the Jesuits in Samar held a great procession asking God to bring the local communities success in their wars against slave raiders from Mindanao. This was done as a way of supplanting a preexisting tradition where the Visayans asked their own gods to provide them with good winds and success in battle.[105] Yet, possibly most powerful of all, was the symbolic act of baptism. Many believed that the holy water used by the priests could have healing powers and was an effective way to counter evil spirits.[106] Stories similarly abound in missionary accounts of native priests or priestesses cursing missionaries. When the person making the curse subsequently fell ill or died, this was used as a way of proving the priests' superiority to pagan magic and convinced many to convert lest they themselves were similarly punished by the Christian God.[107]

Other missionaries used physical objects like Agnus Dei coins, which the indios believed had special powers of healing. The Jesuit Annual Report of 1601–1602 relates a story of a feud between a woman and a native priestess in a town outside Manila that resulted in the woman being cursed by the priestess and falling gravely ill. When her husband came to a Jesuit priest for help, the priest gave him a small Agnus Dei and asked him to have faith that his wife would get better. The priest then fell to his knees and asked the Lord to give him strength of faith and to favor the newly converted Christians.[108] When the woman made a full recovery, many other members of the town came to the priest to ask for similar amulets to protect them from curses and other evil. As noted by Alfred McCoy, amulets became very popular even in some of the more Hispanicized provinces of the Philippines, along with Latin or Latin-sounding words that were thought to have magical powers.[109] Amulets had long held an important place within Philippine religious ceremonies as good luck charms or as protection against evil spirits.[110] Their replacement by Christian tokens like Agnus Dei coins thus was important in establishing the place of Christianity within local religious practice.[111]

Missionaries also made use of Philippine kinship networks. This was particularly successful with regards to native catechists—indios who became proponents of Christianity and used their relationships to spread Christian teachings. At the same time, kinship also presented problems for conversion when it came to questions of salvation and the afterlife. Many were concerned by the fundamental Christian tenet that only those who were baptized could enter heaven. For some, the opportunity to abandon their ancestor connections was a benefit of converting to Christianity—especially when these associations with ancestors were considered to be largely negative and the cause of sickness or bad luck. In these instances, the saints and God acted as positive alternative spirits that indigenous communities could worship in a very similar manner to their ancestor worship. However, for many others, the idea of abandoning or completely severing ties with their ancestors was something that they were unwilling to contemplate and some expressed the preference for entering hell alongside their ancestors.[112]

Missionaries thus had to learn to adapt their strategies to suit local spiritual beliefs. In many cases, this adaptation required missionaries to take on the roles previously played by native priestesses. Yet, this was not a case of supplanting the existing spiritual landscape with a new Christian orthodoxy, but rather the melding of the two. Anthropological research from the twentieth century strongly supports this. In the 1960s, F. Landa Jocano noted that, particularly in rural areas, communities continued to practice spirit worship and to believe in an integral relationship between the environment, the spirit world, ancestors, and the material successes of the community. Religious beliefs colored almost all of the social, economic, and cultural activities that people engaged in—all activities were undertaken in careful consideration of the spirit world.[113] These communities tended to see Christian saints as intermediaries between themselves and God, who was considered unreachable by ordinary people. In this sense, saints were conceived "as supernatural beings with powers similar to those of environmental spirits."[114] Communities would appeal to saints to prevent illness or the destruction of crops and to ensure good luck in activities like fishing or hunting. Ritualistic use of Christian symbolism was seen as a way of improving the communion between the individual and the saint. Additionally, many Filipinos believed that religious artifacts or other objects blessed by a priest had supernatural power and could allow the person who possessed it to achieve extraordinary things. Holy water was still considered to have curative powers, while other objects could heal stomach upsets or exorcise the effects of a witch or evil spirit.[115]

Along with these practices, communities continued to rely on *baylans*, or mediums, who were able to commune with the spirit world, practiced herb medicine and other forms of magic, and superstitious rituals, often within the natural environments of caves or gullies or springs. *Baylans* were seen to be capable of healing the sick and could intervene in other instances where the community suffered misfortune. The belief in the spirit world was maintained through the telling and retelling of stories and legends that elevated ancestors as well as saints to heroic status. Landa Jocano concluded that particularly in regions like Panay the introduction of Catholicism did not lead "to any substantial shift in the emphasis that is placed on folk beliefs, attitudes and practices."[116] His conclusions are reflected in the work of a number of other anthropologists and historians.[117] Alfred McCoy similarly documented numerous instances of spirit and ancestor worship. For example, he notes that in the Western Visayas some communities still believed that it was necessary to make noise through the beating of pots and pans to frighten away evil spirits—a phenomenon that was also witnessed by priests in the seventeenth century. Geomancy and sacrifices were still practiced as a way of placating evil spirits, and ceremonies were still conducted by *baylans* to help negotiate the relationship between men and the spirit world.[118]

While anthropologists have been interested in charting this continuation of pagan beliefs and melding of religious practice, historians have not adequately explained how this might have taken place. Particularly with regard to the early colonial period, a triumphalism remains within a religiously dominated historiography. Of all the corners of Philippine historiography, it is here that we are most likely to find defenders of colonization and the promise of civilizational advancement that it brought.[119] As this chapter has demonstrated, the history of conversion is fraught with violence and resistance. Despite grandiose claims by religious orders to have rapidly baptized and converted hundreds of thousands of indios in the space of a few short decades, conversion clearly remained limited and partial. The efforts of missionaries were limited by their own internal weaknesses—a shortage of priests, the emergence of corruption or abuse—as well as the spiritual landscape in which they operated. This landscape was both physical—etched into the natural environment—and metaphysical, and Philippine communities retained strong connections to it. Religious practice was inscribed into this social world, influencing where people lived, where they grew their crops, and how they traveled across the countryside. Missionaries needed to contend with this reality before they had any real success in conversion.

At the same time, Philippine indios did not automatically accept Christianity into their communities and were at times prepared to violently resist the conversion efforts of Spanish missionaries. This was sometimes a response to the abuse and exploitation that they experienced at the hands of individual priests. Yet religious symbolism was embedded in many of these rebellions, suggesting that these actions were also designed in part as a way of protecting community customs from being swept aside or censored by Christianization. In the end, these actions demonstrate another dimension of Philippine agency, wherein communities were able to choose the elements of Christianity that fit within their existing worldview. The contested nature of conversion forced missionaries to adapt their strategies and to adopt much of the symbolism and spiritual worldview of local indios. What emerged from this by the end of the seventeenth century could only ever be a partial conversion, engendering a new and dynamic spiritual landscape that incorporated elements of both Christianity and indigenous religions.

CHAPTER 4

Slave Raiding and Imperial Retreat

One October night in 1603, the Jesuit Fr. Melchor Hurtado was awoken just before dawn with the news that a great armada of Maguindanao raiders was fast approaching the town of Dulag on the island of Leyte, where he was staying. Dressing hastily, he and his companions fled as quickly as they could into the mountains, accompanied by villagers and guided by a local principal. Although they had a head start, the raiders were soon pursuing them by foot through the forests. In the blink of an eye, Melchor Hurtado found himself alone. He hid among the thick roots of a banyan tree and waited for nightfall. From his hiding place, he watched a woman and child being taken captive, while another Visayan was killed by a raider wielding a kampilan.[1] Eventually, he was discovered and taken prisoner. His captor took him down the mountain to Dulag where he joined hundreds of other captives, who were laden on to the vessels brought by the raiders to be shipped back to Mindanao.[2] He wrote later of how, during the long voyage to Mindanao, his clothes gradually disintegrated, and he became very weak from illness, infested with lice, and covered from head to foot with scabies.[3]

To begin with, Melchor Hurtado remained on board the Moro vessel as captive cargo while the Maguindanao raiders continued to attack coastal settlements on the islands of Leyte and Samar in search of more captives. News had traveled fast throughout the Visayan islands that raiders were approaching and mostly the Maguindanaos found the settlements to be abandoned. Undeterred, they sacked the towns and set fire to their churches. Advance warnings by word of mouth were the best defenses that Visayans had against such raids. Melchor Hurtado wrote of his disappointment that in all the weeks they spent raiding the coasts of the Visayas, they only encountered a handful of Spanish soldiers who were ill prepared to defend against or to pursue the raiders. In one instance, the raiders entered a river mouth where they were confronted by a single, desultory soldier who fired ineffectually at their vessel. The Maguindanaos continued their raiding without opposition before finally sailing for Mindanao. Arriving at the mouth of the Pulangi River, they rowed upstream and fired their arquebuses and artillery in salute outside the houses of local datus in celebration of their triumphant return.[4] In all, Melchor Hurtado spent nearly a year as a captive of the Maguindanaos between 1603 and 1604. He remained the prisoner of Datu Buisan, who was intent on ransoming him for a piece of artillery that the Spanish had previously seized. Eventually an agreement was reached with the Spanish envoy, Cristóbal Gómez, who was sent to negotiate the terms of the ransom. Melchor Hurtado was released in September 1604. [5]

While his treatment may have been exceptional, Melchor Hurtado's experience of being captured by Moro slave raiders was shared by thousands of others during the late sixteenth and seventeenth centuries—mostly by indios from coastal villages across the Visayas, Camarines, Mindoro, and the Calamianes islands.[6] Slave raids were devastating for local communities. Raiders regularly captured hundreds of indios while at the same time often burning villages, looting, and desecrating churches and sometimes burning crops as well. While slave raiding was a common form of warfare throughout Southeast Asia prior to the arrival of the Spanish, the raiding that took place in the seventeenth-century Philippines took on a new political dimension as a response to Spanish expansionary ambitions in the region.

The regular slave raids by Moro raiders were one of a number of external threats that challenged Spanish defensive capabilities during the seventeenth century. The other major threat came from the Dutch, who, in the first half of the century, were embroiled in the Eighty Years' War with Spain. Up until 1648, the tactics employed by the Dutch in the East Indies were clearly designed to intervene in the trade between China and the Philippines in an attempt to force the Spanish to abandon their position. The first confrontation with the Dutch happened in 1600, when the Dutch pirate Olivier van Noort sailed into the Philippines in the hopes of capturing one of the famed silver galleons. On failing to sight the ship, he plundered the coasts of the Visayas and then set up a blockade of Manila, seizing some of the Chinese merchant ships. The Spanish lifted the blockade after winning a naval battle in December 1600.[7] Over the next several decades, the Dutch ran pillaging raids through the Visayas, besieged Manila and the port of Cavite, and engaged the Spanish in several spectacular naval battles.[8] By the 1620s it had become a common occurrence for Dutch ships to blockade the entrance into the archipelago at the Cape of Espiritu Santo and lie in wait for the arrival of the galleons from Acapulco.[9] While the success of Dutch blockades varied from year to year in terms of the quantity of cargo that the Dutch were able to seize, the regularity of the Dutch presence did at times limit trade between Spain and China, compounding the financial woes of the Spanish settlement in Manila.[10]

Yet, while Spanish officials in Manila worried about Dutch attacks on their commercial activities, the slave raiding polities of the southern archipelago were arguably a more consistent threat to the Spanish presence in the Philippines. Not only did they destabilize the process of colonization in the Visayas through their regular attacks on newly formed Spanish settlements, but they also thwarted Spanish ambitions of expanding their influence and reaching further into the Indonesian archipelago. From the vantage point of Manila, the southern archipelago offered a number of opportunities for extending the potential of Spanish power in the region. Royal officials coveted control over the spice trade centered on the Maluku archipelago in Indonesia, while tantalizing rumors abounded that Mindanao was abundant in gold and other riches. Consequently, expansion of Spanish territorial control southward was proposed very shortly after the founding of Manila.

These ambitions were the most clearly articulated by Governor Francisco de Sande, the third governor of the Philippines. Sande was extremely aggressive and had an inflated sense of Spanish military capacity, arguing that if reinforcements were sent from Spain via the Straits of Magellan, they would not only quickly conquer Borneo, Mindanao, and Jolo, but extend Spanish dominion over the spice islands and Java. He also thought that China could be easily conquered in much the same way that the Aztecs were defeated at Tenochtitlán.[11] While few royal officials shared Sande's optimism, many saw great merit in conquering the neighboring Muslim polities and establishing encomiendas throughout those islands.[12] At the same time, both Maguindanao and Jolo stood directly along the sea route between Manila and the Maluku Islands. Shortly after settling in the Visayas and Luzon, Spanish officials began to plan the territorial conquest of the southern archipelago.[13]

Yet, for all these ambitions, Spanish aims were repeatedly frustrated and defeated. The polities of Mindanao, Jolo, Borneo, and Ternate all responded to Spanish military aggression by intensifying their raiding activities. Virtually no community south of Manila was exempt from the yearly assault, but the Visayan territories were the most frequently impacted. Over just three years, between 1599 and 1602, Maguindanao raiders seized 2,300 slaves from Visayan territories,[14] while in 1635, Governor Hurtado de Corcuera estimated that raiders from Borneo and the Camucones had collectively captured around 25,000–30,000 vassals of the king of Spain.[15] On occasion, raiders would even venture close to Manila as a way of demonstrating the weakness of Spanish defenses.[16] This pattern of raiding continued throughout the century up until 1663, when the Spanish withdrew all of their military personnel from Mindanao, Ternate, and the Calamianes.

The conflict between the Spanish and Moro polities in the southern archipelago has often been framed as a religious conflict between Islam and Christianity.[17] This interpretation is evident within many of the earliest Spanish

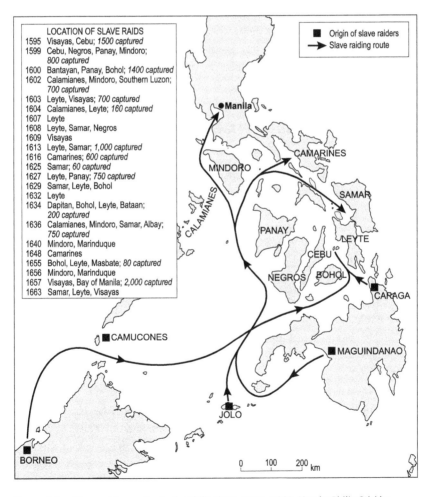

FIGURE 4.1.   Slave raiding routes in the Philippines, 1595–1663. Map by Philip Stickler.

chronicles, where the Moros are painted as barbarians and the Spanish—particularly the priests involved in various religious and military missions—as righteous civilizers.[18] These accounts moreover pivot on a series of "conquest" narratives depicting the defeat of the Maguindanaos in 1637 and the Sulus in 1638 by armies led by Governor Hurtado de Corcuera.[19] Although Hurtado de Corcuera only established a limited Spanish conquest over these polities that lasted less than a decade, his story of military conquest has been enduring, with one historian even dubbing him "the last conquistador."[20] Yet, this interpretation deliberately overemphasizes Spanish military power, overlooking the multiple limitations that the Spanish military faced and the consistent successes of the Moros in countering Spanish attacks. Despite trying for the best part of a century, Spanish forces were never able to overcome these polities. Moreover, Moro raiding on Spanish possessions in the Visayas disrupted Spanish colonial interests. By the end of the century, the original objective of territorial expansion and conquest was abandoned completely in favor of merely holding what could be held in the region.

Slave Raiding Polities in the Southern Archipelago

Maritime raiding was an integral part of the Southeast Asian political economy, tied inexorably to war, slavery, and trade. Spanish chroniclers and royal officials wrote of slave raids in the Visayas as acts of piracy, senseless in their destruction of newly constructed Christian missionary outposts and barbaric for their seizure and sometimes slaughter of whole villages.[21] Yet, these chroniclers seemed unaware of the widespread nature of raiding across Southeast Asia, much less the social function that these raids performed. Throughout the early modern period, raiding took place in a wide geographical region extending from the Malay Peninsula to Indonesia, the Sulu Sea, Borneo, China, and Japan.[22] The physical environment of maritime Southeast Asia—characterized by island archipelagos that conducted a busy trade among one another as well as with continental Asia—made it an ideal place for maritime raiding. Raiders were intimately knowledgeable of the annual monsoonal cycles that would create the right sailing conditions needed for successful raids of other islands.

Raiding was an organized tactic of warfare mobilized by chiefs and kings for the pursuit of power and prestige.[23] The principal objective was the capture of slaves from rival communities. Large fleets of galleys, known as *caracoas*, would arrive at coastal villages laden with thousands of warriors who would plunder and set fire to the village and pursue the inhabitants, taking captives. Coastal and inland fortifications were thus common in the pre-Hispanic Visayas and ranged from impregnable defenses to tree houses constructed fifteen or more meters above the ground. Visayan communities were also known to commonly abandon settlements in the face of sea raiders. If the raid was bad enough, this could result in the complete abandonment of a village and resettlement elsewhere on the island, often in a more inland location that was easier to defend.[24]

The most powerful and well-known of the slave raiding communities were the Maguindanaos of Mindanao and the Sulus of Jolo; however, raids were also conducted semiregularly by raiders from Borneo, Caraga in Eastern Mindanao, and the Camucones, in modern-day Palawan (Calamianes). Many of these polities had converted to Islam by the late sixteenth century.[25] Yet, slave raiding was not a subset of their religion; rather, both the conversion of these polities to Islam and their increased interest in slave raiding reflected their integration into an Indian Ocean trading network that had been dominated by Islamic traders for several centuries.[26] Greater integration into global trading

FIGURE 4.2. The southern archipelago. Map by Philip Stickler.

systems increased the need of these polities for slaves and bondsmen—as both laborers within trading societies and as chattel commodities.[27] The arrival of the Portuguese into this region in the sixteenth century furthered this reliance on slave raiding since the Portuguese were eager slave traders themselves.[28]

At the end of the sixteenth century, the southern archipelago was centered around two major poles of commercial and political influence—Brunei and Ternate. Both were trading entrepôts with extensive connections throughout the Malay world, as well as established trading relationships with China, Siam, the Arabian Peninsula, and, later, the Portuguese. In 1578, Governor Sande wrote that Borneo was situated at the center of Southeast Asian trading routes, attracted many visitors from across the region, and was abundant in birds, food, fruit, wine, and slaves captured in raids.[29] Early Spanish accounts of Brunei described it as a bustling port city—the largest the Spanish had yet seen in Asia—boasting sumptuous palaces belonging to the sultan, thriving shipyards, and a well-armed and militarized population. Brunei was also a center of Islamic learning, with an established mosque and learned men who wrote books in Arabic.[30] In the decades preceding the Spanish settlement of Manila, Brunei had established tributary populations in the Philippines—centered on Manila, Mindoro, and Balayan. Although the sultan of Brunei had previously maintained friendly trading relations with the Portuguese, the invasion of Manila and the hostile defeat of the local Muslim rulers set the Spanish on a path of conflict with Brunei.[31] Yet, for the most part, direct contact between Borneo and the Spanish was relatively rare in the seventeenth century as the two sides engaged in a proxy war.[32]

The Borneans preferred to rely on a tributary population known as the Camucones to conduct raids in the Philippines and bring slaves back for trade in Borneo.[33] The Camucones were said to live in the islands of the Sulu Sea, likely to the south of the Calamianes.[34] Spanish observers described them as nomadic, sea-dwelling communities whose boats acted as their houses, making it likely that they were part of the Sama-Bajau—an ethnic group that extends across the eastern Indonesian archipelago and who were known in later periods to act as mercenaries within the extensive regional slave trade.[35] At the same time, the epithet "Camucones" appears to have been applied liberally in the seventeenth century, suggesting that these raids were not conducted by one community or polity but by many different groups. At times, their armadas were said to be small and weak,[36] while at other times they arrived in large warships capable of carrying hundreds of raiders.[37] What united them in the eyes of the Spanish was how difficult it was to defend against their attacks. Of all the raiders in the seventeenth-century Philippines, the Camucones were the most consistently troubling to the Spanish, owing in part to the fact that—

unlike the Maguindanaos and Sulus—they maintained no centralized political structure with which the Spanish could negotiate, nor a fixed territory that could easily be invaded in reprisal. The Camucones were frequently described by the Spanish as the cruelest and most violent of all raiders since they were as likely to slaughter villagers as capture them.[38] A Jesuit description of a raid in Marinduque in 1625 told of how a priest was captured and had his throat slit, while the raiders used his cap as a drinking vessel. The raiders then went to Catbalogan in Samar, where two priests fled for their lives along with the Visayans. Those who could not flee were captured, including some who were sick with smallpox, who in turn had their heads cut off.[39] Camucones sailed in light vessels that were faster and less cumbersome than Spanish galleys, and easily escaped Spanish pursuit, often dispersing back to sea before news of their raids even reached the Spanish.[40]

Beyond Borneo, the other major pole of influence within the southern archipelago was Ternate, located in the Maluku Islands. Like Brunei, Ternate was a powerful trading entrepôt at the center of the spice trade. As the only clove-producing islands in the world, the Maluku Islands had attracted traders to their ports for centuries.[41] Yet, Ternate's rise to prominence as a regional power in the late sixteenth century was linked to its relationship with the Portuguese, who since 1522 had occupied fortified positions in Ternate and Tidore and had established a unique trading partnership with these islands. In 1570, the sultan of Ternate, Hairun, was assassinated by the Portuguese, initiating a period of anti-colonial rebellion against the Portuguese. Hairun's son, Babullah, took up the position of sultan and was motivated to avenge the death of his father. For the next five years, Babullah laid siege to the Portuguese fort in Ternate, leading to the eventual expulsion of the Portuguese from the island in 1575. Over the course of the next several decades, Babullah and his son Sultan Saïd al-din Berkat Syah set about establishing an extensive tributary network that extended across the majority of island polities throughout the Banda, Celebes, and Molucca Seas.[42] By these means, Ternate consolidated its power in the region, seized greater control over the spice trade from neighboring rivals in Tidore, and ensured that any uninvited future European interventions would be met with considerable resistance. The spice trade continued to thrive without a European monopoly. A 1603 description of Ternate noted the island regularly received traders from Java and Malaya, as well as Turks who traveled via Java and Aceh.[43]

This interaction with lucrative global trading markets meant that Ternate had access to some of the most sophisticated weaponry of the era, including artillery.[44] In most of their engagements with Moros, the Spanish came up against highly militarized and fortified communities, who often had far superior artillery to the Spanish. This made them formidable foes. Governor Sande reported that in their initial encounters with Borneo, Jolo, and Mindanao in 1578 to 1579, the Spanish had seized more than two hundred pieces of artillery, most of which was Portuguese.[45] In 1584, Ternate was said to have fortified its main fort alone with three hundred pieces of artillery, having amassed weaponry through trade with foreign merchants. At that time, the king of Ternate had reportedly ordered that no merchant would be allowed to trade with his vassal states unless they brought artillery with them. By these means, Ternate was able to fortify not only its own forts within the island of Ternate but a large part of the Moluccan archipelago. The principal fort in Ternate was garrisoned with a thousand men who were equipped with coats of mail, doublets, and helmets that they had taken from the Portuguese. Additionally, they were backed by a thousand Javanese, Chinese, Acehnese, and Turks, the latter of whom were experts in firebombs and other explosive weapons.[46]

Importantly for the Spanish in the Philippines, Ternate's influence extended to the island of Mindanao, where the Ternatens retained an alliance with the Maguindanao rulers of the Pulangi River region.[47] Toward the close of the sixteenth century, Ternate was reported to have sent considerable aid to Mindanao in the form of shipbuilders, armorers, gunpowder manufacturers, artillery, and manpower to help the Maguindanaos resist Spanish invasion into their island.[48] In 1597, Governor Tello argued that aid from Ternate had allowed the Maguindanaos to resist conquest by the Spanish and led directly to the death of captain Esteban Rodriguez de Figueroa.[49] The following year, a force of eight hundred Ternatens arrived in the Pulangi River to fight against the invasion force of Juan Ronquillo.[50] The 1606 Spanish conquest of the Maluku Islands, while motivated by a desire to claim control over the spice trade, was also a response to the increasing influence of Ternate on Mindanao; the Spanish hoped that by conquering Ternate, they would cut off the supply of military aid to the Maguindanaos.[51] While the conquest was successful, in that the Spanish succeeded in reclaiming possession of the Portuguese forts in Ternate and Tidore, the Spanish never overcame Ternate's power. The arrival of the Dutch in the Maluku Islands and their alliance with Ternate locked the Spanish into a costly war of attrition that lasted until their final withdrawal from the Maluku Islands in 1663.[52]

While Borneo and Ternate remained centers of trade, political power, and Islamic learning, the Spanish in Manila were more immediately concerned with the Muslim polities based in Jolo and Mindanao. These islands were identified not only as the most obvious strategic sites for expansion into the spice islands but also as major obstacles toward that goal. The Sulu sultanate was centered in Jolo and claimed the longest Islamic tradition in the region, dating back to the early fifteenth century.[53] However, the regional importance of

Jolo predated the arrival of Islam, with evidence of trade with South Chinese ports from the late thirteenth century onward. At this time, Sulu was known to the Chinese as one of the most militarized and warlike populations among the spice island archipelagos, making regular raids on neighboring territories, and particularly Borneo. Spanish observers in the seventeenth century similarly noted that the Sulu capital, Jolo, was one of the largest and wealthiest polities in the entire archipelago.[54]

The Sulu consolidated into a formidable slave raiding empire in the eighteenth century; yet in the late sixteenth century the Spanish believed that the Maguindanao polities, centered around the Pulangi River in Mindanao, were far more powerful. At the turn of the seventeenth century, power in Maguindanao was split between three rulers—Rajah Mura, Sirongan, and Buisan.[55] Although Rajah Mura was the nominal head of the Maguindanao confederacy, the Spanish identified Sirongan, who lived in the Buayan region of Mindanao, as the most important of the three leaders. Buisan was also a powerful warrior who personally led some of the most successful raiding missions of the early seventeenth century. The competition between these three rulers was eclipsed by the rise to power of Cachil Kudarat, the son of Buisan, who became sultan of Mindanao in 1619.[56] The Maguindanao rulers maintained complex systems of vassalage with the itinerant maritime Sama and Ilanun peoples as well as neighboring communities living in the hinterlands of Mindanao, who traded in foraged forest products.[57]

Shortly after founding their settlement in Manila in 1571, Spanish officials began to plan the conquest of all these southern polities, with their eyes firmly set on the prize of the spice trade. Francisco de Sande, the governor of the Philippines, thought that such a conquest would be quick and easy and organized several military expeditions to Borneo, Jolo, and Mindanao in 1578 and 1579.[58] However, he vastly underestimated the strength of the Moro polities and the forces needed not only to conquer but occupy the southern archipelago. In Mindanao, the Maguindanaos retreated into the interior of their island to avoid negotiating with the Spanish envoys.[59] In 1578, a Spanish siege of the Sulu hilltop fort in Jolo resulted in Raja Pangiran agreeing to swear fealty and pay tribute to the Spanish Crown. Pangiran also promised to cease raiding activities within Spanish possessions.[60] Yet, while the Sulus appear to have honored the latter part of the agreement, they never fully recognized vassalage to Spain and did not wish to pay more than a symbolic amount of tribute. Moreover, both the Maguindanaos and the Sulus responded to Spanish subjugation attempts with violent resistance. In 1596, Captain Esteban Rodriguez de Figueroa was killed while leading the first full-scale military invasion of the Pulangi River. His replacement, Captain Juan de la Jara, was so intimidated by the Maguindanaos that he eventually abandoned his position to return to Manila, ordering his soldiers to burn down their palisades and prepare to retreat.[61] Matters proceeded no better with the Sulus. In 1599, thirteen Spanish soldiers were killed in Jolo when Captain Cristóbal Villagra went in search of supplies for the soldiers stationed in Mindanao.[62] In 1602, Captain Juan Juárez Gallinato led a retaliatory mission against the Sulus—however, the Spanish forces were vastly outnumbered, and the Sulus ultimately retreated to their hilltop fort where they were comfortably able to withstand Gallinato's soldiers. In frustration, Gallinato ordered that they destroy all the towns and crops on the island and then withdrew.[63]

In invading Mindanao and Jolo, the authorities in Manila hoped not only to bring the Moros under Spanish vassalage, but also to negotiate an end to slave raiding activities in the region. Yet, these early campaigns had the opposite effect, instead solidifying Moro hostility to the Spanish. Both the Maguindanaos and Sulus increased their raiding activities in the Visayas, beginning in 1599, when three hundred Maguindanaos in fifty vessels sailed under the leadership of Sali and Sirongan, raiding Cebu, Negros, and Panay and taking eight hundred captives.[64] The following year, Sali returned and took another eight hundred captives from Panay and Bohol.[65] In 1602, raiders from Mindanao and Jolo seized and killed another seven hundred people in the Calamianes.[66] The City Council of Manila reported that in the year 1603 alone, raiders had collectively taken two thousand captives, including missionaries.[67]

At the same time, Moro leaders began to use slave raids quite deliberately to destabilize the Spanish presence in the Visayas. In 1603, Datu Buisan led a particularly violent raid on Leyte, taking hundreds captive and giving the local datus a week to find ransom to pay for their release. When he returned, Buisan took the opportunity to entreat the people of Leyte to give up their alliance with Spain, who were clearly unable to protect them from external threats. If they joined in an alliance with the Maguindanaos, he argued, they would no longer have to fear these raids. Buisan asked them to think on this and said he would return within a year for their answer. Seeing reason in this, the datus of Leyte entered into a blood compact with Buisan.[68] In response, the authorities in Manila sent a force of forty Spanish troops to convince the people of Leyte that they would protect them against the raiders. They used the Chinese uprising in Manila as an excuse for why they had not been able to come to their aid earlier and agreed to ransom the rest of those who were still in captivity. The communities of Leyte were able to play the situation to their advantage by bargaining with both sides for better terms.[69] This turn of events was clearly of concern to the Spanish in Manila, as the Maguindanaos appeared to be moving toward building their own tributary populations within the Visayas.[70] Another squadron of *caracoas* from Mindanao and Jolo raided the Calamianes Islands that same year. The raiders negotiated peace treaties with the communities in exchange for them becoming tributaries of Maguindanao. Unlike in Leyte, the Spanish could do nothing about this, having as yet no established presence in the Calamianes.[71]

While the Maguindanaos used raiding as a political tactic to consolidate power and convince territories to break their alliance with Spain, the Sulus realized raiding could also cause economic harm. In November 1627, raiders from the island of Jolo attacked a major Spanish shipyard located in the province of Camarines. The shipyard had been newly established and Chinese and indio laborers had been brought in to work on ship construction, along with great quantities of iron and rice and four pieces of artillery for its defense. That November two thousand raiders in more than thirty large, oared vessels assaulted the shipyards. The Jesuit account reported that the Spanish had carelessly failed to build fortifications or even mount their artillery. Consequently, the battle was short lived. Many of the laborers were captured, while the dozen wounded Spanish overseers fled upriver, leaving the camp to the Sulu raiders. The raiders remained there for several days, feasting and drinking. They sacked the shipyards, seizing the artillery and iron, setting fire to the ships, and throwing the rice into the sea. On their way back to Jolo, the Sulus raided the island of Bantayan, where they met with resistance from a group of Spaniards, including a Jesuit missionary who was later dispatched to Manila to give an account of these events.[72] This raid was particularly brazen. For perhaps the first time, Moro raiders had targeted a strategic Spanish outpost, turning the object of their raiding mission toward one of destroying strategic military assets as well as the capture of slaves.

Between Conquest and Diplomacy: Jolo and Mindanao, 1571–1638

The regularity of slave raids in the Visayas had a substantial impact on Spanish efforts to resettle Visayans into Spanish controlled coastal settlements. Prior to colonization, retaliatory raiding was used by communities as a way of discouraging repeat incursions.[73] However, Spanish missionary attitudes toward indigenous slavery prohibited communities under Spanish control from engaging in such retaliations, thereby leaving most communities weak and exposed to attack.[74] Prevented from engaging in their customary methods of defensive and retaliatory warfare, many Visayan communities would simply leave the Spanish controlled towns in April each year, anticipating the start of the slave raiding season by the change in the direction of the seasonal winds.[75] Particularly in the first decades of the century, the inability of the Spanish to put an end to Moro raids struck a real blow to Spanish authority in many communities. In 1605, Ríos Coronel argued that the prevalence of Moro raids across the archipelago caused fear among Spanish and indigenous populations alike, and few would risk traveling across certain parts of the archipelago. Many local indigenous communities also actively shunned Spanish society by climbing "up into the mountains saying that since the Spanish cannot defend them, they are not going to pay tribute."[76] Ríos Coronel's words were echoed by numerous other royal and ecclesiastic officials.[77]

Finding an effective way of defending against slave raiding was therefore essential to furthering Spanish colonization efforts in the Visayas. Across the archipelago, presidios formed the main line of Spanish defense. They were established in strategic locations to protect major Spanish ports or outposts and to serve as launching bases for expeditions of exploration or conquest.[78] In the Visayas, presidios were established early in Cebu and Oton in Panay, with between 50 and 170 soldiers stationed there throughout the century, alongside contingents of up to a 100 Pampangan soldiers.[79] In 1609 and 1635, two further presidios were established at Caraga and Zamboanga on the island of Mindanao.[80] Collectively these presidios were responsible for defending Visayan communities from slave raiders.

Like all presidios in the Philippines, however, the Visayan outposts suffered from a chronic manpower shortage. The numbers of soldiers stationed there fluctuated according to the priorities and ambitions of different governors. Soldiers were dispatched to the Philippines each year on board the galleons sent from New Spain; on average, 156 soldiers were sent annually, though in practice this number fluctuated widely and, in some years, royal officials in Manila received no reinforcements at all. Recruiting officers in New Spain struggled to find volunteers willing to enlist to serve in the Philippines, thanks to the perceived dangers of the transpacific voyage and a pervasive idea that no one ever returned from such a remote and hostile outpost.[81] Consequently, many of the soldiers that were sent to serve in Philippine presidios were actually recruited through a variety of coerced methods, including capturing vagrants and runaway soldiers and sailors as well as through criminal sentencing to a period of convict labor. The unfree origins of many soldiers serving in Spanish presidios meant that their loyalty to Spanish aims in the archipelago was always questioned. Particularly in remote presidios, soldiers would desert and at times even engaged in episodes of large-scale mutiny.[82]

The unreliability of these soldiers had an impact on Spanish defensive capabilities in the Visayas. In particular, the shortages in recruits made it difficult to contemplate expanding the number of presidios to encompass a wider defensive network. One solution thus was to establish a defensive armada that relied on soldiers drawn from the Oton and Cebu presidios, but which could present a more mobile response to sea raiding activities. In 1602, Governor Acuña wrote that a defensive armada was the only possible way of protecting the Visayas since they lacked the capacity to place a garrison of soldiers in all of the numerous islands of the archipelago.[83] The following year, the governor stationed an armada in Oton under the charge of Ronquillo, who was instructed to pursue and attack any raiding vessels.[84] Nevertheless, most officials soon realized that the defensive armadas were no real match for the well-organized and experienced slave raiding parties. Spanish ships were usually too heavy and cumbersome—requiring large teams of oarsmen to row—and were not light enough to pursue the *caracoas* of the Mindanaos.[85] Fr. Melchor Hurtado observed that the Mindanaos sailed in formation so that the least damage would be done to their fleet should they encounter Spanish vessels.[86] The *oidor* Antonio Ribera Maldonado argued that instead it would be easier to invade and conquer Mindanao.[87]

In the late sixteenth century, several invasions were attempted into the territories of the Maguindanaos and Sulus. Such invasions by nature required a considerable military force and in these instances the Spanish relied on levies of indigenous soldiers, recruited under the auspices of the repartimiento, as outlined in the chapter 2.[88] In one such invasion in 1597, Captain Juan Ronquillo sailed an army of 230 Spanish and 1,500 indigenous soldiers up the Pulangi River to wage an assault on the Maguindanao fort at Buayan.[89] When they arrived, they found that the Maguindanaos presented a formidable defense. They occupied a well-defended fort, garrisoned with many soldiers and artillery, and positioned at the head of a large lake, with a swamp on either side and a wall of more than a thousand steps in length.[90] Although Ronquillo set up a siege of this main fort, he was aware that defeating the Maguindanaos presented a considerable challenge. Writing back to Manila, he reported that, after several skirmishes with the Maguindanaos on his way to the fort, he was running low on ammunition. They had run down to just three thousand bullets, and the soldiers were tired and hungry, and many had fallen sick or were injured. Meanwhile, he believed that the Maguindanaos were willing to fight to the death but would also be able to flee by ship without being easily pursued. Because of this he was reluctant to start a prolonged war and so he sent two captains with terms of a peace treaty.

While Ronquillo was waiting for a response, a force of eight hundred Ternatens sailed up the Pulangi River, coming in aid of the Maguindanaos, who hoped that this powerful force would easily crush Ronquillo's armada.[91] Ronquillo met the Ternatens by land and by river. A major battle ensued in which the Ternatens were soundly defeated and their general, Cachil Babul, was killed.[92] This victory was significant. The Ternatens were widely believed to be undefeatable after they had successfully ousted Portuguese forces from the Maluku Islands in the 1570s. Clearly intimidated by this defeat, the Maguindanaos agreed to sign Ronquillo's treaty and he returned to Manila as a hero.[93] While in 1597 Ronquillo had seemingly managed to achieve what no one before him had, shortly after negotiating the treaty he and his soldiers also abandoned Mindanao. Faced with ongoing rebellion in Cagayan and news of the arrival of Dutch and English ships in the Maluku Islands, the royal officials in Manila felt it prudent to retreat Ronquillo and his forces, but not before instructing him to set fire to as many coconut and sago palms as he could possibly manage—up to fifty thousand trees according to one account—laying waste to Maguindanao food supplies.[94]

Ronquillo's expedition revealed one of the main flaws in Spanish conquest attempts of the southern archipelago: their reliance on levies of indigenous soldiers to bolster meager Spanish armies also meant that a more permanent occupation of captured territory was more difficult. This was especially so when the victory won was not met with equivalent agreement from the other side for genuine peace. Most indigenous soldiers were enlisted for the duration of a particular expedition, but any attempts to further extend this period of service resulted in high levels of desertion and a loss of loyalty to the project of occupation.[95] The Spanish capture of former Portuguese forts in the Maluku Islands following their invasion of Ternate in 1606 represented the only lasting attempt at such an occupation and was widely considered a significant drain on Spanish resources in the Philippines. While they succeeded in maintaining a garrison in the Maluku Islands for nearly six decades, this outpost consumed constant military reinforcements and supplies. Of the hundreds of soldiers stationed there in the seventeenth century, many deserted by preference to the Dutch, fell sick and died, or mutinied.[96] Meanwhile, the main prize—control of the spice trade—was not captured, thanks to the arrival of the Dutch in the Maluku Islands shortly after the initial successful conquest.

Faced with ongoing destabilization in the Visayas coupled with consistent failures to combat Moro raids militarily, the authorities in Manila realized that they desperately needed an alternative solution. In 1605, Governor Acuña appointed the Jesuit missionary, Fr. Melchor Hurtado, to travel as an ambassador to Mindanao, beginning a new era of diplomatic negotiations. Hurtado was an ideal ambassador since he had already spent considerable time in Mindanao following his capture by Datu Buisan in 1603. His time spent as a captive gave him unprecedented knowledge of the Maguindanao leaders. Furthermore, he had gained their trust, if not their friendship.[97] Thus, less than a year after his release from captivity, in August 1605, Melchor Hurtado found himself back in Maguindanao to negotiate peace and the release of more than two thousand Visayan captives. There was considerable disagreement among the three Maguindanao leaders—Sirongan, Buisan, and Raja Mura—over how to deal with these new overtures from the Spanish in Manila. While Sirongan was amenable toward a peace agreement chiefly because the Spanish offered to recognize him as the superior ruler of all the Maguindanao datus, the other two were angered at being considered of only secondary importance. Buisan furthermore was still awaiting the ransom that he had been promised the year before. Ultimately, it was the preparations that the Spanish were making to go to war against Ternate that led to a breakdown in negotiations. Since Maguindanao was an ally of Ternate, and since Ternate was a much closer and, in many ways, more formidable threat to peace in the region, the datus were reluctant to ally themselves with the Spanish. And so, instead of negotiating with Hurtado, they once again took him captive.[98]

This time Melchor Hurtado remained in captivity until word reached the Pulangi River in June 1606 that the Spanish had successfully seized the fort in Ternate and captured Sultan Saïd. Sirongan, Buisan, and Raja Mura collectively wrote to Manila to sue for peace. They released Melchor Hurtado along with thirty other captives and sent him with their peace offer back to Manila.[99] However, Governor Acuña died of suspected poisoning shortly after returning to Manila from his conquest of Ternate. In the upheaval following the governor's death, these peace treaties were never ratified and the Maguindanaos resumed their slave raids.[100] In 1608, the audiencia reported that in April the Maguindanaos had sailed with seventy-seven *caracoas* and attacked the islands of Leyte and Ibabao. They robbed and burnt churches, taking many captives.[101] Melchor Hurtado laid the blame for this situation squarely on Spanish involvement in Ternate. He noted that the Maguindanaos were united with Ternate in religion, friendship, and trade and recognized Ternate as superior. Hurtado warned that it was possible that the Maguindanaos would join the Ternaten alliance with the Dutch and gather together a great armada to sail on Manila. This placed the islands in the greatest danger. Hurtado recommended that more soldiers should be quickly sent to the Visayas to defend them and to prepare a defensive armada.[102] A council of war convened in Manila agreed to increase fortifications in the Visayas and seventy soldiers were sent to join the fifty already stationed there.[103] Following another raid in 1609 a new presidio was established in Caraga, in Eastern Mindanao.[104]

To a degree, this diplomacy was somewhat effective; although raiding did not cease, over the next decade its leadership passed principally to the Sulus, Camucones, and Borneans.[105] Yet, the Spanish were not always so tactful in their dealings with Moro leaders. In the 1620s, a Sulu embassy was sent to

Manila to request their intercession in a dynastic challenge underway in Jolo. The leader of this embassy, Datu Ache received relatively little attention and left Manila soon after arriving. On their way home, the Sulus were intercepted by a search party in pursuit of Camucones raiders. Datu Ache and his entourage were captured and then thrown into prison in Manila and left to starve. Eventually, their case was brought to the attention of the *oidors* by the Jesuits and they were released; however, Datu Ache had three valuable pearls confiscated from his possessions. Angry and humiliated, Datu Ache responded by leading the aforementioned raid on the Spanish naval base in Camarines, inaugurating a renewal of hostilities.[106]

In April 1628, the Spanish organized a major retaliatory attack on the Sulu capital of Jolo, mustering a force of two hundred Spanish soldiers and up to two thousand indios.[107] In the space of half a day, this army ripped through the island, sacking and burning the town, the mosque, and the sepulchers of the Sulu rulers. They destroyed all the fields and set fire to more than a hundred ships that lay in the mouth of the river, and robbed all the small artillery, arquebuses, munitions, and supplies that they could find, in the hopes that this would prevent the Sulus from conducting further raids. Meanwhile, Rajah Bungsu and his vassals retreated to his mountain fort, which the Spanish believed to be impregnable.[108]

The brutality of this attack ultimately led to an escalation in the conflict with the Sulus. Recovering quickly, the following year the Sulus counterattacked, burning more ships in Camarines and then raiding Samar, Leyte, and Bohol.[109] The next year, the Spanish organized yet another military expedition to Jolo, this time involving 350 Spanish and more than 2,500 indigenous soldiers. But when they arrived, they found that Rajah Bungsu had dismantled the town and retreated with the majority of the population to his hill fort. Although the Spanish prepared a raid at dawn, at a time they thought the Sulus were the least prepared, it quickly became apparent that there would be no possibility of conquering the fort. Instead, once again they set about burning the villages and felling the fields in the countryside, slaying anyone that they came across.[110] In 1632, the Sulus again counterattacked, raiding Leyte and this time seizing a Jesuit priest, Fr. Giovanni Domenico Bilanci, who later died in captivity.[111]

Around this time, the Maguindanaos also resumed their raiding, under the leadership of the new and powerful Maguindanao leader, Cachil Kudarat. There had been a period of peace since 1619, when the Jesuits received news from a Franciscan friar living among the Maguindanaos that they had ceased raiding because they were occupied in their own internal affairs.[112] When raiding resumed in 1634, Cachil Kudarat had become the sole ruler of all the Maguindanao communities in the Pulangi River region. Furthermore, Kudarat had managed to establish a political alliance with the Sulus through the marriage of his son to the daughter of the Sulu ruler.[113] In 1634, with a force of 1,500 soldiers, Kudarat's raiding fleet swept through the Visayas seizing captives. A letter from a Jesuit provincial in 1635 indicated the devastating impact of these raids. Not only had a number of senior missionaries lost their lives, but mission churches had been sacked and burned, ornaments and holy images had been desecrated, and Christian communities attacked and scattered, with countless Visayans taken into slavery.[114]

The combined threat of the Maguindanaos and Sulus was of deep concern for the royal officials in Manila. In 1633, the audiencia wrote to the king saying that the Moros posed the greatest risk to the reputation of the Crown and of the entire Spanish nation within the archipelago, describing the raiders as "the vilest people that there are in the surrounding islands."[115] Despite this, the government in Manila had never been able to present an adequate opposition to this threat. When news of the raids reached Manila, it was already too late to send out an armada to pursue them because by this time they would be already on their way back to their own islands. The armadas stationed in Oton and Cebu were ineffective, presenting only a constant drain on the resources of the Royal Treasury.[116] Responding to this request, the king issued a decree dated February 16, 1635 that was received by the Governor Don Sebastián Hurtado de Corcuera instructing him to put in place a final remedy against the Moros from Jolo, the Camucones, and Borneo.[117] Later that year, a military outpost was finally established at Zamboanga—on the southwestern point of Mindanao—that was intended to act as an early warning system for raiding parties sailing from both Mindanao and Jolo.[118]

In 1637 Hurtado de Corcuera prepared an invasion force of 250 Spanish and 3,000 indigenous soldiers and set sail for the Pulangi River. The official accounts of the ensuing battle fail to mention these indigenous soldiers, instead painting a picture of Hurtado de Corcuera valiantly assaulting the Moro towns and fort with just a handful of Spanish soldiers, placing his faith "in the kindness and compassion of God" rather than in the number of soldiers he had.[119] These accounts go on to depict a glorious victory for the Spanish over a heathen people. Cachil Kudarat had fortified himself at the top of a rugged mountain, with very few access paths, allowing him to withstand the initial assaults made by Hurtado de Corcuera's forces; however, eventually a section of the Spanish army managed to sneak through a back entrance that the Moros had considered inaccessible and they seized the fort. Rather than surrender to the Spanish, many of the Moros threw themselves off the mountain, while others fled. Although they captured a number of the Moros and plundered a large amount of artillery and munitions, Cachil Kudarat and most of his subjects escaped. This did not stop Hurtado de Corcuera from returning to Zamboanga and proclaiming victory over the Maguindanaos. He then sent his army to exact pledges of vassalage and tribute from Moro communities across Mindanao.[120] Meanwhile, a Spanish armada comprising more than a thousand mostly indigenous soldiers sailed along the coasts of the island, burning towns and crops, destroying trees, and killing up to seventy or more Mindanaons that came across their path, until they finally reached the Spanish fort in Caraga, on the other side of Mindanao.[121]

Emboldened by his successes, the following year Hurtado de Corcuera set sail for the island of Jolo with an army of five hundred Spanish and three thousand indigenous soldiers. Having heard of the events in Mindanao, the Sulus were prepared for the arrival of the Spanish. They fortified themselves in a high and impregnable hill fort where they waited and watched as the Spanish soldiers built their stockades and attempted to barrage their heavy defenses with little success. Hurtado de Corcuera realized quickly that his forces were insufficient to defeat the fortified position of the Sulus, and so he and his soldiers settled in for a siege in an attempt to starve them out. Initially, the Sulus received food and rice from a tributary population that continued to tend to their harvests in the fields surrounding the battleground. But Spanish incursions into these fields meant that eventually the supply of food to the fort dwindled and those inside were forced to survive principally on salted fish.[122] Suddenly, at the beginning of April 1638, the siege ended after three months. Thousands of Sulus descended from the mountain fort while their leaders negotiated the terms of peace. Even so, while all this was happening a torrential tropical storm blew in over the camp, providing the cover and excuse for most of the Sulus to flee, leaving their possessions behind and the peace treaty in tatters.[123]

The Failed Conquest, 1639–1662

Although both of these conquests in Mindanao and Jolo ended with the flight and escape of the Moro leadership, Hurtado de Corcuera was able to gather sufficient plunder—including captives that he took as slaves—to return to Manila proclaiming a glorious victory. After each of these battles, he held military parades through the streets of Manila, reminiscent of Roman triumphs and designed to demonstrate the might of the Spanish sword.[124] Of all the Spanish conquest attempts, the invasions of 1637 and 1638 came closest to subduing the Moro polities. Governor Hurtado de Corcuera was eager to consolidate his gains and, unlike his predecessors, he did not withdraw his forces following the successful sieges that resulted in the dispersal of Moro leadership.

Despite this, the peace was broken in Mindanao almost immediately. Trouble began in the Buayan region. A dispute over who was to control the Buayan fort led to the local leader Cachil Moncay declaring war on the Spanish. Meanwhile, Kudarat regrouped to the north of the Pulangi River, and the Spanish were concerned that he would join forces with Moncay. The military commander Pedro de Almonte y Verastegui reported that he led an assault on Cachil Moncay's forts in the hills and marshes of Buayan, setting them on fire and destroying his crops. He then forged an alliance with Cachil Manaquior, a rival ruler, reducing him to the obedience of the king of Spain and installing him as a puppet ruler of the Buayan region. Moncay did not give up, however; he rallied his supporters to take back Buayan, attacking the Spanish soldiers stationed there, killing several, including a Jesuit priest. These actions frightened Manaquior, who fled from Buayan and later joined Kudarat in his resistance against the Spanish.[125] While the Spanish continued their occupation of Buayan, Kudarat retook his lands to the north along the Pulangi River, cutting off the supply route between the Spanish fort and the sea. In 1642, he attacked a shipment of supplies sent upriver to Buayan, killing all but six Spanish soldiers, who were taken captive. Although these six captives were later released, the Spanish commander at Zamboanga determined that a continued presence at Buayan was unviable, so they dismantled and abandoned the fort, essentially handing back the territory that they had nominally conquered from Kudarat just five years earlier. Kudarat then proceeded to stir up discontent among other populations along the coasts of Mindanao toward Zamboanga, forcing Spanish missionaries to flee for their lives from Sibuguey and Basilan.[126]

Matters proceeded no more peacefully in Jolo, where Raja Bungsu had retreated into the interior of the island and begun to organize resistance against the Spanish, sending his son to muster support among the other islands in the Sulu archipelago. The Spanish commander, Almonte, organized a second military invasion of Jolo in 1639, attacking Bungsu's new fort.[127] While Bungsu managed to flee, the Spanish slaughtered all the Sulus that they found. A second military force was sent on a circuit of the island, enforcing obedience to the Spanish Crown at sword-point, and leaving the heads of five hundred Sulu resisters hanging from trees across the island. After this, the Spanish sailed to Tawi-Tawi, burning ships and slaughtering more than five hundred people with the intention of cutting off any possible resistance that they might offer. A governor was installed and provided with a contingent of soldiers to occupy the island. Despite this, the Sulus continued to resist and a second military incursion into the interior was organized which also traveled to the island of Parangan, where the Spanish reportedly slaughtered all the inhabitants after their commander was killed in the fighting.[128] The Jesuits reported that in 1640 the Sulus joined with the Borneans in raiding the coast of Marinduque. One of the priests working there at the time described the raiders setting fire to the church, houses, and fields, although they did not capture anyone.[129]

Thus, by 1644, all of the gains made by Hurtado de Corcuera in his "conquests" of 1637 and 1638 had been completely reversed. When the governorship passed to Diego Fajardo in August 1644, the strategy of dealing with Mindanao and Jolo also changed dramatically from one of aggressive military invasion to peace negotiations. Governor Fajardo seemed far more cognizant of the genuine threat posed by ongoing war—not only from the point of view of a dwindling military capacity in the archipelago but also because relations with the Dutch continued to be hostile. He thus appointed the Jesuit missionary, Fr. Alejandro López to travel as an ambassador to Mindanao.[130] In June 1645, López met with Kudarat and was able to negotiate a peace treaty promising perpetual friendship and a military alliance between Kudarat and the king of Spain. Importantly, unlike previous treaties, the Spanish did not attempt to force Kudarat into becoming a vassal of Spain; rather, they recognized his sovereignty over a large part of Mindanao, and the right to maintain his own relationships of vassalage with communities surrounding the Pulangi River, Iranun Bay, and in the hills further inland. Kudarat for his part agreed to cede the territories around Lake Lanao to the Spanish and to allow Jesuit missionaries into his settlements. A similar treaty was signed with the Sulus in April 1646, following a failed Dutch attempt to ally themselves with the Sulus and take Jolo from the Spanish. This event convinced Governor Fajardo that continued occupation of Jolo was untenable. The Sulu treaty was modeled on the one already signed by Kudarat and recognized Sulu sovereignty over most islands in the Sulu archipelago while granting the Spanish access to some of the smaller islands.[131]

The outcome of these treaties was a negotiated conciliation between the Spanish and the two Moro powers. Spanish military forces were tolerated in their outposts at Zamboanga and Caraga, while Jesuit and Augustinian missionaries were allowed to continue evangelizing among the non-Muslim populations in Caraga, Dapitan, Zamboanga, and Lake Lanao. This conciliation lasted four years before the first signs that the truce would not hold. In 1649, the Palapag rebellion began in Samar and spread across much of the Visayas, extending into the territory at Caraga. In response, Spanish soldiers pursued some of the rebels into Kudarat's territory, seizing captives. Kudarat considered this to be a major breach of the peace treaty and responded by preparing his own raiding party. This raid was only averted through the intercession of Fr. López, who traveled to speak to Kudarat and convinced him not to go ahead. In 1653, the new governor Manrique de Lara sent an embassy to Kudarat to confirm their mutual commitment to peace; however, it seems that some of the Maguindanao datus were discontent with their restrictions on raiding. In 1655, Kudarat sent an aggressive embassy to Manila to demand that the governor return some Maguindanao captives that were being held prisoner in Manila, as well as some of the artillery stolen during the campaign of Hurtado de Corcuera. Although Manrique de Lara agreed to these demands, he had little hope of meeting them since he no longer possessed the requested artillery, and the captives were reluctant to be sent back. Fr. López returned to Mindanao to try to negotiate with Kudarat, but the negotiations turned sour when López belabored the point that Kudarat refused to allow Christian missionaries into his lands. López was later killed while traveling through Buayan, reportedly by assassins sent on behalf of Kudarat.[132]

These events meant that the resumption of war was inevitable. Kudarat began to assemble a large alliance, bringing together allies from the Maluku Islands and the Sulu archipelago. Manrique de Lara instructed the commander at Zamboanga to begin preparing for an invasion of the Maguindanao territory.[133] In 1656, the Maguindanaos raided Marinduque, Mindoro, and Camarines without opposition. The Bishop of Nueva Cáceres described this raid on the town of Tayabas in Camarines, saying that all the indios fled into the mountains, followed by their priests. Those that remained were only able to survive the assault because they had previously fortified their church and stocked it with arquebuses and gunpowder. The priests in Camarines Province were so fearful of a return to regular raiding that they organized a militia, suggesting the indios of the region should come to mass armed with bows and arrows and practice firing these weapons in the patio of the church.[134] In 1657, the Sulus also raided the Visayas, taking a thousand captives. In 1658, the Spanish finally counterattacked, raiding the Maguindanao settlements, sacking their houses and ships, and burning their fields.[135] The same year, the Sulus raided Bohol, Leyte, Samar, Masbate, and even traveled as far as Manila Bay.[136] Peace in the region had once again been shattered.

It was within this turbulent context that Koxinga's envoy arrived in Manila in 1662 bearing a letter threatening to rain down blood and fire over the city. All at once the Spanish were confronted by internal rebellions in Northern Luzon, the threat of invasion by the Zheng warlord, and intensifying hostilities with the Maguindanaos and Sulus. Something had to break. Within the space of a year, all Spanish soldiers were withdrawn from the southern archipelago apart from the fort at Caraga on the eastern coast.[137] This decision was taken at a moment of real crisis and regretted bitterly by royal officials in Madrid.[138] But it did finally gain the peace that Governors Fajardo and Manrique de Lara had attempted to broker over the last two decades. As soon as Spanish soldiers left their territories, the Maguindanaos and Sulus ceased raiding in the Visayas.

At the same time, peace with Maguindanao and Jolo following 1663 did not mark a full halt of raiding activities in the archipelago. The Camucones continued to engage in regular raiding throughout the latter half of the seventeenth century. Governor Manrique de Lara reported that they would come in very small and light ships, sailing from island to island, often living at sea with no fixed abode. He called them "ladroncillos rateros"—despicable little thieves.[139] In 1666, Governor Salcedo organized several defensive armadas designed to capture and punish the Camucones raiders, with very limited success.[140] In 1679, the attorney Diego de Villatoro argued that the closure of the Zamboanga presidio had resulted in the islands being "infested" by pirates from the Camucones. The provinces where the villages were most exposed to the sea, such as in Camarines, were most affected by the regular raids, although the Camucones were also known to have raided as far as Mariveles, at the mouth of the Bay of Manila. The indios of Camarines had built themselves an armada of small light vessels and had successfully defended themselves against the pirates.[141] Most officials in Manila believed that the Camucones were ultimately acting on behalf of the Borneans, with whom the Spanish had had only limited direct contact over the course of the previous century. When the sultan of Brunei sent an ambassador to sign a peace agreement with the Spanish and open direct trade with Manila in the early 1680s, it was hoped that this would help to put an end to the regular raids of the Camucones.[142]

Around the same time, in 1685, the governor in Manila received letters from both the kings of Mindanao and Jolo saying that they would conserve the peace with the Spanish while they remained preoccupied with fighting a war among themselves.[143] Combined with a newly established trading relationship with Borneo, this gave many in Manila hope that the Moro wars had come to an end. They had already attempted to intervene into the internal affairs of the Maguindanaos, favoring Prince Curay as the successor to Kudarat and offering in 1671 to provide him with military support against three other rivals for the sultanship.[144] Yet, as the century progressed these internal disputes transformed into a conflict between Maguindanao and Sulu for supremacy over the whole region.[145] In 1690, Governor Abella Fuertes reported that peace with Maguindanao was unstable and that the brother of the ruling sultan had been put to death for wanting to break the peace with Spain. He also reported that the Maguindanaos were pursuing war against Jolo.[146] By the early eighteenth century, the Sulus came out of the conflict triumphant, building the biggest Muslim sultanate yet seen in the Philippine archipelago, that by the late eighteenth century became the largest and most notorious slave raiding entrepôt in maritime Southeast Asia. Slave raiding not only resumed but reached even greater levels of destructiveness.[147]

The Spanish began their involvement in maritime Southeast Asia in the late sixteenth century with great ambitions for extending their control over large parts of Southeast Asia; however, these ambitions died at the maritime frontier with Mindanao and Jolo. For nearly a century, these polities—along with the Camucones, Borneans, and Caragans—beleaguered the Spanish with constant raiding. Although the Spanish tried various tactics, including subjugation by treaty, defensive armadas, and military invasion, they were ultimately repeatedly outmaneuvered by the Moros militarily and diplomatically. Thus, by the end of the century, they were forced to abandon their territorial ambitions and accept the limitations of the frontier established by the Moros. Moreover, although a peaceful conciliation was eventually reached by the end of the seventeenth century, it had been brokered with considerable loss of life on both sides. While some missionary activity continued in Mindanao over the ensuing decades, it was limited and hampered by hostility from the Moros who, after a century of contact with various Spanish missionaries in the guise of diplomats, had developed a distrust for them. When the Spanish reignited their military engagement with Mindanao and Jolo the following century, a new era of violence was ushered in. The Spanish met their match in the southern archipelago, where Moro polities maintained sophisticated military and diplomatic tactics and were ruthless in warfare, ultimately allowing them to retain their own sovereignty and limiting that of the Spanish.

CHAPTER 5

Mountain Refuges

In February 1624, the military commander Don Alonso Martín Quirante found himself standing on a summit deep within the Cordillera mountain range of Northern Luzon. Stretched out before him, as far as the eye could see, was a rugged landscape of pine covered mountains. Quirante marveled at the sight. For two weeks he and his soldiers had climbed slowly but steadily into this wild terrain, following courses cut by mountain streams through rainforest that gradually gave way to the unending tropical pine forest that now surrounded him. Writing later, Quirante described this as an eerie landscape, prone to heavy rains that washed down the mountainsides, accompanied by great booming thunder and lightning, and followed by thick shrouds of fog that made everything damp and humid. He found the endless pine trees oppressive and the climate intolerable even when the sun was shining. Hardly a creature stirred among these pines except for occasional crows and some small birds that Quirante likened to goldfinches. In Quirante's view, this territory was so rugged and barren that he found it almost impossible to believe that any creature lived there, let alone indigenous Igorot communities.[1]

Northern Luzon is defined by its mountains. In the west the Cordillera Mountains stretch for nearly two hundred miles from the plains of Pangasinan in the south to the northern coastline of Cagayan. The mountains rise sharply from the coastline to reach heights of nearly three thousand meters; their ecosystems are defined by higher altitude tropical pine forests and montane rain forests as well as tropical rain forests at lower altitudes. In the southeast, the Cordillera range joins with the eastern Sierra Madre Mountains via a lower mountain range known as the Caraballo Sur. Together these three mountain ranges ring the great expanse of the Cagayan Valley. Despite the Spanish tendency to describe all inhabitants as "Igorots," these mountains were and remain home to numerous ethnic groups. These groups maintained trading relations with their lowland neighbors in Cagayan, Ilocos, and Pangasinan.[2] In the early seventeenth century, Spanish knowledge of the territorial extent and geography of these mountains and the people who lived in them was minimal and derived primarily from information given to them by lowland informants.[3] Rumors of gold mines hidden deep within the Cordillera Mountains were fueled by the regular trade in gold between Igorots and coastal communities in Ilocos and Pangasinan. At the same time, the presence of such a vast, unexplored, and uncontrolled territory hindered efforts to establish control in the neighboring lowlands, particularly in Cagayan. Beginning in the 1590s, numerous attempts were made to penetrate into the Cordillera Mountains, compelled by two principal aims: to capture control of Igorot gold mines and to aid in the pacification of neighboring lowland regions.

Don Quirante led one such expedition in 1624 when he and his soldiers went in search of the famed Igorot gold mines. Previous expeditions had barely managed to penetrate these mountains, overwhelmed both by their geography and the hostility of the communities that lived there. Standing on this summit in 1624 and surveying the vast and rugged territory that rolled away before him, Quirante was perhaps the first Spaniard to truly appreciate the scale of this task. Indeed, the Cordillera remained largely unexplored by Europeans until the nineteenth century, while Igorot and other mountain communities continued to resist colonization into the twentieth century.[4]

The history of the Cordillera region of Northern Luzon is one of systematic resistance, in which its inhabitants used tactics of warfare including raiding, headhunting, and guerrilla warfare to evade colonization as well as to disrupt Spanish lowland settlements.[5] This story has come to define the history of mountain communities in the Philippines, earning the Igorots a mythological status within the annals of Philippine history. Their independence from colonial rule has in turn shaped postindependence calls for autonomy and indigenous sovereignty,[6] and—according to the famous historian of the Cordillera, William Henry Scott—contributed to the "distinction between lowland and highland Filipinos which contrasted submission, conversion, and civilization on the one hand with independence, paganism, and savagery on the other."[7] Nevertheless, this focus on Igorots flattens the history of resistance among multiple different ethnic groups occupying the mountain regions of Northern Luzon.

The Spanish often used the term Igorot, which means "people of the mountains," to refer to all of the inhabitants of upland Northern Luzon. Yet, as Deirdre McKay points out, Igorot is itself a colonial term, derived from the lowlands rather than from the mountain communities themselves.[8] Igorot territory encompasses six different ethnolinguistic groups: Bontoc, Ibaloi, Ifugao, Isneg, Kalinga, and Kankana-ey. A survey conducted in 1989 revealed that among the ethnic groups normally subsumed under the Igorot category, many do not self-identify as "Igorot."[9] At the same time, numerous other indigenous groups inhabited the Cordillera, Caraballo Sur, and Sierra Madre Mountains and the Cagayan Valley including Isinai, Gaddang, Ibanag, Itawis, Yogad, Ilongot, and Aeta.[10] All of these groups had unique and diverse experiences of colonization and resistance; like the Igorots, many of them entered the twentieth century largely outside of colonial control. Their stories have been folded into that of the Igorots, even while they maintain their individual ethnic identities.

The history of Igorot resistance is therefore perhaps less exceptional than at first glance. Neither was this a story unique to Northern Luzon. Particularly in the seventeenth century, mountains across the entire archipelago defined the territorial limits of colonial control.[11] Spanish officials deployed discourses of barbarism and savagery to describe these uncontrolled spaces, using these views to justify their use of excessive violence against mountain communities and to excuse their repeated failures to bring these upland spaces under control.[12] Moreover, while some mountain communities—like the Igorots, Zambales, and Aetas—represent autonomous upland groups that managed to prevent the establishment of colonial rule in their territories, uplands also became the sites of widespread migration from the lowlands, attracting those seeking refuge from the colonial state. In this regard, the role of mountains in Philippine history is not exceptional but is reflected in similar histories of resistance and refuge found across the Spanish empire, particularly in frontier regions where Spanish power was less assured and the balance of power between colonizing forces and local indigenous communities was more equal than sometimes assumed.[13] James Scott has described similar processes in mainland Southeast Asia, linking the Philippine experience to these wider debates on the role of state power and the ability for communities to evade and resist the state.[14]

This chapter thus traces two distinct but related processes that took place in Philippine mountains: the persistent resistance of autonomous mountain communities and the widespread migration of fugitives into the mountains. In some instances, these two distinct groupings of people converged, with autonomous upland groups like the Ifugao and the Aeta providing sanctuary to those fleeing Spanish colonization. In all instances, upland communities—both autochthonous and migrant—presented a fierce and persistent problem for colonial authorities. They used sophisticated tactics including headhunting, raiding, rebellion, alliance building, and open warfare to halt colonial expansion. The effectiveness of these actions is evident not only in their persistence but in the way they severely restricted the scope of Spanish domination during the seventeenth century and well into the eighteenth and nineteenth centuries.

Zones of Refuge

In 1619 the Franciscan Fr. Pedro de San Pablo wrote of the disappointing state of colonial control within the provinces of Camarines, Tayabas, and Laguna de Bay. In the space of just six years, the populations living in Spanish settlements had halved in size. While some indios had gone to work for the Spanish in Manila or elsewhere, many others had simply abandoned the settlements, some establishing bases of resistance in neighboring upland spaces. In Camarines, the Franciscans organized an expedition into the mountains near Labo, where several hundred indios were reported to have fled. Fr. San Pablo described the difficult hike through the dense terrain, saying that they saw neither the sun nor the moon for a whole week due to extensive rain and flooding that turned paths into streams. When they reached the communities in the mountains, they tried to convince them to come back to the Spanish towns. Some said they would go, but many others said that they did not want to because of the great personal labors that the Spanish required of them. In the end, just eighty-one people returned to the lowlands, but many of those eventually went back to the mountains. San Pablo lamented this situation, noting how damaging it was to the spread of the holy faith. He laid the blame on the burdens placed on the indios, who were forced to labor in construction and to provide rice, oil, abaca, wine, beans, and other legumes, none of which was paid for by the Spanish.[15]

Colonial reports like that given by Fr. San Pablo were common. Dozens of reports—from Antipolo, near Manila, to Laguna de Bay, Tayabas, Camarines, Mindoro, and many Visayan islands—describe the upland areas of the Philippines as sites of lawlessness, apostasy, barbarism, and fugitivism (see table 3).[16] The unevenness of Spanish colonization and control within the archipelago opened up opportunities for indios to simply leave the Spanish sphere. Moreover, reports of flight increased in the second half of the century, suggesting that it was an escalating phenomenon. In 1679, the attorney general Don Diego de Villatoro noted the widespread problem of indios fleeing Spanish settlements and running away to live as free people in the mountains. From the uplands, they would often attack Spaniards and loyal indios traveling on the roads between villages. They robbed farms and killed their inhabitants, sometimes

Table 3 Reports of flight, apostasy, and zones of refuge in Luzon and the Visayas, 1574–1744

REGION	PROVINCE	YEARS WHERE FUGITIVISM WAS REPORTED	DESCRIPTION OF FUGITIVISM
Luzon	Antipolo	1601, 1610, 1618, 1649, 1672, 1680, 1699, 1700	The mountains east of Antipolo were inhabited by unsubjugated Aeta communities who harbored fugitives from Manila and Laguna de Bay.[1]
	Baler; Casiguran, and Palanan	1618, 1682, 1688, 1695, 1700, 1733	Ilongots, Aetas, and Irrayas in the Sierra Madre Mountains regularly attacked and raided these settlements and refused conversion.[2]
	Bulacan and Tondo	1582, 1618, 1700, 1702, 1733	Fugitives, heathens, and apostates reported particularly near Meycauayan.[3]
	Cagayan	1598, 1600, 1607, 1608, 1615, 1621, 1622, 1625, 1627, 1661, 1678, 1680, 1686, 1688, 1689, 1690, 1691, 1700, 1701, 1719, 1739, 1742	Regular reports of indios fleeing into the mountains, usually accompanying rebellion and abandonment of Spanish settlements.[4]
	Calamianes	1677, 1695	Reports of fugitives living in the mountains.[5]
	Camarines	1618, 1619, 1656, 1677, 1682, 1683, 1685, 1688, 1697, 1700, 1702, 1726, 1733	Numerous reports of fugitives joining unsubjugated Aeta communities particularly in Mt. Isarog, Lagonoy, Libmanan, and on the outskirts of Nueva Cáceres, regular attacks and raids on Spanish settlements.[6]
	Cavite and Balayan	1604, 1635, 1680, 1706, 1733	Reports of fugitives and apostates living in the mountains close to Maragondon, Balayan, and the cove of Palikpikan.[7]
	Ilocos	1700, 1703, 1737	Reports of fugitivism, apostasy, and attacks on Spanish settlements particularly in Dingras and Bangued.[8]
	Laguna de Bay and Tayabas	1618, 1670, 1677, 1679, 1686, 1688, 1700, 1733	Reports of towns being abandoned and fugitives practicing native religion in the mountains.[9]
	Marinduque	1630, 1661, 1671	Reports of flight away from evangelizing efforts of Jesuits.[10]
	Mindoro	1630, 1635, 1667, 1672, 1679, 1682, 1700	Manguianes used fugitivism to escape evangelization; later in the century communities of apostates formed within the mountains.[11]

Nueva Ecija	1690, 1700, 1717, 1721, 1725, 1737	This region was largely unsubjugated; reports of fugitivism, apostasy, particularly around Gapan.[12]
Pampanga and Zambales	1660, 1665, 1667, 1670, 1679, 1680, 1686, 1688, 1690, 1695, 1699, 1700, 1701, 1733, 1737	Reports of many Pampangans fleeing the province for the mountains or other provinces to escape the burdens of the repartimiento, bandala. Attacks on Spanish settlements from unsubjugated groups as well as fugitives.[13]
Pangasinan	1680, 1688, 1690, 1701, 1733	Reports of fugitivism and apostasy as well as unsubjugated zones; regular attacks by mountain communities.[14]
Visayas		
Bohol	1608, 1621, 1627, 1632, 1639, 1744	Fugitivism increased particularly following the 1621 revolt, with fugitives over ensuing years continuing to make threats against Jesuit-run settlements.[15]
Cebu	1686, 1699, 1700, 1705	Reports of fugitives and apostates living in the mountains.[16]
Leyte	1602, 1603, 1649, 1671, 1688, 1700	Periodic reports of indios fleeing into the mountains and living outside of Spanish control.[17]
Masbate	1649, 1700	Reports of fugitives and unsubjugated areas in the mountains.[18]
Negros	1630, 1633, 1659, 1677, 1688, 1733	Periodic reports of indios fleeing into the mountains, particularly around the mountains of Kabankalan.[19]
Panay	1663, 1671, 1688, 1696, 1700, 1737, 1742	Reports of fugitives living in the mountains among unsubjugated communities; later reports speak of a "conspiracy" among indios to apostatize and retreat into remote mountains and forests.[20]
Samar	1649, 1733	Major episodes of fugitivism during Sumoroy revolt in 1649; later reports of fugitives living in the mountains and attacking Spanish settlements.[21]
Region unspecified[22]	1580, 1582, 1585, 1592, 1618, 1620, 1622, 1630, 1637, 1650, 1665, 1667, 1679, 1683, 1684, 1688, 1690, 1697	Regular reports of indios fleeing into the mountains, usually to escape the burdens of the repartimiento, bandala and tribute payments.[23]

(continued)

Table 3 *(continued)*

[1] Archivo General de Indias (hereafter AGI), Audiencias de Filipinas (hereafter Filipinas), leg. 36, núm. 72; AGI, Filipinas, leg. 75, núm. 41; AGI, Filipinas, leg. 163, núm 33; AGI, Escribanía de Cámara de Justicia (hereafter Escribanía), leg. 404B; Archivo Histórico Nacional (hereafter AHN), Colección Documentos de Indias (hereafter CDI), leg. 26, núm. 28; Archivum Romanum Societatis Iesu (hereafter ARSI), phil. 5, fol. 97v (1601–1602); ARSI, phil. 7., fol. 363r (1646–1649); ARSI, phil. 7, fol. 845v (1665–1672).

[2] AGI, Filipinas, leg. 86, núm. 48; AGI, Filipinas, leg. 125, núm 20; AGI, Filipinas, leg. 144, núm. 9; AGI, Filipinas, leg. 163, núm. 33; AHN, CDI, leg. 26, núm. 28.

[3] AGI, Filipinas, leg. 84, núm. 36; AGI, Filipinas, leg. 144, núm. 9; AGI, Filipinas, leg. 163, núm. 33; AHN, CDI, leg. 26, núm. 28.

[4] AGI, Filipinas, leg. 6, ramo 9, núms. 161, 173; AGI, Filipinas, leg. 7, ramo 5, núm. 65; AGI, Filipinas, leg. 9, ramo 2, núm. 30; AGI, Filipinas, leg. 14, ramo 3, núm. 35; AGI, Filipinas, leg. 18A, ramo 7, núm. 47; AGI, Filipinas, leg. 18B, ramo 1, núm. 2; AGI, Filipinas, leg. 23, ramo 17, núm. 55; AGI, Filipinas, leg. 27, núm. 33; AGI, Filipinas, leg. 76, núm. 18; AGI, Filipinas, leg. 76, núm. 55; AGI, Filipinas, leg. 80, núm. 133; AGI, Filipinas, leg. 83, núms. 27, 52; AGI, Filipinas, leg. 125, núm. 20; AGI, Filipinas, leg. 132, núm. 43; AGI, Filipinas, leg. 148, núm. 18; AGI, Filipinas, leg. 149, núm. 11; AGI, Filipinas, leg. 163, núm. 33; AGI, Filipinas, leg. 331, libro 9, fols. 210v–212r; AGI, Filipinas, leg. 340, libro 3, fols. 406r–406v; "Noticias desde el Junio pasado de 79 hasta el presente de 80," Real Academia de la Historia (hereafter RAH), 9/2668, núm. 66: "Breve relación, y felizes progressos de los Religiosos del Sagrado Orden de Predicadores de las Islas Philipinas," Biblioteca Nacional de España (hereafter BNE). R/33161; "Relación de las plazas, castillos, fuerzas y presidios de las islas Philipinas," BNE, mss/19217; "Misiones de los mandayas en Caraga, por el P. Pedro Jimenez," Archivo de la Provincia del Santísimo Rosario. 58, Sección Cagayan, tomo 13, doc. 4; Felix M. Keesing, *Ethnohistory of Northern Luzon* (Stanford, CA: Stanford University Press, 1962), 175–176, 194, 243; Fr. Diego Aduarte, *Tomo Primero de la Historia de la Provincia del Santo Rosario de Filipinas, Japón, y China, de la sagrada orden de predicadores* (Zaragoza: Por Domingo Gascon, Insançon, Impressor del Santo Hospital Real y General de Nuestra Señora de Gracia, 1693), 315–320, 413–318, 490–494, 550–556; Linda Newson. *Conquest and Pestilence in the Early Spanish Philippines* (Honolulu: University of Hawai'i Press, 2009), 206; Fr. Julian Malumbres, O. P., *Historia de Cagayan* (Manila: Tip. Linotype de Santo Tomás, 1918), 28; Baltasar de Santa Cruz, *Tomo Segundo de la Historia de la Provincia del Santo Rosario de Filipinas, Japón, y China del Sagrado Orden de Predicadores* (Zaragoza: Por Pasqual Bueno, Impressor Reyno, 1693), 18–21.

[5] AGI, Escribanía, leg. 404B; AGI, Filipinas, leg. 125, núm. 20.

[6] "Description of the Philippines. 1618." RAH, 9/3657, núm. 22; AHN, CDI, leg. 26, núm. 28; AGI, Filipinas, leg. 12, ramo 1, núm. 8; AGI, Filipinas, leg. 17, ramo 1, núm. 7; AGI, Filipinas, leg. 76, núms. 145, 155, 156; AGI, Filipinas, leg. 83, núm. 29; AGI, Filipinas, leg. 144, núm. 9; AGI, Filipinas, leg. 331, núm. 9; AGI, Filipinas, leg. 331, libro 8, fols. 11–12r; AGI, Filipinas, leg. 331, libro 9, fols. 102r–104v; AGI, Filipinas, leg. 332, libro 10, fols. 25r–26r; "Informe del Obispo de Nueva Cáceres al Gobierno, sobre los daños que causaban los moros y las vejaciones a los indios por los alcaldes mayores," Archivo Franciscano Ibero-Oriental, 92/7; Norman G. Owen, *Prosperity without Progress: Manila Hemp and Material Life in the Colonial Philippines* (Berkeley: University of California Press, 1984), 22–23.

[7] Francisco Colin, *Labor evangélica, ministerios apostólicos de los obreros de la compañía de Jesus, fundación y progressos de su provincia en las islas filipinas: Historiados por el padre Francisco Colin, provincial de la misma compañía, calificador del santo oficio y su comisario en la governacion de Samboanga y su distrito,* 4 vols. (Madrid: Por Ioseph Fernandez de Buendia, 1668), 459; ARSI, phil. 7, fols. 216r–217v (1634–1635); ARSI, phil. 8, fols. 104v–105r (1697–1706); AGI, Filipinas, leg. 125, núm. 20; AGI, Filipinas, leg. 144, núm. 9.

[8] AGI, Filipinas, leg. 127, núm. 25; AGI, Filipinas, leg. 148, núm. 18; AGI, Filipinas, leg. 163, núm. 33.

[9] AGI, Filipinas, leg. 10, ramo 1, núm. 5; AGI, Filipinas, leg. 13, ramo 1, núm. 13; AGI, Filipinas, leg. 28, núm. 128; AGI, Filipinas, leg. 75, núms. 20, 23; AGI, Filipinas, leg. 125, núm. 20; AGI, Filipinas, leg. 144, núm. 9; AGI, Filipinas, leg. 163, núm. 33; AGI, Filipinas, leg. 331, libro 7, fols. 274r–275r; AGI, Escribanía, leg. 404B; AHN, CDI, leg. 26, núm. 28.

[10] ARSI, phil. 6, fol. 609v (1630); RAH, 9/2668, núm. 42 (1658–1661); RAH, 9/2668, núm. 17 (1665–1671).

[11] ARSI, phil. 6, fol. 611r (1630); ARSI, phil. 7, fols. 218v–219r (1634–1635); AGI, Escribanía, leg. 404B; AGI, Filipinas, leg. 86, núm. 48; AGI, Filipinas, leg. 163, núm. 33; RAH, 9/2668, núm. 17 (1665–1671); RAH, 9/2668, núm. 66 (1679–1680).

[12] AGI, Filipinas, leg. 83, núm. 52; AGI, Filipinas, leg. 134, núm. 12; AGI, Filipinas, leg. 140, núm. 29; AGI, Filipinas, leg. 148, núm. 18; AGI, Filipinas, leg. 163, núm. 33; "Breve apuntamiento de las misiones a cargo de los agustinos calzados en los montes de Pantabangan y Caranglan," BNE, mss/11014, fols. 276r–278v

[13] AGI, Filipinas, leg. 9, ramo 3, núm. 48; AGI, Filipinas, leg. 9, ramo 3, núm. 49; AGI, Filipinas, leg. 10, ramo 1, núm. 4; AGI, Filipinas, leg. 28, núm. 128; AGI, Filipinas, leg. 75, núms. 23, 41; AGI, Filipinas, leg. 81, núm. 109; AGI, Filipinas, leg. 83, núm. 52; AGI, Filipinas, leg. 125, núm. 20; AGI, Filipinas, leg. 144, núm. 9; AGI, Filipinas, leg. 148, núm. 18; AGI, Filipinas, leg. 163, núm. 33; AGI, Filipinas, leg. 193, núm. 22; AGI, Filipinas, leg. 331, libro 7, fols. 274r–275r; AGI, Escribanía, leg. 404B; AGI, Escribanía, leg. 410B.

[14] AGI, Escribanía, leg. 404B; AGI, Filipinas, leg. 83, núm. 52; AGI, Filipinas, leg. 125, núm. 20; AGI, Filipinas, leg. 144, núm. 9.

[15] Colin, *Labor evangélica*, 622; "Insurrections by Filipinos in the Seventeenth Century," in *The Philippine Islands, 1493–1803* (hereafter *B&R*), trans. and ed. Emma Helen Blair and James Alexander Robertson, 55 vols. (Cleveland, OH: A. H. Clark, 1903–9), vol. 38, 87–94; AGI, Filipinas, leg. 76, núm. 13; AGI, Filipinas, leg. 264, núm. 1; AGI, Filipinas, leg. 293, núm. 63; ARSI, phil. 6, fols. 307r–314r (1621); ARSI, phil. 6, fols. 505r–506r (1627); ARSI, phil. 7, fol. 71v (1631–1632); ARSI, phil. 7, fols. 340v–341v (1638–1639).

[16] AGI, Filipinas, leg. 163, núm. 33; AGI, Filipinas, leg. 332, libro 10, fols. 76v–77r; AGI, Filipinas, leg. 332, libro 11, fols. 105r–105v.

[17] ARSI, phil. 5, fols. 94r–113r (1601–1602); Colin, *Labor evangélica*, 473; RAH, 9/2668, núm. 17 (1665–1671); AGI, Filipinas, leg. 125, núm. 20; AGI, Filipinas, leg. 163, núm. 33; "Insurrections by Filipinos in the Seventeenth Century," *B&R*, vol. 38, 101–128.

[18] "Insurrections by Filipinos in the Seventeenth Century," *B&R*, vol. 38, 101–128; AGI, Filipinas, leg. 163, núm. 33.

[19] ARSI, phil. 6, fols. 626v–627r (1630); ARSI, phil. 7, fols. 115r–115v (1633); ARSI, phil. 12, fols. 1r–12r (1660); AGI, Filipinas, leg. 8, ramo 1, núm. 12; AGI, Filipinas, leg. 125, núm. 20; AGI, Filipinas, leg. 144, núm. 9; AGI, Escribanía, leg. 404B.

[20] "Insurrections by Filipinos in the Seventeenth Century," *B&R*, vol. 38, 215–223; AGI, Filipinas, leg. 16, ramo 1, núm. 6; AGI, Filipinas, leg. 71, núm. 1; AGI, Filipinas, leg. 125, núm. 20; AGI, Filipinas, leg. 148, núm. 18; AGI, Filipinas, leg. 163, núm. 33; RAH, 9/2668, núm. 17 (1665–1671); ARSI, phil. 8, fols. 41r–42r (1687–1696); "Relación de las plazas, castillos, fuerzas y presidios de las islas Philipinas," BNE, mss/19217.

[21] "Insurrections by Filipinos in the Seventeenth Century," *B&R*, vol. 38, 101–128; AGI, Filipinas, leg. 144, núm. 9; ARSI, phil. 7, fols. 667v–678r (1646–1649).

[22] Note: Additional reports exist detailing fugitivism in Mindanao, however since this region was so volatile these will be dealt with in other chapters.

[23] AGI, Filipinas, leg. 5, núm 178; AGI, Filipinas, leg. 6, ramo 10, núm. 180; AGI, Filipinas, leg. 7, ramo 5, núm. 67; AGI, Filipinas, leg. 8, ramo 3, núm. 90; AGI, Filipinas, leg. 9, ramo 1, núms. 9, 13; AGI, Filipinas, leg. 9, ramo 3, núm. 44; AGI, Filipinas, leg. 14, ramo 3, núm. 25; AGI, Filipinas, leg. 18B, ramo 2, núm. 19; AGI, Filipinas, leg. 21, ramo 4, núm. 17; AGI, Filipinas, leg. 24, ramo 5, núm. 28; AGI, Filipinas, leg. 26, ramo 6, núm. 25; AGI, Filipinas, leg. 28, núm. 128; AGI, Filipinas, leg. 75, núm. 10; AGI, Filipinas, leg. 80, núm. 41; AGI, Filipinas, leg. 81, núm. 109; AGI, Filipinas, leg. 83, núm. 52; AGI, Filipinas, leg. 84, núms. 13, 46; AGI, Filipinas, leg. 86, núm. 66; AHN, CDI, leg. 26, núm. 30.

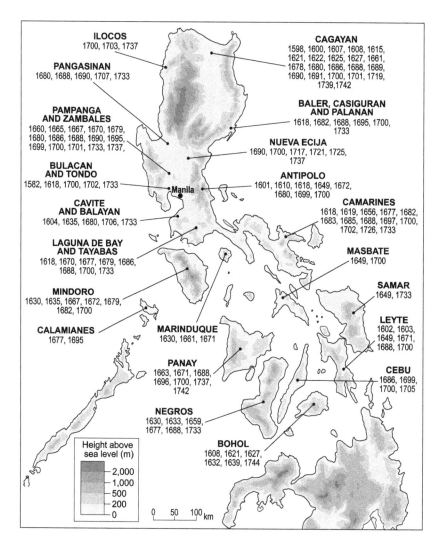

FIGURE 5.1. Reports of flight, apostasy, and zones of refuge in Luzon and the Visayas, 1574–1744. Map by Philip Stickler.

entering towns and burning and sacking them. Displaying his anxiety toward the legitimacy of Spanish colonial rule, Villatoro believed that the greatest danger of this situation was that many indios who remained loyal to the Spaniards would see that those who fled led freer lives.[17]

Outside of Northern Luzon, the region with the most frequent reports of fugitivism was Camarines, particularly in the mountains near Lagonoy and the Caramoan peninsula, Libmanan and Mount Isarog, just outside the Spanish city of Nueva Cáceres.[18] In 1656, the Bishop of Nueva Cáceres wrote that the indios of Camarines regularly ran away into the mountains where they would live off deer hunting and occasionally raiding lowland neighbors. In the mountains, they were supported by Agta communities who would defend the fugitives against Spanish incursions with their bows and arrows.[19] By 1685, regular expeditions against runaways were organized across Camarines and Albay.[20] Similarly, in the 1680s a large number of indio fugitives in the region of Balayan, Laguna de Bay were reported as having abandoned their faith along with their obligations to the Crown. They were also hiding slaves.[21] Not even Manila was exempt from fugitivism. In 1582, a group of principales from the region of Tondo reported that many indios were fleeing their province in order to escape the hardships of Spanish rule, including tribute payments.[22] The nearest uncontrolled upland space to Manila were the mountains between Antipolo and Tanay, where Jesuit missionaries reported substantial unpacified populations.[23] In 1610, Governor Silva organized an incursion into these mountains, ordering soldiers to set fire to fields and houses and to capture as many as possible, sentencing them to ten years of slavery.[24]

A 1691 investigation into fugitivism by the senior *oidor* Don Alonso de Avella y Fuertes noted that it was no wonder these indios sought refuge in the mountains since among the upland communities they were given the kind of safety and protection that was supposedly the centerpiece of the encomienda system but was routinely denied them by brutal encomenderos.[25] Yet, the demands of colonial labor regimes were not the only motivators for abandoning Spanish settlements. Many indios fled into the mountains to escape the evangelizing practices of Spanish missionaries—whether through fear of the new religion, because of abusive behavior of particular priests, or simply because they wished to continue practicing their own religious traditions without persecution.[26] In the Visayas, while indios commonly took to the hills in anticipation of the annual slave raiding activities of the polities in the southern archipelago, at times this was also a tactic used to evade Jesuit missionaries.[27] In 1602 the Jesuits reported that half of the island of Leyte was in uprising and there was a large group of fugitives as well as a band of twelve people who were known killers. Some of the fugitives roved around in gangs around the countryside, sheltering other fugitives and engaging in idolatrous practices that undermined Christianization efforts.[28] In October 1630, news arrived in Manila that many of the indios on the island of Negros had rebelled and fled into the mountains, especially those who belonged within the encomienda of Don Cristóbal de Lugo y Montalvo. Those who had fled into the mountains were engaging in attacks against those who remained within Spanish settlements.[29] In the 1690s the Augustinians reported that there were apostates and fugitives living in the mountains of Panay among other unsubjugated groups that they called "mundos."[30]

In some instances, flight was a response to the arrival of missionaries in communities that had been relatively isolated until quite late in the seventeenth century. This was particularly the case on the islands of Mindoro and Marinduque, where missionary activity was not well consolidated.[31] In 1661, Marinduque was reportedly "infested with *cimarrones* and *forajidos*" who lived in the mountains and had constructed forts so that they could live in freedom.[32] In 1667, the Jesuit Fr. Juan Andres Palavicino undertook a mission to the island of Mindoro where he reported that there were many thousands of "heathens" called Manguianes, living "naked . . . without law or king, and almost without the use of reason," because they had no notion of the Christian God.[33] Two years prior to this, two Jesuits baptized three hundred people. But when the missionaries left, the Manguianes had returned to their pagan customs and retreated back into the mountains to live as they had before.

Terror and violence were the usual responses of Spanish officials to flight into upland spaces.[34] For example, in the 1680s, the governor ordered an armed incursion into the mountains of Pansin, in Laguna de Bay. The alcalde mayor was instructed to take a force of indigenous soldiers to seek out the fugitives, apprehend them along with their slaves, and send them to Manila where they would be brought to justice. If they resisted, he was to respond with force, setting fire to their houses and fields.[35] Similar incursions were organized periodically throughout the century, always with the intention of terrorizing communities and making it difficult for them to live outside Spanish tributary settlements by burning their crops and enforcing harsh penalties of servitude. Such incursions often required the support of indigenous allies who were willing to serve in the Spanish military forces.[36] This was certainly the case in Camarines and Albay, where regular incursions against fugitive runaways were supported by indigenous soldiers motivated principally by the promise that they would be allowed to take captives as their personal slaves.[37] Yet, with the formal abolition of slavery in 1682, these incursions were halted and the mountain communities swelled in number in these provinces.[38]

Writing about the Buid in Mindoro, the anthropologist Thomas Gibson argued that flight was used as a means of avoiding violent encounters because the Buid had little to gain from such confrontations.[39] Yet, in the seventeenth century, there is evidence that flight into upland spaces was often combined with aggressive resistance to colonial rule.[40] In retaliation and responding to the tactics of the colonial state, upland communities actively destabilized Spanish settlements in the lowlands by raiding Spanish villages, attacking indios who stayed loyal to the Spanish, destroying their crops, seizing them as slaves, and sometimes killing them in the process.[41] The regions that suffered the most from such raids were those lowland areas in closest proximity to unconquered mountain ranges. Pampanga in particular suffered from regular raiding by the Zambales, a group of upland communities living in the coastal mountain range between Mariveles and Bolinao.

Upland regions in the Philippines thus acted as sites of freedom where indigenous communities sought refuge from oppressive colonial labor regimes and evangelization efforts. Fugitives were particularly attracted to mountainous regions with established autonomy, where indigenous groups continued to successfully resist colonization attempts. Such upland communities defined and delimited the colonial frontier; from these strategic locations, fugitives joined forces with established unsubjugated communities and often utilized tactics of violence and rebellion to disrupt the colonization process in neighboring lowlands. For these reasons, although Spanish officials and missionaries were concerned with recovering fugitives and apostates, they also realized that such efforts would be ineffective unless these autonomous mountain regions were brought under control. Throughout the seventeenth century, military resources were concentrated on two upland regions in particular: the Cordillera and the Zambales Mountains. Both were considered intractable sites of autonomy, where indigenous groups refused colonization, harbored fugitives from the lowlands, and led headhunting and raiding missions on Spanish settlements. Yet, despite numerous Spanish military incursions into these regions, their strategic use of mountain geographies aided their continued resistance and allowed them to retain their autonomy throughout the century.

Geographies of Resistance in the Cordillera Mountains

Their settlements are in the summits of the mountains . . . from where from very far away they can survey all the paths [leading up to the mountain] so that none can climb up there without being seen by their sentries who are placed there continuously by night and by day. If they fear some kind of danger, they can easily retreat without being discovered, leaving behind no more than their sad shacks . . . They defend where they can by throwing boulders from above that they have placed for this purpose, [along with] bacacayes [a type of spear] and rocks, by which they seek to make the site secure and comfortable.[42]

This 1624 description of Igorot defenses by the military commander Don Alonso Martín Quirante gives a clear insight into the way in which indigenous communities of the Cordillera strategically used mountain geographies to their advantage. Such strategic use of the rugged Cordillera environment contrasted starkly with the limited geographic knowledge of military commanders like Quirante when they began their explorations of the mountains of Northern Luzon. Beginning in the 1590s, Spanish expeditions approached the exploration of the Cordillera from two main directions (see table 4). Initially, Don Luis Pérez Dasmariñas entered the southeast corner of the mountains over what became known as the Balete Pass, before pushing into the southern reaches of the Cagayan Valley.[43] This region was known as Ituy and in this period encompassed much of the southern half of the Cagayan Valley as well as the southeastern edge of the Cordillera and the Caraballo Sur Mountains. In the 1620s, a new approach into the mountains was attempted from the Pangasinan coast, beginning at the settlement of Aringay and penetrating into the mountains of Benguet.[44] Reports from this period make it clear that the Spanish military officials leading these expeditions were uncertain of the geography of the mountains and unaware of how much distance separated these two approaches. This lack of geographic understanding led to early assumptions that pacifying one section of the mountains would quickly lead the rest to fall under Spanish control; most importantly, the Spanish would then be able to exploit the gold mines that they knew were hidden within the Cordillera. All of these expeditions required extensive preparations and large military forces which relied routinely on the mobilization of up to two thousand indigenous soldiers, recruited principally from Pampanga, Pangasinan, and Ilocos. They were similarly reliant on the aid of indigenous guides with knowledge of the mountain terrain. One such guide, Dionisio Capolo, led several missions into Ituy beginning in 1585.[45] Although the early missions into Ituy resulted in a number of communities agreeing to ally themselves with Spain and pay tribute, the Spanish lacked the resources to genuinely settle this region and could not muster the military strength required to consolidate their alliances or regularly collect tribute.

It is clear that geography remained a major factor in limiting Spanish exploration of the mountains, presenting both a natural obstacle to expedition parties and providing local communities with the means to evade, resist, or ambush Spanish forces.[46] Quirante argued that geography was in fact the best defense of the Igorots against colonization. The paths that he and his soldiers traversed through the mountains of Benguet were rugged and treacherous, often passing through reedbeds and over fallen trees, which slowed their progress considerably. Once in the mountains, they were subjected to sweeping rain accompanied by thunder and lightning and great fogs that cloaked the mountains and made the land very humid. Many of the soldiers engaged in these expeditions fell ill, possibly from waterborne diseases. The Spanish viewed the mountains as barren

Table 4 Military expeditions in the Cordillera mountain range, 1585–1667

YEAR	CAPTAIN	REGION EXPLORED	NOTES
1585	Dionisio Capolo	Ituy (Caraballo Sur Mountains)	Reconnaissance mission led by a Pampangan military leader; retreated due to hostility of local communities.[1]
1591	Luis Pérez Dasmariñas	Ituy (Balete Pass, Magat River, southern Cagayan Valley)	First exploration of this region; some violence and resistance from local communities; Dasmariñas claimed to have pacified fifteen thousand tributes.[2]
1591	Pedro de Sid	Ituy (Balete Pass, Magat River, Cagayan Valley)	Second exploration of this region, no significant tribute collected.[3]
1594	Toribio de Miranda	Ituy (Balete Pass, Magat River, Ganano River)	Tribute collection mission; resistance experienced in the southern parts of the Cagayan Valley; fort established in the village of Tuy, but besieged and later abandoned.[4]
160?	Captain Clavijo	Ituy	Attempt at discovering the Igorot gold mines—party was attacked by a thousand indios and turned back.[5]
1606	Unknown	Ituy	A force of Spaniards and indigenous soldiers tried to enter Ituy from Cagayan—one hundred of their soldiers were killed.[6]
1607	Dionisio Capolo	Ituy	Mission sent in reprisal of the soldiers killed the previous year; Capolo convinced seventeen principales to pledge allegiance to Spain.[7]
1620	García de Aldana Cabrera	Benguet	First attempt to control the Igorot gold mines; retreated after the death of Aldana Cabrera.[8]
1623	Francisco Carreño de Valdes	Benguet	Second attempt to control the Igorot gold mines; forced to retreat after Valdes was wounded.[9]
1624	Alonso Martín Quirante	Benguet	Third attempt to control the Igorot gold mines; Spanish encountered serious resistance from local communities; retreated due to limited exploitation of mines.[10]
1667	Pedro Durán de Monforte	Benguet	Final attempt at discovering the Igorot gold mines; no gold was uncovered; expedition retreated after two years.[11]

[1] William Henry Scott, *Discovery of the Igorots: Spanish Contacts with the Pagans of Northern Luzon* (Quezon City: New Day, 1974), 11.

[2] Archivo General de Indias (hereafter AGI), Audiencia de Filipinas (hereafter Filipinas), leg. 6, ramo 7, núm. 86; AGI, Filipinas, leg. 7, ramo 3, núms. 45, 46; AGI, Filipinas, leg. 193, núm. 1.

[3] AGI, Filipinas, leg. 193, núm. 1.

[4] AGI, Filipinas, leg. 7, ramo 3, núm. 45.

[5] The exact date of this expedition is unclear from the source. AGI, Filipinas, leg. 7, ramo 3, núm. 45

[6] Keesing notes that this expedition was led by "an encomendero and two Spaniards." Felix M. Keesing, *Ethnohistory of Northern Luzon* (Stanford, CA: Stanford University Press, 1962), 276.

[7] AGI, Filipinas, leg. 7, ramo 3, núm. 45.

[8] AGI, Filipinas, leg. 7, ramo 5, núm. 59.

[9] AGI, Filipinas, leg. 30, núm. 4.

[10] AGI, Filipinas, leg. 30, núm. 3.

[11] Casimiro Diaz Toledano, *Conquistas de las islas Filipinas la temporal por las armas de nuestros Católicos Reyes de España . . . Parte segunda* (Valladolid, Spain: Imprenta Librería de Luis N. de Gaviria, 1890), 236–253.

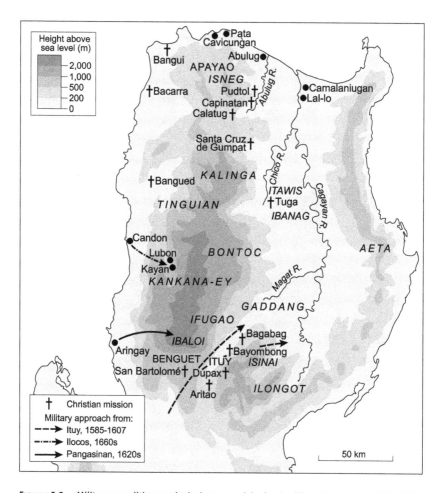

FIGURE 5.2. Military expeditions and missionary work in the Cordillera Mountains, 1575–1700. Map by Philip Stickler.

of all edible flora and fauna, meaning that all provisions had to be hauled by the soldiers themselves. Quirante believed that nothing would grow in such an inhospitable climate, not least because of the deep and extensive root systems belonging to the monotonous pine trees in the higher altitudes.[47]

These same environmental conditions were used effectively by mountain communities to track and evade the approach of Spanish expeditions, who often encountered settlements that had been abandoned or even burnt to the ground prior to their arrival.[48] Quirante described the Igorots of Benguet as highly mobile, having houses that could be easily constructed and fields of sweet potato that took little effort to establish.[49] This meant there was little lost in abandoning their villages in advance of the expeditionary forces. In 1591, the residents of the town of Santa Cruz de Tuy abandoned their settlement after hearing that an alliance with the Spanish would bring them into conflict with neighboring communities. They returned the following day to burn down the village, initiating an armed conflict with Dasmariñas and his army.[50] In other instances, Igorots asked the Spanish directly to leave their lands before disappearing into the mountains. This happened to Aldana Cabrera twice in 1620, with Igorot leaders rejecting Spanish overtures to ally themselves with Spain and stating plainly that they were not interested in Christianity.[51] Quirante found that not only did the Igorots of Benguet burn their own villages, but they also tracked the progress of the Spanish army and set fire to the Spanish campsites. Since Quirante had split his forces into several detachments that marched a day apart, this simple act of sabotage by the Igorots was designed to frustrate their advance into the mountains.[52]

The further they pushed into the mountains, the greater these acts of resistance became. Igorots were able to use the rugged terrain to attack Spanish soldiers, often without warning. For example, Toribio de Miranda's attempt to pacify the mountains surrounding Ituy in 1594 faced resistance from skilled archers who tracked the expedition and fired on them as they made their way through the forest, resulting in the death of a Cagayan indio who had been acting as a guide to the expedition. Resistance continued to increase the further Miranda's party explored into the mountains and the expedition was eventually called to a halt when they could find no one who would agree to pay tribute to the Spanish.[53] On the other side of the Cordillera, five of the indigenous soldiers accompanying Aldana Cabrera in 1620 were attacked while collecting water from a stream and two had their heads cut off. Aldana Cabrera responded by sending a force of five hundred men to seek out these attackers and punish them. The soldiers succeeded in capturing one principal and extracted a small payment of tribute from him.[54] Four years later, during Quirante's expedition, a group of Igorots used a strategic narrow pass that the Spanish soldiers had to travel through to force Quirante and his men into a defensive battle in which some of his soldiers were wounded.[55]

Frequent ambushes combined with the inhospitality of the terrain led to a growing realization among Spanish officials in Manila that occupying these mountains came at a very high cost. The expeditions of the 1620s were initiated with high hopes of gaining control of the Igorot gold mines, with an intended return that would cover the costs of the expeditions and future occupation. Yet, even when the source of the gold was found, the Spanish were unable to extract anything of real value. In April 1624 the treasury official Luis de Vera Encalada wrote a report for the king arguing that the expense devoted to these expeditions was not commensurate with the gains made. Royal officials in

Manila had no hope that the Igorots would swear obedience to the king or that they would engage more peacefully in the future. The king had been informed of the riches of those mountains without consideration for the communities that lived there and the resistance they offered through their use of arrows and lances. Even when they reached the mines, the Spanish could not exploit them without considerable protection. Many soldiers died during the expeditions and, thus, considering that no benefit was going to be realized for the royal treasury, Vera Encalada recommended that it would be of greater service to discontinue the expeditions.[56]

No further attempt was made to penetrate this part of the Cordillera until the late 1660s, when Governor Diego de Salcedo decided that the best way to overcome the tyranny of mountain geography was to establish a permanent, fortified Spanish garrison in the Cordillera, allowing supplies and soldiers to be routinely replenished.[57] Admiral Pedro Durán de Monforte led a series of expeditions involving Spanish and indio soldiers who marched into the mountains from Candon on the Ilocos coast and reached the towns of Kayan and Lubon, where they were instructed to build the fort. The chronicler Casimiro Diaz suggested that this expedition was successful in exploring more than 150 villages in the mountains, mostly located along rivers that all flowed into the Cagayan River. Nearly forty villages apparently agreed to pay tribute, while another fifteen villages paid something in recognition.[58] The missionaries also claimed successes in converting many of the inhabitants and a number were reduced into villages along the Ilocos coast. However, despite these apparent successes, the attempt to establish a permanent presence in the mountains still suffered from problems with supply routes through the rugged terrain. By 1672 Governor Manuel de León ordered a retreat, because the expedition had placed a great strain on both finances and manpower.[59]

Spanish knowledge of the geography of the Cordillera increased gradually over the course of the seventeenth century, thanks to a growing number of missionaries who were attracted to the mountains by the prospect of evangelizing and converting large mountain populations estimated to reach into the tens of thousands (see table 5). Nevertheless, most of these early attempts by missionaries to reduce and convert mountain communities were short lived. Although missionaries were not encumbered by the thousands of hungry soldiers that military expeditions relied on, the remote and difficult terrain of the mountains nevertheless remained obstacles to the establishment of permanent missions. In addition to the hostility of local communities to their evangelizing activities, missionaries had to contend with the seasonality of travel in the mountains. During the rainy season, mountain rivers overflowed

Table 5 Missionary work in the Cordillera Mountains, 1598–1700

YEAR	MISSIONARY ORDER	REGION	NOTES
1598	Augustinians	Bangued, Abra	Augustinian missionaries began working in this region in 1598, setting up a separate ministry in 1612 from where missionaries made trips into the nearby mountains. This work appears to have ceased after the 1620s.[1]
1610	Dominicans	Apayao	Dominican missionaries began trying to convert Isneg inhabitants of the Apayao Mountains, beginning with the founding of Pudtol (1610) and Capinatan (1619). Although these missions were not formally abandoned until the mid-eighteenth century, they were repeatedly rocked by rebellion and Christian converts routinely abandoned the settlements in favor of living in the mountains.[2]
1625	Dominicans	Ituy	Two missionaries based in Pangasinan explored the Ituy region and attempted to convert locals to Christianity.
1632	Dominicans	Ituy	Establishment of Dominican missions in Ituy: Dupax (1633), Dangla (1637), Bugay (Aritao) (1637), and Bagabag or Bayombong (1637). These missions were likely abandoned following the death of Fr. Tomás Gutiérrez.[3]
1652–1654	Dominicans	Ituy	Dominican missionaries with military accompaniment led an abortive attempt to set up a permanent mission in this region. Withdrawn due to ill health among the soldiers and the violent resistance of local communities.[4]
1668	Augustinians	Bacarra and Bangui	This mission was established to evangelize the Isnegs living in the northwestern reaches of the Cordillera Mountains, but many of the initial converts soon retreated back into the mountains.[5]
1685	Dominicans	Lower Kayapa Valley	This mission, known as San Bartolomé, was established in the mountains to the west of Ituy and lasted about two decades before it was abandoned due to the hostility of neighboring Igorots.[6]
1688	Dominicans	Kalinga and Apayao foothills	Two mission bases were established in the foothills of the Cordillera Mountains close to Tuao, on the Chico River: Tuga (1688), at the foothills of Kalinga territory, and Santa Cruz de Gumpat (1693) on the eastern side of the Apayao Mountains, working with Isneg and Kalinga communities. Major rebellions rocked these missions in the 18th century, leading to the abandonment of Santa Cruz.[7]

[1] Felix M. Keesing, *Ethnohistory of Northern Luzon* (Stanford, CA: Stanford University Press, 1962), 126–127.

[2] Fr. Diego Aduarte, *Tomo Primero de la Historia de la Provincia del Santo Rosario de Filipinas, Japón, y China, de la sagrada orden de predicadores* (Zaragoza: Por Domingo Gascon, Insançon, Impressor del Santo Hospital Real y General de Nuestra Señora de Gracia, 1693), 550–556; Baltasar de Santa Cruz, *Tomo Segundo de la Historia de la Provincia del Santo Rosario de Filipinas, Japón, y China del Sagrado Orden de Predicadores* (Zaragoza: Por Pasqual Bueno, Impressor Reyno, 1693), 18–21.

[3] Aduarte, *Tomo Primero*, 636–641; Keesing, *Ethnohistory of Northern Luzon*, 280–281.

[4] Archivo General de Indias, Audiencia de Filipinas, leg. 285, núm. 1, fols. 30r–41v.

[5] Felix M. Keesing, *Ethnohistory of Northern Luzon* (Stanford, CA: Stanford University Press, 1962), 154–156.

[6] Keesing, *Ethnohistory of Northern Luzon*, 71–72.

[7] Keesing, *Ethnohistory of Northern Luzon*, 226–233.

making travel through remote and rugged territory impossible, thus cutting off neophyte communities for half the year.[60]

As a result, most missionaries preferred to establish settlements in the lowlands immediately adjacent to the mountains, often along a river that would allow supplies to be easily brought in, and from where missionaries could encourage mountain-dwelling communities to come down from the mountains to attend mass and hopefully to settle permanently. Among the most enduring of these missionary outposts were the towns of Pudtol and Capinatan, small villages nestled between the Abulug River and the foot of the Apayao Mountains, in the north of the Cordillera range. As with other parts of the Cordillera, the Apayao Mountains were considered dangerous owing to the fierce resistance of the Isnegs. Missionaries were advised not to travel in this region without an armed escort and in the early years they visited this mission field only very infrequently, perhaps only once a year.[61] Yet, as the missionary presence in Apayao became more permanent over the first two decades of the seventeenth century, tensions with the Isnegs grew. A series of violent rebellions that took place in 1625 and 1639—explored in greater detail in the next chapter—led to the retreat of Dominican missionaries from Apayao for the next four decades.[62] Efforts resumed in the 1680s to conquer the Apayao Mountains and pacify the neighboring coastal settlements. Fortifications were established in the coastal town of Cavicungan as well as the two Isneg settlements of Pudtol and Capinatan. Despite this effort to militarize the region, the Isnegs and their coastal neighbors continued to resist Spanish efforts of colonization. Soldiers stationed in Apayao were subject to attacks by armed rebels, leading to the death of at least one soldier, while headhunting attacks on the coastal settlements of Pata and Cavicungan caused many of the townspeople to retreat into the mountains.[63] When the missionary Fr. Pedro Jiménez arrived in Pudtol in 1684, he found the residents of the Spanish settlements living in famine as regular attacks by neighboring mountain groups had prevented them from tending to their fields.[64]

Fr. Jiménez remained in this region for the next three years and is credited with founding a church in the mountains and converting 1,300 Isnegs to Christianity. The neighboring mountain community of Calatug remained hostile and continued to threaten war against anyone who was reduced by the Spanish. In 1688, when Fr. Jiménez became sick and had to return to the lowlands, the people of Calatug took the opportunity to assault the newly founded Christian settlement and killed all but 140 indios, who fled back into the mountains.[65] After this, Dominican missionaries retreated from this region altogether. Although the Spanish continued to occupy the two Isneg settlements of Pudtol and Capinatan into the eighteenth century, they never managed to convince more than a few hundred Isnegs to settle there and continued to need a military presence to protect the

FIGURE 5.3. Idea aproximada del territorio entre Cagayan e Ilocos [Approximate idea of the territory between Cagayan and Ilocos], nineteenth century. Image from the holdings of the Biblioteca Nacional de España.

towns from their upland neighbors. These settlements were eventually abandoned altogether in 1769, with Christian converts transferred to the coastal settlements of Abulug and Camalaniugan and missionaries did not return to Apayao until the early twentieth century.[66] A nineteenth-century map depicting Northern Luzon reveals the territory of Apayao as blank and unmapped with a note stating simply: *alzados (desconocido)*—in uprising, unexplored.[67]

The fierce autonomy of these upland communities and their strategic use of geography to hinder Spanish colonization efforts meant that throughout the seventeenth century the Cordillera attracted a steady stream of lowland migrants escaping Spanish colonization across a very large region. Archaeological work in the Ifugao region of the Cordillera Mountains has confirmed that there was a significant population increase into this section of the mountains between the sixteenth and eighteenth centuries, evidenced through the intensification of landscape modification and the appearance of imported trade ware ceramics, indicating intensified trading interactions between upland regions of Ifugao and their lowland neighbors.[68] Significantly, the archaeologist Stephen Acabado argues that wet-rice cultivation was developed as a strategy that helped upland Ifugao communities to resist colonization, replacing taro cultivation as a better source of sustenance for feeding larger populations. At the same time wet-rice cultivation also became an important part of the cultural identity of these communities.[69] The most evident legacy of this history of resistance are the famous Ifugao rice terraces, now UNESCO world heritage listed. They stand as physical structures emblematic of an indigenous culture that effectively resisted colonization, accepted fugitives from lowlands seeking to evade the excesses of the colonial state and adapted their agricultural technology to allow them to claim sovereignty from state control for hundreds of years.[70]

The rugged and extensive terrain of the mountains presented a natural barrier for Spanish colonization attempts, making the initial military expeditions into the mountains more costly. Permanent settlement or militarization of the mountains also proved difficult without established supply routes through the mountains, since the Spanish did not know how to live in what they saw as a barren and inhospitable landscape. At the same time, the intimate knowledge of the geography held by Igorots and other Cordillera residents meant that these communities made effective and strategic use of the terrain in defending their territory and attacking Spanish expeditions. The mountains furthermore presented a ready escape from missionary settlements established in nearby lowlands, particularly when such settlements were burnt down and abandoned in times of rebellion. Finally, the Ifugao's innovative use of mountain landscapes to create agricultural surpluses meant that mountain settlements could support ever growing numbers of migrants wishing to retreat further away from colonization.

Headhunting and Raiding in the Zambales Mountains

The Cordillera was not the only mountain range to exhibit such fierce resistance to colonization. A similar story can be told of the Zambales, a group of upland communities living in the coastal mountain range between Mariveles and Bolinao. Renowned as fierce headhunters, the Zambales are nonetheless often left out of accounts of the early colonial period.[71] Like the Igorots of the Cordillera, their resistance to colonization and active destabilization of neighboring colonial settlements meant that these mountains became the target for Spanish attempts at pacification throughout the seventeenth century. While geography was also an important factor in Zambales' resistance to these successive conquest attempts, they also made effective use of headhunting and raiding as both a defensive strategy and a way of destabilizing Spanish settlement in the neighboring lowlands of Pampanga and Pangasinan.

The Zambales Mountains rise sharply away from the western coast of Luzon, extending for 120 miles between Mariveles and Bolinao, with peaks rising to more than two thousand meters. To the east lie the long plains of the province of Pampanga, the heartland of Spanish control in the Philippines. In the seventeenth century, the Zambales Mountains were inhabited by groups of hunter-gatherers who were variously referred to as Zambales, Negritos, and Aetas. The Spanish struggled throughout the seventeenth century to establish a foothold among these communities, who initially fell under the administration of the Augustinian Recollects and were later transferred over to the Dominicans in 1679.[72] Both groups of missionaries attempted to reduce the mountain populations into coastal settlements, where they would be more easily controlled. Initial accounts from the Dominicans in the early 1680s paint a picture of a region with a very scattered population. The largest Spanish controlled town consisted of no more than a hundred families, while the second largest comprised only fifty families. These two towns were located on the coast of the province, close to a fort established at Paynauen.[73] The environment of the Zambales hindered colonization efforts. Not only was the region characterized by rugged and high mountains, which became impassable during the monsoonal rains, but the coast was often inaccessible from the sea due to countervailing winds.[74]

Geographic factors alone do not account for the difficulties faced by missionaries and soldiers in this region. Of all the upland communities, the Zambales were regarded by the Spanish as particularly barbarous and uncivilized, and often defined by their custom of headhunting. In 1605, the attorney Hernando de los Ríos Coronel described them as "a people who live naked in the mountains who are highwaymen who want nothing more than to cut off heads so as to slurp up their brains; the most courageous leader is one who has cut off the most heads."[75] By the early seventeenth century, the Zambales Mountains were an infamous site of recalcitrance that many officials believed was almost impossible to conquer. Unlike the Igorots, the Zambales offered no great incentive by way of resources—other than perhaps access to their timber supply—and may well have been left alone were it not for their proximity to the province of Pampanga. Throughout the century, the Zambales actively destabilized lowland neighboring regions by raiding and engaging in acts of headhunting. In 1590, Governor Gómez Pérez Dasmariñas reported a particular incident where twenty-four principales from Tondo were traveling through Zambales territory, carrying some gold and other goods for trade with the Pangasinanes. They were attacked by 250 Zambales armed with axes, spears, and daggers, resulting in twenty-one deaths.[76] In 1606, the attorney Rodrigo Díaz Guiral reported on frequent attacks by the Zambales against the province of Pampanga. He disparaged the Zambales as a brutish people who lived without permanent abodes and engaged in cutting off the heads of other indigenous peoples. The population of Pampanga, by comparison, was known for their sedentary ways and their agriculture, which made them easy targets for the Zambales who would swoop down and attack them while they were working their fields.[77] Spanish missionaries were also targets. Fr. Pedro de Valenzuela fell victim to headhunters while traveling through the Zambales Mountains in 1648. He was shot through with arrows, beheaded, and his skull was later reported to be used as a ceremonial drinking vessel.[78]

Despite the imperial objectives and colonial propaganda, it is evident from these early Spanish accounts that raiding of lowland settlements predated Spanish settlement in the region. Headhunting was widespread among many upland communities in the Philippines, as well as Southeast Asia more broadly.[79] Anthropologists have moved away from colonial discourses of barbarity and civilizational backwardness, placing headhunting instead within a complex Southeast Asian cosmography. Janet Hoskins notes a variety of purposes behind headhunting traditions in Southeast Asia, including mourning rituals, the improvement of community well-being, rites of passage into adulthood, and, occasionally, to be released from debt. She notes that in some societies, it was unimportant whose head was taken and often raiders would take the head of older people, pregnant women, or children, because they were easier targets.[80] Barbara Watson Andaya argues that headhunting raids were almost universally associated with masculinity, the attainment of manhood, and the right to marriage. Women were not excluded from the rituals but performed important roles in the ceremonial reception of the heads, which were associated with fertility and community well-being.[81] Yet, headhunting was also clearly a tactic of intercommunity feuding and warfare, whereby the taking of a head was part of redressing a wrong done to one party and could serve to either conclude or aggravate a conflict.[82] Renato Rosaldo argues that headhunting was as much a symbolic process that allowed communities to relieve themselves from a feeling of weight associated with burdens felt by the community as a whole. "What is ritually removed, Ilongots say, is the weight that grows on one's life like vines on a tree."[83]

Many of the same conclusions can be found within the description of the Zambales communities written by the Dominican priest Fr. Domingo Pérez in 1681. Pérez described the Zambales as much more horizontally structured than their lowland neighbors in Pampanga. Although they maintained some of the same class structures—including slavery—they operated in smaller and more egalitarian units, where age played the greatest role in determining authority. Headhunting was a common way of resolving disputes between groups, where the period of mourning could not be completed until another head had been taken. The taking of a head was often accompanied by a great ritual celebration. Pérez noted that children were inducted into the custom at a very young age, sometimes even as young as three, because it was considered shameful not to have taken a head. At times, communities would purchase slaves for a ritual killing where the children were able to take their first head—often sharing the privilege as a group. This communal killing was continued into adulthood, since it was common for a group to conduct a headhunting raid together and each claimed the kill as their own, regardless of who committed the act. Killings of strangers were sometimes undertaken as preventative measures because the presence of a stranger in a village might signify that that individual was themselves looking for a head to take.[84]

Headhunting was consequently a frequent practice. Pérez believed that three-quarters of deaths among the Zambales were violent, while only a quarter were of natural causes. In order to prevent a constant retaliation—where heads were exchanged for heads in perpetuity—Pérez noted that the family of the murdered were often paid in gold by the murderer to conclude the conflict. Those who were unable to pay this price in gold faced being enslaved by the family of the victim, and so would sometimes capture a substitute to be enslaved or killed in their place. Pérez offers a compelling explanation for why headhunting became a common weapon directed against lowland groups—and later against the Spanish and other indio subjects of the Crown: since those who were not a part of the extended kinship networks in the mountains did not need to be mourned in the same way, taking the head of an outsider was a way of ending the cycle of violence.[85]

The arrival of the Spanish into this mountain region exposed them to the practices of headhunting and set a pattern of violent confrontation between Zambales communities and Spanish missionaries and soldiers that continued for more than a century. In 1592, Dasmariñas sent captains into the region, taking with them 120 Spanish soldiers and more than 3,000 indigenous soldiers.[86] The companies entered the Zambales territory from six different directions in an attempt to surprise and root out their enemies. While the roughness and density of the terrain allowed many of the Zambales to easily escape and hide from the oncoming Spanish armies, the expedition nevertheless resulted in the capture of 2,500 men and boys. The majority of captives were taken while they were out hunting or gathering food in the forests, and this was part of a plan to reduce the Zambales communities to hunger and force them into Spanish settlements further down the mountains. The expedition was eventually called to a halt when the soldiers began to fall ill and die. Three presidios were established during this period on the Pampangan side of the mountains, as well as a fourth on the coast, at Playa Honda.[87] The captains left the presidios of the region well garrisoned, and the governor felt that the mission was a resounding success that would prevent future rebellion in the region.[88] Yet, by 1597, the remaining Zambales had regrouped, killed two alcaldes mayores, and headhunting and raiding of lowland settlements had resumed.[89]

The efforts of the Augustinian Recollects were similarly frustrated. Shortly after their arrival in the islands in 1606, they began work in the Zambales, reducing the indios to the town of Sigayen, where they also made plans to establish a monastery. Yet, in 1612, one of the missionaries was attacked by a Zambal wielding a headhunting knife. Although the Zambal did not succeed in removing the priest's head, he was severely wounded and later died. The attack prompted the entire town to rise up and burn down the church and convent before fleeing into the mountains. The remaining missionaries were escorted out of the area by some friendlier Zambales, leaving the entire area deserted.[90] In 1622, Governor Fajardo de Tenza reported that the Zambales still had not been conquered and continued to engage in the same disturbances as always.[91]

In the second half of the seventeenth century, the Spanish responded with increasing violence and militarization. Over the course of the 1660s, Governors Salcedo and Leon ordered the military occupation of the Zambales Mountains.[92] Four forts were established in the neighboring lowlands and garrisoned with 150 soldiers.[93] Meanwhile, a series of expeditions into the mountains were organized with the intention of forcefully reducing the Zambales and ensuring their obedience. Yet, by 1672, the soldiers had once again been withdrawn from the region, largely as a result of the dense and rough terrain and the distance the soldiers were required to travel, which made the expeditions enormously costly both in terms of money and lives. Many of the soldiers sent to engage in these conquests had become sick and the expeditions had achieved very little.[94] Despite working in the region for seventy years, by 1676, the Recollects had just barely 811 tributes under their control, spread over eighteen different towns in the region. The majority of these towns had fewer than fifty tributes, while several of the smallest had fewer than twenty.[95]

In 1679, the administration of the Zambales region was passed over to the Dominicans.[96] In contrast to the Recollects, the Dominicans had extensive experience of working in rebellious and uncontrolled mountain territories elsewhere in the islands. They were also not averse to the use of force and violence. Thus, shortly after their arrival, a new wave of conquest began. At the beginning of 1680, thirty soldiers, led by the *ayudante* Alonso Martín, marched through the mountains, burning down settlements and destroying crops.[97] In May of that year, the governor reported that the total number of people brought down from the mountains in 1680 was a thousand and that the four new towns were built after burning and destroying the houses and crops that these people had in the mountains.[98]

The report written by Fr. Domingo Pérez in 1680 makes it clear that much of this strategy was in fact the idea of the Dominicans. Pérez advocated the virtues of using force and the threat of violence from soldiers stationed in the fort of Paynauen. He argued that, despite their fearsome reputation, the Zambales were in fact extremely cowardly and used their tactics of flight and hiding in the mountains as their greatest weapon against reduction and conversion. They were frightened of the guns carried by the Spanish soldiers. The Dominicans thus used the soldiers to spread fear, especially by organizing incursions into the mountains and destroying any crops that the Zambales had established. This was designed to look like an invasion into their lands. By contrast, the priests were portrayed as peaceable protectors of the Zambales against the brutality of the soldiers. The priests, therefore, went about instructing the soldiers where to go and what to destroy and then followed this by telling the Zambales that they should only cultivate in designated places near the Spanish settlements. Additional incursions were also organized to try to collect fugitives. Pérez considered these methods to be most effective against the problems of flight and resistance to the reduction process.[99] That same year, the Dominicans wrote that many of the Zambales continued to descend from the mountains and they believed that within a short time three-quarters of the population would be adequately reduced.[100]

Despite his confidence, shortly after Pérez wrote his report, he was shot with an arrow and killed by a Zambal.[101] His death acted as a signal for many of the subjugated Zambales to revolt and flee back into the mountains. For several days following his death, a group of Zambales attempted to assault the convent at Balacbac before retreating.[102] Governor Curucelaegui described the events surrounding Pérez's death as very turbulent, involving Zambales from the mountains sacking, slaughtering, and robbing lowland villages. The Archbishop Fr. Felipe Pardo reported that the region was in uprising and said that many Dominicans were afraid of traveling through the towns around Playa Honda without an escort of soldiers. After the death of Fr. Pérez, they had retreated into the fort at Paynauen, afraid that they would all be killed.[103]

The death of Fr. Pérez marked the end of the last serious attempt to gain military control over the Zambales Mountains. Over the course of the next three decades, the Dominicans became embroiled in a drawn-out contest with the Recollects for control over the region that eventually led to the Recollects regaining administration of the mountains in 1713.[104] Although they never completely abandoned the Zambales, Recollect activities in the eighteenth century were concentrated in the lowlands, along the Zambales coast and in the Tarlac Valley to the east of Zambales.[105] Thus, far from being cowardly and frightened of Spanish guns—as Pérez had so confidently stated—by the close of the seventeenth century the Zambales had successfully defended their territory from military invasion and spiritual conquest with bows and arrows and the headhunting bolo.

Mountains sit at the heart of the story of colonization in the Philippines. As sites of autonomy, rebellion, and freedom, they came to define the physical limits of colonial territorial control and to symbolize the weaknesses of colonial power.[106] Communities utilized upland spaces across the archipelago to evade the colonial state. Fugitives in turn used their position of autonomy to disrupt colonization in neighboring lowland regions, particularly through regular raiding. At the same time, rugged and remote mountain geographies were deployed strategically by fugitive and autonomous indigenous communities to secure upland sites from colonial control. Despite routine and regular attempts to invade these spaces, the Spanish simply lacked the military resources needed to overcome these barriers.

Consequently, the famed story of Cordillera autonomy can be extended to many other mountain spaces that became zones of refuge and autonomy for numerous communities. Early twentieth century anthropologists documented the persistence of these zones of refuge up to the end of Spanish colonial rule. The hilly terrain of Nueva Vizcaya—that connects the southern reaches of the Cordillera, Sierra Madre, and Caraballo Sur Mountains—was recorded in the American census of 1903 as having the highest number of unpacified communities anywhere in the archipelago, with nearly three-quarters of inhabitants described as living "wild."[107] During this same period, the American anthropologist David P. Barrows remarked that even along the mostly peaceful western coastline of Ilocos, Christianized settlements extended only for "two to five miles from the coast," giving way quickly to "rancherias of the *infieles*."[108] When H. Otley Beyer produced the first detailed population study of the archipelago in 1916, he found hill peoples across Central and Southern Luzon and the Visayas who were commonly held to be "descendants of *remontados*, or outlaws from the Christian towns, who have fled to the hills and there mixed with wandering bands of Negritos."[109] The largest such communities were found on the Visayan islands of Negros and Panay where, combined, more than thirty thousand *mundos* continued to adopt non-sedentary lifeways. Unlike the Igorots of Northern Luzon or the myriad indigenous groupings of Mindanao, these *remontados* confronted colonial racial classifications because, as ethnic Malays, they defied expectations about the success of Spanish colonization in the archipelago. The migration of lowlanders into Aeta spaces also led to the emergence of new ethnic formations whose very names—Agta Cimarron, Dumagat Remontados— manifest their histories of resistance to colonial control.[110]

Across the Visayas and Mindanao, these groups were often referred to as Bukidnon, an epithet that—like Igorot—means "people of the mountains."[111] And yet, working with the Sulod Bukidnon in Panay in the 1950s, the anthropologist F. Landa Jocano recovered epic poems that spoke more of the sea than of the mountains, suggesting these groups had migrated inland away from coastal areas.[112] Such histories of migration and movement into mountain spaces are found in folklore from around the islands. Like the Sulod, Ifugao oral histories speak of large rivers the likes of which cannot be found in the mountains, hinting at the path of migration taken by the ancestors of the Ifugao from the Magat and Cagayan River valleys.[113] On the opposite side of the Cordillera, an Iloko-Kankana-ey song recorded in the 1980s tells of a migration up the Amburayan River away from Spanish construction projects that resulted in increased taxation and labor demands.[114] Elsewhere, prominent mountains that were common zones of refuge in the colonial period—like Mount Arayat in Pampanga, Mount Isarog in Camarines, and Mount Makaling in Laguna—feature in local legends as spaces belonging to native gods and local ancestor spirits, terrains that defied and escaped incorporation into new Christian worlds.[115]

Even in areas where colonization eventually took place, substantial histories of resistance can still be told that begin with flight into mountain spaces. One such instance took place on the Visayan island of Bohol, where frequent episodes of flight in the seventeenth century led up to the largest ever rebellion against Spanish rule in the eighteenth century. In 1744, the local leader Dagohoy led Boholanos into the mountains, rejecting Spanish authority completely; they remained outside of colonial control for eighty-five years.[116] Linguists have speculated that this lengthy rebellion may have contributed to the development of Eskaya, a language first identified by linguists in southeastern Bohol in the 1980s.[117] Ulysses B. Aparece notes that Dagohoy is still commemorated as a folk hero and incorporated within ancestor worship on the island of Bohol. He also writes that he grew up with "stories from the distant past . . . of headless Spanish priests walking in empty streets, *condenados* dragging metal chains, and spirit warriors in hot pursuit of Spanish soldiers."[118]

As evidence mounts that patterns of migration away from the colonial state were common across large parts of the archipelago, it is no longer possible to view spaces like the Cordillera mountains as "untouched" indigenous territories with histories separate from the rest of the archipelago. Upland histories were intimately connected to that of their lowland neighbors. Nowhere is this more evident than in the turbulent history of the Cagayan Valley. The chapter that follows thus looks toward the mountains from the perspective of valley communities.

CHAPTER 6

Cagayan Insurgencies, 1572–1745

In March 1691, a group of indigenous leaders from Cagayan, in Northern Luzon, wrote a letter to the Spanish officials in Manila warning them of the imminent risk of an uprising. Fed up with the combined burdens of labor, taxation, and military service, communities across Cagayan were threatening to abandon settlements established by the Spanish and to take to the hills, following a long-standing pattern of resistance to Spanish colonization. Valley communities in Cagayan maintained strong connections to neighboring autonomous mountain zones, channeling weapons, iron, and other goods into the uplands to better aid their independence. The principales warned that if just one village became discontent, they would call on the rebels in the mountains to come down into the lowlands and take everyone whether by choice or by force, killing all others and setting the churches and towns alight. In the meantime, they reported a campaign of agitation from fugitives in the mountains, who would say to the lowlanders of Cagayan, "Miserable slaves, how much better would it be if you came to live amongst us, your brethren that do not suffer as you suffer? Climb up here with us, because you know that amongst us you will be free from such labors."[1]

From the perspective of the Cagayan Valley, the histories of upland and lowland spaces were always intertwined. Beginning in the late sixteenth century, Cagayan was the site of ongoing and extensive rebellion against colonial rule. Communities periodically set fire to their churches and villages and fled into the mountains. Their actions successfully halted the advance of the colonial frontier at the foothills of the mountains. Yet in the majority of histories of the colonial Philippines, Cagayan is notably absent.[2] This is because the history of Cagayan appears as an anomaly in the standard presentation of Philippine colonial history. By divorcing the experiences of upland regions from very similar stories of resistance and flight in neighboring lowlands like Cagayan, a seemingly permanent binary has been established between easily colonized lowland spaces and the autonomous, authentic, indigenous highlands. In the seventeenth century, this binary simply did not exist. Resistance, rebellion, and particularly flight away from colonization were in fact common across the whole breadth of Northern Luzon in the seventeenth century, including the lowland and valley regions. The previous chapter considered the way in which ongoing trade and migration between lowland and upland communities helped upland spaces maintain their independence: this chapter considers the other side—the impact of autonomous indigenous upland spaces on colonization efforts in the lowlands of Cagayan.[3]

In the seventeenth century, the province of Cagayan encompassed the expansive lowland plains and foothills of the Cagayan Valley, stretching from the northern coast of Luzon to the Caraballo Mountains in the south and bordered on both sides by the Cordillera and Sierra Madre mountain ranges. The valley hosted a variety of ethnic and linguistic groups, including Ibanag, Itawis, Gaddang, Yogad, and Aeta communities.[4] The Spanish first visited Cagayan in 1572 and determined that it would be a good defensive location against potential attacks by Chinese or Japanese pirates.[5] Initial explorations of the region revealed a vast and fertile valley, extending for more than 10,000 square miles, that was densely populated by communities spread along numerous waterways that extended down from the mountains and connected the coast with the interior.

What at first looked like a promising region for expanding colonial agricultural resources and spreading evangelization in fact proved to be one of the most persistently unmanageable of all the regions in the archipelago. The extent of resistance to Spanish colonization efforts meant that the majority of Spanish settlements were concentrated along the northern coastline and on the banks of the Cagayan River and its tributary, the Chico River. The capital of the province was established at Lal-lo—then called Nueva Segovia by the Spanish—on the banks of the Cagayan River just inland from the port of Aparri. Despite its designation as a capital city, Lal-lo was never a big settlement. In the 1620s the town boasted just twenty Spanish *vecinos* and forty-eight tributes.[6] Eventually Lal-lo was demoted as a capital when the seat of the bishopric of Nueva Segovia shifted to Vigan in 1756, reflecting the fact that the Spanish presence had not substantially grown in this region in nearly two centuries of attempted occupation.[7]

Spanish maps of the region produced in the late seventeenth and early eighteenth centuries show Spanish controlled fortifications, settlements, and churches extending throughout the provinces. Yet these maps are works of spatial overexaggeration, designed to amplify the reach of Spanish power and minimize the extent of uncontrolled—and unmapped—areas.[8] The further inland these settlements were, the less stable Spanish control was, with rebellions affecting the southern and western missionary outposts in particular. In the seventeenth century, Spanish influence ended at the settlement of Itugud, just past the present-day town of Ilagan, leaving the southern half of the valley virtually unexplored. The history of Spanish colonization in Cagayan is one of constant expansion and contraction of territorial influence, as rebellion after rebellion spread through the valley. Lowland communities made use of their relationships and trading alliances with upland neighbors to solidify their opposition to colonial control.[9]

What follows in this chapter is ultimately a history of ongoing and extraordinary frontier violence that has rarely been acknowledged elsewhere in the historiography of the Philippines. The valley is emblematic of the contested nature of Spanish colonization in Philippine lowlands, revealing in clear detail the patchwork and shifting nature of Spanish power. Historiography of Spanish imperial frontiers has suggested that a defining feature of frontiers is the absence of a single ascendant or hegemonic controlling power.[10] Donna Guy and Thomas Sheridan define the frontier regions of North and South America as "contested ground," as "areas where imperial or, later, national power was too weak to maintain stable patterns of coerced labor."[11] In their comparative collection on the frontier regions of Spanish America, they find consistent patterns of response to the process of colonization, including the presence of indigenous forms of slavery and slave raiding, episodes of violent resistance, and indigenous flight away from colonized spaces, often resulting in the formation of fugitive communities outside of Spain's control. All of these factors meant that the cost of conquest, pacification, and integration into the empire was higher in these frontier regions.

At the same time, it is clear that the relationship between valley communities and upland spaces was what made Cagayan so volatile.[12] All of the different lowland zones of Cagayan maintained a connection with unpacified upland groups—from the Isnegs and Kalingas in the northwest to the Aetas of the Sierra Madre Mountains in the east, and the Ifugaos, Ilongots, and other inhabitants of Nueva Vizcaya in the southern half of the valley. Colonization altered connections that predated Spanish arrival, with established trading networks linking lowland and upland spaces.[13] While missionaries and colonial officials devised ever greater methods of armed coercion, the frontier developed a symbiotic logic of its own based in extensive and profitable trading networks between upland communities and lowland frontier settlements. Active resistance and trade interests, often illicitly pursued against colonial authority, combined to frustrate the aims of the Spanish Crown for control over the vast majority of Northern Luzon.

The Cagayan Frontier

Resistance to Spanish settlement of the Cagayan Valley commenced from the moment the Spanish set foot in the region. In 1574, a contingent of 150 soldiers led by the *maestre de campo* Don Luis de Sagajosa arrived to conquer and settle the province. The mission failed, however, when seventy soldiers died from the hardships of the journey and from the lances and arrows of the Cagayanes. A series of expeditions followed this, all of them resulting in the loss of dozens of soldiers and in one case two galleys. In 1575, Juan Pablo de Carrión managed to establish a town at Camalaniugan—a league from the eventual settlement site of Nueva Segovia—but the Cagayanes resisted and took the Spaniards' supplies. They were so warlike that Carrión was forced to dismantle the settlement and return to Manila, having lost many of his men in the fighting.[14] Gradually, over the course of the 1580s, the Spanish established encomiendas across coastal Cagayan and inland along the length of the Cagayan River. The capital of the province was founded at Lal-lo, and twenty-two different encomenderos were granted the rights to collect tribute.[15]

Yet, by 1589, word reached Manila that communities were in uprising along the length of the Cagayan River, from north to south. Soldiers and encomenderos were killed by bands of Cagayanes resisting tribute collection in all of the recently established encomiendas.[16] A group of Cagayanes even attacked the newly founded capital of the province, threatening to set it on fire, and demanding resources and munitions from the residents of the city. They threatened to incite a mass retreat from Spanish settlements.[17] The Spanish residents of the province petitioned the governor for license to dismantle the city and abandon the settlement of Cagayan because they could no longer sustain themselves; however, the governor refused, responding that to do so would mean risking the reputation of the Spanish in all of the islands.[18] An initial force of sixty Spanish soldiers and more than eight hundred indigenous allies was sent to quell the rebellion in June 1589. Yet, the commander of this expedition, Pedro de Chavez, reported that they had been unable to do much more than cut down palm trees and destroy the crops of the rebels. In return, the Cagayanes burnt down their villages and fled into the mountains, leaving the province as if it had never been pacified. Chavez reported that they had been surrounded by so many enemies and had so few Spaniards that without reinforcements the province would surely be lost.[19]

The new governor Gómez Pérez Dasmariñas, who arrived in the islands in mid-1590, took stock of the situation and within two months sent Captain Fernando Becerra Montaño with eighty soldiers and instructions to pacify the province.[20] Becerra found most of the settlements were deserted, the Cagayanes having retreated into the mountains, while their datus refused to meet with him. During the course of his expedition, Becerra learnt of a particular faction based in Tuguegarao, led by a female datu and her three sons, who were fiercely opposed to the Spanish presence in the province. When Becerra eventually met with the datus of Lal-lo and Pilitan, they told him that the datu of Tuguegarao had destroyed their crops and killed their people to warn them off allying with the Spanish and that she had also done this to other communities. They had been forced to flee from their villages and had retreated to a different site out of fear.[21] This information allowed Becerra to build alliances with particular groups by offering them protection from the faction in Tuguegarao and he returned to Manila claiming to have pacified the province and returned it to peace and vassalage.[22]

Rather than pacification, all that Becerra achieved was to establish a Spanish foothold in the coastal and northern riverine region of the valley, while their influence over the majority of Cagayan remained negligible. Although Spanish missionaries and tribute collectors returned to the province over the coming decades, the peace that Becerra achieved was fleeting (see table 6). Initial unrest was provoked by the behavior of encomenderos, alcaldes mayores, and the contingents of soldiers sent to collect tribute. In 1598, rebellion broke out in Pata and Abulug, on the northern coastline, in response to brutality experienced during tribute collection. The Spanish responded by executing twelve datus and cutting down palm trees and burning crops; however, this, in turn, provoked the rebelling Isnegs to burn down their villages and flee into the Apayao Mountains.[23] In 1605, the Itawis of Lubo, on the Chico River resolved to rise up and kill as many Spanish soldiers as they could.[24] In 1607, the Gaddangs of Simbuey killed their encomendero, Luis Enriquez, after he mistreated them the previous year. They lanced him and used his leg bones to make a stair from which the datu could climb into his house.[25]

As the century progressed, the focus of these rebellions shifted toward the Dominican missionaries, who after 1595 became the drivers of efforts to reduce Cagayanes into Spanish settlements.[26] The Dominican chronicler Diego

Table 6   Rebellions in Cagayan Province, 1575–1639

YEAR	REGION	TOWNS IMPACTED	DESCRIPTION
1575	Coastal Cagayan	Camalaniugan	This town was first established by Juan Pablo de Carrión; however, shortly afterwards the Cagayanes rebelled and stole all of the Spanish supplies, forcing them to dismantle the settlement and return to Manila. Many of the Spanish soldiers were killed.[1]
1589	Isabela	Purao, Culi, Yagun, Pilitan	Generalized rebellion against Spanish control lasting for more than two years. More than twenty-five Spanish soldiers were killed while collecting tribute and attempting to enforce Spanish control.[2]
	Cagayan River	Lallo, Talapa, Gattaran, Capa, Tuguegarao, Iguig	
	Babuyan Islands	Babuyan Islands	
	Coastal Cagayan	Maquin	
1598	Coastal Cagayan	Pata, Abulug	Rebellion against tribute collection. Twelve datus were executed and the Spanish cut down palm trees and destroyed crops. In response, the Cagayanes burned their villages and fled into the mountains.[3]
1605	Cagayan River	Tuguegarao	Rebellion against the encomendero, who was killed. The priest was also ejected from the town.[4]
1607	Chico River	Lobo (Tabang)	Reports that this region was in uprising; the bishop claims that it was always in uprising and tribute had never been satisfactorily collected.[5]
1607	Chico River	Nalfotan	Rebellion led by a priestess against Spanish missionaries, resulting in the town being burned down and the Cagayanes fleeing into the mountains.[6]
	Isabela	Simbuey	The indios of Simbuey killed their encomendero during tribute collection.[7]
1615	Isabela	Abuatan (Tumauini), Bolo (Ilagan), Batavag, Pilitan	Rebellion led by native priestesses against religious conversion, resulting in the abandonment of some of these towns.[8]
1621	Isabela	Abuatan, Bolo, Pilitan	Indios of Abuatan burnt down the town and declared themselves enemies of Spain and God. The rebellion spread into neighboring regions. Missionaries forced out of this region for the next half century.[9]
1625	Apayao	Pudtol, Capinatan	Indios of Capinatan killed two priests and then burned these two towns and fled into the mountains.[10]

| 1639 | Apayao | Capinatan | Rebellion in which twenty-five soldiers were killed, the town was burnt down, and the Cagayanes fled into the mountains. This settlement was abandoned by Dominican missionaries for the next several decades.[11] |

[1] Archivo General de Indias (hereafter AGI), Patronato, leg. 25, ramo 44.

[2] AGI, Patronato, leg. 25, ramo 44; AGI, Audiencia de Filipinas (hereafter Filipinas), leg. 6, ramo 7, núm. 67.

[3] AGI, Filipinas, leg. 6, ramo 9, núms. 144, 161, 173; AGI, Filipinas, leg. 27, núm. 33; Felix M. Keesing, *Ethnohistory of Northern Luzon* (Stanford, CA: Stanford University Press, 1962), 175–176; Linda Newson, *Conquest and Pestilence in the Early Spanish Philippines* (Honolulu: University of Hawai'i Press, 2009), 206.

[4] Fr. Julian Malumbres, O. P. *Historia de Cagayán* (Manila: Tip. Linotype de Santo Tomás, 1918), 28.

[5] AGI, Filipinas, leg. 76, núm. 55.

[6] Fr. Diego Aduarte, *Tomo Primero de la Historia de la Provincia del Santo Rosario de Filipinas, Japón, y China, de la sagrada orden de predicadores* (Zaragoza: Por Domingo Gascon, Insançon, Impressor del Santo Hospital Real y General de Nuestra Señora de Gracia, 1693), 317.

[7] Aduarte, *Tomo Primero*, 315–318.

[8] Aduarte, *Tomo Primero*, 413–418.

[9] Aduarte, *Tomo Primero*, 490–494.

[10] Aduarte, *Tomo Primero*, 550–556; Keesing, *Ethnohistory of Northern Luzon*, 194.

[11] Baltasar de Santa Cruz, *Tomo Segundo de la Historia de la Provincia del Santo Rosario de Filipinas, Japón, y China del Sagrado Orden de Predicadores* (Zaragoza: Por Pasqual Bueno, Impressor Reyno, 1693), 18–21.

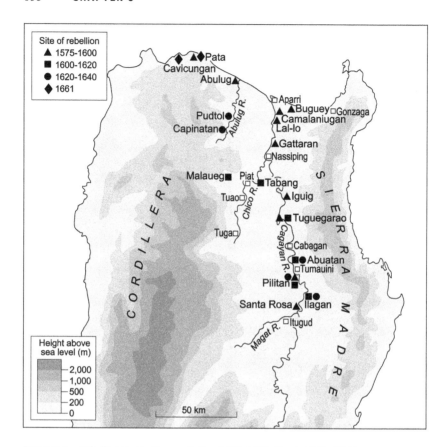

FIGURE 6.1.   Rebellions in the Cagayan Valley, 1575–1661. Map by Philip Stickler.

Aduarte wrote that the conversion of the Cagayanes to Christianity progressed very slowly and many in the town of Nueva Segovia could hear shouts and screams particularly at night emanating from the pagan ceremonies and celebrations that the Cagayanes continued to perform. During this period, the Dominicans built churches in the towns of Pata, Abulug, and Camalaniugan. Aduarte suggested that the indios of these towns accepted the missionaries into their communities when they became convinced that the Christian God was able to cure a contagious illness. Elsewhere, however, the conversion activities of the priests promoted conflict. This was particularly the case in the upper Cagayan Valley. In 1607, a priestess named Caquenga convinced many in the newly founded town of Nalfotan to abandon the Spanish settlement. They set fire to the church at midnight and began profaning religious items, smashing them to pieces and drinking from the chalice "as a people without God, governed by the Devil."[27] They later fled into the mountains. A similar rebellion occurred in the towns of Batavag, Bolo, Pilitan, and Abuatan in 1615—all located around the modern-day settlements of Ilagan and Tumauini—just eight years after these Gaddang towns were founded by the Dominicans. Missionary attempts to eradicate indigenous religious practices and ceremonies performed by local priestesses caused a large number of Gaddangs to flee into the mountains, and it was difficult to convince them to return.[28]

In the 1620s, a new wave of revolt spread over Cagayan and formalized the territorial frontier of Cagayan to Lal-lo and the coast, with soldiers and missionaries abandoning large parts of the Cagayan Valley and foothills for the next half century. The first wave of this rebellion again took place in the Gaddang towns of Pilitan and Abuatan. On November 6, 1621, the Gaddangs burned down the church and towns in this region and declared themselves enemies of Spain and of God. They fled into the nearby mountains and the rebellion spread through the surrounding regions. In panic, the priest stationed in Pilitan decided to leave very early in the morning, but as he was making his escape a large armed crowd of Gaddangs came marching from Abuatan, naked and covered in oil. The priest attempted to reason with this crowd, lecturing all eight hundred of them for more than an hour in the patio of his church. While he was giving his lecture, another group began to set fire to the town and the Gaddangs left him. From there, the rebellion spread throughout the region. Aduarte described the rebels performing sacrilegious acts, dressing in the garb of the priests, and thrusting a knife into the face of the statue of the Virgin Mary to see if she would really bleed. After carousing and celebrating the retreat of the Spaniards, the Gaddangs then retreated into the mountains.[29]

While the Spanish scrambled to respond to these events, a second wave of rebellion commenced in Pudtol and Capinatan, in the Apayao Mountains, beginning on June 8, 1625. The Isnegs of Apayao had attempted on two previous occasions to escape into the mountains but were thwarted in their attempts. This time, they planned their rebellion carefully and kept it secret. In Capinatan the rebellion was led by two datus called Don Miguel Lanab and Alababan, who interrupted two Dominican priests during their evening meal and decapitated them using traditional headhunting knives. One of the blows was not complete and the priest was saved by some friendly Isnegs who tried to place him on a barge to be taken out of the village. The rebels intercepted this and took him instead to their female datu where he was cut to pieces and his body was thrown to be eaten by the pigs. The Isnegs of both Capinatan and Pudtol then set fire to the churches and returned to the mountains.[30]

The government in Manila responded by sending two contingents of soldiers who arrived some ten months after the beginning of this second rebellion.[31] They set about cutting down palm trees throughout the province, to try to destroy the sources of subsistence that the rebels relied on.[32] In the process, the governor claimed that they were able to reduce more than a thousand Isnegs; however, the soldiers left after just two months to undertake the conquest of Taiwan.[33] A report from 1628 suggested that the province remained in rebellion.[34] Although attempts were made over the next decade to return to the region of Capinatan in the foothills of the Apayao Mountains, the Isnegs once again responded with violence. At ten in the morning on March 6, 1639, a group of armed Isnegs attacked the sentry post in Capinatan and killed the sentinel before breaking down the doors of the fort and killing twenty soldiers. Five soldiers managed to escape but later died in a fire. The Isnegs then attacked the convent, although the Dominican chronicler Baltasar de Santa Cruz says that they spared the life of the priest, placing him on board a small boat along with his possessions and sending him out of the town. Once this was done, they burnt down the church and convent and once again returned to the mountains.[35]

Trade and Militarization

It is unsurprising that upland areas provided shelter to people fleeing colonization of the lowlands. Rather than representing two distinct worlds, upland and lowland regions always existed in a symbiotic relationship.[36] The ecology of upland areas had a significant impact on the subsistence patterns of local communities. While many upland communities in the Cordillera Mountains—such as the Ifugao and Isneg—practiced swidden agriculture and rice farming, communities occupying the Sierra Madre Mountains in the east tended to be nomadic hunter-gatherers. These groups are known by different names—Aeta, Agta, Ita, or Negrito, for instance—and have often been referred to as the original inhabitants of the Philippine islands, predating the arrival of Malay migrants. Anthropologists have pointed out that the designation "hunter-gather" to describe the Aeta has granted the communities of the Sierra Madre a false reputation as independent and untouched by lowland society.[37] While anthropological studies of these societies suggest that communities tended to be small and highly mobile, frequently relocating to temporary camps in the rainforest and living off bow and arrow hunting, trapping, fishing, and foraging, such groups nevertheless relied on trade with farming settlements to supplement their subsistence with rice and other necessary staples only found within lowland regions. Upland areas also controlled resources that lowland regions relied on for production, subsistence, and long-distance trade. Thus, mountain communities typically traded meat, honey, wax, resins, and precious metals, including gold, in exchange for subsistence items such as rice and salt, and iron tools, weapons, and manufactured goods.[38]

The upland communities of both the Cordillera and Sierra Madre Mountains were important to the history of resistance in the Cagayan Valley.[39] Yet, there are few written sources describing the history of communities in the Sierra Madre Mountains. This is partly because the Spanish made very few forays into these remote mountains. Most of the contact took place from the eastern coastline, where Franciscan missionaries were stationed in Casiguran. Records from these missions suggest that Spanish contact with upland Aetas was hostile, involving frequent raiding and disruption to missionary travel through the province.[40] In the 1650s, the Dominicans attempted to reduce groups of Aetas in the north of the Sierra Madre, establishing a mission base in modern-day Gonzaga. These efforts were short-lived, with the Aetas returning to the mountains in response to hostilities with lowland neighbors.[41] Yet, although the Spanish had limited contact with the communities of the Sierra Madre, it is evident that this was not the case for indigenous inhabitants of the Cagayan Valley. While Spanish settlements adjacent to Apayao and Kalinga territories maintained connections to the Cordillera uplands, many inland Spanish settlements in Cagayan were on the eastern banks of the Cagayan River, placing them much closer to the Sierra Madre Mountains. Spanish sources are remarkably nonspecific when describing population movements in the Cagayan Valley, a likely consequence of geographic ignorance. It is nevertheless most likely that the frequent references of retreat into the mountains by these communities indicate movement into the Sierra Madre Mountains. Settlements like Tuguegarao, Cabagan, and other Ibanag and Gaddang communities—where many of the most tumultuous rebellions against Spanish rule took place—were positioned close to the foothills of these mountains.

Established trading relations between upland and lowland groups had an impact on colonization efforts in Cagayan but were in turn altered by Spanish attempts at establishing military control. Trade between lowland and upland groups had been reported as early as 1593 when it was uncovered that lowland groups were funneling swords and other arms into the mountains to aid their resistance of Spanish settlement.[42] By the late seventeenth century, this trade was not only supplying uncolonized communities with a ready supply of arms, but also with iron for making their own weapons and farming tools and goods such as clothes and salt and other necessary items that they needed to continue to live their lives autonomously within the mountains.[43] By 1691, the Gaddangs were known to be skilled in the use of Spanish weaponry, including firearms, lances, and shields as well as the arrows used by upland communities. Moreover, they maintained communication and alliances with unpacified groups in the mountains and were able to source gunpowder and munitions from Pampanga and Laguna and from along the coasts of Lampon.[44] Significantly, parts of this trading network were facilitated by the Spanish presence in the province, in part, as we will see, due to the emergence of an illicit black-market trade in weapons and other supplies by corrupt officials in remote outposts.

Following the rebellions of the 1620s, no further attempts were made to push into the interior of Cagayan until the 1670s. These later efforts were led by the Dominicans and marked the most aggressive intervention into the valley to date. The first mission began in the Gaddang region in 1673 and by 1678 the Dominicans had established three new towns on the site of the old mission settlements called Santa Rosa, San Fernando, and Nuestra Señora de la Victoria de Itugud.[45] This was followed by renewed efforts in Pudtol and the Apayao Mountains (1684), the Batanes Islands (1686), and the Chico River region (1688), where they founded the towns of Tuga (1689) and Santa Cruz, near Malaueg (1693).[46]

Even so, by this time the communities of Northern Luzon had accommodated themselves to the existing frontier and were prepared to heavily resist any further expansion into their territories. Reports from this period repeatedly emphasize the continued harassment of newly established lowland settlements by Cagayanes living in upland areas who opposed the Spanish presence.[47] In 1678, the interim governor Francisco de Montemayor y Mansilla estimated that about four thousand previously pacified indios had abandoned Spanish settlements in Cagayan. In response, the Dominicans requested a force of Spanish soldiers to help them to reduce apostate communities, while providing protection to those who wished to return to their towns. Their proposal was met with only a lukewarm response from the military, who argued that, based on past experiences, sending soldiers into Cagayan was a drain on resources and achieved very little. Instead, they suggested that a more effective tactic would be to position soldiers within the missionary settlements and wait until the fugitives returned to the lowlands to conduct trade.[48] Thus a network of forts was established at Lal-lo, Cabagan, Itugud, Tuao, Capinatan, Pudtol, Cavicungan, Aparri, and Buguey, with the intention of supporting tribute collectors and defending the towns from attacks.[49]

Far from protecting the Dominicans and their converts, these forts quickly became outposts within the lucrative trading network that extended throughout the province, connecting Spanish settlements with the unconquered upland interior.[50] The majority of military officers, encomenderos, and alcaldes mayores appeared to be involved in this illicit trade. Fr. Francisco de Olmedo noted that the corporals of the presidios typically employed the Cagayanes in carting goods backward and forward between the provincial capital and the

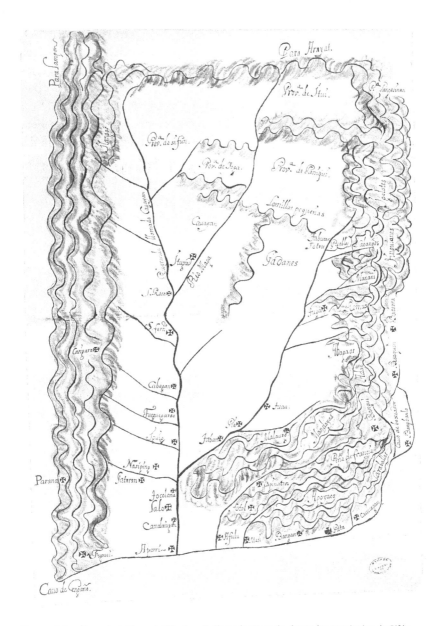

Figure 6.2. Mapa de la Vega del Río Grande llamado Cagayán, hasta las provincias de Sifún, Yoga, Paniqui, Itui, etc., en el que se señalan misiones y pueblos [Map of the plain of the great river called Cagayan until the provinces of Sifún, Yoga, Paniqui, Itui, etc., showing missions and towns], 1690. España. Ministerio de Cultura, Archivo General de Indias, Mapas y Planos, Filipinas, núm. 140.

interior, nominally under the guise of transporting food and materials for the infantry stationed in each of the forts.[51] This aid rarely reached the soldiers and would instead be confiscated by the military commanders and used for trade. Spanish officers took the tobacco, wine, salt, iron, clothes, and other goods destined for the soldiers and sold them to Christian indios, who then took them into the mountains to trade with unconquered and fugitive communities. In return, they would receive wax, gold, and other goods from the mountains. The conduct of this trade placed excessive burdens on the communities under Spanish control, which local principales likened to slavery. Many of the Cagayanes were employed in a constant stream of tasks, from carting and hauling goods through the province, to hunting, harvesting, and cutting timber. Even in the towns without a military outpost, the principales argued, there was at least one Spaniard overseeing this trading network.[52]

Some Cagayanes living within newly established Spanish settlements benefited from this trade. The Christianized indios in the lowlands acted as intermediaries between the Spanish and the unconquered hinterland—suggesting one motivation to convert to Christianity was that of access to trade with lowland Spanish settlements. Moreover, they would trade their own goods as well as the goods given to them by the alcaldes mayores or encomenderos. Fr. Marrón noted that it was consequently in the interest of these Christianized intermediaries to convince other Cagayanes to remain within the mountains. They would often spread rumors of the great labors that indios suffered within Christian settlements through the tribute, repartimiento, and bandala systems. Many encomenderos, military officers, and alcaldes mayores were likewise self-interested in maintaining this situation and would do nothing to aid in reductions or conversions.[53]

Thus, while trading activities in Cagayan may have been mutually profitable for the secular officials, military officers, and their Christian intermediaries, it arguably played a significant role not merely in maintaining the status quo but in actually furthering the anticolonial position of the communities in the unconquered hinterland. The many burdens associated with the ongoing trading activities both dissuaded upland communities to join Spanish settlements and encouraged those who had been recently reduced to flee back into the mountains. Fr. Olmedo argued that the trade conducted by the alcaldes mayores with the unpacified communities provided those communities with no incentive to live among the Christians. At the same time, many of those who had converted to Christianity regularly left for the mountains in order to escape the exploitative taxation and forced labor systems imposed on them by the Spanish soldiers.[54] The Cagayan principales agreed with this, saying that the towns of Nassiping, Gattaran, Tocolana, Capinatan, Pudtol, and Abulug had been destroyed, with the residents joining the communities in the mountains. The principales argued that no one wanted to live in a town where they were treated as the slaves of the corporal of the presidio.[55]

Thus, the fortified outposts established in Cagayan with the intention of securing control over the valley were instead transformed into trading hubs that undermined the advance of Spanish control in Cagayan. Numerous observers noted that these outposts were virtually useless in times of attack or rebellion. Fr. Ginés Barrientos reported that whenever hostile Cagayanes arrived within a town—usually to take a head or set fire to some of the buildings—the corporals and their soldiers were known to retreat into their fort, leaving the townspeople to resist and confront the enemies themselves. He argued that some of the Cagayanes liked to throw spears at the Spanish forts simply to prove that they could do so with impunity. Fr. Francisco de Olmedo similarly reported that a Spanish soldier had been killed at the fort in Capinatan, while another indigenous soldier was killed while on sentry duty at midday in the fort of Pudtol. The soldiers would not come out of the forts to help defend their towns even when the town was on fire. Fr. Bartolomé Marrón had witnessed two indios have their heads cut off by invading forces in Tuao in 1689, while the corporal shut himself and his soldiers into the fort.[56]

The Cagayan principales went even further in their criticism of the presidios. They explained the dysfunction of the forts by describing the low-level conflict that regularly took place between the indigenous people in the Spanish towns and those from the mountains. These unpacified groups would descend from the mountains in parties of between twelve and twenty and would wait, hidden within the dense rainforest, looking for an opportunity to headhunt. When the indios of the town heard about this, they would immediately take up arms and begin to pursue the raiders from the mountains through the forests, shouting to each other as they went. Because those from the town were more familiar with the paths and roads around their village, they were often able to catch up to the intruders and in turn cut off their heads. By contrast, the soldiers in the presidio prevented this speedy pursuit by demanding that the townspeople come to the fort to report the matter to the corporal, who would then call a meeting of the whole town and organize a contingent to pursue the enemies. The pursuit was thus delayed by some time and they were never able to catch up to the enemies or retaliate in any way. Because of this, the principales argued that the mountain communities had become more daring in raiding the towns that housed Spanish presidios because they knew that they were able to attack these towns almost without notice.[57]

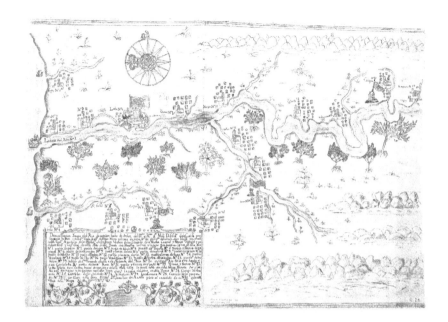

FIGURE 6.3. Mapa del Río y Provincia de Cagayán, en el que se identifica mediante letras la iglesia y fuerza que se construyó en la nueva entrada de dicha provincia (Nordeste de la isla de Luzón, Filipinas) [Map of the river and province of Cagayan that identifies by means of letters the church and fort that were constructed in the new entrance of the said province (northeast of the island of Luzon, Philippines)], 1719. España. Ministerio de Cultura, Archivo General de Indias, Mapas y Planos, Filipinas, núm. 22.

The principales spoke of the presidios as both an impediment and an embarrassment, while the Dominicans believed that the forts were largely responsible for the ongoing instability experienced within the province. Ironically, while they had initially been the greatest proponents of militarization in Cagayan, by the end of the 1680s the Dominicans withdrew their support for the presidios. In 1689, Fr. Alonso Sandín collected a series of petitions from Dominican missionaries stationed in Cagayan advocating for the closure of all of the forts in the province, with the exception of the presidio in the capital, Lal-lo.[58] Nevertheless, the Dominicans continued to believe that the conquest of Cagayan could only be achieved through military means. What became apparent by the 1690s, however, was that the vast, uncontrolled, and largely unexplored territories in the southern half of the Cagayan Valley presented a massive disadvantage to these conquest attempts. In the 1690s, a new proposal emerged to concentrate military efforts in the region known as Ituy that encompassed the mountainous borderlands of the Caraballo Sur between Pangasinan and Cagayan as well as the lower half of the Cagayan Valley. Although its conquest had been attempted several times in the late sixteenth century, this region remained unpacified and was considered to contain an extremely large population that was hostile to the Spanish.[59] Fr. Cristobal Pedroche believed that there were more souls in this region than in the rest of the Philippines combined,[60] while in 1708 Governor Zabalburu estimated the population of Ituy as reaching up to four hundred thousand people.[61] Such a large number of uncontrolled communities in the heartland of Luzon was not only an embarrassment but also presented a serious strategic threat. At that time there was no safe overland passage between Pangasinan and Cagayan, meaning that all military supplies and reinforcements had to enter Cagayan by ship from the northern coastline.[62] The goal to conquer Ituy and build a road connecting Pangasinan with Cagayan thus became the strategic priority of official Spanish policy for the next half century.

The Road through Ituy

Ituy was a very fertile, temperate, and populous land with many large towns of five hundred or more. An eighteenth-century description of the population of Ituy noted that they had their own distinct language and customs, including the sharpening and coloring of teeth and the wearing of ear adornments that reached to their shoulders. Women were particularly respected as spiritual leaders and educated members of their communities.[63] Both the extensive savannahs of the Magat River and the gentle hills of the Caraballo Sur were suitable for rice cultivation, and communities harvested both wet and dry rice and cultivated other crops such as ginger, sweet potato, cotton, and many different types of livestock.[64]

The idea that Ituy was the secret to controlling Cagayan was not new. The abundance of food and other supplies in Ituy meant it was an ideal place for communities to move to when escaping Spanish colonization efforts further up the Cagayan Valley. As early as the 1590s, officials in Manila argued that the pacification of Cagayan could not be completed without the conquest of Ituy, since this region provided a ready haven for anyone wishing to escape Spanish control. This view was based on information provided by indigenous informants like Don Cristóbal Gatavololoc who reported that up to fifteen thousand people lived along the riverbanks alone in Ituy and that these communities provided shelter to those seeking independence from Spain. Some Spanish military officials believed that communities in Ituy were also providing military support for others in Cagayan to resist colonization. When Don Luis Pérez Dasmariñas was sent to explore Ituy in 1591, he was explicitly instructed to lead his men all the way up the Cagayan River, "cleaning out the

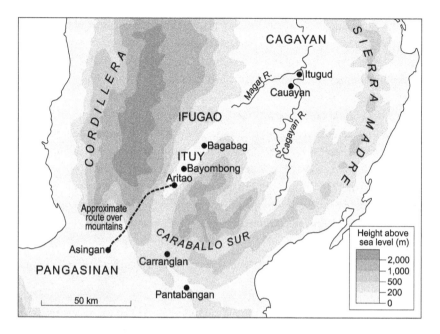

FIGURE 6.4. Ituy and the southern Cagayan Valley. Map by Philip Stickler.

criminality" among the populations that lived along the river, those that made war against the Spanish.[65]

Yet, as noted in the previous chapter, although a number of conquest attempts were made between 1591 and 1609, Ituy remained uncolonized and largely unexplored throughout the seventeenth century. In 1690, Fr. Pedroche proposed establishing a fort in Ituy that would be garrisoned with a thousand indio soldiers—mostly from the province of Pampanga—who would be incentivized to serve in this occupation by being granted an exemption from paying tribute.[66] This call for the militarization of Cagayan and its neighboring regions arose from the increased violence, resistance, and desertion that Dominicans encountered within the communities that they were attempting to convert to Christianity. Fr. Pedroche's proposal eventually gained the support of the secular and military authorities in Manila. In February 1691, Captain Diego de Acosta was given the orders to march with a troop of soldiers to the fort of Itugud and from there to explore the region to the south with the aim of finding the best overland route to Pangasinan. Acosta described raiding at dawn the towns of Afugao, Tafucan, and Amulion. Since he and his soldiers did not have a native guide, they were not completely certain of the locations of the towns, but they nonetheless killed fifteen people and captured four infants. They searched the towns for rice and then burnt them down, inflicting the greatest amount of damage possible.[67] Despite this, shortly after initiating the campaign, Sergeant Major Martin de Leon wrote to Manila to recommend that the Pampangan troops stationed in Itugud should be withdrawn. Most of them were anxious to return to their land in order to harvest their crops and prepare for the annual tribute collection. Leon warned that if they were not allowed to return home they might become upset with the Spanish and choose to simply desert.[68] Taking this threat seriously, the Spanish authorities complied, and the soldiers were retreated on February 24, 1691, just two weeks after they began the mission.[69]

Following this failed attempt, a number of military commanders expressed considerable doubts over the viability of conquering Ituy and pacifying Cagayan. Most captains believed that it was an unwinnable war. Sergeant Major Don Ambrosio Saquin, a native of Itugud, believed it would be a mission of great terror and horror. He offered to act as a guide through the region but reiterated how difficult the occupation of this region would be and that they would need a constant military escort for all their activities in the province. Captain Diego de Acosta reported that he had traveled on a number of occasions to this region to fight against rebel, heathen, and apostate communities. He believed that any attempt to conquer this territory would require a force of five hundred, and that the subjugation of these communities would even then be difficult because they were not afraid of the Spanish weapons, possessed their own firearms, and were experienced in war.[70] Ayudante Sebastian de Acencio added that they would need to find the means of maintaining a permanent presence in the region capable of dealing with the large number of hostile communities, as well as materials for the construction of a fort and labor in the fields to sustain the soldiers stationed there. Thus, by 1700 the proposed conquest of Ituy still had not begun. In explaining the reasons for this to the king, Governor Fausto Cruzat wrote that many experienced persons had argued that it would be an impractical conquest. They would need a significant military force, which they lacked. Consequently, he had not been able to take a resolution on the matter.[71]

Nevertheless, the lack of an overland route that passed through Ituy, allowing soldiers to march easily into rebellious Cagayan, remained a major strategic disadvantage for the Spanish. This was particularly so during moments of violent resistance in the valley. On October 13, 1718, rebellion broke out in the Chico River region of Cagayan. The residents of Tuao, Piat, Malaveg, and Tabang rose up, taking up arms, burning down churches, and fleeing into the mountains. Although the alcalde mayor sent an immediate dispatch to Manila for military aid, within a week the rebellion had spread to neighboring Gaddang and Ibanag territories—centered on Tuguegarao—and by mid-November communities across the entire Cagayan Valley were in uprising. The alcalde mayor wrote to Manila saying it was clear that the rebels intended to eject all the Spaniards from the province. In Manila, royal officials organized a Junta de Guerra on November 15 that resolved to send fifty Spanish soldiers and an unspecified number of Pampangans with three artillerymen and a corporal, as well as sufficient gunpowder and cannonballs.[72]

This episode—reminiscent of the rebellions that swept across the province a century earlier in the 1620s—highlighted once again the remoteness of Cagayan and its disconnection from other centers of Spanish military control. The building of a road that connected Cagayan to Pangasinan thus became an obsession for all of the different groups of Spaniards working on the conquest of Cagayan.[73] When news of the rebellions reached Manila, the governor dispatched Don Luis Estacio Venegas to Cagayan to help quell the rebellion and begin preparations for opening a road south of Itugud; in the meantime Don Miguel Navarro was ordered to march into Ituy from Pampanga and identify the best route for this road through the Caraballo Sur Mountains. Although both men claimed success in their missions, the project to build the road was halted very abruptly in November 1719, when a new rebellion broke out in Pangasinan, on the other side of the mountains. This rebellion was initiated in direct response to the burdens placed on communities in Pangasinan to supply grain and other provisions for the expeditions into Ituy. Three hundred indios seized control of the town of San Jacinto and fortified themselves in the church. The rebellion was only ended when indios loyal to the Spanish succeeded in capturing and killing the leader.[74] At the same time, Augustinian missionaries working in the Caraballo Sur Mountains complained that the mission to open a road between Pangasinan and Cagayan was seriously impacting their missionary work. The militarization of this region had "caused horror" among indigenous neophytes who until that time had descended voluntarily from the mountains thanks to the work of the missionaries.[75] These events spooked officials in Manila; just as they tried to control one region, they lost control of another. The mission to build the road was brought to an end.

The ambivalence that military and secular officials held toward Cagayan and Ituy was not matched by the Dominican missionaries, who continued to extend their efforts through the valley in the eighteenth century. The road between Cagayan and Pangasinan was eventually completed by the Dominican order and apparently without even financial backing from the secular officials in Manila. Dominicans inherited religious jurisdiction over the southern reaches of the Cagayan Valley from the Augustinians in 1736. At this time, Spanish knowledge of the territory was limited to the lands adjacent to the Magat River that linked Itugud with Bayombong. Very little was known about the extent of this section of the valley from east to west, except that it extended into Igorot territory on one side and to that of the Ilongots on the other. When the Dominicans took control of this region, they immediately began attempting to extend control further south from Itugud. In 1737, four friars were chosen to lead an expedition to choose a path for a road linking Cagayan and Pangasinan. They were granted a military escort to ensure their safety. As they marched through the southern reaches of the valley, they encountered hostility and resistance from local communities who forced them to sleep in the open outside of the towns and refused to provide them with provisions or show them the way through their lands. During this period, three missionaries were killed by poisoning by Cagayanes.[76]

Despite these setbacks, the Dominicans managed to solidify powerful alliances with several indigenous leaders from Cauayan, who acted as their escorts and guides through the southern reaches of the valley. The social standing of these leaders also meant that the Dominicans were able to broker peace with communities along the way. Violent resistance continued to be a problem particularly in Bayombong, in the foothills of the Cordillera Mountains. During the course of all of these activities, the missionaries began to wear down a path that linked Ituy with Pangasinan, but the road was very long and winding and was considered of little use for communication or trade. Following this, the Dominicans paid a workforce of indios from Pangasinan to construct a more direct road. The road that they took passed through Igorot territory, along the southeastern slopes of the Cordillera Mountains. The missionaries had to engage in peace treaties that involved accommodating non-Christian religious practices, including the ritual sacrifice of pigs—something that the Dominican chronicler of these expeditions condescendingly described as a "customary celebration [that was] very ridiculous."[77] The road eventually linked Asingan with Aritao and then onward along the Magat River into the Cagayan Valley, bringing to completion a project that had taken a century and a half to achieve.[78]

While the Dominicans viewed the opening of this road as a glorious achievement of a long-delayed milestone, for the inhabitants of Ituy the road brought with it increasing violence and militarization. Missionaries continued to encounter hostility to their presence, with some communities refusing them entrance into their towns, others actively arming themselves against them, and some like those of Bayombong retreating into the nearby mountains to escape the evangelizing of the missionaries. Missionaries were forced to travel through the region with armed escorts and on occasion encountered squadrons of hundreds of indigenous people armed with lances and arrows. In such instances, the missionaries often chose to engage their assailants in dialogue, since attempting to fight them would be certain suicide.[79]

The Dominicans had learned from hard experience over a century and a half of operating in Cagayan that conquest could only be achieved through brute force. The opening of the road allowed the missionaries to explore dense and remote upland areas where it was common for communities to retreat to escape evangelization. The violence of conquest thus shifted into the Caraballo Sur Mountains as Dominicans pursued communities of apostates and fugitives. In the 1740s, one such incursion was made against a group called the Panuypuyes, who inhabited the Caraballo Sur Mountains south of Aritao. This group was known to regularly attack Spanish settlements and was considered by the Dominicans as a primary cause for a lack of constancy among newly converted Christians. The Dominicans organized for a dispatch of soldiers from Pangasinan and Cagayan, who then marched into the mountains where they found the Panuypuyes had constructed a fortification at the top of a mountain and were prepared to defend themselves with lances and rocks. The Spanish stormed this fortification, killing 276 people and fatally wounding another 130. They then sacked and set fire to the town and the neighboring fields and began marching through the mountains reducing to ashes any settlements that they found.[80] These actions set the tone of Dominican activities in this region for the next decades to come.

Yet, as missionaries pushed further into the mountains, communities began to move further away, developing new methods of resistance. It is likely that those who fled frontier violence in Nueva Vizcaya account for the early eighteenth-century mass migration into Ifugao territory that has been documented in the archaeological record by Stephen Acabado and Marlon Martin. Moving further into the mountains allowed these communities to adopt new environmental forms of resistance. As Acabado argues, Ifugaos secured independence from Spain not just through the use of the rugged terrain of the Cordillera Mountains, but also through new agricultural innovations like the development of large-scale rice terracing that could sustain larger populations in the mountains throughout the year. Alongside these developments, the Ifugao developed a culture that placed upland rice agriculture at its center as a symbol of their resistance to Spanish colonization.[81] Thus, despite the gradual opening of roads that connected Cagayan to the rest of Luzon, and despite the increased militarization and the influx of missionaries into the valley in the eighteenth century, indigenous resistance persisted. By the beginning of the twentieth century, barely a quarter of the residents of Nueva Vizcaya had converted to Christianity.[82] In large part, Ituy remained unpacified.

The turbulent history of Cagayan offered many lessons for Spanish officials and missionaries; the principal one of these was that, where consistent resistance was encountered, the colonization process had to rely on the escalating use of violence. At the same time, this history demonstrates that the kind of frontier violence that accompanied colonization in the Philippines was not only a product of military intervention, tribute collection, or labor exploitation. It also followed trade and the evangelizing efforts of missionaries. Over the course of the seventeenth century, the Dominican missionaries operating in Cagayan became the greatest advocates for the increased militarization of the valley. In many instances, their requests for military intervention went far beyond what the secular and military officials in Manila were willing to provide. Moreover, these lessons were not limited to the Dominicans of Cagayan. Across the islands, in locations where colonization was confronted by pockets of resistance, flight, and apostasy, many missionaries similarly advocated violence to subjugate populations.

In 1733, Governor Fernando Valdés Tamón ordered an investigation into the widespread attacks by upland communities on lowland Christian settlements outside of Northern Luzon. This investigation reported that such attacks were common in many regions, ranging from the regular attacks made by the Zambales on lowland communities in Pampanga and Pangasinan, to attacks by fugitives and apostates living in the mountains of Camarines, Catanduanes, Sorsogon, Baler and Casiguran, Taal, Samar, and Negros. In all of these instances, missionaries reported that these upland communities were made up of people who steadfastly refused to convert to Christianity or who had apostatized and moved into the mountains to avoid paying tribute. Many believed that fugitives and apostates were responsible for even worse hostilities against Spaniards and their allies than groups who had never been colonized. They were known to deliberately disrupt Christian settlements through regular raids during which they would kill individuals and steal livestock or produce. They also often had control over the trade of key resources within the provinces. In Negros, such groups impeded woodcutting and prevented water from being taken from the rivers. In Camarines, fugitives used poisoned arrows to attack missionary parties and controlled the supply of abaca and wax in the region. In Pampanga and Pangasinan, where such hostilities were the most frequent, pacified communities reported being unable to travel or tend to their fields without armed escorts, especially at harvest time.[83]

Just as in Cagayan, however, these reports reveal a degree of voluntary communication and regular interaction between lowlanders and uplanders. These interactions suggest there were many lowlanders who admired the freedom of their neighbors and were themselves receptive to the possibility of living outside of Spanish colonial control. For example, Fr. Benito de San Pablo noted that many of the Pampangans and Pangasinanes had regular exchange with the Zambales and were intimately familiar with them and often related through marriage. Many such lowlanders had willingly participated in raids and robberies against vassals of the Crown or harbored fugitives in their houses and farms.[84]

For this reason, the governor proposed in 1733 that the best solution to these attacks was to explicitly restrict trade between unpacified groups and Christian settlements. Most of the religious participants in this investigation believed this solution was insufficient. They advocated for a variety of more aggressive tactics, ranging from the establishment of multiple presidios in regions closest to the Zambales Mountains, to hanging the bodies of offenders along the highways as a warning to others. Fr. Francisco Gensano thought that military incursions into upland areas should focus on burning and destroying the farmlands and gardens of communities in the mountains. The Dominicans Fr. Geronimo Sanz Ortiz, Fr. Juan de Arechederra, and Fr. Bernardo Basco all believed that they should be able to take unpacified uplanders as slaves, describing them as evil beasts who should not be included in the general term indios. Nevertheless, and in an echo of the history of Cagayan, the audiencia of Manila remained reluctant to approve these extreme measures, saying that offensive war and slavery were drastic measures that should only be considered when all other measures had failed.[85]

Lowland and upland communities across the Philippines have shared histories of resistance to empire.[86] Upland spaces offered a site of refuge for individuals and whole communities wishing to escape colonial control across large parts of the archipelago. Upland communities, in turn, used tactics of raiding, headhunting, and defensive fortifications to both defend themselves from outside incursions and destabilize new colonial settlements in the lowlands. Moreover, as the turbulent history of Cagayan demonstrates, these tactics of resistance were not necessarily confined to upland areas. Accounting for a quarter of the entire territory of Luzon and a very large proportion of the island's population, Cagayan was by no means a marginal space. Cagayanes used existing relationships with mountain peoples and spaces to limit the Spanish frontier for the duration of the seventeenth century and beyond.

CHAPTER 7

Manila

The Chinese City

On November 20, 1639, three thousand Chinese farmers from the settlement of Calamba armed themselves with knives, pikes, and farming implements, killed their local alcalde mayor and two priests, and began marching toward Manila.[1] They were part of a group of Chinese laborers who had been forcefully relocated to Calamba—about thirty miles to the south of Manila—to grow rice for the Spanish port city under a scheme established by Governor Sebastián Hurtado de Corcuera. Yet, while the land in Calamba was fertile, during the growing season of 1639 more than three hundred of the settlers died from malaria. The rest were cruelly mistreated by the alcalde mayor, Don Luis de Arias de Mora. Fed up with compounding abuses, the Chinese farmers of Calamba rebelled in protest. Governor Hurtado de Corcuera responded by sending a large force of Spanish cavalry and Spanish and indigenous soldiers against the rebels, attacking their hastily erected fortifications, and pursuing them ruthlessly as they fled through swamps and into ravines and mountain passes. In this first wave of violence, more than fifteen hundred Chinese were killed.

A week later, news of these violent events on Manila's outskirts began circulating in the city and Manila's resident Chinese population rose in solidarity, sparking panic among the Spanish residents of the city. In response, the governor issued a decree ordering that all Chinese residents in the archipelago must be put to death. More than three thousand Chinese were killed in the ensuing violence that engulfed Manila. While others fled for their lives, a group of two hundred Christian Chinese buried themselves in the mud of the marshes beyond Manila's city walls, creeping out only after the slaughter had subsided to beg for mercy. In the meantime, the governor's decree began to circulate within the provinces. In the port of Cavite, rumors of mass killings mingled with the smoke rising across the bay from Manila, creating panic among all the residents. The sergeant major, Alonso García Romero, acted swiftly to restore calm, ushering a thousand Chinese residents into the sanctuary of government buildings where they were promised safety. Once there, missionaries began the work of baptizing those who were not yet Christian and offering sacraments to those who were. Small groups of Chinese were then quietly led out and executed, one by one. It was only after three hundred were killed in this manner that the captive Chinese realized what was happening and broke free, fleeing for their lives. They were pursued to the beaches and into the fields. Some were trapped within fishing corrals and shot, others were put to sword as they fled inland.

Violence of this nature reverberated across Luzon as local officials enacted the pogrom decreed by their governor. Thousands of Chinese fled Manila in an attempt at escape, first to the north, then into the fastness of the mountains of Antipolo, east of Manila, defending themselves as they went with farm implements, rocks, and hastily fashioned pikes made from sharpened sticks. They were hunted down and systematically put to sword by Spanish and indigenous soldiers. By March 15, 1640, twenty-four thousand Chinese were dead.[2] The remaining nearly eight thousand survivors surrendered to their pursuers because they were starving. This episode represents possibly the largest massacre to take place outside of wartime anywhere in the Spanish empire—paralleled only by the events that occurred in Manila just thirty-six years earlier, in which twenty thousand Chinese were similarly slaughtered during a period of rebellion.[3] The chronicler Casimiro Díaz wrote that "the countryside was covered in Chinese corpses, causing for a long time a pestilential stench throughout all the regions. For more than six months, the water from the rivers could not be drunk, [as it was] corrupted by the dead bodies, nor could the fish be eaten for many leagues around, since they were all fattened by human corpses."[4]

In this final chapter we circle back to the port city of Manila to examine the extent and nature of colonial power within the heart of Spanish authority in the archipelago, focusing on the relations between Spanish and Chinese communities in the city. While colonial control unfolded unevenly within the provinces—contested, shaped, and limited by the actions of indigenous communities—Manila was unquestionably a center of Spanish power. It housed the governor, royal audiencia and officials, military, and religious orders, and formed the thriving locus of the galleon trade, the colony's ultimate raison d'être. While a sizable population of Chinese merchants and laborers supported the development of the city and the establishment of viable local and international economies, the Spanish maintained their superiority through spatial segregation, fortifying themselves within the walled city, Intramuros. We might view episodes like the massacre of Chinese that took place in 1639 and 1640 as exemplifying the power of the Spanish state within this space. Violence, after all, is the ultimate expression of state power. And yet, as this chapter will argue, the violence that the Spanish exacted on the Chinese population was also a response to their lack of control over both the urban space and the city's economy.

Behind this violence lies a story of the rise of two parallel cities in Manila during the sixteenth and seventeenth centuries: the Spanish controlled Intramuros and the much larger Chinese settlement in Manila outside of the Spanish city walls. While Manila has typically been seen as a glorious Spanish entrepôt— Spain's "distinguished and ever loyal city"[5]—in reality, Manila was as much a Chinese city as it was Spanish. Shortly after Manila was founded in 1571, Chinese migrants flocked to the city on board Fujianese trading vessels, attracted by the silver trade.[6] The Ming dynasty's adoption of the silver standard combined with newly relaxed regulations on overseas trade made Manila a lucrative port for Fujianese traders.[7] Over the course of the century, the Chinese population of Manila boomed, reaching at its height forty thousand or more, dwarfing the Spanish population, which rarely exceeded two thousand, and was often considerably less.[8] Manila was a significant node in a much larger trading network controlled by Fujianese merchants that extended from Japan to Indonesia to Siam and beyond into the Indian Ocean.[9] Over the first half of the seventeenth century, these trading networks came to be dominated by powerful Fujianese clans, and particularly by the Zheng clan.[10] Historians utilizing Chinese records make a strong case that the Fujianese saw Manila as their city—occupied by their traders and emissaries and an abundant source of wealth thanks to the silver trade. The Spanish, by contrast, were merely the conduits of this silver.[11]

The city expanded dramatically on the back of Chinese migration. Chinese laborers built the city from the ground up. Chinese merchants controlled the silver trade and Chinese artisans, agricultural workers, and tradesmen dominated the local economy, controlling and producing the vast majority of the city's provisions and material supplies. Although Spanish chronicles often presented the Chinese as a faceless mass, the Chinese population of Manila exhibited significant heterogeneity and class divisions between wealthy merchants and the laboring classes.[12] Understanding these divisions helps to shed new light on the politics of seventeenth-century Manila. Vastly outnumbered, the Spanish struggled to govern this diverse population. While elite merchants could be co-opted into Spanish governance structures and convinced to convert to Christianity in exchange for favorable trading relations, the majority of Chinese artisans and laborers showed limited interest in Spanish laws or religious beliefs beyond that which was essential for commercial interaction. Very quickly, therefore, the Spanish grew to distrust and resent the emerging Chinese city outside of their walls; they came to learn that colonial dominance could only be enforced through violence—first through episodic massacres in 1603, 1639, and 1662, and then through policies of forced expulsion.[13]

While the central place of the Chinese community within Manila's economy has long been acknowledged, there is still a tendency to see the Chinese as subordinate to the Spanish who occupied the genuine position of authority in the city. Yet, by viewing the development of Spanish and Chinese Manila as both interconnected and separate parallel processes we gain a more nuanced understanding of how power operated in the city. The Spanish claimed sovereignty over the city and exercised power simultaneously through bureaucratic means—the imposition of legal frameworks and taxation systems for instance—and the threatened and actual use of military force. They were able to exercise control over the city through policies of rigid segregation and restrictions on movement, punctuated by acts of intimidation and violence. Yet it would be a mistake to assume that the Chinese population did not also exercise power over the Spanish in return. Their power lay in the economic functions that they fulfilled as financiers, laborers, merchants, and artisans. Through these roles they came to control the city's food supply and material needs, placing themselves at the center of local circulations of silver currency. While these two competing manifestations of power in the city were interconnected, the Spanish were ultimately more dependent on the Chinese than the other way around.

This situation of dependence lay at the heart of Spanish insecurities and fears in seventeenth-century Manila and was articulated in rich detail by the authors of the many tracts written in favor of expulsion in the second half of the century. This chapter explores the development of Chinese Manila and its impact on Spanish claims to sovereignty over the city. The Fujianese origins of Chinese Manila sets the stage for an examination of how Chinese migrants came to control the city's economy and how the Spanish chose to respond to this situation. In the first instance, the Spanish used a variety of economic and cultural means to try to exert authority over the Chinese, including segregation, taxation, and conversion. When these means failed, they resorted to violent strategies of population control. Although massacre and expulsion were particularly extreme measures used by the Spanish to control the burgeoning Chinese city, they nonetheless did nothing to address the dependence that the

Spanish had on the Chinese for all of the material supplies and services needed for the city to survive. In the end, even brute force did not circumvent the power that the merchants and laborers had over the commercial life of the city.

The Fujianese Origins of Manila

When Diego Calderón y Serrano traveled to Manila from Acapulco to take up his position as *oidor* of the audiencia in 1674, his first experience of a Philippine province surprised and dismayed him. Stopping in Balayan, he noted that most of the towns appeared to be filled with Chinese people who wore their own traditional clothes and carried themselves with great liberty. His traveling companions informed him that the Chinese dominated commercial life throughout the islands and, on arriving in Manila, Calderón y Serrano discovered this to be true. The Chinese ran the city's guilds and controlled the flow of silver and goods not only from China and New Spain but also from other neighboring Asian trading ports like Siam, Golconda, and Bantan. The guilds acted as arbitrators in the buying of goods and in raising and lowering prices. The Spaniards were required to purchase everything from them, and this was the case not only in Manila but across all the provinces. Calderón y Serrano remarked that while there were no more than fifty wealthy Spaniards in all the islands, there were more than ten thousand Chinese who had amassed fortunes—some of them very copious—at the expense of the Spaniards.[14]

Calderón y Serrano's description of economic life in Manila continues to clash with the traditional view of the galleon trade and the boom of Manila as a global port city in the late sixteenth century. The establishment of the Spanish settlement in Manila opened a new trading connection between European and Chinese markets that dwarfed any other comparable trade at the time. Bullion flows across the Pacific accounted for the largest single contribution of silver to China in the early seventeenth century, peaking at more than 110 tons a year.[15] Chinese traders flooded Manila with sumptuous goods that they exchanged for this silver. On their return route to Acapulco, Spanish galleons carried a cargo of silks of almost every variety, from Cantonese crepes to velvets, taffetas, and heavy brocades, some of which were woven with rich silver and gold threads. In addition to bolts of material, the silks were woven into stockings, skirts, cloaks and robes, tablecloths, bed clothes, and tapestries.[16] All of these items were intended primarily for the Spanish-American market. Yet, despite some of the more romanticized images of Manila as "the greatest emporium in all Asia,"[17] Manila was not really a boomtown for the

Spanish. Any profit made in Manila did not remain there, with silver flowing outward to China and the goods purchased from the Chinese junks proceeding onward to Acapulco for resale.[18]

Manila's fortunes were closely tied to Chinese politics and the migration flows of Chinese merchants and traders around Southeast Asia in the sixteenth and seventeenth centuries. Despite an official ban on maritime trade with the establishment of the Ming dynasty in 1368, Chinese merchants had maintained commercial networks across Southeast Asia largely through illegal smuggling and piracy led by Fujianese merchants.[19] In 1567, the ban on maritime trade was lifted. Fujianese merchants were granted licenses to trade across Southeast Asia, and after 1571 trade with Manila became one of the mainstays of these merchants.[20] The voyage from Fujian took fifteen to twenty days, with trading ships arriving in Manila beginning in March each year.[21] Records of ship arrivals compiled by Juan Gil show that in the earliest decades of the trade, the average number of ships arriving in port each year was twenty-five (see table 7). Each of these ships carried with them between two hundred and four hundred crew;[22] furthermore, many did not leave with the ships returning to China but remained in Manila to work as traders, craftsmen, and laborers.[23] The annual population of Manila fluctuated throughout the century, as Chinese migrants

Table 7   Chinese ship arrivals in Manila, 1580–1699

DECADE	TOTAL SHIPS RECORDED	YEARLY AVERAGE
1580s	221*	25
1590s	148*	25
1600s	246	25
1610s	102*	26
1620s	44*	11
1630s	259	26
1640s	153	15
1650s	66†	7
1660s	46†	5
1670s	31*†	3
1680s	88†	9
1690s	155	16
TOTAL	**1559**	**15**

Note: Based on Contaduría records in the Archivo General de Indias as compiled by Juan Gil, *Los Chinos en Manila: Siglos XVI y XVII* (Lisboa: Centro Científico e Cultural de Macau, 2011), 574–639.
*Data missing for the years: 1584, 1590, 1592, 1593, 1594, 1613, 1614, 1615, 1617, 1618, 1619, 1621, 1622, 1623, 1624, 1625, 1626, and 1674.
†No ships arrived in the years 1657, 1667, 1668, 1669, 1670, 1671, 1672, and 1683.

Table 8   Chinese population of Manila, 1584–1662

YEAR	POPULATION	YEAR	POPULATION	YEAR	POPULATION
1584	3,500[1]	1617	11,113[9]	1630	10,533[9]
1589	"About 4,000"[2]	1618	10,423[9]	1631	13,607[9]
1597	"more than 8,000"[3]	1619	13,048[10]	1632	14,460[9]
1600	15,000[4]	1620	14,795[9]	1633	12,639[9]
1604	457[5]	1621	13,115[9]	1634	12,823[9]
1605	1,648[6]	1622	15,665[9]	1635	21,474[9]
1606	8,181[7]	1623	13,310[9]	1636	"more than 25,000"[9]
1607	15,000[8]	1624	9,824[9]	1639	40,000[11]
1612	11,394[9]	1625	7,748[9]	1640	7000[12]
1613	9,735[9]	1626	11,501[9]	1649	15,000[13]
1614	9,950[9]	1627	11,182[9]	1662	14,000[14]
1615	8,964[9]	1628	11,180[9]		
1616	9,400[9]	1629	10,788[9]		

[1] Archivo General de Indias (hereafter AGI), Audiencia de Filipinas (hereafter Filipinas), leg. 18A, ramo 2, núm. 8

[2] "Letter from Santiago de Vera to Felipe II," in *The Philippine Islands, 1493–1803* (hereafter B&R), trans. and ed. Emma Helen Blair and James Alexander Robertson, 55 vols. (Cleveland, OH: A. H. Clark, 1903–9), vol. 7, 89

[3] AGI, Filipinas, leg. 18B, ramo 7, núm. 87

[4] "Early Years of the Dutch in the East Indies," B&R, vol. 15, 305

[5] AGI, Filipinas, leg. 19, ramo 7, núms. 100, 105

[6] AGI, Filipinas, leg. 19, ramo 7, núms. 100, 105

[7] AGI, Filipinas, leg. 19, ramo 7, núms. 100, 105

[8] "Anua de la Provincia de Filipinas de la Compañía de IHS del año de 1607," Real Academia de la Historia, 9/2667, doc. 10

[9] AGI, Filipinas, leg. 8, ramo 3, núm. 55

[10] AGI, Filipinas, leg. 8, ramo 3, núm. 55. In 1619, the total number of licenses in Manila was 10,136, with an additional 2,912 licenses attributed to Chinese living in the provinces.

[11] Juan Gil, *Los Chinos en Manila: Siglos XVI y XVII* (Lisboa: Centro Científico e Cultural de Macau, 2011), 506

[12] Gil, *Los Chinos en Manila*, 506

[13] "Description of Filipinas Islands," B&R, vol. 36, 204

[14] "Avisos necesarios para la conservación de estas islas [Filipinas] y su cristiandad," Biblioteca Nacional de España, mss. 11014, fols. 32r–37v

arrived and left according to the fortunes of the trade, or as a result of the periodic pogroms and expulsions conducted by the Spanish (see table 8). At its height—on the eve of the massacre of 1639 to 1640—the Chinese population of Manila reached forty thousand, making Manila possibly the largest Chinese city outside of China in this period.

While Manila was important for Fujian, it was by no means unique. Throughout the seventeenth century, Fujianese merchants maintained an extensive trading network that spread across mainland and maritime Asia and into the Indian Ocean.[24] The Selden Map—produced between 1606 and 1623 for a leading Fujianese merchant—gives us the most detailed view of this extensive maritime trading network, while also demonstrating the importance of the Manila silver

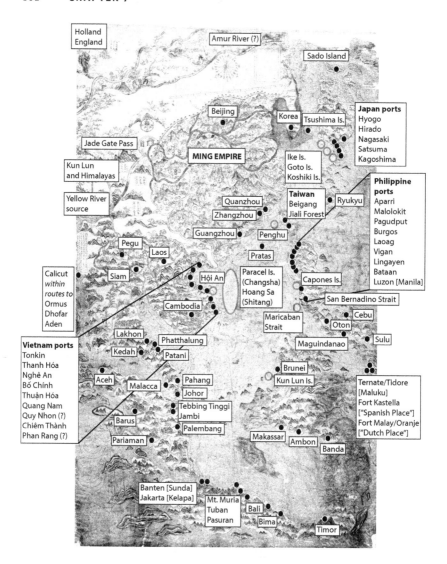

Holland
England

Amur River (?)

Sado Island

Beijing

Korea Tsushima Is.

Japan ports
Hyogo
Hirado
Nagasaki
Satsuma
Kagoshima

Jade Gate Pass

MING EMPIRE

Ike Is.
Goto Is.
Koshiki Is.

Kun Lun
and Himalayas

Yellow River
source

Quanzhou
Zhangzhou

Taiwan
Beigang
Jiali Forest

Ryukyu

Philippine ports
Aparri
Malolokit
Pagudput
Burgos
Laoag
Vigan
Lingayen
Bataan
Luzon [Manila]

Pegu
Laos

Guangzhou

Penghu

Pratas

Calicut
*within
routes to*
Ormus
Dhofar
Aden

Siam

Hội An

Paracel Is.
(Changsha)
Hoang Sa
(Shitang)

Capones Is.

San Bernadino Strait

Cambodia

Maricaban
Strait

Cebu

Oton

Vietnam ports
Tonkin
Thanh Hóa
Nghệ An
Bố Chính
Thuận Hóa
Quang Nam
Quy Nhon (?)
Chiêm Thành
Phan Rang (?)

Lakhon

Kedah

Phatthalung

Patani

Maguindanao

Sulu

Aceh

Malacca

Pahang

Johor

Brunei

Kun Lun Is.

Ternate/Tidore
[Maluku]
Fort Kastella
["Spanish Place"]
Fort Malay/Oranje
["Dutch Place"]

Barus

Tebbing Tinggi
Jambi

Palembang

Makassar

Ambon

Banda

Pariaman

Banten [Sunda]
Jakarta [Kelapa]

Mt. Muria
Tuban
Pasuran

Bali

Bima

Timor

FIGURE 7.1.   The Selden Map of China, with transcription and translation by Robert Batchelor. Solid black dots indicate a labeled circle on the original; the open circles indicate islands that are labeled but lack a circle. Oxford, Bodleian Library, MS Selden Supra 105 (© R. Batchelor. Map reproduced with permission from the Bodleian Library).

market.[25] Additionally, Fujianese traders made use of extensive trading networks within mainland China as well as overseas. Silk and porcelain remained the highest value trade commodities. Silk was sourced from the lower Yangtze region and then spun into fabric in Fujian, while porcelain was imported from Jingdezhen in Jiangxi Province.[26] China annually produced approximately 2,500 tons of silk and exported approximately a third of this to Japan, Manila, and India.[27] A plethora of skilled industries developed in Fujian to support this maritime trade, from shipbuilding to agriculture and mining.[28]

Over the course of the seventeenth century, trade within this extensive maritime network came to be dominated by particular powerful families or clans, including the clan of Li Dan, who may have commissioned the Selden Map.[29] Yet, the most powerful Fujianese traders were the Zheng clan of southern Fujian, who controlled up to 90 percent of the maritime trade by the second half of the seventeenth century.[30] Clans like the Zhengs purchased or acquired bonded servants—called godsons, but often unrelated to the merchant family—who would act as representatives or intermediaries for the family in foreign trading ports. One Chinese chronicler described this arrangement as "Some (people) adopt others as their sons. They do not feel ashamed to let them enter their own clans. When they are in merchant families they are sent all over the world with commercial capital. They travel through many kinds of dangers, some will disappear in enormous storms or fight for one fleeting moment of life with the wind and waves. Their real sons, however, can enjoy its profits without physical danger."[31] Other traders relied on borrowed capital or investments from wealthier individuals in China to finance their operations.[32] All of these arrangements had an impact on the social life of Chinese Manila.

The power and influence of these Fujianese merchant families also meant that the fortunes of Manila fluctuated according to the political situation in mainland China. In the mid-seventeenth century, China—and particularly Fujian—was thrown into a turbulent civil war surrounding the Manchu conquest of China, wherein the Ming dynasty was overthrown by the Qing. The Zheng clan in particular initially remained loyal to the Ming, leading first to war and then outright repression in the province of Fujian. While the Zheng and their followers fled to Taiwan under the leadership of Koxinga, the Qing imposed a brutal maritime ban on Fujian, forcefully evacuating the coastal population up to thirty li (approximately nine miles) from the coast and in the process leading to more than a hundred thousand deaths.[33] Trade in Manila in this period consequently dwindled almost to nothing, with no ships arriving from China between 1667 and 1672, and only thirty-one ships in total for the rest of the 1670s (see table 7). Trade only resumed once again following the successful Qing conquest of Taiwan and the defeat of the Zheng clan in 1683.[34]

From Segregation to Massacre

Manila's fortunes thus were intertwined with Fujian. Very soon after its founding, Manila became a bustling, populous center for Chinese trade, attracting tens of thousands of Fujianese migrants. The Chinese community of Manila—known as the "Sangleys" by the Spanish[35]—was quartered in a separate neighborhood known as the Parian. Located outside of the Spanish Intramuros, but within cannon shot of the city walls, the Parian was founded, razed, and reconstructed numerous times throughout the late sixteenth and seventeenth centuries.[36] It became the thriving commercial hub of the city, where all kinds of trades and supplies were bought and sold. All of this commerce was controlled by Manila's Chinese community. From the outset, Fujianese merchants transported more than just high-value trading commodities; they also brought much-needed supplies including wheat and flour, as well as horses, cattle, and munitions such as saltpeter, sulfur, mercury, copper, iron, and lead.[37] A report from 1588 noted that the ships arriving from China each year carried two hundred thousand pesos worth of merchandise and more than ten thousand pesos in supplies such as flour, sugar, biscuit, butter, oranges, nuts, chestnuts, pine nuts, figs, plums, pomegranates, pears and other fruits, bacons, and hams—enough to sustain the city all year.[38] Moreover, many of the Chinese migrants helped to construct the burgeoning city of Manila, building Spanish houses, churches, and even the city walls that were designed principally to segregate the Spanish from the Chinese.[39] In addition to monopolizing the city's commerce, the Chinese quickly came to occupy all of the skilled trades in the city. Three censuses of Chinese commerce compiled in 1689, 1690, and 1700—although statistically incomplete—indicate the array of trades occupied by members of the Chinese community (see table 9).[40] Such was the industry of the Chinese that many impressed Spanish observers believed no task was beyond them. As Fr. Plácido de Angulo wrote:

> One Sangley might now be a shoemaker, and in the morning if the whim takes him at daybreak a sculptor and silversmith, and among them, this is very customary. All of them know how to count, read, and write in their characters, even if they are the most uncouth fisherman that is never separated from the fishing nets or his boat. Such an outstanding capacity is accompanied by an inexplicable and natural curiosity that these Sangleys have to see everything, walk everywhere, know everything and meet everyone.[41]

In the early days of Spanish colonization, these functions performed by the Chinese were viewed by the Spanish as greatly aiding the establishment of a viable city and trading port. An early description of the population of Manila from 1588 said that there were six hundred Chinese living in the Parian with one hundred and fifty shops between them. Another hundred Chinese lived in vacant land across the river—many of these were married and had converted

Table 9   Trades occupied by the Chinese, 1689, 1690, and 1700

TRADES	1689	1690	1700
Merchants	71	73	73
Silk and cloth merchants			
Craftsmen	191	183	488
Apothecaries, barbers, blacksmiths, box makers, brickmakers, carpenters, dyers, earthenware manufacturers, foundry workers, locksmiths, milliners, ropemakers, sawyers, shoemakers, silversmiths, swordsmiths, tailors, weavers			
Vendors of consumables	195	179	235
Beef merchants, chicken merchants, confectioners, fish merchants, grocers, pork merchants, potato merchants, sugar merchants, wine sellers, and various other vendors of food and drink			
Vendors of other supplies	110	95	299
Booksellers, brass merchants, brick merchants, oil sellers, peddlers, pottery merchants, rattan merchants, straw merchants, tobacconists, wax vendors, wood vendors, and other assorted shopkeepers			
Producers	73	81	301
Agricultural workers, cooks, fishermen, gardeners, rice farmers, slaughterhouse workers, woodcutters, and other types of farmers			
Porters and boatmen	112	59	107
Boatmen, carters of water, porters, runners, and others engaged in transport			
TOTAL	752	670	1,503

Note: The purpose of the table is to represent the diversity of services occupations that were performed by Chinese, rather than as an accurate statistical representation of the Chinese merchant and laboring classes of Manila. This data is taken from three censuses of Chinese merchants and laborers conducted during the expulsion process initiated in 1686 (as discussed later in the chapter). While the data provided during this period is unprecedented for the insights it gives into the variety of jobs performed by Chinese within Manila's local economy, there are some problems with these sources. First, it is likely that the first two years are an incomplete reflection of the total Chinese population, since they were produced to quantify outstanding trading accounts and additionally do not include the Christian Chinese population (as is the case for 1700). Second, these censuses were conducted at a time when the Chinese population of Manila was numerically less than at most other points in the century. Source: Archivo General de Indias, Filipinas, leg. 202.

to Christianity—while three hundred fishermen, market gardeners, hunters, weavers, bricklayers, lime kiln workers, carpenters, and smiths lived outside of the city between the river and the sea. Within the Parian, there were many tailors, shoemakers, bakers, carpenters, candlemakers, pastry chefs, pharmacists, painters, and silversmiths, among others. In the city, there was a public market that every day sold foods including chickens, pigs, ducks, deer, boars, buffalo, fish, bread, as well as firewood and other supplies from China.[42]

Yet, over the course of the century, such favorable portrayals of the commercial life of Manila became exceedingly rare. Increasingly, Spanish officials described the Chinese as maintaining a stranglehold over the commercial life of the city. Their domination of the skilled trades and city's provisions was seen as a sincere threat to Spanish sovereignty not only within Manila but throughout the archipelago. An anonymous report written in the 1660s gave a detailed account of how commerce in Manila was conducted, with the author concluding that the situation was "the most abominable to God and his people that could be imagined."[43] The author wrote that each year ships came from China laden with silks, linens, blankets, ceramics, iron, and other goods. These ships also brought many Chinese migrants who would sell their merchandise to the *vecinos* through the hands of other Chinese, who were their godsons. The Chinese exhibited great unity, obedience, and wisdom. They had their own councilors or consuls, who operated in great secrecy, conducting their meetings at night so that the Spanish could not observe them. During these meetings they determined the prices at which goods would be sold and ensured that everyone in the Parian observed this with uniformity, beating any who broke the monopoly by selling their wares at a cheaper price. The Spanish were obliged to buy from them and, by these means, they came to control both silver and supplies as if they were really the owners of the islands. They bought all of the necessary supplies from the indios or the Spanish and were able to communicate with the indios with greater friendship than the Spaniards.[44] The author concluded that it was almost as if the Spanish were governed by the Chinese and were their tributaries, and not the other way around.[45]

This shift in attitude occurred alongside escalating tensions between the booming Chinese community and the Spanish, which culminated in the rebellion and massacre of 1603. The events of 1603 were not without their precedent. Even prior to the rebellion, many Spanish officials believed that it was wise to limit the numbers of Chinese in the city thanks to their flagrant violation of Spanish laws and lack of respect for Spanish sovereignty over the city.[46] Moreover, some believed the Chinese were prone to acts of violence and treachery. Just three years after the city was founded, the Chinese pirate Limahong attempted to invade and capture Manila.[47] Following this, several groups of Chinese sailors were involved in a series of shipboard mutinies between 1593 and 1597, in which they killed a considerable number of Spanish soldiers.[48] During the mutiny of 1593, Governor Gomez Pérez Dasmariñas had his throat slit by Chinese sailors on board a vessel bound for Ternate.[49] Such acts, combined with the increasing migration of Chinese into Manila and their control of the material supplies of the city, generated great fear among the Spanish. When three Mandarins arrived in Manila in May 1603—looking for a fabled mountain of gold that was said to lie in Cavite—many Spaniards believed this to be a sign that China was preparing to invade and seize control of Manila. Although the Mandarins left soon after, Governor Acuña ordered an immediate increase in military preparations, including the construction of new fortifications.[50]

From the perspective of the Chinese population, by contrast, such actions indicated that the Spanish were preparing for war; and, moreover, that they were the objects of Spanish paranoia. Chinese stonemasons and construction workers set to building the very walls that were designed to keep them out of the city and helped to forge the artillery and munitions that would ultimately be trained on the Parian.[51] Combined with other forms of control, the Spanish were clearly asserting their authority and power within the city. Such actions made many in the Parian nervous. The rebellion which broke out in October 1603 was both a culmination of the heightened tension between the two communities and a contestation over who really controlled Manila.

The rebellion began on October 3, when a large group of Chinese—the audiencia estimated them at ten thousand to twelve thousand—set fire to several houses outside the city walls and then fortified themselves in the district of Tondo, north of the city.[52] The following day, the governor sent a contingent of soldiers led by Don Luis Dasmariñas in search of the rebels; however, the Spanish forces were insufficient, and they were hampered by the marshy terrain. More than a hundred Spanish soldiers died. On October 5, the Chinese armed themselves and "with great force and violence" they attacked the city. Despite their comparatively large numbers, many died during the ensuing battle. The Parian was then set on fire and the Chinese were forced to retreat before dividing into three parties and fleeing into the interior. They were then pursued relentlessly over the next two weeks by Spanish soldiers and a sizable army of indigenous soldiers, who slaughtered all of those they encountered. Those who were not killed during this fighting were sentenced to serve in the galleys.[53] The final death toll is unclear. Estimates of the number of Chinese involved in this rebellion varied widely, ranging from ten thousand to twenty-one thousand;[54] by the close of these events, the Chinese population of Manila had been effectively reduced to just 457, indicating the scale of the slaughter and dispersal.[55]

The events of 1603 set a pattern of interaction between Spaniards and Chinese. Although many officials resolved to never allow the population of the Parian to swell to prerebellion levels, by 1606 there were 8,181 Chinese residents in Manila, and this had increased to more than 25,000 in 1636.[56] The reality was that while the Spanish feared the Chinese community, the city could not function without their labor and commerce. Consequently, over the course of the century, a number of economic and cultural strategies were introduced to try to impose Spanish colonial order. Religious conversion, in particular, was promoted as a way for the Chinese to demonstrate loyalty to the Spanish regime. Despite these efforts, Chinese Manila continued to operate under its own laws

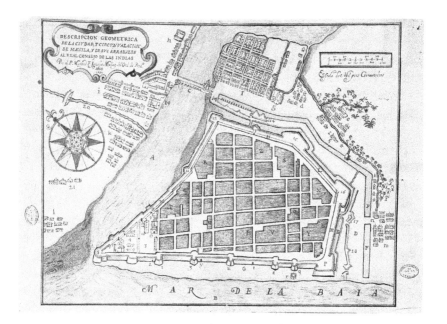

FIGURE 7.2. Descripción geométrica de la ciudad y circunvalación de Manila y de sus arrabales . . . [Geometric description of the city and encirclement of Manila and of its suburbs . . .], 1671. Note: the densely populated Parian occupies the space to the east of the walled city, located at the top of the map. España. Ministerio de Cultura, Archivo General de Indias, Mapas y Planos, Filipinas, núm. 10.

and jurisdictions. Most Chinese residents interacted with the Spanish sphere to the extent that it benefited them commercially. Beyond that, they continued to practice their own customs and very few converted to Christianity.

The most obvious method of control introduced by the Spanish was the forced segregation of the city. The Parian was established in 1581 as Manila's Chinese quarter, set outside the city walls, which acted as an imposed barrier to limit and regulate Chinese–Spanish interaction.[57] The Parian was also clearly designed as a way of containing Chinese interaction with indigenous communities. Many Spanish religious and secular officials believed that the Chinese presented a corrupting influence on the neophyte indio communities, and therefore it was advantageous to place limitations on where they were allowed to live, work, and trade.[58] At the same time, as the century wore on, the Parian was also considered a matter of internal security, to prevent against the threat of Chinese rebellion. The Parian lay just outside the city walls, with artillery aimed at the Chinese at all times, and constant sentinels keeping watch by night and day.[59] While Chinese artisans and laborers did enter the city to trade with the Spanish, they entered through militarized gates defended by a moat and portcullis.

Segregation was accompanied by economic regulations designed to control commercial activities and migration flows into the city. The first such regulation was the *pancada*, introduced in 1586. The *pancada* was an attempt to engage in wholesale bargaining with the Chinese—wherein one Spanish representative would deal with just one Chinese representative and negotiate a price for purchase of all of the goods imported by all merchants that year. This system was intended to undermine Chinese attempts to raise prices. However, the *pancada* was quickly abandoned in favor of a more traditional free-market *feria* (trade fair).[60] Taxation on imported goods (*almojarifazgo*) and mandatory license fees for all Chinese wishing to disembark into the city were also introduced.[61] Both regulations required the inspection of ships arriving each year, and a waystation was established at Mariveles for this purpose, with officials instructed to take a registry of the merchandise and crew. The license fee was set at eight pesos and two reales and was applied indiscriminately to all Chinese in the Parian.[62] In the 1630s, a second license fee—worth ten pesos and two reales—was introduced for Chinese residents outside of the Parian who wished to engage in farming or trade in the provinces.[63] Both taxation and license fees were enormously lucrative for the Crown.[64] Licenses in particular often accounted for the single greatest contribution to Crown revenues, greatly exceeding the tribute collected from indios through royal encomiendas.[65] With these economic advantages came many incentives for extortion, corruption, and evasion. As early as 1605, Hernando de los Rios Coronel argued that officials engaged in inspecting vessels extorted illegal fees from the Chinese.[66] Similar reports were repeated in 1627.[67] More concerning to the authorities were reports of Chinese flaunting the regulations through organized smuggling operations. In the 1660s many Chinese were said to have occupied tracts of land in Mariveles, where they were able to wait for the arrival of the ships from China and give advice to the city that they were arriving, notifying other Chinese of the goods that they were carrying. Because of this, they were able to act as spies and to hide many of the goods in the ships, smuggling them into the Parian little by little, so that when their ships were inspected they did not have to pay taxes. In the same way, many Chinese migrants disembarked and hid among Chinese communities in the provinces before traveling on to Manila in order to avoid paying the license fee.[68]

Segregation was similarly only partially successful. Since the Chinese controlled the city's commerce, the city walls could not prevent daily intermingling between Spanish and Chinese communities.[69] Authorities were particularly concerned about the vice of gambling and poor Spaniards—largely soldiers—consorting with the Chinese.[70] Furthermore, Fr. Ricci accused the Chinese of engaging in the "unspeakable sin" with the poorest Spanish soldiers, "the scum of New Spain [that] come to stay in these islands, the thieves, the criminals, the restless, the expelled, the apostates."[71] Since it was impossible not to rely on such men sent from New Spain, they reasoned that homosexuality could only be prevented by removing the Chinese.[72]

Most concerning to the officials, however, was the intermingling of Chinese and indio communities. The Chinese developed independent commercial and employment relationships with local indigenous communities, typically exchanging commercial wares like cloth, blankets, needles, and tobacco for local produce like chickens, rice, eggs, fruits, and vegetables.[73] In 1613, the City of Manila reported that a parallel trade economy had emerged between Chinese merchants and indigenous communities that they believed was severely damaging to the Spanish republic since indios were less inclined to produce their own goods when they could purchase them from Chinese merchants.[74] The 1663 Council complained that the Chinese would often pay the indios much more—even twice as much—as the Spaniards did for their produce. They argued that when a Spaniard went into an indio village to buy chickens, he would find that there were none for sale; whereas if the Chinese went to the same town, all of the doors would open to them and they would be offered the best produce that they had.[75] Additionally, many of the guilds employed indio laborers in exchange for daily wages. In 1682, Fr. Cristóbal Pedroche described Chinese masters hiring indios as woodcutters, stonemasons, carpenters, and silversmiths. Under this arrangement, Pedroche argued, the Chinese, without ever working, earned ten pesos a month, while the indio believed that he was free and well paid.[76]

Increased interaction between the predominantly male Chinese population and indigenous communities led naturally to intermarriage between the two.[77] Spanish missionaries attempted to enforce a restriction on marriage only between those who had converted to Christianity, but they could ultimately do little about widespread concubinage. Attempts were made throughout the century to limit married and Christianized Chinese to particular settlements outside the Parian, particularly Binondo and Santa Cruz.[78] In 1678, the audiencia went further than that, arguing that no wife should be permitted to live within the Parian and neither should the wives be allowed to enter into their shops or the alleys of the Parian. The same should be observed with the Christian Chinese, prohibiting them from entering the houses of other Chinese or the alleyways or doorways of their houses.[79] Yet, the repetition of these regulations so late in the century only further indicates the degree to which segregation policies had failed.

Although royal policy was for all non-Christian Chinese to be confined to Manila's Parian, licenses were granted early on for the Chinese to live within the provinces.[80] Many of these Chinese were engaged in farming, particularly in the provinces surrounding Manila, like Bulacan and Laguna de Bay.[81] In these locations, they often rented land and were able to supply rice and other produce to the city. Others engaged in commerce, introducing new and unregulated commercial relationships into indigenous communities. Fr. Angulo wrote that many Chinese were attracted to the provinces by the opportunity of tapping into local produce markets. He believed they obtained licenses through bribery and fraud. Once in the province, the Chinese would set up shops, selling items of little value, like tobacco, wine, snacks, and trinkets, through which they gained a familiarity with the local community. However, in time, these shops became the center of commerce in the community. Angulo argued that in this way the Chinese learned all about the goings-on in the town and were able to monopolize trade, sending their earnings and produce to their associates in Manila, where they were resold at a profit. Additionally, Chinese became creditors within the town, lending indios rice when they were short, and selling food and drink on credit in exchange for a cut of the harvest. Angulo concluded that even in the provinces, "the Sangleys, as foreigners, work and can do anything as if they were natives, and the Spaniards themselves, as natives, know nothing and can do nothing, as if they were foreigners."[82]

Spanish officials hoped that a swift conversion of a large number of Chinese would allow Manila to be less reliant on the labor of non-Christian Chinese, referred to as *infieles*.[83] However, this never really eventuated despite concerted attempts and the creation of commercial incentives. The Dominicans were the principal order active in religious conversion in the Parian and Binondo, while the Jesuits had jurisdiction over the Chinese community of Santa Cruz.[84] Christian converts were granted elevated and beneficial positions within colonial society. They were viewed by the Spanish as more respectable and trustworthy, often acting as intermediaries between Spanish and Chinese communities, and some were able to build wealthy commercial empires through these means.[85] After 1627, Christianized Chinese were not required to pay license fees and were reserved from paying tribute for ten years.[86] Despite this, the Christian Chinese population never increased much beyond five hundred.[87] In the 1680s, the archbishop of Manila reported that a survey of the Parian had found no more than three hundred baptized Chinese, but virtually none of them were considered to be genuinely practicing Christians.[88] Some blamed this situation on the controversial requirement of Christian converts to cut their hair—a practice that was considered a humiliation and provoked numerous protests as well as theological debates that continued through the century.[89] In Chinese traditions, maintaining uncut hair was not only seen as necessary for personal health but was also a sign of loyalty to the emperor. Chinese men with short hair were therefore marked as criminals and shunned from Chinese society.[90] Perhaps because of this, the willingness of Chinese converts to cut their hair became a marker of loyalty and a measure of their commitment to their new religion.

At the same time, Dominican missionaries harbored distrust even of those Chinese who did convert to Christianity, believing that their conversion was often motivated principally by temporal and material ends rather than a sincere devotion to Christ. The Chinese converted in order to be granted the right to marry an india, to gain patronage within the Spanish community, which could help in conducting business in Manila, or to gain exemption from paying the license fee.[91] Many Chinese believed that adopting a Christian name allowed them to conduct their commerce more easily and expanded their commercial opportunities.[92] Fr. Jacinto Samper claimed that some Chinese went to confession in order to obtain papers that they then sold to others, while others made up sins that they had never committed since they regarded confession as a hollow and ridiculous action. He noted that every Sunday more than a hundred Christian Chinese came to the Parian from the farmlands or towns closest to the city to hear mass, but they only came under duress and many of them were so bored and frightened that on Sunday morning they hid so as to be free of the hated mass.[93] Fr. Vittorio Ricci noted that temporal motivations behind conversion meant that when the Chinese returned to China, they abandoned their faith and recommenced their idolatrous ways: "in Manila as in Manila, in China as in China." If they were genuine converts, he argued, they would continue to practice as Christians in China, converting their wives, children, servants, and family members; but this did not happen. Rather, many in China were greatly embarrassed to be Christians.[94]

Thus, despite the best efforts of Spanish missionaries, the majority of Chinese in Manila remained unconverted to Christianity and continued to practice their own religious customs.[95] The lunar new year was a focal point for celebration in the Parian, and many of the activities taking place in this period deeply offended Spanish missionaries.[96] Fr. Cristóbal Pedroche said that during this time the Chinese believed that they had to please the spirits and idols in order to have good fortune and profit in the coming year. They made offerings of food to the sky and the earth, for which they went in search of particular things like duck eggs, the heads of pigs or goats, chickens, and wine, which they offered up with some brief, reverent words. During the lunar new year, they invited many of their countrymen to eat together and considered it the greatest discourtesy to refuse these invitations. Pedroche understood that almost all of the Christian Chinese attended these ceremonies and believed it a matter of great embarrassment to reveal that they were Christians.[97] These practices were even more concerning to Spanish missionaries for the impact that they had on the indigenous population. Ricci noted that, although the missionaries and priests preached to them and taught them that there was punishment or reward in the afterlife, they saw that the Chinese ignored this and enjoyed themselves in this life and that they did better than the Spaniards. The Chinese easily persuaded the indios that they did not need to go to confess their sins to the priests because they had no power to absolve them since they were just ordinary men like everyone else. Ricci concluded that because of this many indios continued eating and drinking and sinning and finally died without being pardoned for their sins.[98]

The fears expressed by leading Spanish clergy and royal officials were both a response to the growth and cultural influence of the Chinese community and a reflection of their own impotence in the face of Chinese control over the local economy. The resolution to this conundrum was the ongoing militarization of the city: the Spanish could only assert their power over the city through the permanent threat of violence. The massacre of 1603 therefore set a precedent for the next century. The next time the Chinese rebelled—in 1639—Governor Hurtado de Corcuera responded by ordering a wholesale pogrom of the Chinese community, ordering his soldiers to hunt down and put to sword tens of thousands of people.

The massacres of 1603 and 1639 were the ultimate response to Spanish fears of the Chinese. Purging the city of the Chinese threat was the only means by which the Spanish could truly impose their authority over the city. Yet, at the same time, these periodic pogroms revealed that Manila could not function without Chinese labor. After each massacre, the economy of Manila ground to a halt. Supplies ran short and there was no one to fix the fortifications damaged in war.[99] Moreover, many worried about the impact on trading relations.[100] Consequently, after each massacre, the Parian was allowed to grow once again, rejuvenated by new waves of migrants.

These cycles of massacre and renewal entrenched hostilities at the same time that Chinese control of the economy was cemented. In 1677, Fr. Vittorio Ricci described the Chinese hold over Manila's economy as "an infernal monopoly" designed to swindle the Spanish of all their silver.[101] The Chinese had come to be masters and owners of all commerce, large and small, "so that not even a needle can be found but that it is in their hands."[102] No other nation would believe that the Spaniards—who should be the masters of the lands—had allowed themselves to be subject to such a "vile, traitorous, disloyal, idolatrous and atheistic riffraff with such notable damages to His Majesty's vassals."[103] A report written in the 1660s similarly concluded by asking in what other land would people entrust their meat and bread with their greatest enemies?[104] Many feared another uprising unless population controls were put in place.[105]

Behind many of these Spanish complaints was a deep racism coupled with resentment for the Chinese pursuit of profit through commercial enterprise. Many observers wrote of the humble origins of Chinese migrants, describing them as arriving in Manila with nothing more than the clothes on their backs and therefore needing to "rob" the Spanish of all of their silver in order to survive.[106] Fr. Angulo argued that "almost all of [the Fujianese] were fishermen, seditious men, runaways, thieves, harmful people, who go to other lands in search of riches that they cannot find in theirs."[107] Vittorio Ricci wrote bitterly that the Chinese only ever acted in the pursuit of profit and that their gains were excessive.[108] At the heart of these criticisms was both a judgment about who constituted the "right" sort of Chinese migrant and a lament that the Spanish seemed unable to compete with the commercial practices of the Chinese in the Parian. Most Spanish officials believed that wealth accumulation was reserved for the noble classes. Yet, no matter how hard they tried, the Spanish routinely lost their silver to the Chinese through the acts of everyday trade and commerce. Ricci and many others, therefore, felt that matters would be greatly improved if interaction with the Chinese was restricted only to the elite merchants who engaged in the profitable galleon trade that enhanced Spanish wealth and furthered their interests.[109]

At the same time, the Spanish were genuinely afraid of the lower-class Chinese. As Ricci wrote in 1677, "by their hands we eat, with great risk to ourselves, . . . [and] they could in one day finish with all of the Spaniards if they poisoned the bread, because they are the bakers of the republic and in their hands and will also is the rice, the meat, the birds, the fish, the eggs, the vegetables, the legumes, the fruit and all of the rest needed for the sustenance of human nature."[110] Fear of poisoning was common throughout the century. In 1663, Chinese rice farmers were accused of having mixed their rice with ashes and lime, leading many soldiers to become sick. In 1682, Fr. Jacinto Samper suggested that a number of Chinese had bought poison to put in the snacks sold in the Parian.[111] The bakers were routinely singled out for suspicion, accused of engaging in dirty tricks by mixing seed in the flour to increase the weight—and therefore the price—of the loaves of bread they sold.[112] Numerous regulations were passed to try to control the bakers, placing restrictions on where they worked and slept.[113] The most serious incident involving the bakers occurred in 1686 when they were accused of placing shards of glass in the city's bread supply with the intention of murdering the Spanish. The investigation into this case initially resulted in all of the Chinese bakers being dismissed from their bakeries and replaced. However, when the city's bread supply fell short in the ensuing days, the Chinese were promptly reinstated and the investigation was formally annulled.[114]

Despite the brutality, Spanish attempts at controlling the Chinese population through violence, segregation, economic regulation, and religious conversion largely failed. Throughout the seventeenth century, the Chinese continued to monopolize the city's economy, they consorted freely with indigenous communities, formed relationships with local women, and showed a disinterest in Christianity. In many ways, the Parian was a separate city to Spanish Manila. While the Spanish tried to enforce their authority in the city, they remained unable to establish domination over the Chinese. This impotence led to escalating fears of the Chinese and their control over the local economy and food supply. What might the Chinese do with this power? At what point would they conclude that Spanish sovereignty over Manila was against their interests?

The Economics of Expulsion

All of this helps to explain the panic that arose in May 1662 when Fr. Vittorio Ricci arrived bearing a letter from the Zheng warlord.[115] Koxinga's ultimatum was the strongest sign to date that Manila was a city that belonged as much to the Fujianese—and to the Zheng clan in particular—as to the Spanish. Many of the merchants in Manila were allied to the Zheng clan. After nearly two decades of fighting a losing war against the Qing in Fujian, Koxinga had been forced to retreat to Taiwan. He was sorely in need of both financial and military resources, and it was natural that he would call on his extensive network across Southeast Asia for this purpose. As the largest Fujianese settlement anywhere outside of China, Manila was naturally the first port of call. At the same time, however, Koxinga's threats clearly indicate that he questioned the legitimacy of Spanish rule over Manila. His threatened invasion in 1662 was articulated as a response to decades of abuses that the Chinese of Manila—his vassals—had suffered at the hands of the Spanish. "Now your little, or mean Kingdom," Koxinga wrote in his letter, "has wronged and oppressed my subjects, and my trading *champanes* . . . provoking discord and encouraging revenge."[116] At this tense juncture, foremost in everyone's minds—Spanish, Sangley, and Zheng—were the two previous rebellions of 1603 and 1639 that had both resulted in the deaths of thousands of Chinese. With the arrival of Koxinga's embassy, Spanish fears of renewed rebellion in the Parian were equaled by Chinese fears of repeated violence at the hands of Spanish forces.

Although Koxinga's invasion never took place, the threat alone was enough to provoke a serious emergency in Spanish Manila. Both secular and religious authorities agreed that living under the shadow of this threat was unsustainable; therefore, the Chinese population of Manila had to—once more—be purged by one means or another.[117] The idea of a generalized expulsion was one of the most enduring legacies of this period.[118] Ethnic expulsions were not a new concept for Spanish administrators, who had the precedents of the expulsion of Jewish and Muslim populations following the conquest of Granada in 1492, and the Morisco expulsion edict of 1609 to call on in making their proposal.[119] Authorities in Manila nevertheless had to contend with the fact that the entire colonial economy relied on the labor, skilled trades, and commercial networks controlled by the Chinese. Spanish attempts to assert control over the city were ultimately frustrated by this simple reality—without the Chinese, the colony would not survive.

The original proposal to expel the Chinese was made by a council of religious, secular, and military authorities, convened immediately after the arrival of Koxinga's embassy.[120] Yet, the chief proponent of this proposal was in fact Vittorio Ricci who in 1677 penned his "Discurso y parecer en que se demuestra que no conviene que la nación de China que llaman sangleyes habite ni viva de asiento en las islas Filipinas."[121] In this extensive tract, Ricci put forward six arguments in favor of the complete expulsion of the Chinese from the Philippines, focusing on the spiritual damage associated with the Chinese community, the history of rebellion in Manila, and their control of the local economy and particularly of the silver that came from New Spain each year. For Ricci, the Chinese were greedy idolaters who taught the local indigenous population sinful and heathen customs and who were prone to sedition and rebellion. He saw no value in their continued presence in the city, arguing that while the commerce with China was essential to the colony, this could be limited to specific times of the year and Chinese migration to Manila could be effectively ended.

Ricci's arguments were supported wholeheartedly by Governor Juan de Vargas, the audiencia, and all of the religious orders,[122] with the notable exception of the Jesuits who published a number of anonymous tracts refuting many of Ricci's points.[123] The arguments put forward by Ricci and his supporters were viewed by the Council of Indies, as well as a special theological council convened in Madrid, before a decree was finally issued in 1686, authorizing the expulsion to take place. The decree instructed the governor and the audiencia to ensure that all those Chinese that were not reduced to the Christian faith within two months should leave the islands within a specified time determined by the governor and audiencia, but to be completed as quickly as possible. Additionally, the Chinese that came to trade should only be allowed to remain for the duration of the trade fair and the time that was necessary to prepare their return voyage, without allowing any of them to remain unless they wished to convert to Christianity.[124]

In part, the idea of a generalized expulsion of Chinese was considered feasible and desirable in the 1670s and 1680s because trade with China had diminished dramatically owing to the wars between the Qing and the Zheng clans and the Qing policy of forcefully depopulating coastal Fujian.[125] After the massacre of 1662—which is recounted in detail in chapter 1—the Chinese population of Manila had not recovered as before, with fewer vessels arriving in this period and consequently fewer migrants (see table 7). Ricci and his counterparts believed that it would be wholly possible for Manila to survive with a drastically reduced population in the Parian comprising primarily Christianized Chinese. Central to this was a belief that migration would be restricted to only the right sort of Chinese—largely wealthy merchant elites whose willingness to convert to Christianity was evidence of their respect for Spanish authority. Those who were principally targeted by the expulsion decree were therefore from the lower classes—the artisans, laborers, itinerants, and vagabonds. These same classes of Chinese had always been the object of suspicion.[126] Moreover, they were often the principal movers of the different rebellions that took place.[127]

Yet, it was this very objective of the expulsion decree—to purge Manila of the laboring classes—that ultimately made the decree so problematic. As the Jesuits pointed out in their anonymous rebuttal of Ricci, the Chinese controlled the entire economy of Manila, not just the commerce that formed the backbone of the galleon trade. According to the Jesuits, the Chinese provided all three of the functions necessary for life within the city—skilled trades, provisions, and commerce.[128] Without them, all of the things essential to the republic would cease to be provided, all of the mechanical offices would halt or diminish, and there would be a great shortage in blacksmiths and sawyers, which would have consequences for the construction of ships for the galleon trade, among other things.[129] Moreover, many of the *vecinos* made money from renting property to the Chinese, and there would be certain individuals—widows in particular—who would be impoverished by their departure. All of the value of the lands would diminish without the Chinese to farm them, meaning there would be no one to harvest the sugar cane and there would be no one to rent these lands to. And finally, warned the Jesuits, they ran the risk of all trade from China ceasing altogether.[130] Fierce debate raged among the religious orders over whether or not the skilled trades could be taken over by the indios, with many arguing that this would be advantageous to both the indios themselves and the colony as a whole.[131] But, as the Jesuits pointed out, while this was a good idea in theory, it was not something that could easily be enforced without a period of transition during which time the indios would learn the trades from the Chinese.[132]

The Chinese were acutely aware of the power that they gained from occupying these skilled trades and controlling the city's provisions. In response to the expulsion decree, they produced several petitions politely requesting a suspension of the order.[133] Chief among their reasons for this suspension was the fact that they retained extensive outstanding commercial debts not only with the Spanish population, but also with indios, mestizos, mulattos, and other Chinese. Concluding these complicated accounts would not only take time but required an injection of silver from New Spain. An audit of debt and credit arrangements between Chinese businesses and the rest of the population of Manila revealed that, of 761 different workshops and business operating in the Parian, 63 percent had outstanding accounts with Spanish residents, 59 percent had outstanding accounts with indios, and 75 percent had outstanding accounts with other Chinese. The Chinese pointed out that even with respect to these latter accounts, they could not possibly conclude them until they had tied up their affairs with the Spaniards and the indios. The Justicia Mayor of the Parian and the City of Manila agreed that executing the expulsion decree before these accounts could be concluded would be prejudicial to all parties. Consequently, authorities were instructed to draw up a list of Chinese who did not have outstanding credit or debit arrangements and, in 1689, 341 Chinese were deported on the seven trading ships that had arrived from China that year.[134]

This meager deportation appears to have been the only significant expulsion that occurred in this period. The delays caused by the suspension and a lack of available ships gave the Chinese time to represent their arguments against the decree, centering on their role as essential laborers, suppliers of the city, and creditors to both the Crown and individual Spaniards.[135] By 1695, a substantial shift in politics had occurred, with the audiencia writing to the king to request a clarification on the original decree, citing fears that a complete expulsion posed the risk of completely cutting trade with China while grinding the local economy to a halt.[136] The Council of Indies clarified in October 1696 that the original decree was only meant to reduce the number of Chinese in the colony to six thousand, because this number was needed for the conservation of the islands. They warned that they did not mean for the trade of the islands to diminish; it was never the will of the king for the total expulsion of all of the non-Christian Chinese, and they were leaving it up to the judgment of the audiencia to determine the quality of those that were to remain in the Parian, containing the number to six thousand, as had been established previously.[137] An audit of the Chinese population in 1700 revealed that there were just 2,117 Chinese in Manila, and so the expulsion decree was determined as concluded and put aside.[138]

While forced expulsion was itself a form of violence enacted on the Chinese community of Manila, unlike the earlier massacres it required a considerable bureaucracy. Royal officials were thus afforded plenty of time to consider the consequences of their actions, and ultimately to avoid the mistakes made by the protagonists of the massacres in destroying the city's economy. Like the massacres, however, the expulsion proposal faced the same ultimate quandary: that Manila simply could not function without its Chinese laborers. Despite this, the proposal was resurrected numerous times during the eighteenth century, always by disgruntled Spanish *vecinos* who were jealous of the Chinese monopolization of the city's wealth, or by religious leaders outraged by their heathen and idolatrous ways.[139] Although expulsion did finally take place between 1767 and 1772—following the British occupation of Manila, which many Chinese settlers supported—there is no evidence to suggest that any of these earlier economic problems were resolved. As Salvador Escoto has noted, the economy of Manila fell into a slump in the 1770s and, by 1778, the Spanish were forced to send recruiters directly to Canton to try to convince settlers to come back and fill the skilled trades in the city.[140]

The Role of Violence

As this chapter demonstrates, many leading Spanish figures in Manila exhibited a singular and at times violent hatred for their Chinese counterparts. The violence exacted on the Chinese population of Manila—particularly during the massacres of 1603 and 1639—is in many respects extraordinary in its scope and its indiscriminate nature. Nevertheless, there remain clear parallels between these episodes and the increasing calls for escalating violence, military occupation, and enslavement of uncolonized and unruly spaces and peoples, as explored in preceding chapters. In all these instances, violence was a response to the limitations of colonial control, exemplifying the inability of colonial authorities to find any other more peaceful and longer lasting solution when dealing with communities that refused to cooperate with the colonial state or in some way threatened the hegemony of Spanish rule. What distinguishes the Chinese massacres from frontier violence enacted on indigenous communities was that in Manila the Spanish had the military capacity to bring their violent aims to completion. And yet, it is hard to see how such violence genuinely furthered Spanish aims, followed as it was by economic crises and a continued dependence on Chinese labor for the survival—let alone prosperity—of the city.

Viewed from a different perspective, there is a temptation to see Spanish violence against the Chinese as part of a project of bolstering solidarity between Spanish and indigenous communities: by constructing a Chinese "other," Spaniards and indios were united against a common threat. It is certainly true that indigenous soldiers were recruited in their hundreds to help complete the pogrom of 1639.[141] But we need to be careful when interpreting these numbers. After all, the 1639 rebellion in Calamba was a response to a policy of relocating Chinese laborers into the countryside to make up the shortfalls Manila experienced in agricultural supplies. When we consider the hundreds of thousands of tribute-paying indigenous subjects that the Crown claimed by this time—many of whom paid tribute in-kind in addition to contributing to the forced requisitioning of agricultural products under the bandala—it is hard to understand just how Manila could be experiencing such shortages, especially since the Spanish population of the city was reaching a low point in this period.[142] It therefore seems the case that tributes were not routinely collected; the reliability and loyalty of such subjects was limited to a few communities—the same communities that routinely supplied military labor in times of war or rebellion, and the same communities who would themselves turn to rebellion two decades later, in 1660 and 1661, in response to burdens demanded of them by the colonial state.

By contrast, the wealth of documents produced in the 1660s and 1670s regarding the proposed expulsion of the Chinese emphasize far greater integration rather than hostility or competition between indigenous and Chinese communities. While some Chinese traders set up businesses within local communities, others established direct employment opportunities, offering up to twice the wages that Spaniards offered for the same work.[143] Spanish commentators wrote jealously of these friendly and productive relationships, while noting that the indios often would not work at all for the Spanish.[144] Indeed, the dependence on Chinese labor had its roots in the shortage of local laborers, particularly within manual trades such as masonry, blacksmithing, carpentry, and so on.[145] Seen from this perspective, for every loyal indio that participated in periodic pogroms of the Chinese "other," we can posit an equal or even greater number of communities who preferred to trade and engage with the Chinese. This is borne out by the simple fact that *mestizaje* was always far greater between Chinese and indios than between Spaniards and indios, in stark contrast to most other parts of the empire.[146]

Spanish violence against the Chinese community in the seventeenth century thus exemplifies the most extreme reaction to all these realities. The parallel rise of a separate Chinese Manila challenged Spanish perceptions of their own sovereignty over the urban space. And yet, lacking the ability to operationalize indigenous labor—whether by force or cooperation—they ultimately came to rely on the Chinese for all provisions, material supplies, and labor, largely against their will and better judgment. Such a dependency necessitated giving up a degree of control and to some extent recognizing Chinese sovereignty over the local economy. As this chapter has shown, few if any Spaniards were comfortable with this. Over the course of the century, Spanish officials attempted to control the Chinese community through both economic and cultural regulation, including forced segregation, taxation, licenses, and religious conversion. Yet, Manila's Sangleys remained steadfastly independent, retaining their own governance structures and kinship connections to mainland China, while showing disinterest in Spanish religion. They moreover displayed greater acumen in commercial affairs, dominating the economic life of the city and quickly monopolizing the silver that flowed into domestic markets. The Spanish were acutely aware of how much this threatened their authority in the city and elsewhere in the archipelago. They remained impotent to subvert this imbalance. Periodic massacre may therefore have been the ultimate, and final expression of power. But it was not necessarily a successful one.

Conclusion

In January 2020, I found myself standing amid the dusty ruins of a Spanish-era church in Camalaniugan, Cagayan. My driver and guide, Ramil, was watching me through the front window of his rusty pickup truck, adopting a carefree position with one foot propped on the dashboard and the other dangling in the dust by the open door. Only his squint betrayed what he was really thinking: what was this Australian kid looking for among these piles of old bricks and stone? In truth, I wasn't exactly sure either. I had come to Cagayan to try to make sense of this region that I had spent so many years reading about within Spanish colonial archives, to try to find hints of a four-hundred-year-old history. Having arrived, I found myself on an odd sort of pilgrimage, diligently photographing church plaques and facades and affecting an interest in the layout of ruins like those in Camalaniugan, not far from Lal-lo, the former capital of the archdiocese of Nueva Segovia. At first glance, the signs of this colonial heritage were disappointingly few in this vast agricultural landscape—a far cry from the architectural displays of colonial power that might be seen by visitors to Mexican towns, for instance, where even the urban layout speaks to a standardized colonial imprint repeated hundreds of times over. The modern plaques fixed to the handful of remaining colonial buildings in Cagayan—mostly churches—recorded foundation dates and the name of missionary founders, paralleling the histories written by seventeenth-century missionary chroniclers like Fr. Diego

Aduarte and Fr. Baltasar de Santa Cruz, asserting boldly the success of Christianization and colonial establishment in the valley.

And yet, as I made my way from place to place, I began to think also about what these spaces say about silences within the historical record. The plaque at Camalaniugan, for instance, records a fire that destroyed the church in 1719. Left of out of this commemorative note is the context of widespread rebellion that swept the valley that year, when Gaddangs, Ibanags, and Itawis threatened to expel the Spanish permanently from their communities.[1] In Apayao, I found the burnt-out remains of churches in Pudtol and Capinatan, two missionary settlements that were rocked by frequent rebellions and eventually abandoned by the Dominicans in the late eighteenth century. Communities still worship in these beautiful ruins that were never rebuilt, the rows of church pews within these crumbling facades emblematic of the contested colonization of this region.[2] Downriver and further along the Cagayan coast, more church ruins lie hidden from view in someone's backyard, surrounded by an abundant orchard of tropical fruit trees, and slowly disappearing beneath the regrowth of vegetation. Unadorned with any historical marker, this church was one of the first ever founded in Cagayan, in the coastal town of Pata, now part of the modern settlement of Sanchez-Mira. During the 1661 rebellion, the missionaries stationed in Pata fled for their lives as an army of rebels descended from the nearby Apayao Mountains, killing one priest and leaving his headless body in a ditch by the road. After calm was restored and the local leaders of this rebellion were executed, the missionaries returned to Pata and found the church and its artifacts, as well as their houses and belongings, smashed and cut to pieces.[3] I was unable to confirm whether the ruins I was looking at dated from this moment, but Pata is mostly absent from religious chronicles after this date.

In many ways, this book is all about reading silences within the archives. By reading colonial history through the prism of limitations—shifting the interrogation from *how* to *if* and *where*—it asks for a more specific delineation of what the colonization process actually involved and how successful it really was. This process requires deconstructing the colonial archive and making decisions about how much weight should be given to different kinds of sources and the fragments of evidence that they hold. Gonzalo Lamana describes this method of rereading colonial narratives as a decolonial process: actively seeking to interrogate "a pervasive colonial imprint [that] still permeates accounts of what happened almost 500 years ago" and seeking in its place "to provide an alternative historical narrative that at once examines the imprint and shifts away from it."[4] What emerges is not a repudiation, denial, or rejection of Spanish colonization in the Philippines, but a call for a reassessment of its strengths and limitations. Put another way, the vantage points from which we choose to view the colonial period shape how that history unfolds. If we always situate ourselves firmly within the walls of Intramuros Manila, our view of colonization will be shaped by the perspectives of the colonial bureaucrats and missionary chroniclers that we are surrounded by. The vantage point of Spanish colonial documents and religious chronicles presents a simplistic image of the colonial process, seeking to elevate Spanish successes while glossing over unevenness and limitations.

Listening for silences within these records betrays some of the unspoken realities of the colonization process. As Engseng Ho has so eloquently put it: "There were reasons for writing things down and for not doing so. As well, the gnawing criticism of termites played its part."[5] Tom Simpson has written about absences as a deliberate form of colonial statecraft, relevant particularly in frontier regions, where "strategies of forgetting, overlooking, and occluding" helped with "limiting the spread of certain types of knowledge and willfully disregarding others."[6] Likewise, colonial records—including missionary chronicles, which have long formed the mainstay of Philippine historical research—are political documents. There were incentives for some things to be absent or removed from colonial archives, especially when they demonstrated the weaknesses of the colonial project or the limitations placed on Christian conversion. Spanish documents often speak generically about indios or about the operations of the colonial institutions like the repartimiento and the bandala without specifying who and where they mean. Such vagueness gives the reader the impression of a semblance of the universal spread of such institutions. But when we turn to look for specifics, we will find only a handful of places and people regularly mentioned, with Pampanga being the most common—a fact reinforced by petitions from the Pampangans themselves complaining about shouldering too many of the burdens of the colonial state.[7]

While some archival silences may represent a strategy of colonial statecraft—in this case asserting an uncontested sovereignty over peoples and lands—absences of information can also indicate weaknesses and a lack of knowledge. Sporadic and irregularly organized official inspections of the provinces offer some glimpses into these geographical limits. For instance, in 1723, when the *oidor* Don Joseph Antonio Pavón went to inspect new Augustinian missions in lowland Nueva Ecija and the foothills of the Caraballo Mountains—just beyond the historical province of Pampanga—one of the questions he asked of witnesses was where this region—the region he himself was physically present in—actually was in relation to other parts of Luzon.[8] A century and a half after colonization, Spanish officials genuinely did not know this geography, even within lowland spaces adjacent to those they were clear about controlling. Ironically, for a region that is regarded as so anomalous as to have been written out of many classic accounts of the colonial Philippines,[9] Cagayan has left one of the largest archival footprints of any individual region in this period. For most parts of the archipelago, there is only a limited amount of source materials to be found amid hundreds of volumes of archival records. Does this mean that nothing remarkable happened in these places? That, once religious conversion took place and encomienda lists were drawn up, these communities settled into a neat and unbroken rhythm punctuated by the chiming of church bells? Or do these silences suggest something else? That, perhaps, nothing happened because no one was there to write about it. If perspective matters, then so too must we be careful about essentializing Spanish claims and assuming they applied to "the vast majority of the lowlands." How much of what we know about the early colonial history of the Philippines really only applies to Pampangan and Tagalog communities—and even then, unevenly, subject to intense and often violent contestation?

These limitations—of knowledge, of the geographic spread of colonial institutions, of the successful conversion of communities—are understandable when viewed from the perspective of a limited supply of the agents of empire needed to achieve all of these ends. The strength of the Spanish presence was not fixed; high numbers of missionaries and soldiers in the early seventeenth century were accompanied by optimistic efforts of colonial expansion. But this contrasted starkly with a sudden and rapid decline in all forms of personnel by the mid-century. The Spanish were therefore limited in their abilities to impose wide sweeping control and culture change. Even John Leddy Phelan acknowledged that such chronic shortages in personnel resulted in the uneven spread of colonial control, while nevertheless still proclaiming colonization to be completed by the end of the seventeenth century.[10] Reading beyond grand proclamations of hundreds of thousands of baptisms in the space of a few short years, missionary records reveal that evangelizing activities followed a constant pattern of expansion and retreat, determined to a large extent by the number of missionaries available to travel beyond established settlements and into the hinterlands of provinces and islands where the majority of communities lived. New mission fields were established throughout the century and might be abandoned a number of years or decades later as missionaries died from poor health or grew too elderly to continue to traverse the rough terrain. These records also chart the avenues—both physical and spiritual—that communities used to evade evangelization. Similar patterns of expansion and retreat are mirrored within the efforts of soldiers to occupy, intimidate, and coerce communities into submission, only to find their own limited numbers forcing them to withdraw some weeks or months later. At the same time, the limitations of control within some frontier regions such as Cagayan clearly opened up opportunities for some agents of empire to benefit or profiteer from a lack of centralized oversight.

These weaknesses drove the expansion of violence within the archipelago, with increasing calls for the militarization and terrorization of recalcitrant populations reaching new heights by the beginning of the eighteenth century. Thus, the colonization of the Philippines was not "a relatively bloodless" conquest that was achieved in a few short years, but one that ebbed and flowed for centuries. Within this narrative we find another type of silence that has emerged within modern accounts of the colonial history: the rewriting of missionaries as peaceful arbiters between the violent state and defenseless indigenous communities. While some early missionary efforts to counter indigenous slavery and to uphold indigenous rights certainly reflect this view, as the century wore on missionaries were often the greatest proponents of violent means and were evidently frustrated by the limits placed on their proposals by royal officials, who wanted to uphold imperial law, and military commanders, who knew they could not resource these projects.

Reading the colonial archive against the grain and recognizing it as a record of the expansion and establishment of empire also allows us to see it as an archive of crisis. By the end of the seventeenth century, Spanish colonization of the Philippines remained tenuous. It was widely contested by communities across the archipelago. The limited nature of the Spanish population created a constant sense of unease among Spanish officials. The colonial archives are a documentary record of anxiety similar to that noted by historians of colonial India and the Dutch East Indies.[11] These historians argue that anxiety was a corollary of colonization and that the archival record shows how colonial states often responded with panic to established limits of their control and the threat of rebellion. Yet, if we take seriously the claims of the colonial state in imposing power, why not also the widespread and extensive evidence of community rejection, resistance, evasion, refusal? When looked at together, each of these multiple fronts of contestation combined—attacks by slave raiders, ungovernable Chinese communities, multitudes of fugitives, apostates, and rebels—created a genuine series of crises that threatened the existence of the colonial state and exposed its lack of resources to adequately respond.

As I discovered in Cagayan, silences also extend into the spaces beyond the archive. The history of the seventeenth-century Philippines is one of constant mobility of populations, many of whom fled colonized territories altogether. Spanish sovereignty was far more nodal than suggested by imperial narratives and religious chronicles, with vast swathes of territory remaining outside of colonial control altogether. These territories extended beyond the confines of upland Northern Luzon to include both upland and neighboring lowland spaces across the breadth of the archipelago. Some of these communities furthermore used tactics of headhunting, raiding, rebellion, and killing to erode established bases of Spanish influence. There is an as yet unwritten history of what happened within these autonomous refuge spaces beyond colonial hinterlands. The first glimpse of this history is emerging within archaeological research focused on Cordillera spaces like Ifugao where only now upland connections to the lowlands are being fully explored and rediscovered. Refocusing on the limitations of empire opens the possibility of extending such work into spaces that have hitherto only been understood through the lens of colonization.

These conclusions do not sit comfortably within a historiography that has overwhelmingly focused on how the colonial state exercised power and control. Lowland communities have often been contrasted to their upland neighbors who resisted colonization and retained their pre-Hispanic cultures and traditions. In rejecting colonization, upland communities were thus constructed as bastions of "authentic" indigeneity, in contrast to lowland communities that are often presented as willing receptors of multiple waves of colonial culture and ideology.[12] The anthropologist Fenella Cannell writes poignantly that lowland Filipino communities have typically seen themselves "as having no culture worth the name," as "disturbingly devoid . . . of social backbone," and "'merely imitative' of their two sets of Western colonisers."[13] Arguably, this concept of cultural obliteration within the lowlands has been perpetuated by the historiography of colonial state formation. By asserting a completed and largely uncontested colonization process, by denying agency in the face of religious as well as military and economic colonization, the "people with no culture" are also ultimately, as Agoncillo famously argued, a people with no history.[14] Histories that only focus on the process of Spanish colonization continue to overexaggerate Spanish control. But, more than this, they perpetuate an illusion that Filipinos retained their cultural heritage almost by accident—that indeed the agency of indigenous people was always reactive rather than constructive, that they were secondary actors within their own historical narratives, subjects of empire rather than active agents that shaped their communities and the world around themselves and in turn forced the Spanish empire itself to constantly change and reshape itself.

How we interpret this turbulent period of the seventeenth century matters; it forms the edifice for understanding all those periods that follow. The extraordinary cultural diversity of the archipelago, marked by 182 living languages and a plethora of ethnicities and autonomous political identities, suggests that the process of colonization was far less successful than previously argued; it certainly was no revolution in centralization.[15] As William Henry Scott once argued: "The rich fabric of Filipino life is not a tapestry with a deliberate design, nor even an oil painting executed by some creative artist. Rather, it is like the display of brilliant paints spilled on the floor of the artist's studio. It is, in other words, something of a mess."[16] Like Scott, I argue that this mess is a product of Philippine agency in the face of colonization, witnessed within these myriad stories of constant disruption, failure, contestation, limitation.

NOTES

Abbreviations

AFIO   Archivo Franciscano Ibero-Oriental (Madrid)

AGI   Archivo General de Indias (Seville)

AGN   Archivo General de la Nación (México)

AGPR   Archivo General de Palacio Real (Madrid)

AHN   Archivo Histórico Nacional (Madrid)

APSR   Archivo de la Provincia del Santísimo Rosario (University of Santo Tomas, Manila)

ARSI   Archivum Romanum Societatis Iesu (Rome)

B&R   *The Philippine Islands, 1493–1803: Explorations by Early Navigators, Descriptions of the Islands and Their Peoples, Their History and Records of the Catholic Missions, as Related in Contemporaneous Books and Manuscripts, Showing the Political, Economic, Commercial and Religious Conditions of These Islands from Their Earliest Relations with European Nations to the Beginning of the Nineteenth Century.* Translated and edited by Emma Helen Blair and James Alexander Robertson. 55 vols. Cleveland, OH: A. H. Clark, 1903–9.

BNE   Biblioteca Nacional de España (Madrid)

RAH   Real Academia de la Historia (Madrid)

Introduction

1. "Boxer Codex," Boxer mss. II, 1500–1899, Lilly Library, Indiana University, fols. 28r–28v.

2. The same story was recorded by the anthropologist Mabel Cook Cole in 1916, but this time attributed to the Tagalog region of the Philippines. "The Creation Story," in *Philippine Folk Tales*, ed. Mabel Cook Cole (Chicago: A. C. McClurg, 1916), 187–188.

3. Early accounts of Philippine religion record that the traditions were passed down through song. Pedro Fernández del Pulgar, "Descripción de las Filipinas y de las Malucas e Historia del Archipiélago Maluco desde su descubrimiento," Biblioteca Nacional de España (hereafter BNE), mss. 3002, fol. 27v; Pedro Chirino, *Relación de las islas Filipinas i de lo que en ellas an trabajado los padres de la Compañía de Iesus* (Roma: Por Estevan Paulino, 1604), 296–297.

4. "The Children of the Limokon," in Cole, *Philippine Folk Tales*, 143–144.

5. "The Sun and the Moon," in Cole, *Philippine Folk Tales*, 145–146. The tale of the sun and the moon was also recorded in the Visayas, see "The Sun and the Moon," in Cole, *Philippine Folk Tales*, 201.

6. "The Creation," in Cole, *Philippine Folk Tales*, 99–101.

7. Spanish chroniclers record numerous names for this creator God. Alcina reports that the Ibabao called this God Malaon, while elsewhere it was called Macapatag. See P. Francisco Ignacio Alzina, *Historia de las islas e indios de Bisayas, De la Compañía de Jesús, Año 1668*, Archivo General de Palacio Real (hereafter AGPR). Both Pedro Fernández del Pulgar and Pedro Chirino recorded that this creator God was called Bethala Meycapal in Tagalog and Laon in Visayan. Pedro Fernández del Pulgar, "Descripción de las Filipinas y de las Malucas e Historia del Archipiélago Maluco desde su descubrimiento," BNE, mss. 3002, fols. 27v–29v; Chirino, *Relación de las islas Filipinas*. In 1686, Felipe Pardo recorded that the Zambales believed in a creator God called Poon. Archivo General de Indias (hereafter AGI), Audiencia de Filipinas (hereafter Filipinas), leg. 75, núm. 20.

8. Alzina, *Historia de las islas e indios de Bisayas*, AGPR, 27v–28r.

9. "The Story of the Creation," in Cole, *Philippine Folk Tales*, 139–140.

10. Stephen Acabado, "Zones of Refuge: Resisting Conquest in the Northern Philippine Highlands through Environmental Practice," *Journal of Anthropological Archaeology* 52 (2018): 180–195; William Henry Scott, *The Discovery of the Igorots: Spanish Contacts with the Pagans of Northern Luzon* (Quezon City: New Day, 1974).

11. John Leddy Phelan, *The Hispanization of the Philippines: Spanish Aims and Filipino Responses, 1565–1700* (Madison: University of Wisconsin Press, 1967); Nicholas P. Cushner, *Spain in the Philippines: From Conquest to Revolution* (Quezon City: Ateneo de Manila University, 1971).

12. Ed. C. de Jesus, "Control and Compromise in the Cagayan Valley," in *Philippine Social History: Global Trade and Local Transformations*, eds. Alfred W. McCoy and Ed. C. de Jesus (Quezon City: Ateneo de Manila Press, 1982), 21–39.

13. José Rizal, *Sobre la indolencia de los Filipinos: Estudio Político-Social* (Manila: Nueva Era, 1954).

14. Fenella Cannell, *Power and Intimacy in the Christian Philippines* (Cambridge: Cambridge University Press, 1999), 6–7.

15. Felix M. Keesing, *The Ethnohistory of Northern Luzon* (Stanford, CA: Stanford University Press, 1962), 304.

16. *Breve relacion, y felizes progresos de los Religiosos del Sagrado Orden de Predicadores de las Islas Philipinas, en la Conquista espiritual, y reduccion de los Gentiles de la Provincia de Paniqui q media entre las Provincias de Cagayan y Pangasinan* (Manila: en el Collegio, y Vniversidad del Señor Santo Thomas con lizencia del Superior Govierno por Geronimo Correa de Castro, 1739).

17. Yanna Yannakakis, *The Art of Being In-between: Native Intermediaries, Indian Identity, and Local Rule in Colonial Oaxaca* (Durham, NC: Duke University Press, 2008), 4–5; Anne Laura Stoler and Frederick Cooper, "Between Metropole and Colony: Rethinking a Research Agenda," in *Tensions of Empire: Colonial Cultures in a Bourgeois World*, eds. Frederick Cooper and Ann Laura Stoler (Berkeley: University of California Press, 1997), 6; James C. Scott, *The Art of Not Being Governed: An Anarchist History of Upland Southeast Asia* (New Haven, CT: Yale University Press, 2009), 284.

18. Tsim D. Schneider, "Placing Refuge and the Archaeology of Indigenous Hinterlands in Colonial California," *American Antiquity* 80, no. 4 (2015): 696–697.

19. Lee M. Panich, "Archaeologies of Persistence: Reconsidering the Legacies of Colonialism in Native North America," *American Antiquity* 78, no. 1 (2013): 106–107.

20. Pekka Hämäläinen, *The Comanche Empire: A Study of Indigenous Power* (New Haven, CT: Yale University Press, 2009), 6–7.

21. H. de la Costa, S. J., *Readings in Philippine History* (Manila: Bookmark Inc., 1965), 16–17; William Henry Scott, *Barangay: Sixteenth-Century Philippine Culture and Society* (Quezon City: Ateneo de Manila University Press, 1994), 129. Datu is a pre-Hispanic title signifying "ruler," "chief," or "leader" within Philippine communities.

22. William Lytle Schurz, *The Manila Galleon: The Romantic History of the Spanish Galleons Trading between Manila and Acapulco* (New York: E. P. Dutton, 1959), 16–22, 220–221; Teodoro A. Agoncillo and Oscar M. Alfonso, *History of the Filipino People* (Quezon City: Malaya Books, 1967), 79–83; María Lourdes Díaz-Trechuelo Spínola, *Filipinas: La Gran Desconocida (1565–1898)* (Pamplona: Ediciones Universidad de Navarra, 2001), 40–63; Leandro Rodríguez, "El 'Tornaviaje': motivaciones de la ida y vuelta desde Nueva España a Filipinas y viceversa," in *Camineria Hispánica: Actas del III Congreso Internacional de Caminería Hispánica, Celebrado en Morelia (Michoacán), México, Julio 1996*, ed. Manuel Criado de Val (Guadalajara, Spain: Aache Ediciones, 1996), 315–326; Nicolas Zafra, *The Colonization of the Philippines and the Beginnings of the Spanish City of Manila* (Manila: National Historical Commission, 1974), 15–32.

23. Schurz, *The Manila Galleon*.

24. John Leddy Phelan, "Free versus Compulsory Labor: Mexico and the Philippines 1540–1648," *Comparative Studies in Society and History* 1, no. 2 (1959): 192.

25. It should be noted that each tribute usually represented an entire family and so is generally multiplied by a factor of three or four to find the total population. In this instance Salazar was therefore claiming to have converted 586,800 souls. Archivo Histórico Nacional (hereafter AHN), Colección Documentos de Indias (hereafter CDI), leg. 26, núm. 10.

26. AGI, Filipinas, leg. 79, núm. 22.

27. AGI, Filipinas, leg. 84, núm. 95.

28. AGI, Filipinas, leg. 22, ramo 7, núm. 20.

29. Phelan, *Hispanization of the Philippines*, 161. See also John N. Schumacher, S. J., *Growth and Decline: Essays on Philippine Church History* (Quezon City: Ateneo de Manila University Press, 2009), 1–21; John N. Schumacher, "Syncretism in Philippine Catholicism: Its Historical Causes," *Philippine Studies* 32 (1984): 251–272; Miguel A. Bernad, S. J., *The Christianization of the Philippines: Problems and Perspectives* (Manila: Filipiniana Book Guild, 1972); Victor Lieberman, *Strange Parallels: Southeast Asia in Global Context, c. 800–1830*, vol. 2, *Mainland Mirrors: Europe, Japan, China, South Asia, and the Islands* (Cambridge: Cambridge University Press, 2009), 833–834.

30. Eladio Neira, *Conversion Methodology in the Philippines (1565–1665)* (Manila: University of Santo Tomas, 1966), 4. For a fairly similar analysis see also Ramon C. Reyes, "Religious Experiences in the Philippines: From Mythos through Lagos to Kairos," *Philippine Studies* 33, no. 2 (1985): 203–212.

31. Cushner, *Spain in the Philippines*, 5.

32. Robert R. Reed, *Colonial Manila: The Context of Hispanic Urbanism and Process of Morphogenesis* (Berkeley: University of California Press, 1978), 11.

33. Luis Camara Dery, *Pestilence in the Philippines: A Social History of the Filipino People, 1571–1800* (Quezon City: New Day, 2006), v.

34. Cushner, *Spain in the Philippines*, 5.

35. Agoncillo and Alfonso, *History of the Filipino People*, vi–vii.

36. William Henry Scott, *Cracks in the Parchment Curtain and Other Essays in Philippine History* (Quezon City: New Day, 1982); see also William Henry Scott, *Prehispanic Source Materials for the Study of Philippine History* (Quezon City: New Day, 1984); William Henry Scott, *Slavery in the Spanish Philippines* (Manila: De la Salle University Press, 1991); William Henry Scott, *Looking for the Prehispanic Filipino and Other Essays in Philippine History* (Quezon City: New Day, 1992); Scott, *Barangay*. Scott's work has been expanded on by the historical archaeologist Laura Lee Junker, *Raiding, Trading and Feasting: The Political Economy of Philippine Chiefdoms* (Honolulu: University of Hawai'i Press, 1999).

37. Vicente L. Rafael, *Contracting Colonialism: Translation and Christian Conversion in Tagalog Society Under Early Spanish Rule* (Ithaca, NY: Cornell University Press, 1988). Examples of works in this tradition include Reynaldo Clemeña Ileto, *Pasyon and Revolution: Popular Movements in the Philippines, 1840–1910* (Quezon City: Ateneo de Manila University Press, 1979); D. R. M. Irving, *Colonial Counterpoint: Music in Early Modern Manila* (Oxford: Oxford University Press, 2010); Felice Noelle Rodriguez, "Juan de Salcedo Joins the Native Form of Warfare," *Journal of the Economic and Social History of the Orient* 46, no. 2 (2003): 143–164; Stephanie Mawson, "Philippine *Indios* in the Service of Empire: Indigenous Soldiers and Contingent Loyalty, 1600–1700," *Ethnohistory* 62, no. 2 (2016): 381–413; Charles J. H. Macdonald, "Folk Catholicism and Pre-Spanish Religions in the Philippines," *Philippine Studies* 52, no. 1 (2004): 78–93; Mark Dizon, "Social and Spiritual Kinship in Early-Eighteenth-Century Missions on the Caraballo Mountains," *Philippine Studies* 59, no. 3 (2011): 367–398; Mark Dizon, "Sumpong Spirit Beliefs, Murder, and Religious Change among Eighteenth-Century Aeta and Ilongot in Eastern Central Luzon," *Philippine Studies* 63, no. 1 (2015): 3–38.

38. See for example Scott, *Discovery of the Igorots*; Acabado, "Zones of Refuge"; Keesing, *The Ethnohistory of Northern Luzon*; Oona Paredes, *A Mountain of Difference: The Lumad in Early Colonial Mindanao* (Ithaca, NY: Cornell Southeast Asia Program Publications, 2013); Cesar Adib Majul, *Muslims in the Philippines* (Quezon City: University of the Philippines Press, 1973); Shinzo Hayase, *Mindanao Ethnohistory Beyond Nations: Maguindanao, Sangir, and Bagobo Societies in East Maritime Southeast Asia* (Quezon City: Ateneo de Manila University Press, 2003); Luis Camara Dery, *The Kris in Philippine History: A Study of the Impact of Moro Anti-Colonial Resistance, 1571–1896* (Quezon City: Luis Camara Dery, 1997).

39. See for example Linda Newson, *Conquest and Pestilence in the Early Spanish Philippines* (Honolulu: University of Hawai'i Press, 2009); Tatiana Seijas, *Asian Slaves in Colonial Mexico: From Chinos to Indios* (Cambridge: Cambridge University Press, 2014); José Eugenio Borao Mateo, "Filipinos in the Spanish Colonial Army during the Dutch Wars (1600–1648)," in *More Hispanic Than We Admit: Insights in Philippine Cultural History*, ed. Isaac Donoso (Quezon City: Vibal Foundation, 2008), 74–93; Augusto V. de Viana, *In the Far Islands: The Role of Natives from the Philippines in the Conquest, Colonization and Repopulation of the Mariana Islands, 1668–1903* (Manila: University of Santo Tomas Publishing House, 2004); Danilo M. Gerona, "The Colonial Accommodation

and Reconstitution of Native Elite in the Early Provincial Philippines, 1600–1795," in *Imperios y Naciones en el Pacífico*, vol. 1, eds. Maria Dolores Elizalde, Josep M. Fradera, and Luis Alonso (Madrid: Consejo Superior de Investigaciones Científicas, 2001), 265–276; Luis Ángel Sánchez Gómez, "Las élites nativas y la construcción colonial de Filipinas (1565–1789)," in *España y el Pacífico: Legazpi*, vol. 2, ed. Leoncio Cabrero (Madrid: Sociedad Estatal de Conmemoraciones Culturales, 2004), 37–70.

40. Paredes, *A Mountain of Difference*, 58; Stephen Acabado, "The Archaeology of Pericolonialism: Responses of the 'Unconquered' to Spanish Conquest and Colonialism in Ifugao, Philippines," *International Journal of Historical Archaeology* 21, no. 1 (2017): 1–26.

41. Isaac Donoso, Glòria Cano, and Jorge Mojarro Romero, eds., *More Hispanic Than We Admit: Insights in Philippine Cultural History*, 3 vols. (Quezon City: Vibal Foundation, 2008–2020).

42. Matthew Restall, *Seven Myths of the Spanish Conquest* (Oxford: Oxford University Press, 2021), 64–76.

43. Amy Turner Bushnell, "Gates, Patterns, and Peripheries: The Field of Frontier Latin America," in *Negotiated Empires: Centers and Peripheries in the Americas, 1500–1820*, eds. Christine Daniels and Michael V. Kennedy (New York: Routledge, 2002), 17; Gonzalo Lamana, *Domination without Dominance: Inca Spanish Encounters in Early Colonial Peru* (Durham, NC: Duke University Press, 2008).

44. Juliana Barr and Edward Countryman, "Maps and Spaces, Paths to Connect, and Lines to Divide," in *Contested Spaces of Early America*, eds. Juliana Barr and Edward Countryman (Philadelphia: University of Pennsylvania Press, 2014), 1–28.

45. See figures 6.2 and 6.3 in chapter 6.

46. Amy Turner Bushnell and Jack P. Greene, "Peripheries, Centers, and the Construction of Early Modern American Empires," in *Negotiated Empires: Centers and Peripheries in the Americas, 1500–1820*, eds. Christine Daniels and Michael V. Kennedy (New York: Routledge, 2002), 2; Lauren Benton, *A Search for Sovereignty: Law and Geography in European Empires, 1400–1900* (Cambridge: Cambridge University Press, 2009), 2; Rachel St. John, "Imperial Spaces in Pekka Hämäläinen's 'The Comanche Empire,'" *History and Theory* 52, no. 1 (2013): 79; Pekka Hämäläinen, "What's in a Concept? The Kinetic Empire of the Comanches," *History and Theory* 52, no. 1 (2013): 87; Donna J. Guy and Thomas E. Sheridan, eds., *Contested Ground: Comparative Frontiers on the Northern and Southern Edges of the Spanish Empire* (Tucson: University of Arizona Press, 1998), 11–15; John E. Kicza, *Resilient Cultures: America's Native Peoples Confront European Colonization, 1500–1800* (Upper Saddle River, NJ: Pearson Education, 2003), 57–63, 171–172.

47. Benton, *A Search for Sovereignty*, 2.

48. Mark Christensen has noted that it was common for mendicants and missionaries to uphold exaggerated views of a completed conquest by reporting on "the relative ease of which the gospel was accepted. Indeed, in many instances, the natives appear eager, even impatient, to convert to Christianity." This led to exaggerations like the claim that millions had been converted in just a few years. Mark Christensen, "Recent Approaches in Understanding Evangelization in New Spain," *History Compass* 14, no. 2 (2016): 40.

49. Schumacher, "Syncretism in Philippine Catholicism," 251–272.

50. Newson, *Conquest and Pestilence*, 256.

51. Stephanie Mawson, "Unruly Plebeians and the *Forzado* System: Convict Transportation between New Spain and the Philippines during the Seventeenth Century," *Revista de Indias* 73, no. 259 (2013): 693–730; Stephanie Mawson, "Convicts or *Conquistadores*? Spanish Soldiers in the Seventeenth-Century Pacific," *Past & Present* 232 (2016): 87–125.

52. Benton, *A Search for Sovereignty*, 2.

53. Martin Austin Nesvig, *Promiscuous Power: An Unorthodox History of New Spain* (Austin: University of Texas Press, 2018), 3.

54. The literature on indigenous allies is by now vast. For some key examples see Laura E. Matthew and Michel R. Oudijk, eds., *Indian Conquistadors: Indigenous Allies in the Conquest of Mesoamerica* (Norman: University of Oklahoma Press, 2007); Richard White, *The Middle Ground: Indians, Empires, and Republics in the Great Lakes Region, 1650–1815* (Cambridge: Cambridge University Press, 1991); Simon Schaffer, Lissa Roberts, Kapil Raj, and James Delbourgo, eds., *The Brokered World: Go-Betweens and Global Intelligence, 1770–1820* (Sagamore Beach, MA: Science History Publications, 2009); Alida C. Metcalf, *Go-Betweens and the Colonization of Brazil, 1500–1600* (Austin: University of Texas Press, 2005); Yannakakis, *The Art of Being In-between*; Bradley Benton, *The Lords of Tetzcoco: The Transformation of Indigenous Rule in Postconquest Central Mexico* (Cambridge: Cambridge University Press, 2017).

55. Michel R. Oudijk and Matthew Restall, "Mesoamerican Conquistadors in the Sixteenth Century," in *Indian Conquistadors: Indigenous Allies in the Conquest of Mesoamerica*, eds. Laura E. Matthew and Michel R. Oudijk (Norman: University of Oklahoma Press, 2007), 30–33.

56. Mawson, "Philippine *Indios* in the Service of Empire," 381–413; Borao Mateo, "Filipinos in the Spanish Colonial Army," 74–93.

57. Restall, *Seven Myths of the Spanish Conquest*, 170.

58. Jane Burbank and Frederick Cooper, *Empires in World History: Power and the Politics of Difference* (Princeton, NJ: Princeton University Press, 2010), 14.

59. AGI, Filipinas, leg. 9, ramo 2, núm. 34; AGI, Filipinas, leg. 52, núm. 2.

60. Victor Lieberman and Anthony Reid both conclude that, by contrast to other parts of Southeast Asia, the Philippines were exceptionally exposed to European colonization. For Lieberman, the absence of centralized structures in most parts of the archipelago meant that the introduction of the colonial state in this space was truly "revolutionary," allowing "Hispanization [to proceed] without large-scale opposition." Lieberman, *Strange Parallels*, vol. 2, 831–834; see also Anthony Reid's thesis on a seventeenth-century crisis in Southeast Asia, *Southeast Asia in the Age of Commerce, 1450–1680*, vol. 2, *Expansion and Crisis* (New Haven, CT: Yale University Press, 1993), 267–325.

61. Kicza, *Resilient Cultures*, 57–63, 171–172; David J. Weber, *Bárbaros: Spaniards and their Savages in the Age of Enlightenment* (New Haven, CT: Yale University Press, 2005); Cynthia Radding, *Wandering Peoples: Colonialism, Ethnic Spaces, and Ecological Frontiers in Northwestern Mexico, 1700–1850* (Durham, NC: Duke University Press, 1997).

62. Junker, *Raiding, Trading and Feasting*, 73–74; Newson, *Conquest and Pestilence*, 12.

63. Newson, *Conquest and Pestilence*, 256.

64. Letter from Mateo Sanchez, April 12, 1603, Archivum Romanum Societatis Iesu (hereafter ARSI), phil. 10, fols. 104r–106v; AGI, Filipinas, leg. 84, núm. 46; Phelan, *Hispanization of the Philippines*, 45.

65. Some of these communities may have abandoned their settlements in response to colonization, as discussed in chapters 6 and 7. AGI, Filipinas, leg. 7, ramo 3, núm. 45; AGI, Filipinas, leg. 330, libro 4, fols. 247r–247v; AHN, CDI, leg. 26, núm. 28.

66. AGI, Filipinas, leg. 84, núm. 46.

67. "Carta Annua de la Provincia de las Philippinas desde Junio 1600 hasta el de Junio de 1601 Años," ARSI, phil. 5, fols. 75r–92r; "Carta Annua de la Vice Provincia de las Islas Philippinas desde el mes de Junio de 1601 hasta el Junio de 1602 años," ARSI, fols. 103r–104v; Letter from Mateo Sánchez, April 12, 1603, ARSI, phil. 10, fols. 104r–106v; Letter from Fr. Miguel Gómez, ARSI, phil. 14, fols. 25r–26v.

68. Both Reid and Lieberman express the view that European military superiority allowed this rapid conquest to take place, leading to what Reid has termed a seventeenth-century crisis that saw the collapse of an independent indigenous-led society across most of island Southeast Asia. Reid, *Southeast Asia in the Age of Commerce*, vol. 2, 267–325; Victor Lieberman, "Some Comparative Thoughts on Premodern Southeast Asian Warfare," *Journal of the Economic and Social History of the Orient* 46, no. 2 (2003): 219–220.

69. Mawson, "Convicts or *Conquistadores*?" 87–125; Mawson, "Philippine *Indios* in the Service of Empire," 381–413.

70. Reports about illness, disease, and death among Spanish soldiers are numerous throughout the century. See for example AGI, Filipinas, leg. 6, ramo 7, núm. 82; AGI, Filipinas, leg. 8, ramo 3, núm. 91; AGI, Filipinas, leg. 9, ramo 2, núm. 30; AGI, Filipinas, leg. 19, ramo 3, núm. 47; AGI, Filipinas, leg. 22, ramo 7, núm. 21.

71. AGI, Filipinas, leg. 18B, ramo 7, núms. 56, 57.

72. Weber, *Bárbaros*, 6.

73. Victor Lieberman has argued that the Spanish were able to bring order to the archipelago, ending the "endemic vendettas and blood feuds" that characterized pre-Hispanic Philippine society. "Spanish officials and friars frequently were able to resolve conflicts more or less impartially," for which indigenous elites were "understandably grateful." Lieberman, *Strange Parallels*, vol. 2, 835. This argument is similar in nature to David Henley's Stranger King thesis. See David Henley, *Jealousy and Justice: The Indigenous Roots of Colonial Rule in Northern Sulawesi* (Amsterdam: VU Uitgeverij, 2002).

74. AGI, Filipinas, leg. 9, ramo 2, núms. 30, 34; "Relación breve de lo sucedido en las islas Filipinas y otras adyacentes desde el octubre del año de 1660 hasta el mes de junio del año de 1662," ARSI, phil. 12, fols. 13r–14v.

75. "Relasión del alçamiento de los chinos en la ciudad de Manila por el mes de noviembre del año de 1639, causas del alçamiento y prinsipio del," Real Academia de la Historia, 9/3663, núm. 28; "Relation on the Chinese Insurrection," in *The Philippine Islands, 1493–1803* (hereafter *B&R*), trans. and ed. Emma Helen Blair and James Alexander Robertson, 55 vols. (Cleveland, OH: A. H. Clark, 1903–9), vol. 29, 194–207.

76. Radding, *Wandering Peoples*, 265; Adriana Rocher Salas, "La Montaña: Espacio de Rebelión, Fe y Conquista," *Estudios de Historia Novohispana* 50 (2014): 45–76.

77. Scott, *Art of Not Being Governed*.

78. Stephanie Mawson, "Escaping Empire: Philippine Mountains and Indigenous Histories of Resistance," *American Historical Review* (forthcoming).

79. Nancy M. Farriss, *Maya Society Under Colonial Rule: The Collective Enterprise of Survival* (Princeton, NJ: Princeton University Press, 1984), 72–75; Sara Ortelli, "Entre desiertos y serranías: Población, espacio no controlado y fronteras permeables en el Septentrión novohispano tardocolonial," *Manuscrits. Revista d'Història Moderna* 32 (2014): 86–87; Cynthia Radding, "Colonial Spaces in the Fragmented Communities of Northern New Spain," in *Contested Spaces of Early America*, eds. Juliana Barr and Edward Countryman (Philadelphia: University of Pennsylvania Press, 2014), 115–141; Flávio Gomes, "Indigenas, africanos y comunidades de fugitivos en la Amazonia colonial," *Historia y Espacio* 6, no. 34 (2010): 1–21.

80. Acabado, "The Archaeology of Pericolonialism," 1–26; Paredes, *A Mountain of Difference*, 58.

1. A Moment of Crisis, 1660–1663

1. Archivo General de Indias (hereafter AGI), Audiencia de Filipinas (hereafter Filipinas), leg. 285, núm. 1.

2. Ana Maria Prieto Lucena, *Filipinas durante el gobierno de Manrique de Lara, 1653–1663* (Sevilla: Escuela de Estudios Hispano-Americanos de Sevilla, 1984); Rosario Mendoza Cortes, *Pangasinan, 1572–1800* (Quezon City: University of the Philippines Press, 1972), 145–168; John A. Larkin, *The Pampangans: Colonial Society in a Philippine Province* (Berkeley: University of California Press, 1972), 26–27; Fernando Palanco, "Resistencia y rebelión indígena en Filipinas durante los primeros cien años de soberanía española (1565–1665)," in *España y el Pacífico: Legazpi*, vol. 2, ed. Leoncio Cabrero (Madrid: Sociedad Estatal de Conmemoraciones Culturales, 2004), 92.

3. This account is based on the following sources: AGI, Filipinas, leg. 9, ramo 2, núms. 29, 30, 34; AGI, Filipinas, leg. 32, núm. 2; "Insurrections by Filipinos in the Seventeenth Century," in *The Philippine Islands, 1493–1803* (hereafter *B&R*), trans. and ed. Emma Helen Blair and James Alexander Robertson, 55 vols. (Cleveland, OH: A. H. Clark, 1903–9), vol. 38, 140–180.

4. AGI, Filipinas, leg. 6, ramo 10, núm. 180; AGI, Filipinas, leg. 7, ramo 5, núms. 30, 53; AGI, Filipinas, leg. 8, ramo 1, núm. 4; AGI, Filipinas, leg. 9, ramo 1, núms. 7, 30; AGI, Filipinas, leg. 12, ramo 1, núm. 8; AGI, Filipinas, leg. 14, ramo 3, núm. 38; AGI, Filipinas, leg. 27, núms. 51, 122; AGI, Filipinas, leg. 28, núms. 21, 104, 107, 128; AGI, Filipinas, leg. 34, núms. 38, 75; AGI, Filipinas, leg. 41, núm. 20; AGI, Filipinas, leg. 75, núm. 10; AGI, Filipinas, leg. 80, núms. 41, 130; AGI, Filipinas, leg. 81, núm. 109; AGI, Filipinas, leg. 83, núm. 48; AGI, Filipinas, leg. 84, núms. 13, 36; AGI, Filipinas, leg. 85, núm. 30; AGI, Filipinas, leg. 86, núm. 75; AGI, Filipinas, leg. 193, núm. 22; Archivo Histórico Nacional (hereafter AHN), Colección Documentos de Indias (hereafter CDI), leg. 26, núms. 28, 30; Antonio de Morga, *The Philippine Islands, Moluccas, Siam, Cambodia, Japan and China at the Close of the Sixteenth Century*, trans. Henry E. J. Stanley (Cambridge: Cambridge University Press, 2010), 329; William J. McCarthy, "The Yards at Cavite: Shipbuilding in the Early Colonial Philippines," *International Journal of Maritime History* 7, no. 2 (1995): 149–162; Stephanie Mawson, "Philippine *Indios* in the Service of Empire: Indigenous Soldiers and Contingent Loyalty, 1600–1700," *Ethnohistory* 62, no. 2 (2016): 381–413; John Leddy

Phelan, "Free versus Compulsory Labor: Mexico and the Philippines 1540–1648," *Comparative Studies in Society and History* 1, no. 2 (1959): 189–201.

5. AGI, Filipinas, leg. 22, ramo 9, núm. 50.

6. AGI, Filipinas, leg. 12, ramo 1, núm. 8. On finance see Leslie E. Bauzon, *Deficit Government: Mexico and the Philippine Situado, 1606–1804* (Tokyo: Centre for East Asian Cultural Studies, 1981); C. R. Boxer, "Plata es Sangre: Sidelights on the Drain of Spanish-American Silver in the Far East, 1550–1700," in *European Entry into the Pacific: Spain and the Acapulco-Manila Galleons*, eds. Dennis O. Flynn, Arturo Giráldez, and James Sobredo (Aldershot, UK: Ashgate, 2001), 165–186.

7. AGI, Filipinas, leg. 22, ramo 9, núm. 43; AGI, Filipinas, leg. 81, núm. 109; AGI, Filipinas, leg. 84, núm. 18; AGI, Filipinas, leg. 85, núms. 25, 30; AHN, CDI, leg. 26, núms. 28, 29, 30.

8. Woodcutting is reported to have taken place in Bulacan, Pampanga, Camarines, Laguna de Bay, and in the forests on the eastern edge of the Zambales Mountains, between Pampanga and Pangasinan. AGI, Filipinas, leg. 9, ramo 2, núms. 29, 30, 34; AGI, Filipinas, leg. 32, núm. 2; AGI, Filipinas, leg. 34, núm. 38; AGI, Filipinas, leg. 83, núm. 48; AHN, CDI, leg. 26, núm. 30. Shipyards were established at various points in Oton, Camarines, Balayan, Lampon, Marinduque, Ibalon, Mindoro, Masbate, Leyte, and Cavite, although with the exception of Cavite these were not permanent installations. AGI, Filipinas, leg. 22, ramo 7, núm. 21; AGI, Filipinas, leg. 27, núm. 233; AGI, Filipinas, leg. 29, núm. 32; AGI, Filipinas, leg. 38, núm. 12; "Carta Annua . . . de 1601 hasta . . . 1602 años," Archivum Romanum Societatis Iesu (hereafter ARSI), phil. 5, fol. 110v.

9. In 1658, the attorney Juan de Bolivar y Cruz investigated the extortionate practices wherein communities were asked to contribute more agricultural products than they could reasonably supply under the bandala. Although ostensibly a generalized investigation, Bolivar y Cruz only supplied evidence from the provinces of Pampanga, Laguna de Bay, and Pangasinan, suggesting that problems of overburdening were limited to these regions. AGI, Filipinas, leg. 22, ramo 9, núm. 50.

10. AGI, Filipinas, leg. 22, ramo 9, núm. 50; AGI, Filipinas, leg. 85, núm. 30; AGI, Filipinas, leg. 193, núm. 22. See also H. de la Costa, S. J., *Readings in Philippine History* (Manila: Bookmark Inc., 1965), 56–57.

11. Larkin, *The Pampangans*, 25; Phelan, "Free versus Compulsory Labor," 193; Linda Newson, *Conquest and Pestilence in the Early Spanish Philippines* (Honolulu: University of Hawai'i Press, 2009), 166–169.

12. AGI, Filipinas, leg. 2, núm. 249; AGI, Filipinas, leg. 43, núm. 27; Larkin, *The Pampangans*, 22.

13. AGI, Filipinas, leg. 19, ramo 6, núm. 84; AGI, Filipinas, leg. 27, núm. 51.

14. Nicholas P. Cushner and John A. Larkin, "Royal Land Grants in the Colonial Philippines (1571–1626): Implications for the Formation of a Social Elite," *Philippine Studies* 25, nos. 1–2 (1978): 102–103, 107–108; Newson, *Conquest and Pestilence*, 172.

15. AGI, Filipinas, leg. 193, núm. 22; Mawson, "Philippine *Indios*," 381–413.

16. "Insurrections by Filipinos in the Seventeenth Century," *B&R*, vol. 38, 101–129; H. de la Costa, S. J., *The Jesuits in the Philippines, 1581–1768* (Cambridge, MA: Harvard University Press, 1961), 411–413; Palanco, "Resistencia y rebelión indígena," 89–90.

17. AGI, Filipinas, leg. 22, ramo 9, núms. 43, 50; AGI, Filipinas, leg. 32, núm. 1.

18. AGI, Filipinas, leg. 22, ramo 9, núm. 50. See also de la Costa, *Readings in Philippine History*, 56–57.

19. "Insurrections by Filipinos in the Seventeenth Century," *B&R*, vol. 38, 146.

20. "Insurrections by Filipinos in the Seventeenth Century," *B&R*, vol. 38, 141.

21. AGI, Filipinas, leg. 9, ramo 2, núm. 34.

22. "Insurrections by Filipinos in the Seventeenth Century," *B&R*, vol. 38, 151.

23. "Insurrections by Filipinos in the Seventeenth Century," *B&R*, vol. 38, 162.

24. The chronicler accounts published by Blair and Robertson mark the date for the beginning of the rebellion as December 15, however December 12 is recorded in two separate accounts written in 1661 by Governor Manrique de Lara. AGI, Filipinas, leg. 9, ramo 2, núms. 29, 30.

25. This account is based on the following sources: AGI, Filipinas, leg. 9, ramo 2, núms. 29, 30, 34; AGI, Filipinas, leg. 32, núm. 2; "Insurrections by Filipinos in the Seventeenth Century," *B&R*, vol. 38, 140–216.

26. William Henry Scott, *Discovery of the Igorots: Spanish Contacts with the Pagans of Northern Luzon* (Quezon City: New Day, 1974).

27. Stephanie Mawson, "Escaping Empire: Philippine Mountains and Indigenous Histories of Resistance," *American Historical Review* (forthcoming).

28. AGI, Filipinas, leg. 27, núm. 51. This is discussed in greater depth in chapters 5 and 6 of this book.

29. AGI, Filipinas, leg. 6, ramo 10, núm. 183; AGI, Filipinas, leg. 19, ramo 7, núm. 100; AGI, Filipinas, leg. 144, núm. 9.

30. Casimiro Diaz Toledano, *Conquistas de las Islas Filipinas: la temporal por las armas de nuestros Católicos Reyes de España . . . Parte segunda* (Valladolid: Imprenta Librería de Luis N. de Gaviria, 1890), 164–172.

31. "Insurrections by Filipinos in the Seventeenth Century," *B&R*, vol. 38, 181–205.

32. AGI, Filipinas, leg. 6, ramo 9, núms. 144, 161, 173; AGI, Filipinas, leg. 7, ramo 6, núm. 85; AGI, Filipinas, leg. 27, núm. 33; Fr. Diego Aduarte, *Tomo Primero de la Historia de la Provincia del Santo Rosario de Filipinas, Japón, y China, de la sagrada orden de predicadores* (Zaragoza, Spain: Por Domingo Gascon, Insançon, Impressor del Santo Hospital Real y General de Nuestra Señora de Gracia, 1693), 550–556; Baltasar de Santa Cruz, *Tomo Segundo de la Historia de la Provincia del Santo Rosario de Filipinas, Japón, y China del Sagrado Orden de Predicadores* (Zaragoza, Spain: Por Pasqual Bueno, Impressor Reyno, 1693), 18–21.

33. "Alzamiento en Cagayan en 1660," Archivo de la Provincia del Santísimo Rosario, 58, sección Cagayan, tomo 13, doc. 3; "Annua de las Islas Philipinas: Del Estado de las islas desde el año 658 hasta el de 661," Real Academia de la Historia (hereafter RAH), 9/2668, núm. 1; AGI, Filipinas, leg. 9, ramo 2, núm. 34.

34. "Insurrections by Filipinos in the Seventeenth Century," *B&R*, vol. 38, 167–180.

35. AGI, Filipinas, leg. 9, ramo 2, núm. 34.

36. AGI, Filipinas, leg. 9, ramo 2, núm. 34.

37. "Relación de lo sucedido en la ciudad de Manila donde la embajada que envió Cotzen capitán general de las costas de China y Rey de Isla Hermosa con el Padre Fray Victorio Riccio su embajador el año 1662, hasta la segunda embajada que envió su hijo con el mismo padre y fue despachado a once de Julio de mil y seiscientos y sesenta y

tres," RAH, 9 / 2668, núm. 4; "Breve relación del estado de las islas Filipinas y reinos adiacentes," ARSI, phil. 12, doc. 70.

38. Quoted in Anna Busquets, "Dreams in the Chinese Periphery: Victorio Riccio and Zheng Chenggong's Regime," in *Sea Rovers, Silver, and Samurai: Maritime East Asia in Global History, 1550–1700*, eds. Tonio Andrade and Xing Hang (Honolulu: University of Hawai'i Press, 2016), 214–215. According to Busquets, the only existing copy of the original letter was published by Domingo Fernández de Navarrete in his *Tratados históricos, politics, éticos y religiosos de la monarquía de China* (Madrid, 1676)—this is the version that she has utilized.

39. AGI, Filipinas, leg. 9, ramo 2, núms. 38, 39; "Breve relación del estado de las islas Filipinas y reinos adiacentes," ARSI, phil. 12, doc. 70.

40. Tonio Andrade, *Lost Colony: The Untold Story of China's First Great Victory Over the West* (Princeton, NJ: Princeton University Press, 2011), 124–136.

41. Juan Gil, *Los Chinos en Manila: Siglos XVI y XVII* (Lisbon: Centro Científico e Cultural de Macau, 2011), 506.

42. These events are examined in detail in chapter 7. See Charles J. McCarthy, "Slaughter of Sangleys in 1639," *Philippine Studies* 18, no. 3 (1970): 659–667; José Eugenio Borao, "The Massacre of 1603: Chinese Perception of the Spanish," *Itinerario* 22, no. 1 (1998): 22–40.

43. This account is based on "Relación de lo sucedido en la ciudad de Manila," RAH 9 / 2668, núm. 4. A copy of this same manuscript is held in the Ayer Library and reproduced in "Events in Manila, 1662–63," *B&R*, vol. 36, 218–260; see also "Breve relación del estado de las islas Filipinas y reinos adiacentes," ARSI, phil. 12, doc. 70; "Relación de varios sucesos en estas Yslas Filippinas, desde el año de 1661 hasta este presente de 1664," ARSI, phil. 12, doc. 3; de la Costa, *Jesuits in the Philippines*, 478–479; Gil, *Los Chinos en Manila*, 514–527; Busquets, "Dreams in the Chinese Periphery," 202–225.

44. "Relación de lo sucedido en la ciudad de Manila," RAH 9 / 2668, núm. 4.

45. "Relación de lo sucedido en la ciudad de Manila," RAH 9 / 2668, núm. 4.

46. "Relación de lo sucedido en la ciudad de Manila," RAH 9 / 2668, núm. 4.

47. Gil, *Los Chinos en Manila*, 520.

48. AGI, Filipinas, leg. 9, ramo 2, núms. 30, 34, 38, 39; AGI, Filipinas, leg. 9, ramo 3, núm. 42; "Anuas de las islas Philipinas: Del Estado de las islas desde el año 658 hasta el de 661," RAH, 9 / 2668, núm. 1; "Breve relación del estado de las islas Filipinas y reinos adiacentes," ARSI, phil. 12, doc. 70.

49. Stephanie Mawson, "Convicts or *Conquistadores*? Spanish Soldiers in the Seventeenth-Century Pacific," *Past & Present* 232 (2016): 87–125; Stephanie Mawson, "Unruly Plebeians and the *Forzado* System: Convict Transportation between New Spain and the Philippines during the Seventeenth Century," *Revista de Indias* 73, no. 259 (2013): 693–730.

50. AGI, Filipinas, leg. 9, ramo 2, núm. 30; AGI, Filipinas, leg. 23, ramo 2, núm. 4; AGI, Filipinas, leg. 32, núm. 2.

51. AGI, Filipinas, leg. 9, ramo 2, núm. 30.

52. AGI, Filipinas, leg. 9, ramo 3, núm. 42.

53. Busquets, "Dreams in the Chinese Periphery," 217–218.

54. AGI, Filipinas, leg. 9, ramo 2, núm. 39; AGI, Filipinas, leg. 86, núm. 20; Andrade, *Lost Colony*, 299–301; Busquets, "Dreams in the Chinese Periphery," 218–219.

55. Francisco Combes, *Historia de las islas de Mindanao, Jolo y sus adyacentes. Progresos de la religión y armas católicas. Compuesto por el padre Francisco Combes, de la compañía de Iesus, Cathedratico de Prima de Theologia en su Colegio y Universidad de a la Ciudad de Manila* (Madrid: Por los herederos de Pablo de Val, Año de 1667), 375–400, 432–439, 471–510; "Informe del Obispo de Nueva Cáceres al Gobierno, sobre los daños que causaban los moros y las vejaciones a los indios por los alcaldes mayores," Archivo Franciscano Ibero-Oriental, 92/7; "Traslado de una carta que el Señor D. Sabiniano Manrique de Lara Governador, y Capitán General de las Islas Filipinas, y presidente de la Audiencia Real, que en ellas reside, escribe al padre Magino Sola, de la Compañía de Iesus, residente en la Real Corte de Madrid, Fecha en Cabite, Puerto de dichas Islas, en 24 de Iulio del año de 1658 y recibida en Madrid en 19 de Iunio de 1659," ARSI, phil. 11, fols. 353r–366r.

56. Mawson, "Convicts or *Conquistadores?*" 112–119; Gary William Bohigian, "Life on the Rim of Spain's Pacific-American Empire: Presidio Society in the Molucca Islands, 1606–1663" (PhD diss., University of California, Los Angeles, 1994), 71–76.

57. AGI, Filipinas, leg. 23, ramo 8, núm. 24; AGI, Filipinas, leg. 330, libro 6, fols. 129r–131r, 150v–152v; AGI, Filipinas, leg. 331, libro 7, fols. 205r–206v, 353v–355v; AGI, Filipinas, leg. 341, libro 7, fols. 147v–149v.

58. "Breve relación del estado de las islas Filipinas y reinos adiacentes," ARSI, phil. 12, doc. 70.

59. AGI, Filipinas, leg. 10, ramo 1, núm. 7.

2. Slavery, Debt, and Colonial Labor Regimes

1. Archivo General de Indias (hereafter AGI), Audiencia de Filipinas (hereafter Filipinas), leg. 52, núm. 2; Luciano P. R. Santiago, "The Filipino Indio Encomenderos (ca. 1620–1711)," *Philippine Quarterly of Culture and Society* 18, no. 3 (1990): 173–176.

2. This argument is consistent with the broader literature on labor regimes elsewhere in the Spanish empire. Particularly in the Andes, Raquel Gil Montero notes that the labor systems introduced by the Spanish were based heavily on existing practices of tribute that was often paid in terms of labor or military service as well as the provision of particular goods. Raquel Gil Montero, "Free and Unfree Labour in the Colonial Andes in the Sixteenth and Seventeenth Centuries," *International Review of Social History* 56, special issue S19 (2011–12): 297–318; Raquel Gil Montero, "Mecanismos de reclutamiento indígena en la minería de plata: Lípez (sur de la actual Bolivia), siglo XVII," *America Latina en la Historia Económica* 21, no. 1 (2014): 5–30. See also Jeremy Ravi Mumford, *Vertical Empire: The General Resettlement of Indians in the Colonial Andes* (Durham, NC: Duke University Press, 2012); Steve J. Stern, *Peru's Indian Peoples and the Challenge of Spanish Conquest: Huamanga to 1640* (Madison: University of Wisconsin Press, 1982); William L. Sherman, *Forced Native Labor in Sixteenth-Century Central America* (Lincoln: University of Nebraska Press, 1979), 218–232.

3. Laura Lee Junker, *Raiding, Trading and Feasting: The Political Economy of Philippine Chiefdoms* (Honolulu: University of Hawai'i Press, 1999), 73–74.

4. AGI, Filipinas, leg. 6, ramo 2, núm. 16; AGI, Filipinas, leg. 34, núm. 8; AGI, Filipinas, leg. 84, núms. 15, 18, 21; Pedro Chirino, *Relación de las islas Filipinas i de lo que en ellas an trabajado los padres de la Compañía de Iesus* (Roma: Por Estevan Paulino, 1604), 363–

364; Fray Juan Francisco de San Antonio, *Crónicas de la Provincia de San Gregorio Magno*, trans. Don Pedro Picornell (Manila: Historical Conservation Society, 1977), 161.

5. "Boxer Codex," Boxer mss. II, 1500–1899, Lilly Library, Indiana University, fols. 29v–30r.

6. Junker, *Raiding, Trading and Feasting*, 123–126. Scott notes that *timawa* in Luzon referred to a third tier of freemen who were not noble and did perform productive labor, which adds further to the confusion provided by these early ethnographic accounts. See William Henry Scott, "*Oripun* and *Alipin* in the Sixteenth Century Philippines," in *Slavery, Bondage and Dependency in Southeast Asia*, ed. Anthony Reid (St. Lucia: University of Queensland Press, 1983), 146.

7. Scott, "*Oripun* and *Alipin*," 138–155; Junker, *Raiding, Trading, and Feasting*, 131.

8. Anthony Reid, ed., *Slavery, Bondage and Dependency in Southeast Asia* (St. Lucia: University of Queensland Press, 1983); Gwyn Campbell and Alessandro Stanziani, *Bonded Labour and Debt in the Indian Ocean World* (London: Pickering & Chatto, 2013); Stephanie Mawson, "Slavery, Conflict, and Empire in the Seventeenth Century Philippines," in *Slavery and Bonded Labor in Asia, 1250–1900*, ed. Richard B. Allen (Leiden: Brill, 2022), 260–266.

9. Anthony Reid, "Introduction: Slavery and Bondage in Southeast Asian History," in *Slavery, Bondage and Dependency in Southeast Asia*, ed. Anthony Reid (St. Lucia: University of Queensland Press, 1983), 8.

10. P. Francisco Ignacio Alzina, *Historia de las islas e indios de Bisayas, De la Compañía de Jesús, Año 1668*, Archivo General de Palacio Real (hereafter AGPR); Chirino, *Relación de las islas Filipinas*, 363–364; Antonio de Morga, *The Philippine Islands, Moluccas, Siam, Cambodia, Japan and China at the Close of the Sixteenth Century*, trans. Henry E. J. Stanley (Cambridge: Cambridge University Press, 2010), 298–300; Miguel de Loarca, "Relación de las Yslas Filipinas," in *The Philippine Islands, 1493–1803* (hereafter *B&R*), trans. and ed. Emma Helen Blair and James Alexander Robertson, 55 vols. (Cleveland, OH: A. H. Clark, 1903–9), vol. 5, 136–144; Juan de Plasencia, "Customs of the Tagalogs," *B&R*, vol. 7, 164–176; AGI, Filipinas, leg. 6, ramo 2, núm. 16; AGI, Filipinas, leg. 18A, ramo 2, núm. 9; AGI, Filipinas, leg. 34, núm. 8; AGI, Filipinas, leg. 84, núms. 18, 21.

11. Tatiana Seijas, *Asian Slaves in Colonial Mexico: From Chinos to Indios* (Cambridge: Cambridge University Press, 2014); Andrés Reséndez, "An Early Abolitionist Crusade," *Ethnohistory* 64, no.1 (2017): 19–40; see also Mawson, "Slavery, Conflict, and Empire," 258–260.

12. AGI, Escribanía de Cámara de Justicia (hereafter Escribanía), leg. 954; AGI, Escribanía, leg. 957; AGI, Escribanía, leg. 1027B; AGI, Escribanía, leg. 1027C; AGI, Escribanía, leg. 1028A; AGI, Filipinas, leg. 8, ramo 1, núm. 12; AGI, Filipinas, leg. 19, ramo 7, núms. 100, 105; AGI, Filipinas, leg. 24, ramo 5, núm. 28; AGI, Filipinas, leg. 27, núms. 51, 52, 63; AGI, Filipinas, leg. 285, núm. 1, fols. 30r–41v; Seijas, *Asian Slaves in Colonial Mexico*; William Henry Scott, *Slavery in the Spanish Philippines* (Manila: De la Salle University Press, 1991), 27–35; Déborah Oropeza Keresey, "La esclavitud asiática en el virreinato de la Nueva España, 1565–1673," *Historia Mexicana* 61, no. 1 (2011): 5–57.

13. Scott, *Slavery in the Spanish Philippines*, 3; see also John Leddy Phelan, "Free versus Compulsory Labor: Mexico and the Philippines 1540–1648," *Comparative Studies in Society and History* 1, no. 2 (1959): 197.

14. Hans Hägerdal, "The Slaves of Timor: Life and Death on the Fringes of Early Colonial Society," *Itinerario* 34, no. 2 (2010): 24.

15. Angela Schottenhammer, "Slaves and Forms of Slavery in Late Imperial China (Seventeenth to Early Twentieth Centuries)," *Slavery & Abolition* 24, no. 2 (2003): 143.

16. Reid, "'Closed' and 'Open' Slave Systems in Pre-Colonial Southeast Asia," in *Slavery, Bondage and Dependency in Southeast Asia*, ed. Anthony Reid (St. Lucia: University of Queensland Press, 1983), 159; Schottenhammer, "Slaves and Forms of Slavery," 144; Peter Boomgaard, "Human Capital, Slavery and Low Rates of Economic and Population Growth in Indonesia, 1600–1910," *Slavery & Abolition* 24, no. 2 (2003): 88–89; Bryce Beemer, "Southeast Asian Slavery and Slave-Gathering Warfare as a Vector for Cultural Transmission: The Case of Burma and Thailand," *Historian* 71, no. 3 (2009): 490; Gwyn Campbell and Alessandro Stanziani, "Introduction," in *Bonded Labour and Debt in the Indian Ocean World*, ed. Gwyn Campbell and Alessandro Stanziani (London: Pickering & Chatto, 2013), 3.

17. Beemer, "Southeast Asian Slavery," 490; Hägerdal, "Slaves of Timor," 20–21.

18. Hägerdal, "Slaves of Timor," 20–21.

19. Campbell and Stanziani, "Introduction," 4.

20. Mawson, "Slavery, Conflict, and Empire," 260–266.

21. Chirino, *Relación de las Islas Filipinas*, 363–364; Morga, *The Philippine Islands*, 298–300; Loarca, "Relación de las Yslas Filipinas," *B&R*, vol. 5, 136–144; Plasencia, "Customs of the Tagalogs," *B&R*, vol. 7, 164–176; AGI, Filipinas, leg. 6, ramo 2, núm. 16; AGI, Filipinas, leg. 18A, ramo 2, núm. 9; AGI, Filipinas, leg. 34, núm. 8; AGI, Filipinas, leg. 84, núms. 18, 21.

22. Morga, *The Philippine Islands*, 299; AGI, Filipinas, leg. 24, ramo 5, núm. 28; Mawson, "Slavery, Conflict, and Empire," 260–266.

23. Alzina, *Historia de las islas e indios de Bisayas*, AGPR; Chirino, *Relación de las Islas Filipinas*, 363–364; Morga, *The Philippine Islands*, 298–300; Loarca, "Relación de las Yslas Filipinas," *B&R*, vol. 5, 136–144; Plasencia, "Customs of the Tagalogs," *B&R*, vol. 7, 164–176; Scott, *"Oripun and Alipin,"* 138–155.

24. Junker, *Raiding, Trading and Feasting*, 130.

25. A *gobernadorcillo* was a local judge or governor; a *juez de sementeras* was a superintendent of the harvests.

26. AGI, Filipinas, leg. 2, núm. 249; AGI, Filipinas, leg. 43, núm. 27; William Henry Scott, *Discovery of the Igorots: Spanish Contacts with the Pagans of Northern Luzon* (Quezon City: New Day, 1974), 11–12; Luciano P. R. Santiago, "The Houses of Lakandula, Matandá and Solimán (1571–1898): Genealogy and Group Identity," *Philippine Quarterly of Culture and Society* 18, no. 1 (1990): 44–45, 52–53.

27. Sherman, *Forced Native Labor*, 11; Patricio Hidalgo Nuchera, "¿Esclavitud o liberación? El fracaso de las actitudes esclavistas de los conquistadores de Filipinas," *Revista Complutense de Historia de América* no. 20 (1994): 61–63; Nancy E. van Deusen, *Global Indios: The Indigenous Struggle for Justice in Sixteenth-Century Spain* (Durham, NC: Duke University Press, 2015), 216–230.

28. Van Deusen, *Global Indios*, 3; Reséndez, "An Early Abolitionist Crusade," 20; Sherman, *Forced Native Labor*, 85–152.

29. 1585: AGI, Filipinas, leg. 339, libro 1, fols. 325v–326r. 1594: AGI, Filipinas, leg. 339, libro 2, fol. 65r. 1608: AGI, Filipinas, leg. 340, libro 3, fols. 26r–26v, 28v–30r. 1609:

AGI, Filipinas, leg. 329, libro 2, fols. 83r–85r. 1639: AGI, Filipinas, leg. 330, libro 4, fols. 122v–123r. 1656: AGI, Filipinas, leg. 330, libro 5, fols. 87v–88v. 1660: AGI, Filipinas, leg. 330, libro 5, fols. 190r–194r; AGI, Filipinas, leg. 341, libro 6, fols. 261v–262r. 1662: AGI, Filipinas, leg. 330, libro 6, fols. 23v–44r. 1677: AGI, Filipinas, leg. 341, libro 7, fols. 246r–255v. 1679: AGI, Filipinas, leg. 331, libro 7, fols. 276r–277r. 1696: AGI, Filipinas, leg. 331, libro 9, fol. 209r. 1697: AGI, Filipinas, leg. 332, libro 10, fols. 26r–26v.

30. Scott, *Slavery in the Spanish Philippines*, 21–23.

31. AGI, Escribanía, leg. 403A; AGI, Filipinas, leg. 20, ramo 4, núm. 31; AGI, Filipinas, leg. 84, núms. 18, 21; H. de la Costa, "Church and State in the Philippines during the Administration of Bishop Salazar, 1581–1594," *Hispanic American Historical Review* 30, no. 3 (1950): 314–335; Hidalgo Nuchera, "¿Esclavitud o liberación?" 61–74.

32. AGI, Escribanía, leg. 403A.

33. AGI, Filipinas, leg. 18A, ramo 3, núm. 12; Scott, *Slavery in the Spanish Philippines*, 21–26.

34. James S. Cummins and Nicholas P. Cushner, "Labor in the Colonial Philippines: The Discurso Parenético of Gómez de Espinosa," *Philippine Studies* 22, nos. 1–2 (1975): 149–150; Patricio Hidalgo Nuchera, *Encomienda, tributo y trabajo en Filipinas (1570–1608)* (Madrid: Ediciones Polifemo, 1995), 241–243; Nicholas P. Cushner, *Spain in the Philippines: From Conquest to Revolution* (Quezon City: Ateneo de Manila University, 1971), 114, 118–119.

35. Nicholas P. Cushner, *Landed Estates in the Colonial Philippines* (New Haven, CT: Yale University Southeast Asia Studies, 1976), 51; Phelan, "Free versus Compulsory Labor," 193.

36. *Alcaldes mayores* were regional magistrates. *Vecinos* were Spaniards of noble heritage who had the status of citizens of the Philippines,

37. AGI, Filipinas, leg. 83, núm. 52.

38. A tribute often represented an entire family of four or more people.

39. AGI, Filipinas, leg. 27, núm. 31; Hidalgo Nuchera, *Encomienda, tributo y trabajo*, 166–168.

40. AGI, Filipinas, leg. 27, núm. 31. Hidalgo Nuchera notes that there were slight differences in how tribute payments were calculated across different documents produced in the late sixteenth century. See Hidalgo Nuchera, *Encomienda, tributo y trabajo*, 142–144.

41. AGI, Filipinas, leg. 34, núm. 38. *Gantas, brazas*, and *maes* are all units of measurement unique to the Spanish Philippines. A *ganta* is a weight equivalent to about 2.3 dry liters; a *braza* is a length a little more than five and a half feet; a *mae* is a weight worth approximately 3.1 grams.

42. Patricio Hidalgo Nuchera, "La encomienda en Filipinas," in *España y el Pacífico: Legazpi*, vol. 1, ed. Leoncio Cabrero (Madrid: Sociedad Estatal de Conmemoraciones Culturales, 2004), 477.

43. AGI, Filipinas, leg. 27, núm. 31. Major inflation in prices shortly after colonization was noted by a number of commentators: see for example AGI, Filipinas, leg. 6, ramo 10, núm. 180.

44. AGI, Patronato, leg. 25, ramo 46.

45. AGI, Filipinas, leg. 27, núm. 44. It should be noted that the role of silver in the colonial economy functioned very differently in the Philippines than in other parts of

the empire, where the widespread introduction of silver currency helped compel indigenous communities into work in order to pay their tribute and participate in new commercial markets. See for example Raquel Gil Montero, "Migración y tributación en los Andes: Chichas y Lípez a fines del siglo XVII," *Anuario de Estudios Americanos* 70, no. 1 (2013): 58. Since the silver supply was monopolized by the Chinese community of Manila, as discussed in chapter 7, there is strong archival evidence that very little silver filtered through to the provinces of the Philippines and thus pre-Hispanic models of debt servitude remained the predominant principle of economic organization within most communities.

46. AGI, Filipinas, leg. 85, núm. 55.

47. AGI, Filipinas, leg. 80, núm. 130.

48. AGI, Filipinas, leg. 80, núm. 133.

49. Mawson, "Slavery, Conflict, and Empire," 270–274.

50. Luis Alonso Álvarez, "Repartimientos y economía en las islas filipinas bajo dominio español, 1565–1815," in *El repartimiento forzoso de mercancías en México, Perú y Filipinas*, ed. Margarita Menegus (México: Instituto de Investigaciones Dr. José María Luis Mora Centre de Estudios sobre la Universidad, UNAM, 2000), 170–215; William J. McCarthy, "Yards at Cavite: Shipbuilding in the Early Colonial Philippines," *International Journal of Maritime History* 7, no. 2 (1995): 149–162.

51. AGI, Filipinas, leg. 12, ramo 1, núm. 8.

52. Archivo Histórico Nacional (hereafter AHN), Colección Documentos de Indias (hereafter CDI), leg. 26, núm. 28. In 1616, the Crown was reported to owe 71,705 pesos to Pampangans and 41,874 pesos to indios from Pintados, Ilocos, and the Tagalogs for rice, wood, and other goods. AGI, Filipinas, leg. 85, núm. 30.

53. AGI, Filipinas, leg. 193, núm. 22.

54. AGI, Filipinas, leg. 27, núm. 122; AGI, Filipinas, leg. 80, núm. 41; AGI, Filipinas, leg. 81, núm. 109; AGI, Filipinas, leg. 84, núm. 13.

55. AGI, Filipinas, leg. 75, núm. 10.

56. Cummins and Cushner, "Labor in the Colonial Philippines," 117–120.

57. AGI, Filipinas, leg. 22, ramo 9, núm. 43; AGI, Filipinas, leg. 81, núm. 109; AGI, Filipinas, leg. 84, núm. 18; AGI, Filipinas, leg. 85, núms. 25, 30; AHN, CDI, leg. 26, núms. 28, 29 30.

58. AGI, Filipinas, leg. 84, núm. 18.

59. AHN, CDI, leg. 26, núm. 28. Stephanie Mawson, "Escaping Empire: Philippine Mountains and Indigenous Histories of Resistance," *American Historical Review* (forthcoming).

60. AGI, Filipinas, leg. 6, ramo 10, núm. 180; AGI, Filipinas, leg. 8, ramo 3, núm. 90; AGI, Filipinas, leg. 18A, ramo 7, núm. 47; AGI, Filipinas, leg. 27, núm. 89; AGI, Filipinas, leg. 28, núm. 128; AGI, Filipinas, leg. 75, núms. 10, 18; AGI, Filipinas, leg. 80, núms. 41, 133; AGI, Filipinas, leg. 83, núm. 52; AGI, Filipinas, leg. 84, núm. 13; AGI, Filipinas, leg. 85, núm. 25; AHN, CDI, leg. 26, núms. 28, 29, 30; Salvador Gómez de Espinosa, *Discurso Parenético* (1657), reprinted in Cummins and Cushner, "Labor in the Colonial Philippines," 159.

61. AGI, Filipinas, leg. 81, núm. 109.

62. AGI, Filipinas, leg. 193, núm. 22.

63. AGI, Filipinas, leg. 6, ramo 10, núm. 180; see also AGI, Filipinas, leg. 19, ramo 3, núm. 31; de la Costa, "Church and State in the Philippines," 314–316.

64. AGI, Filipinas, leg. 19, ramo 3, núm. 31.

65. McCarthy, "Yards at Cavite," 157–158.

66. AGI, Filipinas, leg. 193, núm. 22.

67. McCarthy, "Yards at Cavite," 154–155.

68. The majority of these were not permanent installations. AGI, Filipinas, leg. 22, ramo 7, núm. 21; AGI, Filipinas, leg. 27, núm. 233; AGI, Filipinas, leg. 29, núm. 32; AGI, Filipinas, leg. 38, núm. 12; "Carta Annua . . . de 1601 hasta . . . 1602 años," Archivum Romanum Societatis Iesu (hereafter ARSI), phil. 5, fol. 110v.

69. Stephanie Mawson, "Philippine *Indios* in the Service of Empire: Indigenous Soldiers and Contingent Loyalty, 1600–1700," *Ethnohistory* 62, no. 2 (2016): 381–413.

70. AGI, Filipinas, leg. 6, ramo 10, núm. 180.

71. AHN, CDI, leg. 26, núm. 28.

72. AGI, Filipinas, leg. 22, ramo 9, núm. 50.

73. A *cavan* is a Philippine unit of measurement for rice worth about 55 liters.

74. AGI, Filipinas, leg. 22, ramo 9, núm. 50.

75. AGI, Filipinas, leg. 83, núm. 52.

76. AGI, Filipinas, leg. 83, núm. 52.

77. One of the earliest such rebellions occurred in Leyte in 1601 and took two years to defeat. See Fernando Palanco, "Resistencia y rebelión indígena en Filipinas durante los primeros cien años de soberanía española (1565–1665)," in *España y el Pacífico: Legazpi*, vol. 2, ed. Leoncio Cabrero (Madrid: Sociedad Estatal de Conmemoraciones Culturales, 2004), 79–80. There was additionally another major rebellion in Pampanga in 1645 that acted as a precursor to later events. See "Insurrections by Filipinos in the Seventeenth Century," *B&R*, vol. 38, 97–98; Felix M. Keesing, *Ethnohistory of Northern Luzon* (Stanford, CA: Stanford University Press, 1962), 71.

78. "Insurrections by Filipinos in the Seventeenth Century," *B&R*, vol. 38, 101–128; H. de la Costa, S. J., *The Jesuits in the Philippines, 1581–1768* (Cambridge, MA: Harvard University Press, 1961), 411–413; Palanco, "Resistencia y rebelión," 89–90.

79. "Insurrections by Filipinos in the Seventeenth Century," *B&R*, vol. 38, 107.

80. An *oidor* is a judge of the royal audiencia. Gómez de Espinosa, *Discurso Parenético*, 148–203. The original copy is held in the library of the Archivo General de Indias, Biblioteca I.A. 43 / 28. There is a second copy held by the Vatican Film Library—ARSI, phil. 11, doc. 88—however the pages in this copy are out of order. Cummins and Cushner additionally note two other copies of the *Discurso* in the priory of Santo Domingo, Quezon City, Philippines and in the Archivo General de la Nación (México).

81. Gómez de Espinosa, *Discurso Parenético*, 148.

82. José Miranda, "La función económica del encomendero en los orígenes del régimen colonial, Nueva España (1525–1531)," *Anales del Instituto Nacional de Antropología e Historia*, Sexta época (1939–1966), 2 (1946): 421–422; Sherman, *Forced Native Labor*, 85–152; Águeda Jiménez Pelayo, "Condiciones del trabajo de repartimiento indígena en la Nueva Galicia en el siglo XVII," *Historia Mexicana* 38, no. 3 (1989): 455; Hidalgo Nuchera, *Encomienda, tributo y trabajo*, 137–138, 232.

83. Hidalgo Nuchera, *Encomienda, tributo y trabajo*, 233–243; Cushner, *Spain in the Philippines*, 114.

84. AGI, Filipinas, leg. 6, ramo 10, núm. 180; AGI, Filipinas, leg. 7, ramo 5, núm. 64; AGI, Filipinas, leg. 8, ramo 1, núm. 4; AGI, Filipinas, leg. 18B, ramo 2, núm. 19; AGI,

Filipinas, leg. 18B, ramo 7, núm. 58; AGI, Filipinas, leg. 27, núm. 51; AGI, Filipinas, leg. 28, núm. 105; AGI, Filipinas, leg. 28, núm. 128; AGI, Filipinas, leg. 34, núm. 38; AGI, Filipinas, leg. 75, núm. 18; AGI, Filipinas, leg. 80, núm. 41; AGI, Filipinas, leg. 83, núm. 52; AGI, Filipinas, leg. 84, núms. 13, 36; AGI, Filipinas, leg. 85, núm. 25.

85. Gómez de Espinosa, *Discurso Parenético*, 189–190.

86. Gómez de Espinosa, *Discurso Parenético*, 190.

87. Gómez de Espinosa, *Discurso Parenético*, 190.

88. Gómez de Espinosa, *Discurso Parenético*, 160; AGI, Filipinas, leg. 18B, ramo 2, núm. 19; AGI, Filipinas, leg. 28, núm. 105; AGI, Filipinas, leg. 34, núm. 38.

89. Gómez de Espinosa, *Discurso Parenético*, 162; AGI, Filipinas, leg. 28, núm. 105.

90. Gómez de Espinosa, *Discurso Parenético*, 159–163.

91. AGI, Filipinas, leg. 18B, ramo 2, núm. 19.

92. AGI, Filipinas, leg. 84, núm. 13.

93. Gómez de Espinosa, *Discurso Parenético*, 180–182.

94. Gómez de Espinosa, *Discurso Parenético*, 170.

95. AGI, Filipinas, leg. 18B, ramo 2, núm. 19.

96. Gómez de Espinosa, *Discurso Parenético*, 160.

97. AGI, Filipinas, leg. 21, ramo 4, núm. 17.

98. Eighty different decrees were passed dealing with different aspects of indigenous labor, tribute payments, and other forms of treatment by royal officials and missionaries in the years 1574, 1575, 1580, 1584, 1585, 1594, 1596, 1602, 1604, 1608, 1609, 1613, 1618, 1620, 1624, 1627, 1628, 1631, 1632, 1638, 1639, 1641, 1643, 1656, 1660, 1661, 1662, 1673, 1677, 1679, 1681, 1685, 1686, 1690, 1696, 1697, 1698. See AGI, Filipinas, leg. 329, libros 1, 2, 3; AGI, Filipinas, leg. 330, libros 4, 5, 6; AGI, Filipinas, leg. 331, libros 7, 8, 9; AGI, Filipinas, leg. 332, libro 10; AGI, Filipinas, leg. 339, libros 1, 2; AGI, Filipinas, leg. 340, libros 3, 4; AGI, Filipinas, leg. 341, libros 6, 7.

99. AGI, Filipinas, leg. 22, ramo 9, núms. 43, 51.

100. AGI, Filipinas, leg. 22, ramo 9, núm. 51.

101. Gómez de Espinosa, *Discurso Parenético*, 200–202.

102. Cummins and Cushner, "Labor in the Colonial Philippines," 138. A decade after this attack, Fr. Francisco Solier was publicly accused of violently abusing four indios in Sampaloc, as will be discussed in chapter 3. See AGI, Filipinas, leg. 10, ramo 1, núm. 5.

103. Cummins and Cushner, "Labor in the Colonial Philippines," 137–143. The author of the pamphlet refers to the way in which Bartolomé Las Casas was used by imperial rivals to undermine the reputation and authority of the Spanish empire. See Margaret R. Greer, Walter D. Mignolo, and Maureen Quilligan, eds., *Rereading the Black Legend: The Discourses of Religious and Racial Difference in the Renaissance Empires* (Chicago: University of Chicago Press, 2007).

104. AGI, Filipinas, leg. 22, ramo 9, núm. 51.

105. Cummins and Cushner, "Labor in the Colonial Philippines," 143–145.

106. AGI, Filipinas, leg. 22, ramo 9, núm. 51.

107. AGI, Escribanía, leg. 410A; Cummins and Cushner, "Labor in the Colonial Philippines," 146.

108. AGI, Filipinas, leg. 24, ramo 5, núm. 28.

109. Sherman, *Forced Native Labor*, 11; Hidalgo Nuchera, "¿Esclavitud o liberación?" 61–63; Van Deusen, *Global Indios*, 216–230.

110. Reséndez, "An Early Abolitionist Crusade," 19–40; Walter Hanisch Espíndola, S. J., "Esclavitud y libertad de los indios de Chile, 1608–1696," *Historia* no. 16 (1981): 5–65.

111. AGI, Filipinas, leg. 24, ramo 5, núm. 28.

112. AGI, Filipinas, leg. 24, ramo 5, núm. 28.

113. Mawson, "Slavery, Conflict, and Empire," 276–281.

3. Contested Conversions

1. "Insurrections by Filipinos in the Seventeenth Century," in *The Philippine Islands, 1493–1803* (hereafter *B&R*), trans. and ed. Emma Helen Blair and James Alexander Robertson, 55 vols. (Cleveland, OH: A. H. Clark, 1903–9), vol. 38, 87–94; Pedro Murillo Velarde, *Historia de la Provincia de Philipinas de la compañia de Jesús: Segunda Parte, que comprehende los progresos de esta provincia desde el año de 1616 hasta el de 1716* (Manila: Imprenta de la Compañía de Jesús, por D. Nicolas de la Cruz Bagay, 1749), 17–19; Fray Juan de Medina, *Historia de los sucesos de la orden de N. Gran P.S. Agustín de estas Islas Filipinas, desde que se descubrieron y se poblaron por los españoles, con las noticias memorables* (Manila: Tipo-Litografía de Chofre y Comp., 1893), 226–228; Archivo General de Indias (hereafter AGI), Audiencia de Filipinas (hereafter Filipinas), leg. 76, núm. 13; "Annua Societatis Iesu Provinciae Philippinarum Insularum, Anni 1621," Archivum Romanum Societatis Iesu (hereafter ARSI), phil. 6, fols. 307r–314r.

2. "Carta Annua de Philipinas desde el año de 1665 hasta el de 1671," Real Academia de la Historia (hereafter RAH), 9/2668, núm. 17.

3. "Insurrections by Filipinos in the Seventeenth Century," *B&R*, vol. 38, 87–94; Murillo Velarde, *Historia de la Provincia*, 17–19; Medina, *Historia de los Sucesos*, 226–228; AGI, Filipinas, leg. 76, núm. 13; "Annua Societatis Iesu Provinciae Philippinarum Insularum, Anni 1621," ARSI, phil. 6, fols. 307r–314r; "Carta Annua . . . de 1665 hasta . . . 1671," RAH, 9/2668, núm. 17.

4. AGI, Filipinas, leg. 75, núm. 20; Pedro Fernández del Pulgar, "Descripción de las Filipinas y de las Malucas e Historia del Archipiélago Maluco desde su descubrimiento," Biblioteca Nacional de España (hereafter BNE), mss. 3002, fol. 28v. This was not unique to the Philippines, see Barbara Watson Andaya, "The Changing Religious Role of Women in Pre-Modern South East Asia," *South East Asia Research* 2, no. 2 (1994): 102.

5. By contrast there were nineteen men involved in these practices. AGI, Filipinas, leg. 75, núm. 23.

6. Carolyn Brewer, "From Animist 'Priestess' to Catholic Priest: The Re/Gendering of Religious Roles in the Philippines, 1521–1685," in *Other Pasts: Women, Gender and History in Early Modern Southeast Asia*, ed. Barbara Watson Andaya (Honolulu: Center for Southeast Asian Studies, University of Hawai'i at Manoa, 2000), 69–86; see also Marya Svetlana Camacho, "The *Baylan* and *Catalonan* in the Early Spanish Colonial Period," in *Un mar de islas, un mar de gentes: Poblacion y diversidad en las islas Filipinas*, eds. Marta María Manchado López and Miguel Luque Talaván (Córdoba: Servicio de Publicaciones Universidad de Córdoba, 2014), 127–144.

7. Alfred McCoy, "Baylan, Animist Religion and Philippine Peasant Ideology," *Philippine Quarterly of Culture and Society* 10 (1982): 165–166.

8. John Leddy Phelan, *Hispanization of the Philippines: Spanish Aims and Filipino Responses, 1565–1700* (Madison: University of Wisconsin Press, 1967); Francisco Javier

Campos y Fernández de Sevilla, "Las órdenes mendicantes en Filipinas: agustinos, franciscanos, dominicos y recoletos," in *España y el Pacífico: Legazpi*, vol. 2, ed. Leoncio Cabrero (Madrid: Sociedad Estatal de Conmemoraciones Culturales, 2004), 251–280; Cayetano Sánchez Fuertes, "La Iglesia y sus relaciones con los Filipinos en los siglos XVI y XVII," in *España y el Pacífico: Legazpi*, vol. 2, ed. Leoncio Cabrero (Madrid: Sociedad Estatal de Conmemoraciones Culturales, 2004), 319–357; Eladio Neira, *Conversion Methodology in the Philippines (1565–1665)* (Manila: University of Santo Tomas, 1966); John N. Schumacher, S. J., "Syncretism in Philippine Catholicism: Its Historical Causes," *Philippine Studies* 32 (1984): 251–272; John N. Schumacher, S. J., *Growth and Decline: Essays on Philippine Church History* (Quezon City: Ateneo de Manila University Press, 2009); Ramon C. Reyes, "Religious Experiences in the Philippines: From Mythos through Lagos to Kairos," *Philippine Studies* 33, no. 2 (1985): 203–21; Pedro Borges Morán, "Aspectos Característicos de La Evangelización de Filipinas," in *España y el Pacífico: Legazpi*, vol. 2, ed. Leoncio Cabrero (Madrid: Sociedad Estatal de Conmemoraciones Culturales, 2004), 285–318; Pablo Fernandez, O. P., *History of the Church in the Philippines (1521–1898)* (Manila: National Book Store Publishers, 1979).

9. Charles J. H. Macdonald, "Folk Catholicism and Pre-Spanish Religions in the Philippines," *Philippine Studies* 52, no. 1 (2004): 78–93; Richard W. Lieban, *Cebuano Sorcery: Malign Magic in the Philippines* (Berkeley: University of California Press, 1967); Fenella Cannell, *Power and Intimacy in the Christian Philippines* (Cambridge: Cambridge University Press, 1999); Charles Macdonald, "Invoking the Spirits in Palawan: Ethnography and Pragmatics," in *Sociolinguistics Today: International Perspectives*, eds. Kingsley Bolton and Helen Kwok (London: Routledge, 1992), 244–260; Stephen K. Hislop, "Anitism: A Survey of Religious Beliefs Native to the Philippines," *Asian Studies* 9 (1971): 144–156; F. Landa Jocano, "Filipino Catholicism: A Case Study in Religious Change," *Asian Studies* 5, no. 1 (1967): 42–64; F. Landa Jocano, "Conversion and the Patterning of Christian Experience in Malitbog, Central Panay, Philippines," *Philippine Sociological Review* 13, no. 2 (1965): 96–119; McCoy, "Baylan, Animist Religion," 141–194; Charles Macdonald, "Cleansing the Earth: The *Pangarris* Ceremony in Kulbi-Kanipaqan, Southern Palawan," *Philippine Studies* 45 (1997): 408–422; Thomas Gibson, *Sacrifice and Sharing in the Philippine Highlands: Religion and Society among the Buid of Mindoro* (London: Athlone Press, 1986); Penelope Graham, *Iban Shamanism: An Analysis of the Ethnographic Literature*, Occasional Paper of the Department of Anthropology, Research School of Pacific Studies (Canberra: Australian National University, 1987).

10. Phelan, *Hispanization of the Philippines*; Campos y Fernández de Sevilla, "Las órdenes mendicantes," 251–283; Sánchez Fuertes, "La Iglesia y sus relaciones," 319–357; Schumacher, *Growth and Decline*, 1–21; Neira, *Conversion Methodology*, 4. As should be evident from this discussion, this perspective is most strongly put forward by Church historians; by contrast, ethnohistorians have presented a more complex view of the conversion process, in which Philippine communities exhibited agency over their interpretation of Christianity. See for example Vicente L. Rafael, *Contracting Colonialism: Translation and Christian Conversion in Tagalog Society Under Early Spanish Rule* (Ithaca, NY: Cornell University Press, 1988); Mark Dizon, "Social and Spiritual Kinship in Early-Eighteenth-Century Missions on the Caraballo Mountains," *Philippine Studies* 59, no. 3 (2011): 367–398; Mark Dizon, "Sumpong Spirit Beliefs, Murder, and Religious Change among

Eighteenth-Century Aeta and Ilongot in Eastern Central Luzon," *Philippine Studies* 63, no. 1 (2015): 3–38.

11. Campos y Fernández de Sevilla, "Las órdenes mendicantes," 251.

12. Neira, *Conversion Methodology*, 4; see also Reyes, "Religious Experiences in the Philippines," 203–212.

13. Campos y Fernández de Sevilla, "Las órdenes mendicantes," 252; Sánchez Fuertes, "La Iglesia y sus relaciones," 319–357; Schumacher, *Growth and Decline*, 1–21.

14. Schumacher has argued that "no whole people, at least prior to the late nineteenth century, had ever in the history of the Church been so thoroughly evangelized as were the Filipinos." Schumacher, "Syncretism in Philippine Catholicism," 252. Miguel A. Bernad argues by contrast that, while evangelization had progressed to an impressive extent, the full Christianization of the islands could not be considered complete since native Filipinos were denied access to entering the clergy. Despite this, he calls the Christianization process a "stupendous feat." See Miguel A. Bernad, S. J., *The Christianization of the Philippines: Problems and Perspectives* (Manila: Filipiniana Book Guild, 1972).

15. McCoy, "Baylan, Animist Religion," 146–154.

16. McCoy, "Baylan, Animist Religion," 164.

17. McCoy, "Baylan, Animist Religion," 161–165.

18. Rafael, *Contracting Colonialism*.

19. Historians associated with the Jesuit order: José S. Arcilla, S. J., Miguel A. Bernad, S. J., Pierre de Charentenay, S. J., Horacio de la Costa, S. J., Nicholas Cushner, S. J., Francisco R. Demetrio, S. J., Francis X. Hezel, S. J., Thomas J. O'Shaugnessy, S. J., W. C. Repetti, S. J., and John N. Schumacher, S. J., Associated with the Augustinian Order: Francisco Javier Campos y Fernández de Sevilla. Associated with the Franciscan Order: Cayetano Sánches Fuertes. Associated with the Dominican order: Pablo Fernandez, O. P., Eladio Neira, and Pedro V. Salgado. Associated with the Missionaries of the Sacred Heart: Peter Schreurs.

20. "Carta Annua de la Vice Provincia de las Islas Philippinas desde el mes de junio de 1601 hasta el junio de 1602 años," ARSI, phil. 5, fols. 105r–106v.

21. See for example AGI, Filipinas, leg. 79, núms. 22, 69, 73.

22. On the shortage of priests, see Archivo Histórico Nacional (hereafter AHN), Colección Documentos de Indias (hereafter CDI), leg. 26, núm. 10; AGI, Filipinas, leg. 19, ramo 2, núm. 29; AGI, Filipinas, leg. 79, núms. 22, 35, 37; AGI, Filipinas, leg. 84, núms. 46, 95; Letter from Mateo Sanchez, April 12, 1603, ARSI, phil. 10, fols. 104r–106v.

23. Dizon, "Sumpong Spirit Beliefs," 18.

24. Pedro Chirino, *Relación de las islas Filipinas i de lo que en ellas an trabajado los padres de la Compañía de Iesus* (Roma: Por Estevan Paulino, 1604), 297–298; Pedro Fernández del Pulgar, "Descripción de las Filipinas y de las Malucas e Historia del Archipiélago Maluco desde su descubrimiento," BNE, mss. 3002, fols. 27v–29v.

25. Pedro Fernández del Pulgar, "Descripción de las Filipinas y de las Malucas e Historia del Archipiélago Maluco desde su descubrimiento," BNE, mss. 3002, fols. 27v–29v.

26. Chirino, *Relación de las islas Filipinas*, 299.

27. AGI, Filipinas, leg. 75, núms. 20, 23.

28. AGI, Filipinas, leg. 75, núms. 20, 23; AGI, Filipinas, leg. 13, ramo 1, núm. 13.

29. Antonio de Morga, *The Philippine Islands, Moluccas, Siam, Cambodia, Japan and China at the Close of the Sixteenth Century*; trans. Henry E. J. Stanley (Cambridge:

Cambridge University Press, 2010), 306; Chirino, *Relación de las islas Filipinas*, 300; Pedro Fernández del Pulgar, "Descripción de las Filipinas y de las Malucas e Historia del Archipiélago Maluco desde su descubrimiento," BNE, mss. 3002, fol. 28v.

30. Chirino, *Relación de las islas Filipinas*, 298–299. Fernández del Pulgar says that the Augustinians responded to this by removing the rock and putting in its place a cross and a chapel with the image of San Nicolas de Tolentino. Pedro Fernández del Pulgar, "Descripción de las Filipinas y de las Malucas e Historia del Archipiélago Maluco desde su descubrimiento," BNE, mss. 3002, fol. 27v.

31. AGI, Filipinas, leg. 75, núms. 20, 23; AGI, Filipinas, leg. 13, ramo 1, núm. 13.

32. Chirino, *Relación de las islas Filipinas*, 297–298.

33. AGI, Filipinas, leg. 75, núms. 20, 23; AGI, Filipinas, leg. 13, ramo 1, núm. 13.

34. Chirino, *Relación de las islas Filipinas*, 297–298.

35. Pedro Fernández del Pulgar, "Descripción de las Filipinas y de las Malucas e Historia del Archipiélago Maluco desde su descubrimiento," BNE, mss. 3002, fols. 27v–29v.

36. AGI, Filipinas, leg. 75, núms. 20, 23.

37. Chirino, *Relación de las islas Filipinas*, 300–301; Pedro Fernández del Pulgar, "Descripción de las Filipinas y de las Malucas e Historia del Archipiélago Maluco desde su descubrimiento," BNE, mss. 3002, fol. 28v.

38. AGI, Filipinas, leg. 75, núms. 20, 23.

39. AGI, Filipinas, leg. 75, núm. 20.

40. AGI, Filipinas, leg. 75, núms. 20, 23; AGI, Filipinas, leg. 13, ramo 1, núm. 13.

41. AHN, CDI, leg. 26, núm. 10; AHN, CDI, leg. 27, núm. 36; AGI, Filipinas, leg. 18A, ramo 3, núm. 15; AGI, Filipinas, leg. 19, ramo 2, núm. 29; AGI, Filipinas, leg. 79, núms. 22, 35, 37, 73; AGI, Filipinas, leg. 80, núm. 69; AGI, Filipinas, leg. 84, núms. 46, 95; ARSI, phil. 10, doc. 47; Letter from Mateo Sanchez, April 12, 1603, ARSI, phil. 10, fols. 104r–106v.

42. See for example Jeremy Ravi Mumford, *Vertical Empire: The General Resettlement of Indians in the Colonial Andes* (Durham, NC: Duke University Press, 2012).

43. AHN, CDI, leg. 26, núm. 10; AGI, Filipinas, leg. 19, ramo 2, núm. 29; AGI, Filipinas, leg. 79, núms. 22, 35, 37; AGI, Filipinas, leg. 84, núms. 46, 95; Letter from Mateo Sanchez, April 12, 1603, ARSI, phil. 10, fols. 104r–106v.

44. Letter from Mateo Sanchez, April 12, 1603, ARSI, phil. 10, fols. 104r–106v; AGI, Filipinas, leg. 84, núm. 46; Phelan, *Hispanization of the Philippines*, 45.

45. AGI, Filipinas, leg. 7, ramo 3, núm. 45; AGI, Filipinas, leg. 330, libro 4, fols. 247r–247v; AHN, CDI, leg. 26, núm. 28.

46. Letter from Mateo Sanchez, April 12, 1603, ARSI, phil. 10, fols. 104r–106v.

47. "Carta Annua de la Provincia de las Philippinas desde junio 1600 hasta el de junio de 1601 Años," ARSI, phil. 5, fols. 75r–92r.

48. Murillo Velarde, *Historia de la Provincia*, 148r, 258r–258v; Letter from Ignacio Alcina, June 24, 1660, ARSI, phil. 12, fols. 1r–12r.

49. Letter from Ignacio Alcina, June 24, 1660, ARSI, phil. 12, fols. 1r–12r.

50. AGI, Filipinas, leg. 86, núm. 48.

51. AGI, Filipinas, leg. 86, núm. 48.

52. AGI, Filipinas, leg. 26, ramo 1, núm. 3.

53. AGI, Filipinas, leg. 76, núm. 145.

54. AGI, Filipinas, leg. 10, ramo 1, núm. 5. Notably, Fr. Francisco Solier was one of the most vocal opponents of the *Discurso Parenético*, which sought to highlight the abusive treatment of priests toward indigenous communities, as discussed in chapter 2.

55. Barbara Watson Andaya, "Between Empires and Emporia: The Economics of Christianization in Early Modern Southeast Asia," *Journal of the Economic and Social History of the Orient* 53, nos. 1/2 (2010): 363–364.

56. It should be noted that in this instance the alcalde mayor was reported as being indigenous rather than Spanish, as was normally the case in other provinces.

57. AGI, Filipinas, leg. 10, ramo 1, núm. 5.

58. The same indios reported that the Recollects had demonstrated little interest in teaching them the Holy Gospel—teaching them only basic commandments and, even then, only poorly so that many believed that fornication was not a sin unless the priest specifically said it was. AGI, Filipinas, leg. 75, núms. 20, 23.

59. AGI, Filipinas, leg. 75, núms. 20, 23; AGI, Filipinas, leg. 13, ramo 1, núm. 13.

60. AGI, Filipinas, leg. 75, núms. 20, 23; AGI, Filipinas, leg. 13, ramo 1, núm. 13.

61. AGI, Filipinas, leg. 76, núm. 145.

62. Archivo General de la Nación (México) (hereafter AGN), Indiferente Virreinal, caja 3436, exp. 22.

63. Letter from Valerio de Ledesma, March 10, 1601, ARSI, phil. 10, fols. 41r–42r.

64. Letter from Mateo Sanchez, April 12, 1603, ARSI, phil. 10, fols. 104r–106v. For an extended discussion on the views held by Catholic missionaries regarding indigenous women and their sexuality, see Carolyn Brewer, *Shamanism, Catholicism and Gender Relations in Colonial Philippines, 1521–1685* (Aldershot, UK: Ashgate, 2004).

65. AGI, Filipinas, leg. 75, núms. 20, 23.

66. Letter from Andres de la Cruz, April 30, 1615, ARSI, phil. 11, fols. 51r–54v.

67. AGN, Indiferente Virreinal, caja 4154, exps. 30, 35; AGI, Filipinas, leg. 18B, ramo 8, núm. 91. For comparative studies on this from New Spain and Spain see Zeb Tortorici, *Sins Against Nature: Sex and Archives in Colonial New Spain* (Durham, NC: Duke University Press, 2018); Stephen Haliczer, *Sexuality in the Confessional: A Sacrament Profaned* (Oxford: Oxford University Press, 1996).

68. AGN, Indiferente Virreinal, caja 3436, exp. 22, 28, 42; AGN, Indiferente Virreinal, caja 3871, exp. 11; AGN, Indiferente Virreinal, caja 4052, exps. 26, 29; AGN, Indiferente Virreinal, caja 4154, exps. 1, 5, 18, 20, 21, 26, 32; AGN, Inquisición, vol. 220, exp. 8; AGN, Inquisición, vol. 282, exp. 7; AGN, Inquisición, vol. 293, exp. 19; AGN, Inquisición, vol. 336, exp. 1.

69. AGN, Indiferente Virreinal, caja 4052, exp. 26.

70. AGN, Indiferente Virreinal, caja 4154, exp. 20.

71. AGN, Indiferente Virreinal, caja 4154, exp. 5.

72. AGN, Indiferente Virreinal, caja 4154, exp. 21.

73. AGN, Indiferente Virreinal, caja 4052, exp. 29, fols. 29r–30v.

74. AGI, Escribanía de Cámara de Justicia (hereafter Escribanía), leg. 404B; Damon L. Woods, "Out of the Silence, the Men of Naujan Speak: Tagalog Texts from the Seventeenth Century," *Philippine Studies* 63, no. 3 (2015): 303–340.

75. "Carta Annua . . . de 1665 hasta . . . 1671," RAH, 9/2668, núm. 17; AGI, Filipinas, leg. 75, núm. 20.

76. Woods, "Out of the Silence," 303–340.

77. "Insurrections by Filipinos in the Seventeenth Century," *B&R*, vol. 38, 87–94; Murillo Velarde, *Historia de la provincia*, 17–19; Fray Juan de Medina, *Historia de los sucesos de la orden de N. Gran P.S. Agustín de estas Islas Filipinas, desde que se descubrieron y se poblaron por los españoles, con las noticias memorables* (Manila: Tipo-Litografía de Chofre y Comp., 1893), 226–228; AGI, Filipinas, leg. 76, núm. 13; "Annua Societatis Iesu Provinciae Philippinarum Insularum, Anni 1621," ARSI, phil. 6, fols. 307r–314r.

78. "Insurrections by Filipinos in the Seventeenth Century," *B&R*, vol. 38, 87–94; Murillo Velarde, *Historia de la Provincia*, 17–19; Medina, *Historia de los sucesos*, 226–228; AGI, Filipinas, leg. 76, núm. 13; "Annua Societatis Iesu Provinciae Philippinarum Insularum, Anni 1621," ARSI, phil. 6, fols. 307r–314r.

79. "Annua de la provincia de Philippinas del año de 1627," ARSI, phil. 6, fols. 438r–525r.

80. "Annua de la provincia de Philippinas del año de 1638–1639," ARSI, phil. 7, fols. 311r–394v. Bohol was later the site of the Philippines' longest rebellion against Spanish colonization, led by Dagohoy and lasting for eighty-five years between 1744 and 1829. Renato Constantino, *The Philippines: A Past Revisited* (Quezon City: Tala Publishing Services, 1975), 102–103.

81. Oona Paredes, *A Mountain of Difference: The Lumad in Early Colonial Mindanao* (Ithaca, NY: Cornell Southeast Asia Program Publications, 2013), 83–119; Peter Schreurs, *Caraga Antigua, 1521–1910: The Hispanization and Christianization of Agusan, Surigao and East Davao* (Cebu City: University of San Carlos, 1989), 146–161; AHN, CDI, leg. 25, núm. 62; "Informaciones acerca de la vida del venerable fray Alonso Orozco," BNE, mss. 3828, fols. 213r–216v; Fernando Palanco, "Resistencia y rebelión indígena en Filipinas durante los primeros cien años de soberanía española (1565–1665)," in *España y el Pacífico: Legazpi*, vol. 2, ed. Leoncio Cabrero (Madrid: Sociedad Estatal de Conmemoraciones Culturales, 2004), 85–86; AGI, Filipinas, leg. 8, ramo 1, núm. 16; "Insurrections by Filipinos in the Seventeenth Century," *B&R*, vol. 38, 128–131.

82. "Relación de lo sucedido en las islas Filipinas y otras partes circunvecinas desde el mes de Julio de 1630 hasta el de 1632," RAH, 9/3657, núm. 15.

83. AGI, Filipinas, leg. 27, núm. 184. In 1649, a major revolt extended across the Visayas, involving communities in Samar, Camarines, Masbate, Cebu, Caraga, Iligan and Leyte. "Insurrections by Filipinos in the Seventeenth Century," *B&R*, vol. 38, 101–128; H. de la Costa, S. J., *Jesuits in the Philippines, 1581–1768* (Cambridge, MA: Harvard University Press, 1961), 411–413; Palanco, "Resistencia y rebelión," 89–90.

84. "Insurrections by Filipinos in the Seventeenth Century," *B&R*, vol. 38, 215–223.

85. "Insurrections by Filipinos in the Seventeenth Century," *B&R*, vol. 38, 220.

86. "Insurrections by Filipinos in the Seventeenth Century," *B&R*, vol. 38, 215–223.

87. "Insurrections by Filipinos in the Seventeenth Century," *B&R*, vol. 38, 215–223.

88. AGI, Escribanía, leg. 404B.

89. AGI, Escribanía, leg. 404B; AGI, Filipinas, leg. 82, núm. 91.

90. "Carta Annua de Philipinas desde el año de 1665 hasta el de 1671," RAH, 9/2668, núm. 17; "Carta Annua de la Vice Provincia de las Islas Philippinas desde el mes de junio de 1601 hasta el junio de 1602 años," ARSI, phil. 5, fol. 97v.

91. Letter from Ignacio Alcina, June 24, 1660, ARSI, phil. 12, fols. 1r–12r.

92. AGI, Filipinas, leg. 18A, ramo 3, núm. 19.

93. "Letter from Fr. Diego de Jesús, dated 1680", AGI, Escribanía, leg. 404B, doc. 4, fol. 1r.

94. "Letter from Fr. Diego de Jesús, dated 1680", AGI, Escribanía, leg. 404B, doc. 4, fol. 1r.

95. AGI, Filipinas, leg. 82, núm. 91.

96. AGI, Escribanía, leg. 404B.

97. AGI, Filipinas, leg. 75, núms. 20, 23. This episode is analyzed by Carolyn Brewer, although her source—which she refers to as the "Bolinao Manuscript"—appears to have been only a partial copy of the full archival sources available in Seville. See Brewer, *Shamanism*, 143–188.

98. AGI, Filipinas, leg. 75, núm. 20. This case has also been described in detail in Marta María Manchado López, "Cristianización y persistencia cultural en Filipinas: El caso de la provincia de la Laguna de Bay en la segunda mitad del siglo XVII," in *Filipinas y el Pacífico: Nueva miradas, nuevas reflexiones*, eds. Salvador Bernabéu Albert, Carmen Mena García, and Emilio José Luque Azcona (Sevilla: Editorial Universidad de Sevilla, 2016), 421–440.

99. A *Mestiza de Sangley* is someone of mixed Chinese and Filipino heritage.

100. AGI, Filipinas, leg. 75, núms. 20, 23; AGI, Filipinas, leg. 13, ramo 1, núm. 13.

101. AGI, Filipinas, leg. 75, núms. 20, 23; AGI, Filipinas, leg. 13, ramo 1, núm. 13.

102. Dizon, "Sumpong Spirit Beliefs," 27–29, 33.

103. "Carta Annua de la Vice Provincia de las Islas Philippinas desde el mes de junio de 1601 hasta el junio de 1602 años," ARSI, phil. 5, fol. 107r.

104. McCoy, "Baylan, Animist Religion," 155–156.

105. "Carta Annua de la Vice Provincia de las Islas Philippinas desde el mes de junio de 1601 hasta el junio de 1602 años," ARSI, phil. 5, fols. 104r–104v.

106. Dizon, "Sumpong Spirit Beliefs," 27–29.

107. "Carta Annua de la Vice Provincia de las Islas Philippinas desde el mes de junio de 1601 hasta el junio de 1602 años," ARSI, phil. 5, fols. 101v–102v.

108. "Carta Annua de la Vice Provincia de las Islas Philippinas desde el mes de junio de 1601 hasta el junio de 1602 años," ARSI, phil. 5, fol. 96r.

109. McCoy, "Baylan, Animist Religion," 155–156.

110. McCoy, "Baylan, Animist Religion," 156; Landa Jocano, "Filipino Catholicism," 54; Axel Borchgrevink, "Ideas of Power in the Philippines: Amulets and Sacrifice," *Cultural Dynamics* 15, no. 1 (2003): 41–69.

111. Reynaldo Ileto has demonstrated how amulets continued to hold spiritual significance during the revolutionary era. See Reynaldo Clemeña Ileto, *Pasyon and Revolution: Popular Movements in the Philippines, 1840–1910* (Quezon City: Ateneo de Manila University Press, 1979).

112. Dizon, "Social and Spiritual Kinship," 367–398.

113. Landa Jocano, "Conversion," 96–119.

114. Landa Jocano, "Filipino Catholicism," 48.

115. Landa Jocano, "Filipino Catholicism," 42–64.

116. Landa Jocano, "Conversion," 106.

117. Cannell, *Power and Intimacy*; Macdonald, "Invoking the Spirits," 244–246; Francisco R. Demetrio, S. J., "Shamans, Witches and Philippine Society," *Philippine Studies* 36, no. 3 (1998): 372–380; Lieban, *Cebuano Sorcery*.

118. McCoy, "Baylan, Animist Religion," 146–154.

119. Campos y Fernández de Sevilla, "Las órdenes mendicantes," 251; Neira, *Conversion Methodology*, 4; Reyes, "Religious Experiences in the Philippines," 203–212.

4. Slave Raiding and Imperial Retreat

1. A type of long-sword used by Philippine communities.

2. "Copia de una del padre Melchor Hurtado escrita al Padre Gregorio Lopez Vice Provincial de Philipinas dandole quenta de su captiverio, October 1604," Archivum Romanum Societatis Iesu (hereafter ARSI), phil. 10, fols. 159r–188v.

3. De la Costa concluded however that the illness was likely dysentery. H. de la Costa, S. J., *Jesuits in the Philippines, 1581–1768* (Cambridge, MA: Harvard University Press, 1961), 292; "Copia de una del padre Melchor Hurtado . . . October 1604," ARSI, phil. 10, fols. 159r–188v.

4. "Copia de una del padre Melchor Hurtado . . . October 1604," ARSI, phil. 10, fols. 159r–188v.

5. Francisco Colin, *Labor evangélica, ministerios apostólicos de los obreros de la compañía de Iesus, fundación y progressos de su provincia en las islas filipinas: Historiados por el padre Francisco Colin, provincial de la misma compañía, calificador del santo oficio y su comisario en la governacion de Samboanga y su distrito*, 4 vols. (Madrid: Por Ioseph Fernandez de Buendia, Año de 1668), Libro III, 467–472, 506–510.

6. Cesar Adib Majul, *Muslims in the Philippines* (Quezon City: University of the Philippines Press, 1973); Francisco Mallari, "Muslim Raids in Bicol, 1580–1792," *Philippine Studies* 34, no. 3 (1986): 257–286; Luis Camara Dery, *The Kris in Philippine History: A Study of the Impact of Moro Anti-Colonial Resistance, 1571–1896* (Quezon City: Luis Camara Dery, 1997);; Carlos Martínez-Valverde, "Sobre la guerra contra moros, en filipinas, en el siglo XVI y en el XVII: expediciones de Don Sebastián Hurtado de Corcuera a Mindanao y Jolo," *Revista de Historia Militar* 29, no. 59 (1985): 9–56; Vicente Barrantes, *Guerras piráticas de Filipinas contra mindanaos y joloanos* (Madrid: Imprenta de Manuel G. Hernandez, 1878); José Montero y Vidal, *Historia de la piratería malayo-mahometana en Mindanao, Jolo y Borneo* (Madrid: M. Tello, 1888); Domingo M. Non, "Moro Piracy during the Spanish Period and Its Impact," *Southeast Asian Studies* 30, no. 4 (1993): 401–419.

7. William Lytle Schurz, *The Manila Galleon: The Romantic History of the Spanish Galleons Trading between Manila and Acapulco* (New York: E. P. Dutton, 1959), 344–345; José Eugenio Borao Mateo, *The Spanish Experience in Taiwan, 1626–1642* (Hong Kong: Hong Kong University Press, 2009), 10–11; Otto van den Muijzenberg, "A Short History of Social Connections between the Philippines and the Netherlands," *Philippine Studies* 51, no. 3 (2003): 339–340; Peter Borschberg, "From Self-Defense to an Instrument of War: Dutch Privateering Around the Malay Peninsula in the Early Seventeenth Century," *Journal of Early Modern History* 17, no. 1 (2013): 35–52.

8. Archivo General de Indias (hereafter AGI), Audiencia de Filipinas (hereafter Filipinas), leg. 20, ramo 4, núm. 31; Schurz, *The Manila Galleon*, 346–348; Borao Mateo, *The Spanish Experience in Taiwan*, 13.

9. AGI, Filipinas, leg. 7, ramo 5, núm. 64.

10. AGI, Filipinas, leg. 7, ramo 5, núm. 64; AGI, Filipinas, leg. 20, ramo 18, núm. 118; AGI, Filipinas, leg. 85, núm. 57; Ruurdje Laarhoven and Elizabeth Pino Witter-

mans, "From Blockade to Trade: Early Dutch Relations with Manila, 1600–1750," *Philippine Studies* 33, no. 4 (1985): 491–492.

11. AGI, Filipinas, leg. 6, ramo 3, núm. 35. This proposal was repeated by Governor Gonzalo Ronquillo de Peñalosa in 1582: AGI, Filipinas, leg. 6, ramo 4, núm. 49; Manel Ollé, *La impresa de China: de la armada invencible al galeón de Manila* (Barcelona: Acantilado, 2002).

12. AGI, Filipinas, leg. 18A, ramo 3, núm. 19.

13. AGI, Filipinas, leg. 6, ramo 6, núm. 60; AGI, Filipinas, leg. 6, ramo 7, núm. 79; AGI, Filipinas, leg. 18A, ramo 6, núm. 36; AGI, Filipinas, leg. 18B, ramo 5, núm. 45.

14. De la Costa, *Jesuits in the Philippines*, 282–285; Majul, *Muslims in the Philippines*, 116–122; Camara Dery, *The Kris in Philippine History*, 15–16.

15. AGI, Filipinas, leg. 8, ramo 3, núm. 82.

16. AGI, Filipinas, leg. 28, núm. 128; see also Mallari, "Muslim Raids in Bicol," 257–286.

17. Majul, *Muslims in the Philippines*; Ethan P. Hawkley, "Reviving the Reconquista in Southeast Asia: Moros and the Making of the Philippines, 1565–1662," *Journal of World History* 25, nos. 2–3 (2014): 285–310; Mallari, "Muslim Raids in Bicol," 257–286; Thomas J. O'Shaughnessy, "Philippine Islam and the Society of Jesus," *Philippine Studies* 4, no. 2 (1956): 215–239; Najeeb M. Saleeby, *Studies in Moro History, Law, and Religion* (Manila: Bureau of Public Printing, 1905); Najeeb M. Saleeby, *History of Sulu* (Manila: Bureau of Public Printing, 1908); Camara Dery, *The Kris in Philippine History*; John Leddy Phelan, *The Hispanization of the Philippines: Spanish Aims and Filipino Responses, 1565–1700* (Madison: University of Wisconsin Press, 1967); Martínez-Valverde, "Sobre la guerra contra moros," 9–56.

18. Francisco Combes, *Historia de las islas de Mindanao, Jolo y sus adyacentes. Progresos de la religión y armas católicas. Compuesto por el padre Francisco Combes, de la compañía de Iesus, Cathedratico de Prima de Theologia en su Colegio y Universidad de a la Ciudad de Manila* (Madrid: Por los herederos de Pablo de Val, 1667); José Montero y Vidal, *Historia de la piratería malayo-mahometana en Mindanao, Jolo y Borneo* (Madrid: M. Tello, 1888); Pedro Murillo Velarde, *Historia de la provincia de Philipinas de la Compañía de Jesús: Segunda Parte, que comprehende los progresos de esta provincia desde el año de 1616 hasta el de 1716* (Manila: Imprenta de la Compañía de Jesús, por D. Nicolas de la Cruz Bagay, 1749).

19. AGI, Filipinas, leg. 8, ramo 3, núm. 82; AGI, Filipinas, leg. 27, núm. 233; AGI, Filipinas, leg. 8, ramo 3, núm. 97; AGI, Filipinas, leg. 27, núm. 224; Archivo Histórico Nacional (hereafter AHN), Colección Documentos de Indias (hereafter CDI), leg. 26, núm. 70; "Copia de una carta del Padre Juan López, rector del colegio de la compañía de Jesús de Cavite para los Padres Diego de Bobadilla y Simón Cotta, procuradores de la provincia de Philipinas para Roma," Real Academia de la Historia (hereafter RAH), 9/2667, doc. 51; "Sucesos Felices que por mar y tierra ha dado N.S. a las armas españolas," ARSI, phil. 11, fols. 150r–164v; AGI, Filipinas, leg., 8, ramo 3, núm. 97; AGI, Filipinas, leg. 27, núm. 233; AHN, CDI, leg. 26, núm. 74; Letter from Zamboanga, dated April 23, 1638, RAH, 9/3657, doc. 34; "Continuación de los felices successos," ARSI, phil. 11, fols. 167r–174v.

20. De la Costa, *The Jesuits in the Philippines*, 373–398.

21. AGI, Filipinas, leg. 7, ramo 6, núm. 85; AGI, Filipinas, leg. 8, ramo 1, núm. 9; AGI, Filipinas, leg. 30, núm. 12; AGI, Filipinas, leg. 74, núm. 47.

22. Anthony Reid, *Slavery, Bondage and Dependency in Southeast Asia* (St. Lucia: University of Queensland Press, 1983); Robert J. Antony, "Turbulent Waters: Sea Raiding in Early Modern South East Asia," *Mariner's Mirror* 99, no. 1 (2013): 23–38; Bryce Beemer, "Southeast Asian Slavery and Slave-Gathering Warfare as a Vector for Cultural Transmission: The Case of Burma and Thailand," *Historian* 71, no. 3 (2009): 481–506; Peter Boomgaard, "Human Capital, Slavery and Low Rates of Economic and Population Growth in Indonesia, 1600–1910," *Slavery & Abolition* 24, no. 2 (2003): 83–96; Angela Schottenhammer, "Slaves and Forms of Slavery in Late Imperial China (Seventeenth to Early Twentieth Centuries)," *Slavery & Abolition* 24, no. 2 (2003): 143–154; Gwyn Campbell and Alessandro Stanziani, *Bonded Labour and Debt in the Indian Ocean World* (London: Pickering & Chatto, 2013); Bok-rae Kim, "Debt Slaves in Old Korea," in Campbell and Stanziani, *Bonded Labour and Debt*, 165–172; Yoko Matsui, "The Debt-Servitude of Prostitutes in Japan during the Edo Period, 1600–1868," in Campbell and Stanziani, *Bonded Labour and Debt*, 173–186; Hans Hägerdal, "The Slaves of Timor: Life and Death on the Fringes of Early Colonial Society," *Itinerario* 34, no. 2 (2010): 19–44; Rila Mukherjee, "Mobility in the Bay of Bengal World: Medieval Raiders, Traders, States and the Slaves," *Indian Historical Review* 36, no. 1 (2009): 109–129; Joseph MacKay, "Pirate Nations: Maritime Pirates as Escape Societies in Late Imperial China," *Social Science History* 37, no. 4 (2013): 551–573; Tatiana Seijas, *Asian Slaves in Colonial Mexico: From Chinos to Indios* (Cambridge: Cambridge University Press, 2014); Anthony Reid, "'Closed' and 'Open' Slave Systems in Pre-Colonial Southeast Asia," in *Slavery, Bondage and Dependency in Southeast Asia*, ed. Anthony Reid (St. Lucia: University of Queensland Press, 1983), 156–181.

23. Antony, "Turbulent Waters," 23–25, 32–33.

24. William Henry Scott, *Barangay: Sixteenth-Century Philippine Culture and Society* (Quezon City: Ateneo de Manila University Press, 1994), 147–157; Laura Lee Junker, *Raiding, Trading and Feasting: The Political Economy of Philippine Chiefdoms* (Honolulu: University of Hawai'i Press, 1999), 336–369.

25. Isaac Donoso Jiménez, "El Islam en Filipinas (Siglos X–XIX)" (PhD diss., Universidad de Alicante, 2011).

26. Donoso Jiménez, "El Islam en Filipinas"; Howard M. Federspiel, *Sultans, Shamans, and Saints: Islam and Muslims in Southeast Asia* (Honolulu: University of Hawai'i Press, 2007).

27. James Warren has made this argument for emergence of the Sulu archipelago in the late eighteenth century as the most aggressive slaving empire in the history of Southeast Asia. James Francis Warren, *Iranun and Balangingi: Globalization, Maritime Raiding and the Birth of Ethnicity* (Singapore: Singapore University Press, 2002); James Francis Warren, *The Sulu Zone: The World Capitalist Economy and the Historical Imagination* (Amsterdam: VU University Press, 1998).

28. In 1578, Governor Sande noted that the Portuguese were trading large quantities of slaves in the region and were among the largest purchasers of slaves from Borneo. He had heard that the Portuguese had purchased two hundred slaves that the Borneans had captured during raiding missions in the Philippines. AGI, Filipinas, leg. 6, ramo 3, núm. 29; see also Tatiana Seijas, "The Portuguese Slave Trade to Spanish Manila: 1580–1640," *Itinerario* 31, no. 1 (2008): 19–38; William Henry Scott, *Slavery in the Spanish Philippines* (Manila: De la Salle University Press, 1991), 27–29.

29. AGI, Filipinas, leg. 6, ramo 3, núm. 31. Sande mentioned people from the following places as regularly coming to trade in Borneo: Chincheo, Canton, Cambodia, Caviche, Siam, Patani, Parsan, Melaka, India, Bengal, Pegu, Sumatra, Manancabo, Aceh, Java, Batachina, Maluku, Mindanao, Linboton, and many other islands close to Mindanao.

30. AGI, Filipinas, leg. 6, ramo 3, núm. 34; Shinzo Hayase, *Mindanao Ethnohistory Beyond Nations: Maguindanao, Sangir, and Bagobo Societies in East Maritime Southeast Asia* (Quezon City: Ateneo de Manila University Press, 2003), 18–20.

31. AGI, Filipinas, leg. 6, ramo 3, núms. 29, 30, 31, 34, 35, 36; AGI, Filipinas, leg. 29, núm. 29; Majul, *Muslims in the Philippines*, 81–82, 110–113; Donoso Jiménez, "El Islam en Filipinas," 459–469; de la Costa, *Jesuits in the Philippines*, 150; Graham Saunders, *A History of Brunei* (Kuala Lumpur: Oxford University Press, 1994), 54–57.

32. In the late 1570s, the Spanish organized a number of failed military interventions against the sultan of Brunei. AGI, Filipinas, leg. 6, ramo 3, núms. 29, 30, 31, 34, 35, 36; AGI, Filipinas, leg. 29, núm. 29; de la Costa, *Jesuits in the Philippines*, 150; Majul, *Muslims in the Philippines*, 110–111; Saunders, *A History of Brunei*, 54–57; Alicia Castellanos Escudier, "Expediciones españolas a Borneo en el siglo XVI," in *Filipinas y el Pacífico: Nueva miradas, nuevas reflexiones*, eds. Salvador Bernabéu Albert, Carmen Mena García, and Emilio José Luque Azcona (Sevilla: Editorial Universidad de Sevilla, 2016), 21–52.

33. AGI, Filipinas, leg. 18B, ramo 9, núm. 132; AGI, Filipinas, leg. 285, núm. 1, fols. 30r–41v.

34. AGI, Filipinas, leg. 7, ramo 1, núm. 8.

35. Jennifer L. Gaynor, *Intertidal History in Island Southeast Asia: Submerged Genealogy and the Legacy of Coastal Capture* (Ithaca, NY: Cornell University Press, 2016), 45; Warren, *Iranun and Balangingi*; James Francis Warren, "The Balangingi Samal: The Global Economy, Maritime Raiding and Diasporic Identities in the Nineteenth-Century Philippines," *Asian Ethnicity* 4, no. 1 (2003): 7–29.

36. "Relación del estado de las islas Philipinas y otras partes circunvecinas del año de 1626," RAH, 9/3657, doc. 11.

37. "Relación de lo que ha sucedido en las islas Filipinas desde el mes de Junio de 1617 hasta el presente de 1618," RAH, 9/3657, doc. 7; see also ARSI, phil. 11, doc. 54; "Sucesos de las islas Philipinas desde Agosto de 1627 hasta Junio de 1628," RAH, 9/2667, doc. 40.

38. "Relación . . . de 1617 hasta . . . 1618," RAH, 9/3657, doc. 7; see also ARSI, phil. 11, doc. 54.

39. "Relación . . . del año de 1626," RAH, 9/3657, doc. 11. One incident from 1627 indicates that the term Camucones could be applied to almost any foreign invader, regardless of their appearance or even intention to raid. In this episode, the Spanish captured a ship filled with "Camucones" raiders who reportedly traveled naked and without firearms or even any iron nails in their ship. They were armed only with stones and slingshots and a bone chisel was later found in their ship. The Spanish captured the vessel and killed everyone, leaving just six alive that they took with their ship to Cebu. They interrogated these indios, but they could not understand any of the languages that they spoke. "Relación del estado de las islas Philipinas y otros reinos y provincias circunvecinas desde el mes de Julio de 1627 hasta el de 1628," RAH, 9/3657, doc. 12.

40. "Relación . . . de 1617 hasta . . . 1618," RAH, 9/3657, doc. 7; see also ARSI, phil. 11, doc. 54; "Relación . . . del año de 1626," RAH, 9/3657, doc. 11; AGI, Filipinas, leg.

8, ramo 3, núm. 82; AGI, Filipinas, leg. 74, núm. 112; "Sucesos . . . de 1627 hasta . . . 1628," RAH, 9/2667, doc. 40.

41. Hayase, *Mindanao Ethnohistory Beyond Nations*, 21–25; R. A. Donkin, *Between East and West: The Moluccas and the Traffic in Spices up to the Arrival of Europeans* (Philadelphia: American Philosophical Society, 2003). A similar story can be told of the neighboring nutmeg producing Banda Islands. Roy Ellen, *On the Edge of the Banda Zone: Past and Present in the Social Organization of a Moluccan Trading Network* (Honolulu: University of Hawai'i Press, 2003).

42. AGI, Patronato, leg. 46, ramo 18; Leonard Y. Andaya, *The World of Maluku: Eastern Indonesia in the Early Modern Period* (Honolulu: University of Hawaii Press, 1993), 131–133, 137.

43. AGI, Patronato, leg. 46, ramo 18.

44. AGI, Filipinas, leg. 7, ramo 1, núm. 9; AGI, Filipinas, leg. 18A, ramo 6, núm. 36; AGI, Filipinas, leg. 84, núm. 115; AGI, Patronato, leg. 46, ramo 18.

45. AGI, Filipinas, leg. 6, ramo 3, núm. 36.

46. AGI, Patronato, leg. 46, ramo 18; P. Gregorio de San Esteban, *Memoria y relación de lo sucedido en las islas Malucas . . .* , 1609–1619, Archivo Franciscano Ibero-Oriental (hereafter AFIO), 21/12.

47. Ruurdje Laarhoven, *Triumph of Moro Diplomacy: The Maguindanao Sultanate in the 17th Century* (Quezon City: New Day Publishers, 1989), 29–30.

48. AGI, Filipinas, leg. 18A, ramo 6, núm. 36; AGI, Filipinas, leg. 6, ramo 7, núm. 79.

49. AGI, Filipinas, leg. 18B, ramo 7, núm. 57.

50. AGI, Filipinas, leg. 6, ramo 8, núm. 119; AGI, Filipinas, leg. 6, ramo 9, núms. 144, 146, 162; AGI, Filipinas, leg. 18B, ramo 7, núm. 60.

51. AGI, Filipinas, leg. 1, núm. 82; AGI, Filipinas, leg. 7, ramo 1, núms. 23, 29; Bartolomé Leonardo de Argensola, *Conquista de las Islas Malucas* (En Madrid por Alonso Martín, 1609); Andaya, *World of Maluku*, 140–141.

52. Gary William Bohigian, "Life on the Rim of Spain's Pacific-American Empire: Presidio Society in the Molucca Islands, 1606–1663" (PhD diss., University of California, Los Angeles, 1994); John Villiers, "Manila and Maluku: Trade and Warfare in the Eastern Archipelago, 1580–1640," *Philippines Studies* 34, no. 2 (1986): 146–161.

53. Scott, *Barangay*, 178.

54. Junker, *Raiding, Trading and Feasting*, 100, 106–107.

55. AGI, Filipinas, leg. 6, ramo 8, núm. 119; AGI, Filipinas, leg. 18B, ramo 7, núm. 60; de la Costa, *Jesuits in the Philippines*, 150–151, 276–279.

56. See de la Costa, *Jesuits in the Philippines*, 295.

57. Scott, *Barangay*, 175.

58. AGI, Filipinas, leg. 6, ramo 3, núms. 29, 30, 31, 34, 35, 36; AGI, Filipinas, leg. 29, núm. 29; de la Costa, *Jesuits in the Philippines*, 150; Majul, *Muslims in the Philippines*, 112.

59. AGI, Filipinas, leg. 6, ramo 3, núms. 35, 36; AGI, Filipinas, leg. 6, ramo 6, núm. 60; de la Costa, *Jesuits in the Philippines*, 150; Majul, *Muslims in the Philippines*, 112; Hayase, *Mindanao Ethnohistory Beyond Nations*, 49.

60. De la Costa, *Jesuits in the Philippines*, 150.

61. De la Jara was imprisoned by Governor Tello for these actions. AGI, Filipinas, leg. 6, ramo 9, núm. 162; AGI, Filipinas, leg. 18B, ramo 6, núms. 51, 53; AGI, Filipinas, leg. 18B, ramo 7, núms. 56, 57; de la Costa, *Jesuits in the Philippines*, 150–151, 276.

62. AGI, Filipinas, leg. 6, ramo 9, núm. 162; AGI, Filipinas, leg. 19, ramo 1, núm. 6; de la Costa, *Jesuits in the Philippines*, 276.

63. AGI, Filipinas, leg. 19, ramo 3, núm. 32; de la Costa, *Jesuits in the Philippines*, 279–280; Majul, *Muslims in the Philippines*, 117.

64. De la Costa, *Jesuits in the Philippines*, 279.

65. De la Costa, *Jesuits in the Philippines*, 279; Majul, *Muslims in the Philippines*, 116–117.

66. AGI, Filipinas, leg. 19, ramo 3, núm. 53; de la Costa, *Jesuits in the Philippines*, 281–282.

67. AGI, Filipinas, leg. 27, núm. 44.

68. De la Costa, *Jesuits in the Philippines*, 295; Peter Schreurs, *Caraga Antigua, 1521–1910: The Hispanization and Christianization of Agusan, Surigao and East Davao* (Cebu City: University of San Carlos, 1989), 116–117; Majul, *Muslims in the Philippines*, 117–118.

69. De la Costa, *Jesuits in the Philippines*, 302.

70. AGI, Patronato, leg. 46, ramo 18; Andaya, *World of Maluku*, 137.

71. AGI, Filipinas, leg. 7, ramo 1, núm. 17; de la Costa, *Jesuits in the Philippines*, 301.

72. Among the three hundred captives was a Spanish noblewoman named Doña Lucia. "Relación . . . de 1627 hasta . . . 1628," RAH, 9/3657, doc. 12; "Sucesos . . . de 1627 hasta . . . 1628," RAH, 9/2667, doc. 40; AGI, Filipinas, leg. 30, núm. 12; Majul, *Muslims in the Philippines*, 126; de la Costa, *Jesuits in the Philippines*, 321.

73. Scott, *Barangay*, 153.

74. Scott, *Slavery in the Spanish Philippines*, 52–54.

75. De la Costa, *Jesuits in the Philippines*, 282.

76. AGI, Filipinas, leg. 27, núms. 51, 52, 63.

77. AGI, Filipinas, leg. 7, ramo 3, núm. 37; AGI, Filipinas, leg. 21, ramo 7, núm. 23; AGI, Filipinas, leg. 74, núm. 47.

78. Stephanie Mawson, "Convicts or *Conquistadores?* Spanish Soldiers in the Seventeenth-Century Pacific," *Past & Present* 232 (2016): 106–109.

79. Mawson, "Convicts or *Conquistadores?*" 109.

80. AGI, Filipinas, leg. 8, ramo 3, núms. 48, 76; Schreurs, *Caraga Antigua*, 133.

81. Stephanie Mawson, "Unruly Plebeians and the *Forzado* System: Convict Transportation between New Spain and the Philippines during the Seventeenth Century," *Revista de Indias* 73, no. 259 (2013): 693–730.

82. Mawson, "Convicts or *Conquistadores?*" 112–119; Stephanie Mawson, "Rebellion and Mutiny in the Mariana Islands, 1680–1690," *Journal of Pacific History* 50, no. 2 (2015): 128–148.

83. AGI, Filipinas, leg. 19, ramo 3, núm. 53.

84. AGI, Filipinas, leg. 7, ramo 1, núm. 12.

85. AGI, Filipinas, leg. 7, ramo 1, núm. 8.

86. "Copia de una del padre Melchor Hurtado . . . October 1604," ARSI, phil. 10, fols. 159r–188v.

87. AGI, Filipinas, leg. 19, ramo 4, núm. 73; see also AGI, Filipinas, leg. 74, núm. 47; AGI, Filipinas, leg. 84, núm. 117.

88. Stephanie Mawson, "Philippine *indios* in the Service of Empire: Indigenous Soldiers and Contingent Loyalty, 1600–1700," *Ethnohistory* 62, no. 2 (2016): 381–413.

89. AGI, Filipinas, leg. 6, ramo 8, núm. 119; AGI, Filipinas, leg. 6, ramo 9, núm. 162; AGI, Filipinas, leg. 18B, ramo 7, núms. 56, 57, 60; AGI, Filipinas, leg. 18B, ramo 8,

núm. 99; Combes, *Historia de las islas*, 80–84; Majul, *Muslims in the Philippines*, 113–115; de la Costa, *Jesuits in the Philippines*, 276–279; Martínez-Valverde, "Sobre la guerra contra moros," 16–17.

90. AGI, Filipinas, leg. 18B, ramo 7, núms. 56, 57.

91. AGI, Filipinas, leg. 6, ramo 8, núm. 119; AGI, Filipinas, leg. 18B, ramo 7, núm. 60.

92. AGI, Filipinas, leg. 6, ramo 9, núm. 162.

93. AGI, Filipinas, leg. 18B, ramo 8, núm. 99.

94. AGI, Filipinas, leg. 6, ramo 9, núms. 144, 146, 162; AGI, Filipinas, leg. 19, ramo 1, núm. 6; AGI, Filipinas, leg. 35, núm. 42; de la Costa, *Jesuits in the Philippines*, 276–277.

95. For instance, many indigenous soldiers serving in the Spanish attempt to colonize Taiwan deserted to the Dutch. See "Action Taken by Sebastián Hurtado de Corcuera to Explain the Fall of Isla Hermosa," in *Spaniards in Taiwan: Documents*, 2 vols., trans. Pol Heyns and Carlos Gómez, ed. José Eugenio Borao Mateo (Taipei: SMC Publishing, 2001), vol. 2, 430.

96. Mawson, "Convicts or *Conquistadores?*" 112–119; Bohigian, "Life on the Rim," 71–76.

97. AGI, Filipinas, leg. 7, ramo 1, núm. 26; de la Costa, *Jesuits in the Philippines*, 301–304.

98. Letter from Pedro de Acuña, March 6, 1606, ARSI, phil. 14, fols. 30r–31r; Letter from Melchor Hurtado, April 18, 1606, ARSI, phil. 10, fols. 203r–203v; Letter from Melchor Hurtado, April 18, 1606, ARSI, phil. 10, fols. 205r–212r; de la Costa, *Jesuits in the Philippines*, 303–305.

99. De la Costa, *Jesuits in the Philippines*, 303–305; Colin, *Labor evangélica*, Libro IV, 608–612.

100. De la Costa, *Jesuits in the Philippines*, 307–308; Majul, *Muslims in the Philippines*, 120.

101. AGI, Filipinas, leg. 7, ramo 3, núm. 37; AGI, Filipinas, leg. 20, ramo 2, núm. 23; AGI, Filipinas, leg. 60, núm. 10; Letter from Juan Domingo Bilancio, April 24, 1608, ARSI, phil. 10, fols. 235r–235v.

102. Letter from Melchor Hurtado, July 4, 1608, ARSI, phil. 10, fols. 270r–270v.

103. AGI, Filipinas, leg. 60, núm. 10; AGI, Filipinas, leg. 20, ramo 2, núm. 21.

104. Schreurs, *Caraga Antigua*, 133.

105. De la Costa, *Jesuits in the Philippines*, 310.

106. "Relación . . . de 1627 hasta . . . 1628," RAH, 9/3657, doc. 12; de la Costa, *Jesuits in the Philippines*, 320–321; Majul, *Muslims in the Philippines*, 125.

107. The various reports give differing accounts of the number of indio allies that accompanied this mission, ranging from sixteen hundred to two thousand. "Relación . . . de 1627 hasta . . . 1628," RAH, 9/3657, doc. 12; "Sucesos . . . de 1627 hasta . . . 1628," RAH, 9/2667, doc. 40; AGI, Filipinas, leg. 30, núm. 12.

108. "Relación . . . de 1627 hasta . . . 1628," RAH, 9/3657, doc. 12; "Sucesos . . . de 1627 hasta . . . 1628," RAH, 9/2667, doc. 40; AGI, Filipinas, leg. 30, núm. 12; de la Costa, *Jesuits in the Philippines*, 321.

109. "Relación de los sucesos de las islas Philipinas y otros reinos desde el mes de Julio de 1628 hasta el de 1629," RAH, 9/3657, doc. 13; de la Costa, *Jesuits in the Philippines*, 321–322; Majul, *Muslims in the Philippines*, 127.

110. AGI, Filipinas, leg. 8, ramo 1, núm. 9; de la Costa, *Jesuits in the Philippines*, 322.

111. De la Costa, *Jesuits in the Philippines*, 322.

112. "Relación de lo sucedido en las islas Philipinas y otras provincias y reinos vecinos desde el Julio de 1618 hasta el presente de 1619," RAH, 9/3657, doc. 8.

113. Majul, *Muslims in the Philippines*, 128.

114. De la Costa, *Jesuits in the Philippines*, 324.

115. AGI, Filipinas, leg. 21, ramo 7, núm. 23.

116. AGI, Filipinas, leg. 21, ramo 7, núm. 23; Martínez-Valverde, "Sobre la guerra contra moros," 18.

117. AGI, Filipinas, leg. 8, ramo 3, núm. 76. Note that Mindanao was missing from the original decree, but this omission was ignored by Hurtado de Corcuera.

118. AGI, Filipinas, leg. 8, ramo 3, núms. 48, 76; de la Costa, *Jesuits in the Philippines*, 323–324; Majul, *Muslims in the Philippines*, 132.

119. AGI, Filipinas, leg. 8, ramo 3, núm. 82.

120. AGI, Filipinas, leg. 8, ramo 3, núms. 82, 97; AGI, Filipinas, leg. 27, núms. 224, 233; AHN, CDI, leg. 26, núm. 70; "Copia de una carta del Padre Juan Lopez, rector del colegio de la compañía de Jesús de Cavite para los Padres Diego de Bobadilla y Simón Cotta, procuradores de la provincia de Philipinas para Roma," RAH, 9/2667, doc. 51; "Sucesos Felices que por mar y tierra ha dado N.S. a las armas españolas," ARSI, phil. 11, fols. 150r–164v; Martínez-Valverde, "Sobre la guerra contra moros," 25–36.

121. AGI, Filipinas, leg. 8, ramo 3, núm. 82.

122. AGI, Filipinas, leg. 8, ramo 3, núm. 97; AGI, Filipinas, leg. 27, núm. 233; AHN, CDI, leg. 26, núm. 74; de la Costa, *Jesuits in the Philippines*, 387–389.

123. Among the debris left behind after the storm included a number of infants and small children that the Spanish seized as slaves. AGI, Filipinas, leg. 8, ramo 3, núm. 97; AGI, Filipinas, leg. 27, núm. 233; AHN, CDI, leg. 26, núm. 74; Letter from Zamboanga, dated April 23, 1638, RAH, 9/3657, doc. 34; "Continuación de los felices successos," ARSI, phil. 11, fols. 167r–174v.

124. AGI, Filipinas, leg. 8, ramo 3, núms. 82, 97; AGI, Filipinas, leg. 27, núms. 224, 233; AHN, CDI, leg. 26, núms. 70, 74; "Copia de una carta del Padre Juan Lopez, rector del colegio de la compañía de Jesús de Cavite para los Padres Diego de Bobadilla y Simón Cotta, procuradores de la provincia de Philipinas para Roma," RAH, 9/2667, doc. 51; "Sucesos Felices que por mar y tierra ha dado N.S. a las armas españolas," ARSI, phil. 11, fols. 150r–164v; Letter from Zamboanga, dated April 23, 1638, RAH, 9/3657, doc. 34; "Continuación de los felices successos," ARSI, phil. 11, fols. 167r–174v; Martínez-Valverde, "Sobre la guerra contra moros," 36–38, 42–44.

125. "Pedro de Almonte y Verastegui, 1644," RAH, 9/3729, doc. 10; Combes, *Historia de las islas*, 235–265; de la Costa, *Jesuits in the Philippines*, 388–390.

126. Combes, *Historia de las islas*, 265–306; de la Costa, *Jesuits in the Philippines*, 388–390.

127. "Pedro de Almonte y Verastegui, 1644," RAH, 9/3729, doc. 10.

128. Combes, *Historia de las islas*, 307–373; de la Costa, *Jesuits in the Philippines*, 391–392.

129. "Carta annua de la Provincia de Filipinas de la Compañía de Jesús del año 1640 y parte del de 1641," ARSI, phil. 8, fols. 1r–23v.

130. Murillo Velarde, *Historia de la provincia*, 239–248.

131. Combes, *Historia de las islas*, 375–400; de la Costa, *Jesuits in the Philippines*, 436–438.

132. Combes, *Historia de las islas*, 432–439, 471–503; de la Costa, *Jesuits in the Philippines*, 441–443; Majul, *Muslims in the Philippines*, 156–157.

133. Combes, *Historia de las islas*, 503–510; de la Costa, *Jesuits in the Philippines*, 443.

134. "Informe del Obispo de Nueva Cáceres al Gobierno, sobre los daños que causaban los moros y las vejaciones a los indios por los alcaldes mayores," AFIO, 92/7.

135. "Traslado de una carta que el Señor D. Sabiniano Manrique de Lara Governador, y Capitán General de las Islas Filipinas, y presidente de la Audiencia Real, que en ellas reside, escribe al padre Magino Sola, de la Compañía de Iesus, residente en la Real Corte de Madrid, Fecha en Cabite, Puerto de dichas Islas, en 24 de Iulio del año de 1658 y recibida en Madrid en 19 de Iunio de 1659," ARSI, phil. 11, fols. 353r–366r.

136. De la Costa, *Jesuits in the Philippines*, 443.

137. AGI, Filipinas, leg. 9, ramo 3, núm. 42.

138. AGI, Filipinas, leg. 23, ramo 8, núm. 24; AGI, Filipinas, leg. 330, libro 6, fols. 129r–131r, 150v–152v; AGI, Filipinas, leg. 331, libro 7, fols. 205r–206v, 353v–355v; AGI, Filipinas, leg. 341, libro 7, fols. 147v–149v.

139. AGI, Filipinas, leg. 9, ramo 2, núm. 38.

140. AGI, Filipinas, leg. 9, ramo 3, núms. 48, 50.

141. AGI, Filipinas, leg. 28, núm. 128.

142. AGI, Filipinas, leg. 11, ramo 1, núms. 9, 50, 54; AGI, Filipinas, leg. 12, ramo 1, núm. 11; AGI, Filipinas, leg. 13, ramo 1, núm. 3; AGI, Filipinas, leg. 15, ramo 1, núm. 7.

143. AGI, Filipinas, leg. 12, ramo 1, núm. 27. Ruurdje Laarhoven has detailed the political continuity and development of the Maguindanao sultanate following the Spanish withdrawal, arguing that this did not signal a decline as has sometimes been assumed by historians like Majul. During this period the Maguindanaos continued to trade with the Dutch and, briefly, with the English. See Laarhoven, *Triumph of Moro Diplomacy*.

144. AGI, Filipinas, leg. 10, ramo 1, núm. 7.

145. AGI, Filipinas, leg. 24, ramo 9, núm. 45; AGI, Filipinas, leg. 127, núm. 12; AGI, Filipinas, leg. 129, núm. 38.

146. AGI, Filipinas, leg. 14, ramo 2, núm. 15.

147. James Warren, "The Iranun and Balangingi Slaving Voyage: Middle Passages in the Sulu Zone," in *Many Middle Passages: Forced Migration and the Making of the Modern World*, eds. Emma Christopher, Cassandra Pybus, and Marcus Rediker (Berkeley: University of California Press, 2007), 66.

5. Mountain Refuges

1. Archivo General de Indias (hereafter AGI), Audiencia de Filipinas (hereafter Filipinas), leg. 30, núm. 3.

2. Laura Lee Junker, *Raiding, Trading and Feasting: The Political Economy of Philippine Chiefdoms* (Honolulu: University of Hawai'i Press, 1999), 239–245.

3. AGI, Filipinas, leg. 7, ramo 3, núm. 45; AGI, Filipinas, leg. 193, núm. 1.

4. William Henry Scott, *Discovery of the Igorots: Spanish Contacts with the Pagans of Northern Luzon* (Quezon City: New Day, 1974).

5. Stephanie Mawson, "Escaping Empire: Philippine Mountains and Indigenous Histories of Resistance," *American Historical Review* (forthcoming).

6. Miriam Coronel Ferrer, *Region, Nation and Homeland: Valorization and Adaptation in the Moro and Cordillera Resistance Discourses* (Singapore: ISEAS Publishing, 2020).

7. Scott, *Discovery of the Igorots*, 7. Scott was a prolific writer on many aspects of Philippines history, anthropology, and culture. Select works on the mountain communities of Northern Luzon include William Henry Scott, "Class Structure in the Unhispanized Philippines," *Philippine Studies* 72, no. 2 (1797): 137–159; William Henry Scott, "The Igorot: An Integrated Cultural Minority," *Philippine Sociological Review* 20, no. 4 (1972): 356–360; William Henry Scott, "An Historian Looks into the Philippine Kaleidoscope," *Philippine Studies* 24, no. 2 (1976): 220–227; William Henry Scott, "The Word Igorot," *Philippine Studies* 10, no. 2 (1962): 234–248; William Henry Scott, "Igorot Responses to Spanish Aims: 1576–1896," *Philippine Studies* 18, no. 4 (1970): 695–717; John Flameygh and William Henry Scott, "An Ilocano–Igorot Peace Pact of 1820," *Philippine Studies* 26, no. 3 (1978): 285–295; Francisco Antolin and William Henry Scott, "Notices of the Pagan Igorots in 1789," *Asian Folklore Studies* 29 (1970): 177–249; Francisco Antolin, William Henry Scott, and Fray Manuel Carillo, "Notices of the Pagan Igorots in 1789: Part Two," *Asian Folklore Studies* 30, no. 2 (1971): 27–132; William Henry Scott, *A Sagada Reader* (Quezon City: New Day, 1988).

8. Deirdre McKay, "Rethinking Locality in Ifugao: Tribes, Domains and Colonial Histories," *Philippine Studies* 53, no. 1 (2005): 479–480; Scott, "The Word Igorot," 234–248.

9. See Steven Rood, "Summary Report on a Research Programme: Issues on Cordillera Autonomy," *Sojourn: Journal of Social Issues in Southeast Asia* 7, no. 2 (1992): 320.

10. Felix M. Keesing, *Ethnohistory of Northern Luzon* (Stanford, CA: Stanford University Press, 1962).

11. Mawson, "Escaping Empire."

12. Similar discourses about mountain spaces were evident across the Spanish empire, see Adriana Rocher Salas, "La Montaña: Espacio de Rebelión, Fe y Conquista," *Estudios de Historia Novohispana* 50 (2014): 45–76; Edgardo Pérez Morales, "La naturaleza como percepción cultural: Montes y selvas en el Nuevo Reino de Granada, siglo XVIII," *Fronteras de la Historia* 11 (2006): 57–84; David J. Weber, *Bárbaros: Spaniards and Their Savages in the Age of Enlightenment* (New Haven, CT: Yale University Press, 2005).

13. See for example Sara Ortelli, "Entre desiertos y serranías: Población, espacio no controlado y fronteras permeables en el Septentrión novohispano tardocolonial," *Manuscrits. Revista d'Història Moderna* 32 (2014): 85–107; Sean F. McEnroe, "Sites of Diplomacy, Violence, and Refuge: Topography and Negotiation in the Mountains of New Spain," *Americas* 69, no. 2 (2012): 179–202; Cynthia Radding, *Wandering Peoples: Colonialism, Ethnic Spaces, and Ecological Frontiers in Northwestern Mexico, 1700–1850* (Durham, NC: Duke University Press, 1997). Mawson, "Escaping Empire."

14. James C. Scott, *The Art of Not Being Governed: An Anarchist History of Upland Southeast Asia* (New Haven, CT: Yale University Press, 2009).

15. Archivo Histórico Nacional (hereafter AHN), Colección Documentos de Indias (hereafter CDI), leg. 26, núm. 28.

16. For maps depicting the full extent of Philippine zones of refuge see Mawson, "Escaping Empire."

17. AGI, Filipinas, leg. 28, núm. 128.

18. "Description of the Philippines, 1618," Real Academia de la Historia (hereafter RAH), 9/3657, núm. 22; AHN, CDI, leg. 26, núm. 28; AGI, Filipinas, leg. 12, ramo 1,

núm. 8; AGI, Filipinas, leg. 17, ramo 1, núm. 7; AGI, Filipinas, leg. 76, núms. 145, 155, 156; AGI, Filipinas, leg. 83, núm. 29. Mawson, "Escaping Empire."

19. "Informe del Obispo de Nueva Caceres al Gobierno, sobre los daños que causaban los moros y las vejaciones a los Indios por los Alcaldes mayores," Archivo Franciscano Ibero-Oriental (hereafter AFIO), 92/7.

20. AGI, Filipinas, leg. 12, ramo 1, núm. 8.

21. AGI, Filipinas, leg. 125, núm. 20.

22. AGI, Filipinas, leg. 84, núm. 36.

23. "Carta Annua de la Vice Provincia de las islas Philipinas desde el mes de junio 1601 hasta el junio de 1602 años," Archivum Romanum Societatis Iesu (hereafter ARSI), phil. 5, fol. 97v; "Anuas de las islas Philipinas: Del Estado de las islas desde el año 658 hasta el de 661," RAH, 9/2668, núm. 42.

24. AGI, Filipinas, leg. 36, núm. 72.

25. AGI, Filipinas, leg. 14, ramo 3, núm. 25.

26. AGI, Filipinas, leg. 10, ramo 1, núm. 5; AGI, Filipinas, leg. 17, ramo 1, núm. 7; AGI, Filipinas, leg. 76, núm. 145. Mawson, "Escaping Empire."

27. AGI, Filipinas, leg. 27, núms. 51, 52, 63; "Carta Annua de Philipinas desde el año de 1665 hasta el de 1671," RAH, 9/2668, núm. 17; H. de la Costa, S. J., *Jesuits in the Philippines, 1581–1768* (Cambridge, MA: Harvard University Press, 1961), 282.

28. "Carta Annua de la Vice Provincia de las Islas Philippinas desde el mes de junio de 1601 hasta el junio de 1602 años," ARSI, phil. 5, fols. 94r–113r.

29. AGI, Filipinas, leg. 8, ramo 1, núm. 12.

30. AGI, Filipinas, leg. 16, ramo 1, núm. 6; see also Letter from Manuel de Villabona de la Compañía de Jesús, procurador general de las provincias de Indias, RAH, 9/2668, núm. 50; "Carta Annua de Philipinas desde el año de 1665 hasta el de 1671," RAH, 9/2668, núm. 17; AGI, Filipinas, leg. 71, núm. 1; de la Costa, *Jesuits in the Philippines,* 459–461.

31. "Anuas de las islas Philipinas: Del Estado de las islas desde el año 658 hasta el de 661," RAH, 9/2668, núm. 42; "Carta Annua de Philipinas desde el año de 1665 hasta el de 1671," RAH, 9/2668, núm. 17; AGI, Escribanía de Cámara de Justicias (hereafter Escribanía), leg. 404B; AGI, Filipinas, leg. 86, núm. 48.

32. "Anuas de las islas Philipinas: Del Estado de las islas desde el año 658 hasta el de 661," RAH, 9/2668, núm. 42. Where *forajidos* means "outlaws," the term *cimarrones* is usually translated as "maroons," linking the phenomenon of indigenous flight to the widespread practice of maroonage among African slaves in the Americas. See Mawson, "Escaping Empire."

33. "Carta Annua de Philipinas desde el año de 1665 hasta el de 1671," RAH, 9/2668, núm. 17.

34. Mawson, "Escaping Empire."

35. AGI, Filipinas, leg. 125, núm. 20.

36. AGI, Filipinas, leg. 125, núm. 20; AGI, Filipinas, leg. 83, núm. 52; Stephanie Mawson, "Philippine *Indios* in the Service of Empire: Indigenous Soldiers and Contingent Loyalty, 1600–1700," *Ethnohistory* 62, no. 2 (2016): 381–413; José Eugenio Borao Mateo, "Filipinos in the Spanish Colonial Army during the Dutch Wars (1600–1648)," in *More Hispanic Than We Admit: Insights in Philippine Cultural History,* ed. Isaac Donoso (Quezon City: Vibal Foundation, 2008), 74–93.

37. "Informe del Obispo de Nueva Cáceres al Gobierno, sobre los daños que causaban los moros y las vejaciones a los indios por los alcaldes mayores," AFIO, 92/7.

38. AGI, Filipinas, leg. 12, ramo 1, núm. 8.

39. Janet Hoskins, "Introduction: Headhunting as Practice and as Trope," in *Headhunting and the Social Imagination in Southeast Asia*, ed. Janet Hoskins (Stanford, CA: Stanford University Press, 1996), 7; Thomas Gibson, "Raiding, Trading and Tribal Autonomy in Insular Southeast Asia," in *The Anthropology of War*, ed. J. Haas (Cambridge: Cambridge University Press, 1990), 125–145.

40. Mawson, "Escaping Empire."

41. AGI, Filipinas, leg. 19, ramo 7, núm. 100; AGI, Filipinas, leg. 27, núm. 51; AGI, Filipinas, leg. 28, núm. 128.

42. AGI, Filipinas, leg. 30, núm. 3.

43. AGI, Filipinas, leg. 6, ramo 7, núms. 86, 94; AGI, Filipinas, leg. 7, ramo 3, núms. 45, 46; AGI, Filipinas, leg. 18B, ramo 2, núm. 5; AGI, Filipinas, leg. 193, núm. 1; AGI, Filipinas, leg. 285, núm. 1, vols. 30r–41v.

44. AGI, Filipinas, leg. 7, ramo 5, núms. 59, 61; AGI, Filipinas, leg. 30, núms. 3, 4.

45. AGI, Filipinas, leg. 7, ramo 3, núm. 45.

46. Mawson, "Escaping Empire."

47. AGI, Filipinas, leg. 30, núm. 3.

48. Mawson, "Escaping Empire."

49. AGI, Filipinas, leg. 30, núm. 3.

50. AGI, Filipinas, leg. 6, ramo 7, núm. 86.

51. AGI, Filipinas, leg. 7, ramo 5, núm. 59.

52. AGI, Filipinas, leg. 30, núm. 3.

53. AGI, Filipinas, leg. 7, ramo 3, núm. 45.

54. AGI, Filipinas, leg. 7, ramo 5, núm. 59.

55. AGI, Filipinas, leg. 30, núm. 3.

56. AGI, Filipinas, leg. 30, núm. 4.

57. AGI, Filipinas, leg. 9, ramo 3, núm. 50.

58. Casimiro Diaz Toledano, *Conquistas de las Islas Filipinas la temporal por las armas de nuestros Católicos Reyes de España . . . Parte segunda* (Valladolid, Spain: Imprenta Librería de Luis N. de Gaviria, 1890), 236–253.

59. AGI, Filipinas, leg. 10, ramo 1, núms. 4, 13.

60. Fr. Francisco de Zamora, *Memorial del P. Francisco de Zamora al Gobernador de Manila, sobre los Progresos de las Misiones de los Agustinos en las Naciones Italón y Abaca* (Barcelona: [s.n.], 1905 [1708]); AGI, Filipinas, leg. 132, núm. 33; AGI, Filipinas, leg. 134, núm. 12; AGI, Filipinas, leg. 140, núm. 29.

61. Fr. Diego Aduarte, *Tomo Primero de la Historia de la Provincia del Santo Rosario de Filipinas, Japón, y China, de la sagrada orden de predicadores* (Zaragoza: Por Domingo Gascon, Insançon, Impressor del Santo Hospital Real y General de Nuestra Señora de Gracia, 1693), 329.

62. Aduarte, *Tomo Primero*, 550–556; Baltasar de Santa Cruz, *Tomo Segundo de la Historia de la Provincia del Santo Rosario de Filipinas, Japón, y China del Sagrado Orden de Predicadores* (Zaragoza: Por Pasqual Bueno, Impressor Reyno, 1693), 18–21.

63. AGI, Filipinas, leg. 75, núm. 18; AGI, Filipinas, leg. 83, núm. 52.

64. Fray Pedro Jiménez, O. P., "Relación del principio de la misión de los Mandayas, hecha por mi, Fr. Pedro Jiménez, vicario de Fottol y Capinatan, como a quien le toca, por habérmelo mandado por ordenaciones, por ser frontera de estos pueblos, como otros muchos PP: Vicarios la tienen, para procurer la reducción de sus vecinos," *Philippiniana Sacra* 10, no. 30 (1975): 351–364.

65. Vicente de Salazar, *Historia de la Provincia de el Santíssimo Rosario de Philipinas, China y Tunking, de el Sagrado Orden de Predicadores. Tercera Parte, en que se tratan los sucesos de dicha Provincia desde el año de 1669 hasta el de 1700. Compuesta por el R. P. Fr. Vicente de Salazar, Rector de el Collegio de Santo Thomas de la Ciudad de Manila y Chancellario de Su Universidad* (Manila: Impressa en la Imprenta de dicho Collegio y Universidad de Santo Thomas de las misma Ciudad, 1742), 384–397.

66. Keesing, *Ethnohistory of Northern Luzon*, 199–200.

67. "Idea Aproximada del Territorio entre Cagayan e Ilocos [Material cartográfico]," Biblioteca Nacional de España, MR/42/588. See also: Mawson, "Escaping Empire."

68. Stephen Acabado, "The Archaeology of Pericolonialism: Responses of the 'Unconquered' to Spanish Conquest and Colonialism in Ifugao, Philippines," *International Journal of Historical Archaeology* 21, no. 1 (2017): 1–16; Stephen Acabado, "Zones of Refuge: Resisting Conquest in the Northern Philippine Highlands through Environmental Practice," *Journal of Anthropological Archaeology* 52 (2018): 180–195.

69. Marlon Martin, Stephen Acabado, and Raymond Aquino Macapagal, "Hongan di Pa'ge: The Sacredness and Realism of Terraced Landscape in Ifugao Culture, Philippines," in *Indigenous Perspectives on Sacred Natural Sites: Culture, Governance and Conservation*, eds. Jonathan Liljeblad and Bas Verschuuren (London: Routledge, 2018), 167–179; Dominic Glover and Glenn Davis Stone, "Heirloom Rice in Ifugao: An 'Anti-Commodity' in the Process of Commodification," *Journal of Peasant Studies* 45, no. 4 (2018): 776–804.

70. Acabado, "Zones of Refuge," 180–195. See also: Mawson, "Escaping Empire."

71. Marta María Manchado López wrote about the persistence of idolatries in the Zambales Mountains in the late seventeenth century; however her chapter does not consider the wider context of ongoing rebellion and resistance. See Marta María Manchado López, "Los Zambales filipinos en la segunda mitad del siglo XVII: Evangelización, idolatría y sincretismo," in *Un mar de islas, un mar de gentes: población y diversidad en las islas Filipinas*, eds. Marta María Manchado López, and Miguel Luque Talaván (Córdoba: Servicios de Publicaciones Universidad de Córdoba, 2014), 145–174. Carolyn Brewer devotes two chapters to the Zambales region in her study; however these chapters suffer from a lack of contextualization, with the region being used as representative of the remainder of the Philippines, thus losing its historical specificity. See Carolyn Brewer, *Shamanism, Catholicism and Gender Relations in Colonial Philippines, 1521–1685* (Aldershot, UK: Ashgate, 2004), 143–188. The Zambales receive a smattering of references in the following sources: Mawson, "Escaping Empire." Scott, *Discovery of the Igorots*, 2–4, 49–50; Fernando Palanco, "Resistencia y rebelión indígena en Filipinas durante los primeros cien años de soberanía española (1565–1665)," in *España y el Pacífico: Legazpi*, vol. 2, ed. Leoncio Cabrero (Madrid: Sociedad Estatal de Conmemoraciones Culturales, 2004), 77, 81; John A. Larkin, *The Pampangans: Colonial Society in a Philippine Province* (Berkeley: University of California Press, 1972), 30–31; Borao Mateo, "Filipinos in the Spanish Colonial Army," 78–79; Linda Newson, *Con-*

quest and Pestilence in the Early Spanish Philippines (Honolulu: University of Hawai'i Press, 2009), 171–172; Renato Constantino, *The Philippines: A Past Revisited* (Quezon City: Tala, 1975), 100–101.

72. AGI, Escribanía, leg. 404B; Salazar, *Historia de la Provincia de el Santissimo Rosario*, 131–133.

73. Located in present-day Botolan.

74. Domingo Pérez, O. P. "Relation of the Zambals [1680]," in *The Philippine Islands, 1493–1803* (hereafter *B&R*), trans. and ed. Emma Helen Blair and James Alexander Robertson, 55 vols. (Cleveland, OH: A. H. Clark, 1903–9), vol. 47, 310–311.

75. AGI, Filipinas, leg. 27, núm. 51.

76. AGI, Filipinas, leg. 6, ramo 10, núm. 183.

77. AGI, Filipinas, leg. 19, ramo 7, núm. 100.

78. Diaz Toledano, *Conquistas de las Islas Filipinas*, 164–172.

79. Renato Rosaldo, *Ilongot Headhunting, 1883–1974: A Study in Society and History* (Stanford, CA: Stanford University Press, 1980); Michelle Zimbalist Rosaldo, *Knowledge and Passion: Ilongot Notions of Self and Social Life* (Cambridge: Cambridge University Press, 1980); Shu-Yuan Yang, "Headhunting, Christianity, and History among the Bugkalot (Ilongot) of Northern Luzon, Philippines," *Philippine Studies* 59, no. 2 (2011): 155–186; Janet Hoskins, ed., *Headhunting and the Social Imagination in Southeast Asia* (Stanford, CA: Stanford University Press, 1996); Barbara Watson Andaya, "History, Headhunting and Gender in Monsoon Asia: Comparative and Longitudinal Views," *Southeast Asia Research* 12, no. 1 (2004): 13–52; Kenneth M. George, "Headhunting, History and Exchange in Upland Sulawesi," *Journal of Asian Studies* 50, no. 3 (1991): 536–564; Ricardo Roque, *Headhunting and Colonialism: Anthropology and the Circulation of Human Skulls in the Portuguese Empire, 1870–1930* (New York: Palgrave Macmillan, 2010).

80. Hoskins, "Introduction," 12–13.

81. Andaya, "History, Headhunting and Gender," 19.

82. Rosaldo, *Ilongot Headhunting*, 61–62.

83. Rosaldo, *Ilongot Headhunting*, 140.

84. Pérez, "Relation of the Zambals," *B&R*, vol. 47, 310–311, 320–322.

85. Pérez, "Relation of the Zambals," *B&R*, vol. 47, 310–314.

86. AGI, Filipinas, leg. 6, ramo 7, núm. 108. This followed two other military expeditions, the first organized in 1590 under the leadership of Captain Francisco Pacheco. Despite early signs of success, the Zambales who promised to come and live in the new Spanish settlements never showed up. AGI, Filipinas, leg. 6, ramo 7, núms. 69, 74; AGI, Filipinas, leg. 6, ramo 10, núm. 183; AGI, Filipinas, leg. 18B, ramo 1, núm. 2. A second expedition was led by Captain Don Alonso de Sotomayor, following the killing of a missionary and several other Spaniards. Yet, the Zambales continued to refuse to recognize Spanish rule and persisted in attacking and raiding lowland villages. Sotomayor was able to capture three principales and quartered them as punishment for killing the friar, but the expedition was ultimately a failure. AGI, Filipinas, leg. 6, ramo 7, núms. 69, 74.

87. AGI, Filipinas, leg. 6, ramo 7, núm. 108.

88. AGI, Filipinas, leg. 18B, ramo 1, núm. 2; AGI, Filipinas, leg. 18B, ramo 2, núm. 5.

89. AGI, Filipinas, leg. 18B, ramo 7, núm. 57.

90. Andrés de San Nicolas, *Historia General de los religiosos descalzos del orden de los hermitaños del gran padre y doctor de la iglesia San Agustín de la Congregación de España y de*

las Indias, vol. 1 (Madrid: por Andrés García de la Iglesia, 1664), 475; Palanco, "Resistencia y rebelión," 81.

91. AGI, Filipinas, leg. 7, ramo 5, núm. 67.

92. AGI, Filipinas, leg. 9, ramo 3, núms. 44, 48, 49; AGI, Filipinas, leg. 10, ramo 1, núm. 13.

93. AGI, Filipinas, leg. 9, ramo 3, núms. 44, 49.

94. AGI, Filipinas, leg. 10, ramo 1, núm. 13.

95. AGI, Escribanía, leg. 404B, fols. 16r–25v.

96. AGI, Escribanía, leg. 404B, fols. 16r–25v; Salazar, *Historia de la Provincia de el Santissimo Rosario*, 131–133.

97. An *ayudante* is a senior military officer, usually assistant to the *maestre de campo*.

98. AGI, Escribanía, leg. 404B.

99. Pérez, "Relation of the Zambals," *B&R*, vol. 47, 327–330.

100. AGI, Escribanía, leg. 404B.

101. Pérez, "Relation of the Zambals," *B&R*, vol. 47, 331–332.

102. Juan de la Concepción, "Extracts from Juan de la Concepción's Historia," *B&R*, vol. 41, 252.

103. AGI, Filipinas, leg. 75, núm. 20.

104. AGI, Filipinas, leg. 75, núm. 20; AGI, Filipinas, leg. 13, ramo 1, núm. 13; AGI, Filipinas, leg. 75, núm. 23; AGI, Filipinas, leg. 296, núm. 101; Concepción, "Extracts from Juan de la Concepción's Historia," *B&R*, vol. 41, 232–272.

105. AGI, Filipinas, leg. 144, núm. 9; Lino L. Dizon, *East of Pinatubo: Former Recollect Missions in Tarlac and Pampanga (1712–1898)* (Tarlac: Center for Tarlaqueño Studies, Tarlac State University 1998).

106. Mawson, "Escaping Empire".

107. *Census of the Philippine Islands: Taken Under the Direction of the Philippine Commission in the Year 1903, in Four Volumes*, vol. 2 (Washington, DC: United States Bureau of the Census, 1905), 123.

108. Cited in Keesing, *Ethnohisory of Northern Luzon*, 11. *Infieles* literally translates as heathens, referring in this case to communities who, by the twentieth century, had not converted to the Christian religion.

109. H. Otley Beyer, *Population of the Philippine Islands in 1916* (Manila: Philippine Education, 1917), 60–64.

110. Francis X. Lynch, "Some Notes on a Brief Field Survey of the Hill People of Mt. Iriga, Camarines Sur, Philippines," *Primitive Man* 21, nos. 3–4 (1948): 65–73; N. U. Gatchalin, "The Non-Christian Tagalogs of Rizal Province," *Asian Folklore Studies* 28, no. 1 (1969): 94–98; Timoteo S. Oracion, "The Magahats of Southern Negros, Philippines: Problems and Prospects," *Philippine Quarterly of Culture and Society* 2, nos. 1–2 (1974): 38–46. Mawson, "Escaping Empire."

111. F. Landa Jocano, "The Sulod: A Mountain People in Central Panay, Philippines," *Philippine Studies* 6, no. 4 (1958): 405.

112. F. Landa Jocano, *Sulod Society: A Study in the Kinship System and Social Organization of a Mountain People of Central Panay* (Quezon City: University of the Philippines Press, 1968), 20.

113. F. Lambrecht, "The Hudhud of Dinulawan and Bugan at Gonhadan," *Saint Louis Quarterly* 5 (1967): 527–571.

114. Florentino H. Hornedo, "'Indayuan,' An Amburayan Migration Song," *Philippine Studies* 38, no. 3 (1990): 358–368; see also Daniel J. Scheans, "A Remontado Legend from Ilocos Norte," *Philippine Studies* 15, no. 3 (1967): 496–497.

115. Resil B. Mojares, *Waiting for Mariang Makiling: Essays in Philippine Cultural History* (Quezon City: Ateneo de Manila University Press, 2002), 5–7; Julieta C. Mallari, "King Sinukwan Mythology and the Kapampangan Psyche," *Coolabah* 3 (2009): 227–234; Francisco A. Mallari, "The Remontados of Isarog," *Kinaadman* 5 (1983): 103–117. Mawson, "Escaping Empire."

116. AGI, Filipinas, leg. 293, núm. 63; Juan de la Concepción, *Historia General de Philipinas* (Manila: A. de la Rosa y Balagtas, 1788), 76–107.

117. Piers Kelly, *The Last Language on Earth: Linguistic Utopianism in the Philippines* (Oxford: Oxford University Press, 2022).

118. Ulysses B. Aparece, "Retrieving a Folk Hero through Oral Narratives: The Case of Francisco Dagohoy in the *Sukdan* Rituals," *Philippine Quarterly of Culture and Society* 41, nos. 3–4 (2013): 143–162.

6. Cagayan Insurgencies, 1572–1745

1. Archivo General de Indias (hereafter AGI), Audiencia de Filipinas (hereafter Filipinas), leg. 83, núm. 52.

2. Nicholas P. Cushner, *Spain in the Philippines: From Conquest to Revolution* (Quezon City: Ateneo de Manila University, 1971); Renato Constantino, *The Philippines: A Past Revisited* (Quezon City: Tala, 1975); John Leddy Phelan, *Hispanization of the Philippines: Spanish Aims and Filipino Responses, 1565–1700* (Madison: University of Wisconsin Press, 1967); Rosario Mendoza Cortes, Celestina Puyal Boncan, and Ricardo Trota Jose, *The Filipino Saga: History as Social Change* (Quezon City: New Day, 2000). Newson is the only historian to include Cagayan within a generalist history of the seventeenth-century Philippines. See Linda Newson, *Conquest and Pestilence in the Early Spanish Philippines* (Honolulu: University of Hawai'i Press, 2009), 201–217. Cagayan features prominently in Keesing's regional ethnohistory of Northern Luzon. Felix M. Keesing, *Ethnohistory of Northern Luzon* (Stanford, CA: Stanford University Press, 1962). Ed. C. de Jesus wrote about the history of Cagayan in the eighteenth and nineteenth century; however his treatment of the earlier period makes no mention of widespread rebellion or problems in controlling the lowlands. He concludes that the Spanish became the dominant force in the region because of their superior weaponry. See Ed. C. de Jesus, "Control and Compromise in the Cagayan Valley," in *Philippine Social History: Global Trade and Local Transformations*, eds. Alfred W. McCoy and Ed. C. de Jesus (Quezon City: Ateneo de Manila Press, 1982), 21–39. There are two local histories of Cagayan: Pedro V. Salgado, *Cagayan Valley and the Eastern Cordillera, 1581–1898* (Quezon City: Rex Commercial, 2002); Fr. Julian Malumbres, O. P., *Historia de Cagayan* (Manila: Tip. Linotype de Santo Tomás, 1918). See also Stephanie Mawson, "Escaping Empire: Philippine Mountains and Indigenous Histories of Resistance," *American Historical Review* (forthcoming).

3. Mawson, "Escaping Empire."

4. The Spanish never distinguish these different ethnicities within archival sources, referring instead to indigenous peoples as simply "Cagayanes." Despite the inadequacy

of this description, I have chosen to keep this term in preference to the even more generic "indios."

5. AGI, Patronato, leg. 25, ramo 44; Keesing, *Ethnohistory of Northern Luzon*, 170–171.

6. AGI, Filipinas, leg. 74, núm. 90; "Sobre encomiendas," Archivo de la Provincia del Santísimo Rosario (hereafter APSR), 56, sección Cagayan, tomo 9, doc. 3.

7. AGI, Filipinas, leg. 293, núm. 79.

8. AGI, Mapas y Planos, Filipinas, núm. 22; AGI, Mapas y Planos, Filipinas, núm. 140.

9. Mawson, "Escaping Empire."

10. Fabricio Prado, "The Fringes of Empires: Recent Scholarship on Colonial Frontiers and Borderlands in Latin America," *History Compass* 10, no. 4 (2012): 318–333; Caroline A. Williams, "Opening New Frontiers in Colonial Spanish American History: New Perspectives on Indigenous–Spanish Interactions on the Margins of Empire," *History Compass* 6, no. 4 (2008): 1121–1139; Donna J. Guy and Thomas E. Sheridan, eds., *Contested Ground: Comparative Frontiers on the Northern and Southern Edges of the Spanish Empire* (Tucson: University of Arizona Press, 1998); Amy Turner Bushnell and Jack P. Greene, "Peripheries, Centers, and the Construction of Early Modern American Empires," in *Negotiated Empires: Centers and Peripheries in the Americas, 1500–1820*, eds. Christine Daniels and Michael V. Kennedy (New York: Routledge, 2002), 1–14.

11. Guy and Sheridan, *Contested Ground*, 10–11.

12. Mawson, "Escaping Empire."

13. Laura L. Junker, *Raiding, Trading and Feasting: The Political Economy of Philippine Chiefdoms* (Honolulu: University of Hawai'i Press, 1999), 239–245; Laura L. Junker, "Economic Specialization and Inter-Ethnic Trade between Foragers and Farmers in the Prehispanic Philippines," in *Forager-Traders in South and Southeast Asia: Long-Term Histories*, eds. Kathleen D. Morrison and Laura L. Junker (Cambridge: Cambridge University Press, 2002), 203–241; Laura Lee Junker, "Hunter-Gatherer Landscapes and Lowland Trade in the Prehispanic Philippines," *World Archaeology* 27, no. 3 (1996): 389–410.

14. AGI, Patronato, leg. 25, ramo 44. Mawson, "Escaping Empire."

15. The tribute lists note that most of the encomiendas were in rebellion in 1591. AGI, Patronato, leg. 25, ramo 38.

16. AGI, Patronato, leg. 25, ramo 44. Mawson, "Escaping Empire."

17. AGI, Filipinas, leg. 18A, ramo 7, núms. 47, 49.

18. AGI, Patronato, leg. 25, ramo 44.

19. AGI, Filipinas, leg. 18A, ramo 7, núms. 47, 49.

20. AGI, Patronato, leg. 25, ramo 44. Although not mentioned in the original archival record, it is almost certain that Becerra was accompanied by an unknown number of indigenous soldiers.

21. AGI, Filipinas, leg. 6, ramo 7, núm. 67.

22. AGI, Patronato, leg. 25, ramo 44.

23. AGI, Filipinas, leg. 6, ramo 9, núms. 144, 161, 173; AGI, Filipinas, leg. 27, núm. 33; Keesing, *Ethnohistory of Northern Luzon*, 175–176.

24. AGI, Filipinas, leg. 76, núm. 55.

25. Fr. Diego Aduarte, *Tomo Primero de la Historia de la Provincia del Santo Rosario de Filipinas, Japón, y China, de la sagrada orden de predicadores* (Zaragoza: Por Domingo

Gascon, Insançon, Impressor del Santo Hospital Real y General de Nuestra Señora de Gracia, 1693), 315–318.

26. AGI, Filipinas, leg. 18B, ramo 5, núm. 45; AGI, Filipinas, leg. 79, núm. 73; "El gobernador interino, Luis Pérez Dasmariñas, y el Cabildo de Manila conceden a los dominicos la evangelización del valle de Cagayan," APSR, 56, sección Cagayan, tomo 9, doc. 1.

27. Aduarte, *Tomo Primero*, 317.

28. Aduarte, *Tomo Primero*, 413–418.

29. Aduarte, *Tomo Primero*, 490–494.

30. Aduarte, *Tomo Primero*, 550–556.

31. AGI, Filipinas, leg. 7, ramo 6, núm. 85; Newson, *Conquest and Pestilence*, 208.

32. Aduarte, *Tomo Primero*, 556–562.

33. Aduarte, *Tomo Primero*, 556–562; AGI, Filipinas, leg. 7, ramo 6, núm. 85.

34. "Relación del estado de las islas Philipinas y otros reinos y provincias circun-vecinas desde el mes de Julio de 1627 hasta el de 1628," Real Academia de la Historia, 9/3657, núm. 12.

35. Baltasar de Santa Cruz, *Tomo Segundo de la Historia de la Provincia del Santo Rosario de Filipinas, Japón, y China del Sagrado Orden de Predicadores* (Zaragoza: Por Pasqual Bueno, Impressor Reyno, 1693), 18–21.

36. Stephanie Mawson, "Escaping Empire."

37. Thomas N. Headland, "The Wild Yam Question: How Well Could Independent Hunter-Gatherers Live in a Tropical Rain Forest Ecosystem?" *Human Ecology* 15, no. 4 (1987): 463–491; P. Bion Griffin, "Agta Foragers: Alternative Histories, and Cultural Autonomy in Luzon," *Australian Journal of Anthropology* 8, no. 3 (1987): 259–269.

38. Junker, *Raiding, Trading and Feasting*, 239–245; Junker, "Hunter-Gatherer Landscapes," 389–410; Junker, "Economic Specialization," 203–241.

39. Mawson, "Escaping Empire."

40. Thomas N. Headland, "Why Foragers Do Not Become Farmers: A Historical Study of a Changing Ecosystem and Its Effect on a Negrito Hunter-Gatherer Group in the Philippines" (PhD diss., University of Hawaii, 1986), 202–204.

41. Keesing, *Ethnohistory of Nothern Luzon*, 215.

42. AGI, Patronato, leg. 25, ramo 44.

43. AGI, Filipinas, leg. 75, núm. 18.

44. AGI, Filipinas, leg. 83, núm. 52.

45. Vicente de Salazar, *Historia de la Provincia de el Santissimo Rosario de Philipinas, China y Tunking, de el Sagrado Orden de Predicadores. Tercera Parte, en que se tratan los sucesos de dicha Provincia desde el año de 1669 hasta el de 1700. Compuesta por el R. P. Fr. Vicente de Salazar, Rector de el Collegio de Santo Thomas de la Ciudad de Manila y Chancellario de Su Universidad* (Manila: Impressa en la Imprenta de dicho Collegio y Universidad de Santo Thomas de las misma Ciudad, 1742), 158–164; AGI, Filipinas, leg. 23, ramo 17, núm. 55.

46. Salazar, *Historia de la Provincia de el Santissimo Rosario*, 22, 35, 158–164; AGI, Filipinas, leg. 83, núms. 27, 52; "Licencia del obispo para fundar la iglesia de Peñafrancia (apayaos)," APSR, 56, sección Cagayan, tomo 9, doc. 7; "Mas sobre esta Fundación," APSR, 56, sección Cagayan, tomo 9, doc. 7a; "Lista de adultos bautizados en la misión de Ormag, Itaves," APSR, 56, sección Cagayan, tomo 9, doc. 6; "Misiones de los mandayas en 1684,

por el P. Pedro Jiménez," APSR, 58, sección Cagayan, tomo 13, doc. 4; AGI, Mapas y Planos, Filipinas, núm. 140.

47. AGI, Filipinas, leg. 23, ramo 17, núm. 55; AGI, Filipinas, leg. 83, núm. 52.

48. AGI, Filipinas, leg. 23, ramo 17, núm. 55.

49. AGI, Filipinas, leg. 75, núm. 18. The last three forts, all located on the coast, had a corporal but did not host a permanent garrison of soldiers. They were largely established for coastal defense.

50. Mawson, "Escaping Empire."

51. AGI, Filipinas, leg. 75, núm. 18.

52. AGI, Filipinas, leg. 83, núm. 52.

53. AGI, Filipinas, leg. 83, núm. 52.

54. AGI, Filipinas, leg. 75, núm. 18.

55. AGI, Filipinas, leg. 83, núm. 52.

56. AGI, Filipinas, leg. 83, núm. 52.

57. AGI, Filipinas, leg. 83, núm. 52.

58. AGI, Filipinas, leg. 75, núm. 18.

59. AGI, Filipinas, leg. 7, ramo 3, núm. 45; "Expeditions to the Province of Tuy," in *The Philippine Islands, 1493–1803*, trans. and ed. Emma Helen Blair and James Alexander Robertson, 55 vols. (Cleveland, OH: A. H. Clark, 1903–9), vol. 14, 301–315; William Henry Scott, *The Discovery of the Igorots: Spanish Contacts with the Pagans of Northern Luzon* (Quezon City: New Day, 1974), 9–20; Keesing, *Ethnohistory of Northern Luzon*, 271–277.

60. AGI, Filipinas, leg. 83, núm. 52.

61. AGI, Filipinas, leg. 129, núm. 23.

62. AGI, Filipinas, leg. 14, ramo 3, núm. 35; AGI, Filipinas, leg. 83, núm. 52; AGI, Filipinas, leg. 122, núm. 28; AGI, Filipinas, leg. 129, núm. 23; Salazar, *Historia de la Provincia de el Santissimo Rosario*, 158–164; Newson, *Conquest and Pestilence*, 225.

63. *Breve relacion, y felizes progresos de los Religiosos del Sagrado Orden de Predicadores de las Islas Philipinas, en la Conquista espiritual, y reduccion de los Gentiles de la Provincia de Paniqui q media entre las Provincias de Cagayan y Pangasinan* (Manila: en el Collegio, y Universidad del Señor Santo Thomas con lizencia del Superior Govierno por Geronimo Correa de Castro, 1739).

64. AGI, Filipinas, leg. 6, ramo 7, núm. 94; AGI, Filipinas, leg. 193, núm. 1.

65. AGI, Filipinas, leg. 193, núm. 1.

66. AGI, Filipinas, leg. 83, núm. 52.

67. AGI, Filipinas, leg. 14, ramo 3, núm. 35.

68. The *oidor* Avella Fuertes, who was visiting the region at the time, reiterated this advice, and the Pampangans themselves also wrote a petition. AGI, Filipinas, leg. 14, ramo 3, núm. 35.

69. AGI, Filipinas, leg. 14, ramo 3, núm. 35.

70. AGI, Filipinas, leg. 14, ramo 3, núm. 35.

71. AGI, Filipinas, leg. 122, núm. 28.

72. AGI, Filipinas, leg. 132, núm. 43; Malumbres, *Historia de Cagayan*, 55–57.

73. AGI, Filipinas, leg. 141, núm. 6.

74. AGI, Filipinas, leg. 132, núm. 43. Mawson, "Escaping Empire."

75. AGI, Filipinas, leg. 132, núm. 33.

76. *Breve relacion, y felizes progresos.*

77. *Breve relacion, y felizes progresos.*

78. *Breve relacion, y felizes progresos;* AGI, Filipinas, leg. 150, núm. 11. Mawson, "Escaping Empire."

79. Fr. Bernardo Ustariz, *Relación de los sucessos, y progressos de la mission de Santa Cruz de Paniqui y de Ytuy, medias entre las de Pangasinan, Cagayan, y Pampanga: año de 1745* (s.n., 1745?).

80. Ustariz, *Relación de los sucessos.*

81. Stephen Acabado, "The Archaeology of Pericolonialism: Responses of the 'Unconquered' to Spanish Conquest and Colonialism in Ifugao, Philippines," *International Journal of Historical Archaeology* 21, no. 1 (2017): 1–26; Stephen Acabado, "Zones of Refuge: Resisting Conquest in the Northern Philippine Highlands through Environmental Practice," *Journal of Anthropological Archaeology* 52 (2018): 180–195.

82. *Census of the Philippine Islands: Taken Under the Direction of the Philippine Commission in the Year 1903, in Four Volumes,* vol. 2 (Washington, DC: United States Bureau of the Census, 1905), 123.

83. AGI, Filipinas, leg. 144, núm. 9. Mawson, "Escaping Empire."

84. AGI, Filipinas, leg. 144, núm. 9.

85. AGI, Filipinas, leg. 144, núm. 9.

86. Stephanie Mawson, "Escaping Empire."

7. Manila, The Chinese City

1. "Relasión del alçamiento de los chinos en la ciudad de Manila por el mes de noviembre del año de 1639, causas del alçamiento y prinsipio del," Real Academia de la Historia (hereafter RAH), 9/3663, núm. 28; "Relación verdadera del levantamiento de los Sangleyes en las Filipinas y de las vitorias que tuvo contra ellos el Governador don Sebastián Hurtado de Corcuera el año pasado de 1640 y 1641," Biblioteca Nacional de España (hereafter BNE), mss. 2371 fols. 602–604; "Relation on the Chinese Insurrection," in *The Philippine Islands, 1493–1803* (hereafter *B&R*), trans. and ed. Emma Helen Blair and James Alexander Robertson, 55 vols. (Cleveland, OH: A. H. Clark, 1903–9), vol. 29, 194–207; Archivo General de Indias (hereafter AGI), Indiferente General, leg. 113, núm. 47; Juan López, "Events in the Philippines from August 1639 to August 1640," *B&R*, vol. 29, 208–258; Casimiro Diaz Toledano, *Conquista de las Islas Filipinas la temporal por las armas de nuestros Católicos Reyes de España . . . Parte segunda* (Valladolid, Spain: Imprenta Librería de Luis N. de Gaviria, 1890), 401–430; Vicente de Salazar, *Historia de la Provincia de el Santíssimo Rosario de Philipinas, China y Tunking, de el Sagrado Orden de Predicadores. Tercera Parte, en que se tratan los sucesos de dicha Provincia desde el año de 1669 hasta el de 1700. Compuesta por el R. P. Fr. Vicente de Salazar, Rector de el Collegio de Santo Thomas de la Ciudad de Manila y Chancellario de Su Universidad* (Manila: Impressa en la Imprenta de dicho Collegio y Universidad de Santo Thomas de las misma Ciudad, 1742), 149; AGI, Audiencia de Filipinas (hereafter Filipinas), leg. 2, núms. 37, 38; AGI, Filipinas, leg. 28, núms. 21, 25; Charles J. McCarthy, "Slaughter of Sangleys in 1639," *Philippine Studies* 18, no. 3 (1970): 659–667.

2. A total of 1,300 were killed in Cavite, 500 in the farmlands around Manila, 450 in Marigondon and Silang, 300 in Bulacan, 600 in Pampanga, 200 in Pangasinan, 500 in Tal

and Balayan, and 600 along the coasts of Zambales and elsewhere. "Relación verdadera del levantamiento . . . ," BNE mss. 2371, fols. 602–604. Gil notes that the total number of Chinese killed is inconsistent across sources, although the two main sources—the RAH manuscript cited in note 1 and a residencia completed in 1644 (see AGI, Escribanía de Cámara de Justicia, leg. 409D)—cite the figure of 24,000. Juan Gil, *Los Chinos en Manila: Siglos XVI y XVII* (Lisboa: Centro Científico e Cultural de Macau, 2011), 506.

3. AGI, Filipinas, leg. 19, ramo 4, núm. 73; see also AGI, Filipinas, leg. 7, ramo 1, núms. 12, 15, 21, 28; AGI, Filipinas, leg. 19, ramo 5, núm. 76; AGI, Filipinas, leg. 19, ramo 6, núms. 83, 92; AGI, Filipinas, leg. 20, ramo 4, núm. 34; AGI, Filipinas, leg. 27, núm. 45; AGI, Filipinas, leg. 84, núms. 117, 118, 119, 120, 122, 127, 128; AGI, Filipinas, leg. 329, libro 2, fols. 96r–96v; José Eugenio Borao, "The Massacre of 1603: Chinese Perception of the Spanish on the Philippines," *Itinerario* 22, no. 1 (1998): 29–30.

4. Diaz Toledano, *Conquistas de las Islas Filipinas*, 427.

5. "Insigne y Siempre Leal Ciudad"—this was the official title granted to the city by its first governor, Miguel López de Legazpi, and then ratified by royal decree in 1572. AGI, Filipinas, leg. 339, libro 1, fols. 50r–51v.

6. James K. Chin, "Junk Trade, Business Networks, and Sojourning Communities: Hokkien Merchants in Early Maritime Asia," *Journal of Chinese Overseas* 6, no. 2 (2010): 189–190.

7. Dennis O. Flynn and Arturo Giráldez, "Silk for Silver: Manila–Macao Trade in the 17th Century," *Philippine Studies* 44, no. 1 (1996): 52–68; Craig A. Lockard, "'The Sea Common to All': Maritime Frontiers, Port Cities, and Chinese Traders in the Southeast Asian Age of Commerce, ca. 1400–1750," *Journal of World History* 21, no. 2 (2010): 225; Tonio Andrade and Xing Hang, "Introduction: The East Asian Maritime Realm in Global History, 1500–1700," in *Sea Rovers, Silver, and Samurai: Maritime East Asia in Global History, 1550–1700*, eds. Tonio Andrade and Xing Hang (Honolulu: University of Hawai'i Press, 2016), 8.

8. Stephanie Mawson, "Convicts or *Conquistadores*? Spanish Soldiers in the Seventeenth-Century Pacific," *Past & Present* 232 (2016): 109; Juan Mesquida Oliver, "La población de Manila y las capellanías de misas de los Españoles: Libro de registros, 1642–1672," *Revista de Indias* 70, no. 249 (2010): 471; Inmaculada Alva Rodríguez, *Vida municipal en Manila (siglos XVI–XVII)* (Córdoba: Universidad de Córdoba, 1997), 30–31.

9. Robert Batchelor, "The Selden Map Rediscovered: A Chinese Map of East Asian Shipping Routes, c. 1619," *Imago Mundi: The International Journal for the History of Cartography* 65, no. 1 (2013): 37–65; Chin, "Junk Trade," 193.

10. Andrade and Hang, "Introduction," 11; Anna Busquets, "Dreams in the Chinese Periphery: Victorio Riccio and Zheng Chenggong's Regime," in *Sea Rovers, Silver, and Samurai: Maritime East Asia in Global History, 1550–1700*, eds. Tonio Andrade and Xing Hang (Honolulu: University of Hawai'i Press, 2016), 202–225; Manel Ollé Rodríguez, "Manila in the Zheng Clan Maritime Networks," *Review of Culture* 29 (2009): 91–103.

11. Joshua Eng Sin Kueh, "The Manila Chinese: Community, Trade and Empire, c. 1570–c. 1770" (PhD diss., Georgetown University, 2014); Albert Chan, "Chinese–Philippine Relations in the Late Sixteenth Century to 1603," *Philippine Studies* 26, nos. 1–2 (1978): 81; Lin Ren-Chuan, "Fukien's Private Sea Trade in the 16th and 17th Centuries," in *Development and Decline of Fukien Province in the 17th and 18th Cen-*

turies, trans. Barend ter Haar, ed. E. B. Vermeer (Leiden: E. J. Brill, 1990), 183; Chin, "Junk Trade," 187–188; Lucille Chia, "The Butcher, the Baker, and the Carpenter: Chinese Sojourners in the Spanish Philippines and Their Impact on Southern Fujian," *Journal of the Economic and Social History of the Orient* 49, no. 4 (2006): 509–534; Manel Ollé, "La proyección de Fujian en Manila: los sangleyes del parián y el comercio de la Nao de China," in *Un océano de seda y plata: el universo económico del Galeón de Manila,* eds. Salvador Bernabéu Albert and Carlos Martínez Shaw (Sevilla: Consejo Superior de Investigaciones Científicas, 2013), 155–178.

12. Jonathan Gebhardt, "Chinese Migrants, Spanish Empire, and Globalization in Early Modern Manila," *Journal of Medieval and Early Modern Studies* 46, no. 1 (2017): 167–192; Ryan Dominic Crewe, "Pacific Purgatory: Spanish Dominicans, Chinese Sangleys, and the Entanglement of Mission and Commerce in Manila, 1580–1620," *Journal of Early Modern History* 19, no. 4 (2015): 347–348; Chia, "The Butcher, the Baker, and the Carpenter," 509–534; Birgit Tremml-Werner, *Spain, China, and Japan in Manila, 1571–1644: Local Comparisons and Global Connections* (Amsterdam: Amsterdam University Press, 2015), 284–286; Kueh, "The Manila Chinese," 53–66.

13. A rebellion that took place in 1686 is often listed by historians alongside these three other examples as the fourth massacre of the Chinese to take place in the seventeenth century. Nevertheless, while a considerable number of Chinese did lose their lives during skirmishes with the military and through execution at the end of a criminal investigation, these events are categorically different to the preceding examples. The skirmishes were small scale, isolated, and conducted as part of an investigation into the criminal trial; they do not represent indiscriminate, government-sanctioned slaughter. See AGI, Filipinas, leg. 67; AGI, Filipinas, leg. 3, núm. 172; "Diario de los novedades de Filipinas desde Junio de 86 hasta el de 87," RAH, 9/2668, libro 2, núm. 122; AGI, Filipinas, leg. 83, núm. 41; Gebhardt, "Chinese Migrants," 167–192.

14. "Diego Calderón y Serrano, 10 April 1677," AGI, Filipinas, leg. 28, núm. 131, fols. 978r–980v; see also Archivo Histórico Nacional (hereafter AHN), Consejo de Inquisición, leg. 5348, exp. 3.

15. Flynn and Giráldez, "Silk for Silver," 53; Birgit M. Tremml, "The Global and the Local: Problematic Dynamics of the Triangular Trade in Early Modern Manila," *Journal of World History* 23, no. 3 (2012): 567–568; John E. Wills Jr., "Maritime Europe and the Ming," in *China and Maritime Europe, 1500–1800: Trade, Settlement, Diplomacy, and Missions,* ed. John E. Wills Jr. (Cambridge: Cambridge University Press, 2012), 53–54.

16. In addition to Chinese produced goods, the galleons sometimes brought cottons from India and rugs and carpets from Persia as well as numerous other small commodities, including fans, combs, and jewelry. William Lytle Schurz, *The Manila Galleon: The Romantic History of the Spanish Galleons Trading between Manila and Acapulco* (New York: E. P. Dutton, 1959), 32–33.

17. Raquel A. G. Reyes, "Flaunting It: How the Galleon Trade Made Manila, circa 1571–1800," *Early American Studies: An Interdisciplinary Journal* 15, no. 4 (2017): 697.

18. Carmen Yuste López, *El comercio de la Nueva España con Filipinas, 1590–1785* (México: Departamento de Investigaciones Históricas, 1984), 32–34.

19. Chang Pin-Tsun, "Maritime Trade and Local Economy in Late Ming Fukien," in *Development and Decline of Fukien Province in the 17th and 18th Centuries,* ed. Eduard B. Vermeer (Leiden: Brill, 1990), 65–66.

20. Chin, "Junk Trade," 187–190. Chinese chronicler, Li Guangjin, claimed that up to 90 percent of the male population was engaged in overseas maritime trade. Crewe, "Pacific Purgatory," 345.

21. Antonio de Morga, *The Philippine Islands, Moluccas, Siam, Cambodia, Japan and China at the Close of the Sixteenth Century,* trans. Henry E. J. Stanley (Cambridge: Cambridge University Press, 2010), 337.

22. Schurz, *The Manila Galleon,* 71.

23. Chin, "Junk Trade," 157–158.

24. Chin, "Junk Trade," 193; Lockard, "The Sea Common to All," 223.

25. Batchelor, "The Selden Map Rediscovered," 37–65; Robert K. Batchelor, *London: The Selden Map and the Making of a Global City, 1549–1689* (Chicago: University of Chicago Press, 2014); Timothy Brook, *Mr. Selden's Map of China: Decoding the Secrets of a Vanished Cartographer* (New York: Bloomsbury Press, 2013).

26. Pin-Tsun, "Maritime Trade," 72–74.

27. Flynn and Giráldez, "Silk for Silver," 54.

28. Pin-Tsun, "Maritime Trade," 72–74.

29. Robert Batchelor, "Maps, Calendars, and Diagrams: Space and Time in Seventeenth-Century Maritime East Asia," in *Sea Rovers, Silver, and Samurai: Maritime East Asia in Global History, 1550–1700,* eds. Tonio Andrade and Xing Hang (Honolulu: University of Hawai'i Press, 2016), 90–91.

30. Busquets, "Dreams in the Chinese Periphery," 202–225; Cheng-heng Lu, "Between Bureaucrats and Bandits: The Rise of Zheng Zhilong and His Organization, the Zheng Ministry (Zheng Bu)," in *Sea Rovers, Silver, and Samurai: Maritime East Asia in Global History, 1550–1700,* eds. Tonio Andrade and Xing Hang (Honolulu: University of Hawai'i Press, 2016), 132–155; Cheng K'o-ch'eng, "Chen Ch'eng-kung's Maritime Expansion and Early Ch'ing Coastal Prohibition," in *Development and Decline of Fukien Province in the 17th and 18th Centuries,* trans. Burchard Mansvelt Beck, ed. Eduard B. Vermeer (Leiden: Brill, 1990), 217–244; Xing Hang, *Conflict and Commerce in Maritime East Asia: The Zheng Family and the Shaping of the Modern World, c. 1620–1720* (Cambridge: Cambridge University Press, 2016).

31. Quoted from Lung-hsi hsien-chih in Ren-Chuan, "Fukien's Private Sea Trade," 187; see also Chin, "Junk Trade," 202–203.

32. Ren-Chuan, "Fukien's Private Sea Trade," 189–191.

33. Dahpon David Ho, "The Empire's Scorched Shore: Coastal China, 1633–1683," *Journal of Early Modern History* 17, no. 1 (2013): 53–74.

34. Chin, "Junk Trade," 191; Ng Chin-Keong, "The South Fukienese Junk Trade at Amoy from the Seventeenth to the Early Nineteenth Centuries," in *Development and Decline of Fukien Province in the 17th and 18th Centuries,* ed. E. B. Vermeer (Leiden: E. J. Brill, 1990), 300–301.

35. William Henry Scott argues that the origin of this term is from the Chinese words "*chang* and *lai* . . . meaning 'regularly come,' that is, itinerants who could be trusted to keep commercial contracts from one trading season to the next." William Henry Scott, *Barangay: Sixteenth-Century Philippine Culture and Society* (Quezon City: Ateneo de Manila University Press, 1994), 190.

36. Marcelino A. Foronda Jr. and Cornelio R. Bascara, *Manila* (Madrid: Editorial MAPFRE, 1992), 111; Alberto Santamaria, O. P., "The Chinese Parian (El Parian de

los Sangleyes)," in *The Chinese in the Philippines, 1570–1770*, ed. Alfonso Felix Jr. (Manila: Solidaridad Publishing House, 1966), 67–118.

37. AGI, Filipinas, leg. 18A, ramo 3, núm. 12; AGI, Filipinas, leg. 34, núm. 75; AGI, Filipinas, leg. 35, núm. 3; Chan, "Chinese–Philippine Relations," 61; Alva Rodríguez, *Vida municipal en Manila*, 37–38.

38. AHN, Colección Documentos de Indias (hereafter CDI), leg. 26, núm. 10.

39. "Pregunta y propuesta . . . ," BNE, mss. 11014, fols. 42r–65v.

40. Chia, "The Butcher, the Baker, and the Carpenter," 521–522; Tremml-Werner, *Spain, China, and Japan in Manila*, 284–286.

41. "Copia de un capítulo en que se noticia de la nación China, que llaman sangleyes, que residen en el parían de la Ciudad de Manila, y demás Islas Filipinas, su natural, y daños que ocasionan en vivir en los pueblos y ciudades de aquellas provincias, y a su continuación esta la respuesta, haciendo juicio de esta representación," AGI, Filipinas, leg. 28, núm. 131, fols. 1015r–1018v.

42. AHN, CDI leg. 26, núm. 10.

43. "Avisos de el comercio de Filipinas, [en manos de los sangleyes], y su estilo hasta hoy," BNE, mss. 11014, fols. 66r–68v.

44. Specific goods cited included gold, amber, civet, rice, tortoiseshells, beans, sesame seeds, cotton, sugar, wax, abaca, betel nut, wine, coconut oil, cured meat, and blankets, among many other things.

45. "Avisos de el comercio . . . ," BNE, mss. 11014, fols. 66r–68v.

46. AGI, Filipinas, leg. 18B, ramo 7, núms. 72, 74; AGI, Filipinas, leg. 19, ramo 2, núm. 21; AGI, Filipinas, leg. 79, núm. 32.

47. Berthold Laufer, *The Relations of the Chinese to the Philippine Islands*, Smithsonian Miscellaneous Collections, vol. 50 (Washington: Smithsonian Institution, 1908), 259–261; Igawa Kenji, "At the Crossroads: Limahon and Wakō in Sixteenth-Century Philippines," in *Elusive Pirates, Pervasive Smugglers: Violence and Clandestine Trade in the Greater China Seas*, ed. Antony J. Roberts (Hong Kong: Hong Kong University Press, 2010), 73–84; Rafael Bernal, "The Chinese Colony in Manila, 1570–1770," in *The Chinese in the Philippines, 1570–1770*, ed. Alfonso Felix Jr. (Manila: Solidaridad Publishing House, 1966), 50.

48. The first of these mutinies took place on board a ship bound for Ternate in 1593. See AGI, Filipinas, leg. 18B, ramo 4, núm. 24; AGI, Filipinas, leg. 79, núm. 32. A second mutiny occurred after a Spanish ship was captured by a Siamese ship in 1594. See AGI, Filipinas, leg. 18B, ramo 4, núm. 28. The third incident took place on board a vessel sent to Mindanao in 1597. See AGI, Filipinas, leg. 6, ramo 9, núm. 141.

49. In reviewing Chinese records for these events, Laufer makes the point that the Spanish sources conveniently omit the fact that the Chinese sailors were cruelly mistreated by Dasmariñas during the voyage, leading to the death of several. See Laufer, *Relations of the Chinese*, 261–266; AGI, Filipinas, leg. 18B, ramo 4, núm. 24; AGI, Filipinas, leg. 79, núm. 32; Marcelino A. Foronda Jr., *Insigne y Siempre Leal: Essays on Spanish Manila* (Manila: De La Salle University History Department, 1986), 97–99; Milagros C. Guerrero, "The Chinese in the Philippines, 1570–1770," in *The Chinese in the Philippines, 1570–1770*, ed. Alfonso Felix Jr. (Manila: Solidaridad Publishing House, 1966), 17–18.

50. AGI, Filipinas, leg. 7, ramo 1, núms. 6, 8, 12; AGI, Filipinas, leg. 19, ramo 4, núms. 56, 67; AGI, Filipinas, leg. 27, núm. 44.

51. AGI, Filipinas, leg. 7, ramo 1, núm. 12.

52. This account is based primarily on the account given by the audiencia immediately after the close of the events. AGI, Filipinas, leg. 19, ramo 4, núm. 73; see also AGI, Filipinas, leg. 7, ramo 1, núms. 12, 15, 21, 28; AGI, Filipinas, leg. 19, ramo 5, núm. 76; AGI, Filipinas, leg. 19, ramo 6, núms. 83, 92; AGI, Filipinas, leg. 20, ramo 4, núm. 34; AGI, Filipinas, leg. 27, núm. 45; AGI, Filipinas, leg. 84, núms. 117, 118, 119, 120, 122, 127, 128; AGI, Filipinas, leg. 329, libro 2, fols. 96r–96v; Borao, "The Massacre of 1603," 29–30.

53. AGI, Filipinas, leg. 7, ramo 1, núm. 28; AGI, Filipinas, leg. 20, ramo 4, núm. 34; AGI, Filipinas, leg. 329, libro 2, fols. 96r–96v.

54. The audiencia estimated ten to twelve thousand: AGI, Filipinas, leg. 19, ramo 4, núm. 73. The Cabildo *eclesiástico* estimated twenty thousand: AGI, Filipinas, leg. 84, núm. 118. The Augustinians estimated twenty-one thousand: AGI, Filipinas, leg. 84, núm. 119. The Dominicans claimed there were thirty thousand in the Parian prior to the rebellion: AGI, Filipinas, leg. 84, núm. 120.

55. AGI, Filipinas, leg. 19, ramo 7, núms. 100, 105.

56. AGI, Filipinas, leg. 19, ramo 7, núms. 100, 105; AGI, Filipinas, leg. 8, ramo 3, núm. 55.

57. Crewe, "Pacific Purgatory," 348; Dana Leibsohn, "*Dentro y fuera de los muros*: Manila, Ethnicity, and Colonial Cartography," *Ethnohistory* 61, no. 2 (2014): 229–251.

58. Angulo argued that it was not appropriate to allow newly converted indios to be confronted by the pagan Chinese who were prone to excess and all manner of vices and who were able through the course of ordinary trade "to influence and introduce among the indios . . . their customs and pagan rites, their little esteem for the laws of God, or respect for those of the Church, their idolatries, their deceits, weaknesses, drunkenness," all of which was opposed to what the indios learned from the evangelical ministers. "Copia de un capítulo . . . ," AGI, Filipinas, leg. 28, núm. 131, fols. 1015r–1018v.

59. Foronda and Bascara, *Manila*, 111.

60. Schurz, *The Manila Galleon*, 74–78.

61. Crewe, "Pacific Purgatory," 361.

62. "Sobre sacar los sangleyes licencias," Archivo de la Provincia del Santísimo Rosario (hereafter APSR), 40, tomo 1, doc. 3.

63. AGI, Filipinas, leg. 8, ramo 3, núm. 54. This fee was later merged into the half-yearly tribute, applied to Chinese living outside of Manila. See AGI, Filipinas, leg. 10, ramo 1, núm. 7; AGI, Filipinas, leg. 41, núm. 50.

64. AGI, Filipinas, leg. 7, ramo 3, núm. 42.

65. BNE, mss. 2939, fols. 160r–164v; "Lo que cuesta a su majestad cada año las islas Filipinas," BNE mss. 3010; AGI, Filipinas, leg. 8, ramo 3, núms. 54, 55.

66. AGI, Filipinas, leg. 27, núm. 76.

67. AGI, Filipinas, leg. 80, núm. 135.

68. "Avisos necesarios . . . ," BNE, mss. 11014, fols. 32r–37v.

69. Although most evidence speaks of the dangers of intermingling between Chinese and lower-class Spaniards and indios, even elite Spaniards maintained close commercial relationships with their Chinese counterparts. See for example AGI, Filipinas, leg. 27, núm. 73. When Fr. Plácido de Angulo arrived in Manila in 1652, he found that many Chinese were living and sleeping within the walls of the city, and he was so shocked by this that he resolved to write a document representing the dangers that

this placed on the city, with such a large number of Chinese living inside the walls. "Copia de un capítulo . . . ," AGI, Filipinas, leg. 28, núm. 131, fols. 1015r–1018v.

70. "Informe de fray Jacinto Samper, dominico, sobre que no se permita vivir en Filipinas a los chinos infieles, dejando sólo a los cristianos," AGI, Filipinas, leg. 28, núm. 131, fols. 1114r–1121r.

71. "Discurso y parecer en que se demuestra que no conviene que la nación de China que llaman sangleyes habite ni viva de asiento en las islas Filipinas . . . ," AGI, Filipinas, leg. 28, núm. 131, fols. 982r–995v.

72. The homosexual activities of Chinese were a common source of ire among Spanish missionaries, and many Chinese were also commonly accused of engaging in sodomy with indios. See AGI, Filipinas, leg. 10, ramo 1, núm. 7; AGI, Filipinas, leg. 18A, ramo 2, núm. 9; AGI, Filipinas, leg. 126, núm. 1; "Relación del estado de las islas Philipinas y otros reinos y provincias circunvecinas desde el mes de Julio de 1627 hasta el de 1628," RAH, 9/3657, núm. 12, fol. 17v; "Pregunta y propuesta . . . ," BNE, mss. 11014, fols. 42r–65v; "Diego Calderón y Serrano, 10 April 1677," AGI, Filipinas, leg. 28, núm. 131, fols. 978r–980v; "Informe de fray Jacinto Samper, dominico . . . ," AGI, Filipinas, leg. 28, núm. 131, fols. 1114r–1121r; "Consulta del Cabildo, Justicia y regimiento de Manila a la Audiencia, suplicando que, en consideración a las razones que alegan, se mande que todos los sangleyes infieles y cristianos que no fueren casados se reduzcan a vivir en su parián, y los sangleyes cristianos casados a los pueblos de Binondo y Santa Cruz, con las condiciones expresadas," AGI, Filipinas, leg. 28, núm. 131, fols. 999r–1000v; Raquel A. G. Reyes, "Sodomy in Seventeenth-Century Manila: The Luck of a Mandarin from Taiwan," in *Sexual Diversity in Asia, c. 600–1950*, eds. Raquel A. G. Reyes and William G. Clarence-Smith (New York: Routledge, 2012), 127–140. It should be noted that sodomy was not considered a vice in China, see Chan, "Chinese–Philippine Relations," 70–71; D. E. Mungello, *The Great Encounter of China and the West, 1500–1800* (Plymouth: Rowman & Littlefield, 2009), 114–116.

73. "Pregunta y propuesta . . . ," BNE, mss. 11014, fols. 42r–65v; Linda Newson, *Conquest and Pestilence in the Early Spanish Philippines* (Honolulu: University of Hawai'i Press, 2009), 124; Alva Rodríguez, *Vida municipal en Manila*, 39–40.

74. AGI, Filipinas, leg. 27, núm. 89.

75. "Pregunta y propuesta . . . ," BNE, mss. 11014, fols. 42r–65v.

76. "Informe de fray Cristóbal Pedroche, a favor de la expulsión. Hospital de San Gabriel, 10 de junio de 1682," AGI, Filipinas, leg. 28, núm. 131, fols. 970r–977r.

77. AGI, Filipinas, leg. 22, ramo 9, núm. 43.

78. "Diego de Villatoro, 21 July 1678," AGI, Filipinas, leg. 28, núm. 131, fol. 997r; Chia, "The Butcher, the Baker, and the Carpenter," 520–522; Gil, *Los Chinos en Manila*, 121–140.

79. "Consulta del Cabildo . . . ," AGI, Filipinas, leg. 28, núm. 131, fols. 999r–1000v.

80. License data from the period 1619 to 1634 indicates that there were approximately 2,000 licenses granted annually for Chinese to live within the provinces (with a range from 1,503 licenses granted in 1624 to 2,934 granted in 1634). AGI, Filipinas, leg. 8, ramo 3, núm. 55; Larkin, *The Pampangans: Colonial Society in a Philippine Province* (Berkeley: University of California Press, 1972), 48–50.

81. AGI, Filipinas, leg. 8, ramo 1, núm. 7.

82. "Copia de un capítulo . . . ," AGI, Filipinas, leg. 28, núm. 131, fols. 1015r–1018v.

83. In 1597, Luis Pérez Dasmariñas argued that as more and more Chinese were converted to Christianity, they were to be appointed to replace the *infieles* in the trades and other occupations, so that the latter might be removed from the islands. AGI, Filipinas, leg. 18B, ramo 7, núm. 72; AGI, Filipinas, leg. 19, ramo 2, núm. 21.

84. Crewe, "Pacific Purgatory," 351; H. de la Costa, S. J., *Jesuits in the Philippines, 1581–1768* (Cambridge, MA: Harvard University Press, 1961), 369–371.

85. Chia, "The Butcher, the Baker, and the Carpenter," 522. Jonathan Gebhardt has traced the lives of two specific merchants, Don Juan Felipe de León Tiamnio and Don Pedro Quintero Tiongnio, demonstrating how they were able to build themselves a trading empire by developing close connections with important Spanish officials, including the governor of Manila. Both men were at various points embroiled in accusations of corruption, smuggling, and of providing false accusations of sedition against other Chinese, possibly to remove some of their political rivals in the Parian. See Gebhardt, "Chinese Migrants," 167–192.

86. AGI, Filipinas, leg. 80, núm. 123.

87. Crewe, "Pacific Purgatory," 357.

88. "Informe de fray Cristóbal Pedroche . . . ," AGI, Filipinas, leg. 28, núm. 131, fols. 970r–977r.

89. AGI, Filipinas, leg. 34, núm. 75; AGI, Filipinas, leg. 80, núm. 123; AHN, CDI, leg. 26, núm. 45; "Que los sangleyes de las islas se corten el Cabello," APSR, 40, tomo 1, doc. 9; "Sobre lo mismo del documento anterior, hacia 1630," APSR, 40, tomo 1, doc. 10; Tremml-Werner, *Spain, China, and Japan in Manila*, 304–305; Lorena Álvarez Delgado, "Los sangleyes y los problemas de la diversidad cultural en una colonial imperial (Filipinas, siglos XVI–XVII)," in *Actas de la XI reunión científica de la fundación española de historia moderna: Comunicaciones, Volumen I: El estado absoluto y la monarquía*, eds. Antonio Jiménez Estrella and Julián J. Lozano Navarro (Granada: Universidad de Granada, 2012), 915–924.

90. Chan, "Chinese–Philippine Relations," 67.

91. "Pregunta y propuesta . . . ," BNE, mss. 11014, fols. 42r–65v; "Informe de fray Jacinto Samper, a favor de la expulsion. Parián de Manila, 5 de junio de 1682," AGI, Filipinas, leg. 28, núm. 131, fols. 962r–968v; APSR, 45, sección San Gabriel, tomo 13, doc. 1; "Discurso y parecer . . . ," AGI, Filipinas, leg. 28, núm. 131, fols. 982r–995v; "Informe de fray Cristóbal Pedroche . . . ," AGI, Filipinas, leg. 28, núm. 131, fols. 970r–977r.

92. "Discurso y parecer . . . ," AGI, Filipinas, leg. 28, núm. 131, fols. 982r–995v. Fr. Cristóbal Pedroche gave an example of a Chinese who was baptized in order to gain patronage: he took as his patron Manuel Suarez and adopted his first name when baptized, becoming Manuel Simue. This patronage relationship allowed him to gather a great deal of fortune. "Informe de fray Cristóbal Pedroche . . . ," AGI, Filipinas, leg. 28, núm. 131, fols. 970r–977r.

93. "Informe de fray Jacinto Samper, a favor . . . ," AGI, Filipinas, leg. 28, núm. 131, fols. 962r–968v; APSR, 45, seccion San Gabriel, tomo 13, doc. 1.

94. "Discurso y parecer . . . ," AGI, Filipinas, leg. 28, núm. 131, fols. 982r–995v.

95. "Pregunta y propuesta . . . ," BNE, mss. 11014, fols. 42r–65v.

96. Crewe, "Pacific Purgatory," 360.

97. "Informe de fray Cristóbal Pedroche . . . ," AGI, Filipinas, leg. 28, núm. 131, fols. 970r–977r.

98. "Discurso y parecer . . . ," AGI, Filipinas, leg. 28, núm. 131, fols. 982r–995v.

99. Tremml, "The Global and the Local," 571; Alva Rodríguez, *Vida municipal en Manila*, 40–41.

100. Crewe, "Pacific Purgatory," 363. Surprisingly, trading relations were not impacted by the 1603 massacre. Most historians have suggested that this was because the trade itself was not government sponsored, and so the Ming dynasty had no interest in reprisals against the Spanish for the slaughter of tens of thousands of Fujianese merchants. See Borao, "The Massacre of 1603," 31–33. Anna Busquets notes, however, that in the 1650s the powerful Fujianese merchant and warlord Zheng Chenggong banned trade with the Philippines under penalty of death after hearing about the abuses that Chinese merchants received at the hands of the Spanish. See Busquets, "Dreams in the Chinese Periphery," 202–225. In their response to later expulsion proposals, the Jesuits also continuously raised the threat of lost trade with China, questioning whether merchants would continue to return to Manila if they were treated so badly. See "Razones que se ofrecen para que los sangleyes de esta república de Manila no sean desterrados de ella," BNE, mss. 11014, fols. 38r–41r; "Juicio del papel escrito en 25 de marzo de 1677 [por Vitorino Ricci), sobre que no se permitan de asiento los sangleyes en las islas. Impreso favorable al asentamiento de los sangleyes. Sin fecha," AGI, Filipinas, leg. 28, núm. 131, fols. 1003r–1014v.

101. "Discurso y parecer . . . ," AGI, Filipinas, leg. 28, núm. 131, fols. 982r–995v.

102. "Discurso y parecer . . . ," AGI, Filipinas, leg. 28, núm. 131, fols. 982r–995v. One additional consequence to this situation was that the Chinese also commonly became moneylenders to the Spanish population. Tremml-Werner, *Spain, China, and Japan in Manila*, 288; Kueh, "The Manila Chinese," 85–93.

103. "Discurso y parecer . . . ," AGI, Filipinas, leg. 28, núm. 131, fols. 982r–995v.

104. "Avisos de el comercio . . . ," BNE, mss. 11014, fols. 66r–68v.

105. AGI, Filipinas, leg. 27, núm. 207.

106. AGI, Filipinas, leg. 18B, ramo 7, núm. 74; AGI, Filipinas, leg. 28, núm. 128; "Pregunta y propuesta . . . ," BNE, mss. 11014, fols. 42r–65v.

107. "Copia de un capítulo . . . ," AGI, Filipinas, leg. 28, núm. 131, fols. 1015r–1018v.

108. "Discurso y parecer . . . ," AGI, Filipinas, leg. 28, núm. 131, fols. 982r–995v.

109. "Discurso y parecer . . . ," AGI, Filipinas, leg. 28, núm. 131, fols. 982r–995v.

110. "Discurso y parecer . . . ," AGI, Filipinas, leg. 28, núm. 131, fols. 982r–995v.

111. "Informe de fray Jacinto Samper, a favor . . . ," AGI, Filipinas, leg. 28, núm. 131, fols. 962r–968v; APSR, 45, seccion San Gabriel, tomo 13, doc. 1.

112. AGI, Filipinas, leg. 27, núm. 161; Antonio García-Abásolo, "Conflictos en el abasto de Manila en 1686: multiculturalidad y pan," in *El municipio indiano: relaciones interétnicas, económicas y sociales: Homenaje a Luis Navarro García*, eds. Manuela Cristian García Bernal and Sandra Olivero Guidobono (Sevilla: Secretariado de Publicaciones de la Universidad, 2009), 289; Chia, "The Butcher, the Baker, and the Carpenter," 509–534.

113. AGI, Filipinas, leg. 27, núm. 161.

114. AGI, Filipinas, leg. 69.

115. See chapter 1 for details of the events surrounding this threatened invasion.

116. Quoted in Busquets, "Dreams in the Chinese Periphery," 214. A *champan* was a large, flat bottomed sailing vessel commonly used in China, Japan, and some Spanish colonies.

117. "Pregunta y propuesta . . . ," BNE, mss. 11014, fols. 42r–65v.

118. The idea of expelling the Chinese was repeated over and over again throughout the following century. "Pregunta y propuesta . . . ," BNE, mss. 11014, fols. 42r–65v; "Avisos de el comercio . . . ," BNE, mss. 11014, fols. 66r–68v; "Discurso y parece . . . ," AGI, Filipinas, leg. 28, núm. 131, fols. 982r–995v; "Auto acordado del Consejo sobre la expulsión de los sangleyes," AGI, Filipinas, leg. 28, núm. 131, fols. 1126r–1127r; "Consulta del Consejo," AGI, Filipinas, leg. 202, fols. 10r–16r; "Carta de los vecinos de Manila, 30 June 1729," AGI, Filipinas, leg. 202, fols. 490r–493v; "Carta de la Audiencia de Manila: Juan Francisco de Velasco y Francisco Fernández Torivio (sic por Toribio) remitiendo testimonio de autos sobre las providencias de la junta que se mando formar en cumplimiento de la cédula de 30 de mayo de 1734 y la conveniencia de la expulsión de los sangleyes," AGI, Filipinas, leg. 202, fols. 494r–502v; AGI, Filipinas, leg. 292, núms. 60, 65; AGI, Filipinas, leg. 713; AGI, Filipinas, leg. 714; AGI, Filipinas, leg. 715; AGI, Filipinas, leg. 716; Salvador P. Escoto, "Expulsion of the Chinese and Readmission to the Philippines: 1764–1779," *Philippine Studies* 47, no. 1 (1999): 48–76.

119. Henry Kamen, *Spain, 1469–1714: A Society of Conflict* (London: Routledge, 2014), 37–39, 202–206.

120. "Pregunta y propuesta . . . ," BNE, mss. 11014, fols. 42r–65v. It should be noted that this was not the first time expulsion was raised as a possible solution. Similar proposals were made as early as 1597 (see AGI, Filipinas, leg. 18B, ramo 7, núm. 72; AGI, Filipinas, leg. 19, ramo 2, núm. 21) and following the 1603 uprising (see AGI, Filipinas, leg. 27, núm. 45; AGI, Filipinas, leg. 19, ramo 4, núm. 73).

121. "Discurso y parecer . . . ," AGI, Filipinas, leg. 28, núm. 131, fols. 982r–995v.

122. "Diego Calderón y Serrano, 10 April 1677," AGI, Filipinas, leg. 28, núm. 131, fols. 978r–980v; see also AHN, Consejo de Inquisición, leg. 5348, exp. 3; "Andrés González Cano, 30 May 1682," AGI, Filipinas, leg. 28, núm. 131, fols. 1052r–1052v; "Informe de fray Jacinto Samper, a favor . . . ," AGI, Filipinas, leg. 28, núm. 131, fols. 962r–968v; APSR, 45, sección San Gabriel, tomo 13, doc. 1; "Informe de fray Jacinto Samper, dominico . . . ," AGI, Filipinas, leg. 28, núm. 131, fols. 1114r–1121r; "Informe de fray Cristóbal Pedroche . . . ," AGI, Filipinas, leg. 28, núm. 131, fols. 970r–977r; "Diego de Aguilar, 24 June 1682," AGI, Filipinas, leg. 28, núm. 131, fols. 1102r; "Juan de Vargas, 20 June 1682," AGI, Filipinas, leg. 28, núm. 131, fols. 1099r–1100v; "Audiencia of Manila, 25 June 1682," AGI, Filipinas, leg. 28, núm. 131, fols. 1122r–1124r.

123. "Juicio del papel . . . ," AGI, Filipinas, leg. 28, núm. 131, fols. 1003r–1014v; see also "Luis Morales, 13 September 1686," AGI, Filipinas, leg. 28, núm. 131, fols. 1129r–1129v.

124. "Auto acordado . . . ," AGI, Filipinas, leg. 28, núm. 131, fols. 1126r–1127r; "Consulta del Consejo," AGI, Filipinas, leg. 202, fols. 10r–16r.

125. Ho, "Empire's Scorched Shore," 53–74; Roderich Ptak and Hu Baozhu, "Between Global and Regional Aspirations: China's Maritime Frontier and the Fujianese in the Early Seventeenth Century," *Journal of Asian History* 47, no. 2 (2013): 211.

126. "Memorial de los sangleyes dando razones para no ser expulsados," AGI, Filipinas, leg. 202, fols. 410r–412r.

127. Kueh, "The Manila Chinese," 19–20, 39–40, 98, 117, 125–126; Chia, "The Butcher, the Baker, and the Carpenter," 519–520.

128. "Juicio del papel . . . ," AGI, Filipinas, leg. 28, núm. 131, fols. 1003r–1014v; Chia, "The Butcher, the Baker, and the Carpenter," 517–518.

129. "Razones que se ofrecen . . . ," BNE, mss. 11014, fols. 38r–41r.

130. "Razones que se ofrecen . . . ," BNE, mss. 11014, fols. 38r–41r.

131. "Avisos necesarios . . . ," BNE, mss. 11014, fols. 32r–37v; "Andrés Gonzalez Cano, 30 May 1682," AGI, Filipinas, leg. 28, núm. 131, fols. 1052r–1052v; "Informe de fray Cristóbal Pedroche . . . ," AGI, Filipinas, leg. 28, núm. 131, fols. 970r–977r.

132. "Juicio del papel . . . ," AGI, Filipinas, leg. 28, núm. 131, fols. 1003r–1014v.

133. "Compulsa de los autos hechos en virtud de la real cédula de 14 de noviembre de 1686 sobre la expulsión de los sangleyes infieles," AGI, Filipinas, leg. 202, fols. 28r–165r; "Traslado de los autos obrados en cumplimiento de la cédula de expulsión de los sangleyes," AGI, Filipinas, leg. 202, fols. 174r–409r; "Memorial de los sangleyes . . . ," AGI, Filipinas, leg. 202, fols. 410r–412r.

134. Officials at the time reported that they had successfully deported 1,181 Chinese; however this figure is misleading since this included the original 840 crew who had arrived that year onboard these vessels and who were never granted licenses to remain in the city. "Traslado de los autos obrados . . . ," AGI, Filipinas, leg. 202, fols. 174r–409r.

135. "Traslado de los autos obrados . . . ," AGI, Filipinas, leg. 202, fols. 174r–409r; "Carta de la Audiencia de Manila, 25 June 1690," AGI, Filipinas, leg. 202, fols. 168r–172r; "Audiencia de Manila, 25 June 1691," AGI, Filipinas, leg. 202, fols. 413r–416v; "Audiencia de Manila, 18 June 1695," AGI, Filipinas, leg. 202, fols. 1r–3v; "Audiencia de Manila, 20 June 1700," AGI, Filipinas, leg. 202, fols. 421r–421v; Antonio García-Abásolo, "Relaciones entre españoles y chinos en Filipinas: Siglos XVI y XVII," in *España y el Pacífico: Legazpi*, vol. 2, ed. L. Cabrero (Madrid: Sociedad Estatal de Conmemoraciones Culturales, 2004), 242.

136. "Audiencia de Manila, 18 June 1695," AGI, Filipinas, leg. 202, fols. 1r–3v.

137. "Acordado sobre la expulción de los sangleyes," AGI, Filipinas, leg. 202, fols. 418r–420v.

138. "Traslado de la cédula en que se aprueba lo obrado sobre la expulsión de los sangleyes y lo que se ha ejecutado en su conformidad y padrón de los sangleyes," AGI, Filipinas, leg. 202, fols. 423r–456v.

139. The proposal was resurrected in 1729, 1734, 1744, 1753–1757, and 1764–1779. AGI, Filipinas, leg. 97, núm. 39; AGI, Filipinas, leg. 160, núm. 21; AGI, Filipinas, leg. 202; AGI, Filipinas, leg. 292, núms. 34, 60, 65; AGI, Filipinas, leg. 333, libro 13, fols. 157r–163r; AGI, Filipinas, leg. 334, libro 15, fols. 303r–322r; AGI, Filipinas, leg. 335, libro 17, fols. 352r–356v; AGI, Filipinas, leg. 336, libro 18, fols. 86v–88v; AGI, Filipinas, leg. 386, núm. 3; AGI, Filipinas, leg. 713; AGI, Filipinas, leg. 714; AGI, Filipinas, leg. 715; AGI, Filipinas, leg. 716; Escoto, "Expulsion of the Chinese," 48–76.

140. Escoto, "Expulsion of the Chinese," 48–76.

141. The exact extent of indigenous participation in these events is unclear. Where some sources claim that up to ten thousand indios participated in the pogrom, the most detailed account of the events refers more explicitly to an initial levy of one hundred Pampangans and four hundred Tagalogs to help in the attack on the fortifications near Calamba. A second levy of eighteen hundred Pampangans and Zambales took place

as the Chinese fled north toward Pampanga. In this instance, it was said that the indios were offered rewards for every severed head that they delivered. See "Relasión del alçamiento de los chinos en la ciudad de Manila por el mes de noviembre del año de 1639, causas del alçamiento y prinsipio del," RAH, 9/3663, núm. 28; "Relation on the Chinese Insurrection," B&R, vol. 29, 194–207; AGI, Filipinas, leg. 28, núm. 21.

142. In 1638, there were just 90 *vecinos* recorded in the city of Manila, down from 283 in 1634—a number which would continue to drop to just 30 in the decades to come. See Mesquida Oliver, "La población de Manila y las capellanías de misas de los españoles," 471; Alva Rodríguez, *Vida Municipal en Manila*, 30–31. In 1636, the city hosted 466 Spanish soldiers, where normal levels would have been closer to 800–900; see Mawson, "Convicts or *Conquistadores?*" 109.

143. "Pregunta y propuesta . . . ," BNE, mss. 11014, fols. 42r–65v; "Informe de fray Cristóbal Pedroche . . . ," AGI, Filipinas, leg. 28, núm. 131, fols. 970r–977r.

144. "Avisos de el comercio . . . ," BNE, mss. 11014, fols. 66r–68v.

145. "Razones que se ofrecen . . . ," BNE, mss. 11014, fols. 38r–41r.

146. Richard Chu, *Chinese and Chinese Mestizos of Manila: Family, Identity, and Culture, 1860s–1930s* (Leiden: Brill, 2010). *Mestizaje* is an analytical term that refers to the intermixing of different cultures; unlike the direct English translation (miscegenation), the term has generally positive connotations.

Conclusion

1. Archivo General de Indias (hereafter AGI), Audiencia de Filipinas (hereafter Filipinas), leg. 132, núm. 43.

2. Felix M. Keesing, *Ethnohistory of Northern Luzon* (Stanford, CA: Stanford University Press, 1962), 199–200. See also chapters 5 and 6 of this book.

3. 1685: "Alzamiento en Cagayan en 1660," Archivo de la Provincia del Santísimo Rosario, 58, sección Cagayan, tomo 13, doc. 3.

4. Gonzalo Lamana, *Domination without Dominance: Inca Spanish Encounters in Early Colonial Peru* (Durham, NC: Duke University Press, 2008), 1.

5. Engseng Ho, *The Graves of Tarim: Genealogy and Mobility Across the Indian Ocean* (Berkeley: University of California Press, 2006), xxiii.

6. Thomas Simpson, *The Frontier in British India: Space, Science, and Power in the Nineteenth Century* (Cambridge: Cambridge University Press, 2021), 6.

7. AGI, Filipinas, leg. 193, núm. 22.

8. AGI, Filipinas, leg. 140, núm. 29.

9. See note 2, chapter 6.

10. John Leddy Phelan, *The Hispanization of the Philippines: Spanish Aims and Filipino Responses, 1565–1700* (Madison: University of Wisconsin Press, 1967), 161.

11. Ann Laura Stoler, *Along the Archival Grain: Epistemic Anxieties and Colonial Common Sense* (Princeton, NJ: Princeton University Press, 2010); Kim A. Wagner, "'Treading Upon Fires': The 'Mutiny'-Motif and Colonial Anxieties in British India," *Past & Present* 218, no. 1 (2013): 159–197; Robert Peckham, *Empires of Panic: Epidemics and Colonial Anxieties* (Hong Kong: Hong Kong University Press, 2015).

12. Fenella Cannell, *Power and Intimacy in the Christian Philippines* (Cambridge: Cambridge University Press, 1999), 6–7.

13. Cannell, *Power and Intimacy*, 1.

14. Teodoro A. Agoncillo and Oscar M. Alfonso, *History of the Filipino People* (Quezon City: Malaya Books, 1967), vi–vii.

15. Victor Lieberman was particularly forceful in his assertion that Spanish colonization brought with it centralization and a state-building project that conveyed numerous benefits to Philippine communities that they accepted willingly and without opposition. He argues that "In local terms, Philippine unification was obviously revolutionary." Lieberman, *Strange Parallels: Southeast Asia in Global Context, c. 800–1830*, vol. 2, *Mainland Mirrors: Europe, Japan, China, South Asia, and the Islands* (Cambridge: Cambridge University Press, 2009), 832.

16. William Henry Scott, "An Historian Looks into the Philippine Kaleidoscope," *Philippine Studies* 24, no. 2 (1976): 220.

BIBLIOGRAPHY

Archival Sources

Archivo Franciscano Ibero-Oriental (Madrid)
Archivo General de Indias (Seville)
    Audiencia de Filipinas
    Escribanía de Cámara de Justicia
    Indiferente General
    Mapas y Planos
    Patronato Real
Archivo General de la Nación (México)
    Indiferente Virreinal
    Inquisición
Archivo General de Palacio Real (Madrid)
Archivo Histórico Nacional (Madrid)
Archivo de la Provincia del Santísimo Rosario (University of Santo Tomas, Manila)
Archivum Romanum Societatis Iesu (Rome)
Biblioteca Nacional de España (Madrid)
Bodleian Library (Oxford)
Lilly Library, Indiana University (Bloomington)
Real Academia de la Historia (Madrid)

Printed Primary Sources

Aduarte, Fr. Diego. *Tomo Primero de la Historia de la Provincia del Santo Rosario de Filipinas, Japón, y China, de la sagrada orden de predicadores.* Zaragoza: Por Domingo Gascon, Insançon, Impressor del Santo Hospital Real y General de Nuestra Señora de Gracia, 1693.

Argensola, Bartolomé Leonardo de. *Conquista de las Islas Malucas.* En Madrid por Alonso Martín, 1609.

Breve relacion, y felizes progresos de los Religiosos del Sagrado Orden de Predicadores de las Islas Philipinas, en la Conquista espiritual, y reduccion de los Gentiles de la Provincia de Paniqui q media entre las Provincias de Cagayan y Pangasinan. Manila: en el Collegio, y Universidad del Señor Santo Thomas con lizencia del Superior Govierno por Geronimo Correa de Castro, 1739.

Census of the Philippine Islands: Taken Under the Direction of the Philippine Commission in the Year 1903, in Four Volumes. Vol. 2. Washington, DC: United States Bureau of the Census, 1905.

Chirino, Pedro. *Relación de las islas Filipinas i de lo que en ellas an trabajado los padres de la Compañía de Iesus.* Roma: Por Estevan Paulino, 1604.

Colin, Francisco. *Labor evangélica, ministerios apostólicos de los obreros de la compañía de Iesus, fundación y progressos de su provincia en las islas filipinas: Historiados por el padre Francisco Colin, provincial de la misma compañía, calificador del santo oficio y su comisario en la governacion de Samboanga y su distrito.* 4 vols. Madrid: Por Ioseph Fernandez de Buendia, 1668.

Combes, Francisco. *Historia de las islas de Mindanao, Jolo y sus adyacentes. Progresos de la religión y armas católicas. Compuesto por el padre Francisco Combes, de la compañía de Iesus, Cathedratico de Prima de Theologia en su Colegio y Universidad de a la Ciudad de Manila.* Madrid: Por los herederos de Pablo de Val, 1667.

Concepción, Juan de la. *Historia General de Philipinas.* Manila: A. de la Rosa y Balagtas, 1788.

Diaz Toledano, Casimiro. *Conquista de las Islas Filipinas la temporal por las armas de nuestros Católicos Reyes de España . . . Parte segunda.* Valladolid, Spain: Imprenta Librería de Luis N. de Gaviria, 1890.

Jiménez, Fray Pedro, O. P. "Relación del principio de la misión de los Mandayas, hecha por mi, Fr. Pedro Jiménez, vicario de Fottol y Capinatan, como a quien le toca, por habérmelo mandado por ordenaciones, por ser frontera de estos pueblos, como otros muchos PP: Vicarios la tienen, para procurer la reducción de sus vecinos." *Philippiniana Sacra* 10, no. 30 (1975): 351–364.

Medina, Fray Juan de. *Historia de los sucesos de la orden de N. Gran P.S. Agustín de estas Islas Filipinas, desde que se descubrieron y se poblaron por los españoles, con las noticias memorables.* Manila: Tipo-Litografía de Chofre y Comp., 1893.

Morga, Antonio de. *The Philippine Islands, Moluccas, Siam, Cambodia, Japan and China at the Close of the Sixteenth Century.* Translated by Henry E. J. Stanley. Cambridge: Cambridge University Press, 2010.

Murillo Velarde, Pedro. *Historia de la Provincia de Philipinas de la compañía de Jesús: Segunda Parte, que comprehende los progresos de esta provincia desde el año de 1616 hasta el de 1716.* Manila: Imprenta de la Compañía de Jesús, por D. Nicolas de la Cruz Bagay, 1749.

The Philippine Islands, 1493–1803: Explorations by Early Navigators, Descriptions of the Islands and Their Peoples, Their History and Records of the Catholic Missions, as Related in Contemporaneous Books and Manuscripts, Showing the Political, Economic, Commercial and Religious Conditions of Those Islands from Their Earliest Relations with European Nations to the Beginning of the Nineteenth Century. Translated and edited by Emma Helen Blair and James Alexander Robertson. 55 vols. Cleveland, OH: A. H. Clark, 1903–9.

Rizal, José. *Sobre la indolencia de los Filipinos: Estudio Político-Social.* Manila: Nueva Era, 1954.

Salazar, Vicente de. *Historia de la Provincia de el Santíssimo Rosario de Philipinas, China y Tunking, de el Sagrado Orden de Predicadores. Tercera Parte, en que se tratan los sucesos de dicha Provincia desde el año de 1669 hasta el de 1700. Compuesta por el R. P. Fr. Vicente de Salazar, Rector de el Collegio de Santo Thomas de la Ciudad de Manila y Chancellario de Su Universidad.* Manila: Impressa en la Imprenta de dicho Collegio y Universidad de Santo Thomas de las misma Ciudad, 1742.

San Antonio, Fray Juan Francisco de. *Crónicas de la Provincia de San Gregorio Magno.* Translated by Don Pedro Picornell. Manila: Historical Conservation Society, 1977.

San Nicolas, Andrés de. *Historia General de los religiosos descalzos del orden de los hermitaños del gran padre y doctor de la iglesia San Agustín de la Congregación de España y de las Indias.* Vol. 1. Madrid: por Andrés García de la Iglesia, 1664.

Santa Cruz, Baltasar de. *Tomo Segundo de la Historia de la Provincia del Santo Rosario de Filipinas, Japón, y China del Sagrado Orden de Predicadores.* Zaragoza: Por Pasqual Bueno, Impressor Reyno, 1693.

Ustariz, Fr. Bernardo. *Relación de los sucessos, y progressos de la mission de Santa Cruz de Paniqui y de Ytuy, medias entre las de Pangasinan, Cagayan, y Pampanga: año de 1745.* s.n., 1745?

Zamora, Fr. Francisco de. *Memorial del P. Francisco de Zamora al Gobernador de Manila, sobre los Progresos de las Misiones de los Agustinos en las Naciones Italón y Abaca.* Barcelona: s.n., 1905 [1708].

Secondary Sources

Acabado, Stephen. "The Archaeology of Pericolonialism: Responses of the 'Unconquered' to Spanish Conquest and Colonialism in Ifugao, Philippines." *International Journal of Historical Archaeology* 21, no. 1 (2017): 1–26.

Acabado, Stephen. "Zones of Refuge: Resisting Conquest in the Northern Philippine Highlands through Environmental Practice." *Journal of Anthropological Archaeology* 52 (2018): 180–195.

Agoncillo, Teodoro A., and Oscar M. Alfonso. *History of the Filipino People.* Quezon City: Malaya Books, 1967.

Alonso Álvarez, Luis. "Repartimientos y economía en las islas filipinas bajo dominio español, 1565–1815." In *El repartimiento forzoso de mercancías en México, Perú y Filipinas.* Edited by Margarita Menegus, 170–215. México: Instituto de Investigaciones Dr. José María Luis Mora Centre de Estudios sobre la Universidad, UNAM, 2000.

Álvarez Delgado, Lorena. "Los sangleyes y los problemas de la diversidad cultural en una colonial imperial (Filipinas, siglos XVI–XVII)." In *Actas de la XI reunión científica de la fundación española de historia moderna: Comunicaciones, Volumen I: El estado absoluto y la monarquía.* Edited by Antonio Jiménez Estrella and Julián J. Lozano Navarro, 915–924. Granada: Universidad de Granada, 2012.

Alva Rodríguez, Inmaculada. *Vida municipal en Manila (siglos XVI–XVII).* Córdoba: Universidad de Córdoba, 1997.

Andaya, Barbara Watson. "Between Empires and Emporia: The Economics of Christianization in Early Modern Southeast Asia." *Journal of the Economic and Social History of the Orient* 53, nos. 1/2 (2010): 357–392.

Andaya, Barbara Watson. "The Changing Religious Role of Women in Pre-Modern South East Asia." *South East Asia Research* 2, no. 2 (1994): 99–116.

Andaya, Barbara Watson. "History, Headhunting and Gender in Monsoon Asia: Comparative and Longitudinal Views." *Southeast Asia Research* 12, no. 1 (2004): 13–52.

Andaya, Leonard Y. *The World of Maluku: Eastern Indonesia in the Early Modern Period*. Honolulu: University of Hawai'i Press, 1993.

Andrade, Tonio. *Lost Colony: The Untold Story of China's First Great Victory Over the West*. Princeton, NJ: Princeton University Press, 2011.

Andrade, Tonio, and Xing Hang. "Introduction: The East Asian Maritime Realm in Global History, 1500–1700." In *Sea Rovers, Silver, and Samurai: Maritime East Asia in Global History, 1550–1700*. Edited by Tonio Andrade and Xing Hang, 1–27. Honolulu: University of Hawai'i Press, 2016.

Antolin, Francisco, and William Henry Scott. "Notices of the Pagan Igorots in 1789." *Asian Folklore Studies* 29 (1970): 177–249.

Antolin, Francisco, William Henry Scott, and Fray Manuel Carillo. "Notices of the Pagan Igorots in 1789: Part Two." *Asian Folklore Studies* 30, no. 2 (1971): 27–132.

Antony, Robert J. "Turbulent Waters: Sea Raiding in Early Modern South East Asia." *Mariner's Mirror* 99, no. 1 (2013): 23–38.

Aparece, Ulysses B. "Retrieving a Folk Hero through Oral Narratives: The Case of Francisco Dagohoy in the *Sukdan* Rituals." *Philippine Quarterly of Culture and Society* 41, nos. 3–4 (2013): 143–162.

Barr, Juliana, and Edward Countryman. "Maps and Spaces, Paths to Connect, and Lines to Divide." In *Contested Spaces of Early America*. Edited by Juliana Barr and Edward Countryman, 1–28. Philadelphia: University of Pennsylvania Press, 2014.

Barrantes, Vicente. *Guerras piráticas de Filipinas contra mindanaos y joloanos*. Madrid: Imprenta de Manuel G. Hernandez, 1878.

Batchelor, Robert K. *London: The Selden Map and the Making of a Global City, 1549–1689*. Chicago: University of Chicago Press, 2014.

Batchelor, Robert. "Maps, Calendars, and Diagrams: Space and Time in Seventeenth-Century Maritime East Asia." In *Sea Rovers, Silver, and Samurai: Maritime East Asia in Global History, 1550–1700*. Edited by Tonio Andrade and Xing Hang, 86–113. Honolulu: University of Hawai'i Press, 2016.

Batchelor, Robert. "The Selden Map Rediscovered: A Chinese Map of East Asian Shipping Routes, c. 1619." *Imago Mundi: The International Journal for the History of Cartography* 65, no. 1 (2013): 37–65.

Bauzon, Leslie E. *Deficit Government: Mexico and the Philippine Situado, 1606–1804*. Tokyo: Center for East Asian Cultural Studies, 1981.

Beemer, Bryce. "Southeast Asian Slavery and Slave-Gathering Warfare as a Vector for Cultural Transmission: The Case of Burma and Thailand." *Historian* 71, no. 3 (2009): 481–506.

Benton, Bradley. *The Lords of Tetzcoco: The Transformation of Indigenous Rule in Postconquest Central Mexico*. Cambridge: Cambridge University Press, 2017.

Benton, Lauren. *A Search for Sovereignty: Law and Geography in European Empires, 1400–1900*. Cambridge: Cambridge University Press, 2009.

Bernad, Miguel A., S. J. *The Christianization of the Philippines: Problems and Perspectives*. Manila: Filipiniana Book Guild, 1972.

Bernal, Rafael. "The Chinese Colony in Manila, 1570–1770." In *The Chinese in the Philippines, 1570–1770*. Edited by Alfonso Felix Jr., 40–66. Manila: Solidaridad Publishing House, 1966.

Bohigian, Gary William. "Life on the Rim of Spain's Pacific-American Empire: Presidio Society in the Molucca Islands, 1606–1663." PhD diss., University of California, Los Angeles, 1994.

Boomgaard, Peter. "Human Capital, Slavery and Low Rates of Economic and Population Growth in Indonesia, 1600–1910." *Slavery and Abolition* 24, no. 2 (2003): 83–96.

Borao Mateo, José Eugenio. "Filipinos in the Spanish Colonial Army during the Dutch Wars (1600–1648)." In *More Hispanic Than We Admit: Insights in Philippine Cultural History*. Edited by Isaac Donoso, 74–93. Quezon City: Vibal Foundation, 2008.

Borao, José Eugenio. "The Massacre of 1603: Chinese Perception of the Spanish on the Philippines." *Itinerario* 22, no. 1 (1998): 22–40.

Borao Mateo, José Eugenio, ed. *Spaniards in Taiwan: Documents*. Vols. 1 and 2. Translated by Pol Heyns and Carlos Gómez. Taipei: SMC, 2001.

Borao Mateo, José Eugenio. *The Spanish Experience in Taiwan, 1626–1642*. Hong Kong: Hong Kong University Press, 2009.

Borchgrevink, Axel. "Ideas of Power in the Philippines: Amulets and Sacrifice." *Cultural Dynamics* 15, no. 1 (2003): 41–69.

Borges Morán, Pedro. "Aspectos Características de La Evangelización de Filipinas." In *España t el Pacífico: Legazpi*. Vol. 2. Edited by Leoncio Cabrero, 285–318. Madrid: Sociedad Estatal de Conmemoraciones Culturales, 2004.

Borschberg, Peter. "From Self-Defense to an Instrument of War: Dutch Privateering Around the Malay Peninsula in the Early Seventeenth Century." *Journal of Early Modern History* 17, no. 1 (2013): 35–52.

Boxer, C. R. "Plata es Sangre: Sidelights on the Drain of Spanish-American Silver in the Far East, 1550–1700." In *European Entry into the Pacific: Spain and the Acapulco-Manila Galleons*. Edited by Dennis O. Flynn, Arturo Giráldez, and James Sobredo, 165–186. Aldershot, UK: Ashgate, 2001.

Brewer, Carolyn. "From Animist 'Priestess' to Catholic Priest: The Re / Gendering of Religious Roles in the Philippines, 1521–1685." In *Other Pasts: Women, Gender and History in Early Modern Southeast Asia*. Edited by Barbara Watson Andaya, 69–86. Honolulu: Center for Southeast Asian Studies, University of Hawai'i at Manoa, 2000.

Brewer, Carolyn. *Shamanism, Catholicism and Gender Relations in Colonial Philippines, 1521–1685*. Aldershot, UK: Ashgate, 2004.

Brook, Timothy. *Mr. Selden's Map of China: Decoding the Secrets of a Vanished Cartographer*. New York: Bloomsbury, 2013.

Burbank, Jane, and Frederick Cooper. *Empires in World History: Power and the Politics of Difference*. Princeton, NJ: Princeton University Press, 2010.

Bushnell, Amy Turner. "Gates, Patterns, and Peripheries: The Field of Frontier Latin America." In *Negotiated Empires: Centers and Peripheries in the Americas, 1500–1820*. Edited by Christine Daniels and Michael V. Kennedy, 15–28. New York: Routledge, 2002.

Bushnell, Amy Turner, and Jack P. Greene. "Peripheries, Centers, and the Construction of Early Modern American Empires." In *Negotiated Empires: Centers and Peripheries in the Americas, 1500–1820*. Edited by Christine Daniels and Michael V. Kennedy, 1–14. New York: Routledge, 2002.

Busquets, Anna. "Dreams in the Chinese Periphery: Victorio Riccio and Zheng Chenggong's Regime." In *Sea Rovers, Silver, and Samurai: Maritime East Asia in Global History, 1550–1700*. Edited by Tonio Andrade and Xing Hang, 202–225. Honolulu: University of Hawai'i Press, 2016.

Camacho, Marya Svetlana. "The *Baylan* and *Catalonan* in the Early Spanish Colonial Period." In *Un mar de islas, un mar de gentes: Población y diversidad en las islas Filipinas*. Edited by Marta María Manchado López and Miguel Luque Talaván, 127–144. Córdoba: Servicio de Publicaciones Universidad de Córdoba, 2014.

Camara Dery, Luis. *The Kris in Philippine History: A Study of the Impact of Moro Anti-Colonial Resistance, 1571–1896*. Quezon City: Luis Camara Dery, 1997.

Camara Dery, Luis. *Pestilence in the Philippines: A Social History of the Filipino People, 1571–1800*. Quezon City: New Day, 2006.

Campbell, Gwyn, and Alessandro Stanziani. *Bonded Labour and Debt in the Indian Ocean World*. London: Pickering & Chatto, 2013.

Campbell, Gwyn, and Alessandro Stanziani. "Introduction." In *Bonded Labour and Debt in the Indian Ocean World*. Edited by Gwyn Campbell and Alessandro Stanziani, 1–20. London: Pickering & Chatto, 2013.

Campos y Fernández de Sevilla, Francisco Javier. "Las órdenes mendicantes en Filipinas: agustinos, franciscanos, dominicos y recoletos." In *España y el Pacífico: Legazpi*. Vol. 2. Edited by Leoncio Cabrero, 251–280. Madrid: Sociedad Estatal de Conmemoraciones Culturales, 2004.

Cannell, Fenella. *Power and Intimacy in the Christian Philippines*. Cambridge: Cambridge University Press, 1999.

Castellanos Escudier, Alicia. "Expediciones españolas a Borneo en el siglo XVI." In *Filipinas y el Pacífico: Nueva miradas, nuevas reflexiones*. Edited by Salvador Bernabéu Albert, Carmen Mena García, and Emilio José Luque Azcona, 21–52. Sevilla: Editorial Universidad de Sevilla, 2016.

Chan, Albert. "Chinese–Philippine Relations in the Late Sixteenth Century to 1603." *Philippine Studies* 26, nos. 1–2 (1978): 74–81.

Chia, Lucille. "The Butcher, the Baker, and the Carpenter: Chinese Sojourners in the Spanish Philippines and Their Impact on Southern Fujian." *Journal of the Economic and Social History of the Orient* 49, no. 4 (2006): 509–534.

Chin, James K. "Junk Trade, Business Networks, and Sojourning Communities: Hokkien Merchants in Early Maritime Asia." *Journal of Chinese Overseas* 6, no. 2 (2010): 157–215.

Chin-Keong, Ng. "The South Fukienese Junk Trade at Amoy from the Seventeenth to the Early Nineteenth Centuries." In *Development and Decline of Fukien Province in the 17th and 18th Centuries*. Edited by E. B. Vermeer, 297–316. Leiden: E. J. Brill, 1990.

Christensen, Mark. "Recent Approaches in Understanding Evangelization in New Spain." *History Compass* 14, no. 2 (2016): 39–48.

Chu, Richard. *Chinese and Chinese Mestizos of Manila: Family, Identity, and Culture, 1860s–1930s*. Leiden: Brill, 2010.

Cole, Mabel Cook, ed. *Philippine Folk Tales*. Chicago: A. C. McClurg, 1916.

Constantino, Renato. *The Philippines: A Past Revisited*. Quezon City: Tala, 1975.

Coronel Ferrer, Miriam. *Region, Nation and Homeland: Valorization and Adaptation in the Moro and Cordillera Resistance Discourses*. Singapore: ISEAS, 2020.

Cortes, Rosario Mendoza. *Pangasinan, 1572–1800*. Quezon City: University of the Philippines Press, 1974.

Cortes, Rosario Mendoza, Celestina Puyal Boncan, and Ricardo Trota Jose. *The Filipino Saga: History as Social Change*. Quezon City: New Day, 2000.

Crewe, Ryan Dominic. "Pacific Purgatory: Spanish Dominicans, Chinese Sangleys, and the Entanglement of Mission and Commerce in Manila, 1580–1620." *Journal of Early Modern History* 19, no. 4 (2015): 337–365.

Cummins, James S., and Nicholas P. Cushner. "Labor in the Colonial Philippines: The *Discurso Parenetico* of Gomez de Espinosa." *Philippine Studies* 22, nos. 1–2 (1974): 117–203.

Cushner, Nicholas P. *Landed Estates in the Colonial Philippines*. New Haven, CT: Yale University Southeast Asia Studies, 1976.

Cushner, Nicholas P. *Spain in the Philippines: From Conquest to Revolution*. Quezon City: Ateneo de Manila University, 1971.

Cushner, Nicholas P., and John A. Larkin. "Royal Land Grants in the Colonial Philippines (1571–1626): Implications for the Formation of a Social Elite." *Philippine Studies* 25, nos. 1–2 (1978): 102–111.

De la Costa, H. "Church and State in the Philippines during the Administration of Bishop Salazar, 1581–1594." *Hispanic American Historical Review* 30, no. 3 (1950): 314–335.

De la Costa, H., S. J. *The Jesuits in the Philippines, 1581–1768*. Cambridge, MA: Harvard University Press, 1961.

De la Costa, H., S. J. *Readings in Philippine History*. Manila: Bookmark, 1965.

Demetrio, Francisco R., S. J. "Shamans, Witches and Philippine Society." *Philippine Studies* 36, no. 3 (1998): 372–380.

De Viana, Augusto V. *In the Far Islands: The Role of Natives from the Philippines in the Conquest, Colonization and Repopulation of the Mariana Islands, 1668–1903*. Manila: University of Santo Tomas Publishing House, 2004.

Díaz-Trechuelo Spínola, María Lourdes. *Filipinas: La Gran Desconocida (1565–1898)*. Pamplona: Ediciones Universidad de Navarra, 2001.

Dizon, Lino L. *East of Pinatubo: Former Recollect Missions in Tarlac and Pampanga (1712–1898)*. Tarlac: Center for Tarlaqueño Studies, Tarlac State University, 1998.

Dizon, Mark, "Social and Spiritual Kinship in Early-Eighteenth-Century Missions on the Caraballo Mountains." *Philippine Studies* 59, no. 3 (2011): 367–398.

Dizon, Mark. "Sumpong Spirit Beliefs, Murder, and Religious Change among Eighteenth-Century Aeta and Ilongot in Eastern Central Luzon." *Philippine Studies* 63, no. 1 (2015): 3–38.

Donkin, R. A. *Between East and West: The Moluccas and the Traffic in Spices up to the Arrival of Europeans*. Philadelphia: American Philosophical Society, 2003.

Donoso, Isaac, Glòria Cano, and Jorge Mojarro Romero, eds. *More Hispanic Than We Admit: Insights in Philippine Cultural History*. 3 vols. Quezon City: Vibal Foundation, 2008–2020.

Donoso Jiménez, Isaac. "El Islam en Filipinas (Siglos X–XIX)." PhD diss., Universidad de Alicante, 2011.

Ellen, Roy. *On the Edge of the Banda Zone: Past and Present in the Social Organization of a Moluccan Trading Network*. Honolulu: University of Hawai'i Press, 2003.

Escoto, Salvador P. "Expulsion of the Chinese and Readmission to the Philippines: 1764–1779." *Philippine Studies* 47, no. 1 (1999): 48–76.

Farriss, Nancy M. *Maya Society Under Colonial Rule: The Collective Enterprise of Survival*. Princeton, NJ: Princeton University Press, 1984.

Federspiel, Howard M. *Sultans, Shamans, and Saints: Islam and Muslims in Southeast Asia*. Honolulu: University of Hawai'i Press, 2007.

Fernandez, Pablo, O. P. *History of the Church in the Philippines (1521–1898)*. Manila: National Book Store Publishers, 1979.

Flameygh, John, and William Henry Scott. "An Ilocano-Igorot Peace Pact of 1820." *Philippine Studies* 26, no. 3 (1978): 285–295.

Flynn, Dennis O., and Arturo Giráldez. "Silk for Silver: Manila-Macao Trade in the 17th Century." *Philippine Studies* 44, no. 1 (1996): 52–68.

Foronda, Marcelino A. Jr. *Insigne y Siempre Leal: Essays on Spanish Manila*. Manila: De La Salle University History Department, 1986.

Foronda, Marcelino A. Jr., and Cornelio R. Bascara. *Manila*. Madrid: Editorial MAPFRE, 1992.

García-Abásolo, Antonio. "Conflictos en el abasto de Manila en 1686: multiculturalidad y pan." In *El municipio indiano: relaciones interétnicas, económicas y sociales: Homenaje a Luis Navarro García*. Edited by Manuela Cristian García Bernal and Sandra Olivero Guidobono, 283–299. Sevilla: Secretariado de Publicaciones de la Universidad, 2009.

García-Abásolo, Antonio. "Relaciones entre españoles y chinos en Filipinas: Siglos XVI y XVII." In *España y el Pacífico: Legazpi*. Vol. 2. Edited by L. Cabrero, 231–248. Madrid: Sociedad Estatal de Conmemoraciones Culturales, 2004.

Gatchalin, N. U. "The Non-Christian Tagalogs of Rizal Province." *Asian Folklore Studies* 28, no. 1 (1969): 94–98.

Gaynor, Jennifer L. *Intertidal History in Island Southeast Asia: Submerged Genealogy and the Legacy of Coastal Capture*. Ithaca, NY: Cornell University Press, 2016.

Gebhardt, Jonathan. "Chinese Migrants, Spanish Empire, and Globalization in Early Modern Manila." *Journal of Medieval and Early Modern Studies* 46, no. 1 (2017): 167–192.

George, Kenneth M. "Headhunting, History and Exchange in Upland Sulawesi." *Journal of Asian Studies* 50, no. 3 (1991): 536–564.

Gerona, Danilo M. "The Colonial Accommodation and Reconstitution of Native Elite in the Early Provincial Philippines, 1600–1795." In *Imperios y Naciones en el Pacífico*. Vol. 1. Edited by Maria Dolores Elizalde, Josep M. Fradera, and Luis Alonso, 265–276. Madrid: Consejo Superior de Investigaciones Científicas, 2001.

Gibson, Thomas. "Raiding, Trading and Tribal Autonomy in Insular Southeast Asia." In *The Anthropology of War*. Edited by J. Haas, 125–145. Cambridge: Cambridge University Press, 1990.

Gibson, Thomas. *Sacrifice and Sharing in the Philippine Highlands: Religion and Society among the Buid of Mindoro*. London: Athlone, 1986.

Gil, Juan. *Los Chinos en Manila: Siglos XVI y XVII*. Lisboa: Centro Científico e Cultural de Macau, 2011.

Gil Montero, Raquel. "Free and Unfree Labour in the Colonial Andes in the Sixteenth and Seventeenth Centuries." *International Review of Social History* 56, special issue S19 (2011–12): 297–318.

Gil Montero, Raquel. "Mecanismos de reclutamiento indígena en la minería de plata: Lípez (sur de la actual Bolivia), siglo XVII." *America Latina en la Historia Económica* 21, no. 1 (2014): 5–30.

Gil Montero, Raquel. "Migración y tributación en los Andes: Chichas y Lípez a fines del siglo XVII." *Anuario de Estudios Americanos* 70, no. 1 (2013): 39–65.

Glover, Dominic, and Glenn Davis Stone. "Heirloom Rice in Ifugao: An 'Anti-Commodity' in the Process of Commodification." *Journal of Peasant Studies* 45, no. 4 (2018): 776–804.

Gomes, Flávio. "Indigenas, africanos y comunidades de fugitivos en la Amazonia colonial." *Historia y Espacio* 6, no. 34 (2010): 1–21.

Graham, Penelope. *Iban Shamanism: An Analysis of the Ethnographic Literature.* Occasional Paper of the Department of Anthropology, Research School of Pacific Studies. Canberra: Australian National University, 1987.

Greer, Margaret R., Walter D. Mignolo, and Maureen Quilligan, eds. *Rereading the Black Legend: The Discourses of Religious and Racial Difference in the Renaissance Empires.* Chicago: University of Chicago Press, 2007.

Griffin, P. Bion. "Agta Foragers: Alternative Histories, and Cultural Autonomy in Luzon." *Australian Journal of Anthropology* 8, no. 3 (1987): 259–269.

Guerrero, Milagros C. "The Chinese in the Philippines, 1570–1770." In *The Chinese in the Philippines, 1570–1770.* Edited by Alfonso Felix, 15–39. Manila: Solidaridad, 1966.

Guy, Donna J., and Thomas E. Sheridan, eds. *Contested Ground: Comparative Frontiers on the Northern and Southern Edges of the Spanish Empire.* Tucson: University of Arizona Press, 1998.

Hägerdal, Hans. "The Slaves of Timor: Life and Death on the Fringes of Early Colonial Society." *Itinerario* 34, no. 2 (2010): 19–44.

Haliczer, Stephen. *Sexuality in the Confessional: A Sacrament Profaned.* Oxford: Oxford University Press, 1996.

Hämäläinen, Pekka. *The Comanche Empire: A Study of Indigenous Power.* New Haven, CT: Yale University Press, 2009.

Hämäläinen, Pekka. "What's in a Concept? The Kinetic Empire of the Comanches." *History and Theory* 52, no. 1 (2013): 81–90.

Hang, Xing. *Conflict and Commerce in Maritime East Asia: The Zheng Family and the Shaping of the Modern World, c. 1620–1720.* Cambridge: Cambridge University Press, 2016.

Hanisch Espíndola, Walter, S. J. "Esclavitud y libertad de los indios de Chile, 1608–1696." *Historia* no. 16 (1981): 5–65.

Hawkley, Ethan P. "Reviving the Reconquista in Southeast Asia: Moros and the Making of the Philippines, 1565–1662." *Journal of World History* 25, nos. 2–3 (2014): 285–310.

Hayase, Shinzo. *Mindanao Ethnohistory Beyond Nations: Maguindanao, Sangir, and Bagobo Societies in East Maritime Southeast Asia.* Quezon City: Ateneo de Manila University Press, 2003.

Headland, Thomas N. "Why Foragers Do Not Become Farmers: A Historical Study of a Changing Ecosystem and Its Effect on a Negrito Hunter-Gatherer Group in the Philippines." PhD diss., University of Hawaii, 1986.

Headland, Thomas N. "The Wild Yam Question: How Well Could Independent Hunter-Gatherers Live in a Tropical Rain Forest Ecosystem?" *Human Ecology* 15, no. 4 (1987): 463–491.

Henley, David. *Jealousy and Justice: The Indigenous Roots of Colonial Rule in Northern Sulawesi.* Amsterdam: VU Uitgeverij, 2002.

Hidalgo Nuchera, Patricio. *Encomienda, tributo y trabajo en Filipinas (1570–1608).* Madrid: Ediciones Polifemo, 1995.

Hidalgo Nuchera, Patricio. "¿Esclavitud o liberación? El fracaso de las actitudes esclavistas de los conquistadores de Filipinas." *Revista Complutense de Historia de América* no. 20, (1994): 61–74.

Hidalgo Nuchera, Patricio. "La encomienda en Filipinas." In *España y el Pacífico: Legazpi.* Vol. 1. Edited by Leoncio Cabrero, 465–484. Madrid: Sociedad Estatal de Conmemoraciones Culturales, 2004.

Hislop, Stephen K. "Anitism: A Survey of Religious Beliefs Native to the Philippines." *Asian Studies* 9 (1971): 144–156.

Ho, Dahpon David. "The Empire's Scorched Shore: Coastal China, 1633–1683." *Journal of Early Modern History* 17, no. 1 (2013): 53–74.

Ho, Engseng. *The Graves of Tarim: Genealogy and Mobility Across the Indian Ocean.* Berkeley: University of California Press, 2006.

Hornedo, Florentino H. "'Indayuan,' An Amburayan Migration Song." *Philippine Studies* 38, no. 3 (1990): 358–368.

Hoskins, Janet, ed. *Headhunting and the Social Imagination in Southeast Asia.* Stanford, CA: Stanford University Press, 1996.

Hoskins, Janet. "Introduction: Headhunting as Practice and as Trope." In *Headhunting and the Social Imagination in Southeast Asia.* Edited by Janet Hoskins, 1–49. Stanford, CA: Stanford University Press, 1996.

Ileto, Reynaldo Clemeña. *Pasyon and Revolution: Popular Movements in the Philippines, 1840–1910.* Quezon City: Ateneo de Manila University Press, 1979.

Irving, D. R. M. *Colonial Counterpoint: Music in Early Modern Manila.* Oxford: Oxford University Press, 2010.

Jesus, Ed. C. de. "Control and Compromise in the Cagayan Valley." In *Philippine Social History: Global Trade and Local Transformations.* Edited by Alfred W. McCoy and Ed. C. de Jesus, 21–39. Quezon City: Ateneo de Manila Press, 1982.

Jiménez Pelayo, Águeda. "Condiciones del trabajo de repartimiento indígena en la Nueva Galicia en el siglo XVII." *Historia Mexicana* 38, no. 3 (1989): 455–470.

Junker, Laura L. "Economic Specialization and Inter-Ethnic Trade between Foragers and Farmers in the Prehispanic Philippines." In *Forager-Traders in South and Southeast Asia: Long-Term Histories.* Edited by Kathleen D. Morrison and Laura L. Junker, 203–241. Cambridge: Cambridge University Press, 2002.

Junker, Laura Lee. "Hunter-Gatherer Landscapes and Lowland Trade in the Prehispanic Philippines." *World Archaeology* 27, no. 3 (1996): 389–410.

Junker, Laura Lee. *Raiding, Trading and Feasting: The Political Economy of Philippine Chiefdoms.* Honolulu: University of Hawai'i Press, 1999.

Kamen, Henry. *Spain, 1469–1714: A Society of Conflict.* London: Routledge, 2014.

Keesing, Felix M. *The Ethnohistory of Northern Luzon.* Stanford, CA: Stanford University Press, 1962.

Kelly, Piers. *The Last Language on Earth: Linguistic Utopianism in the Philippines.* Oxford: Oxford University Press, 2022.

Kenji, Igawa. "At the Crossroads: Limahon and Wakō in Sixteenth-Century Philippines." In *Elusive Pirates, Pervasive Smugglers: Violence and Clandestine Trade in the Greater China Seas.* Edited by Antony J. Roberts, 73–84. Hong Kong: Hong Kong University Press, 2010.

Kicza, John E. *Resilient Cultures: America's Native Peoples Confront European Colonization, 1500–1800.* Upper Saddle River, NJ: Pearson Education, 2003.

Kim, Bok-rae. "Debt Slaves in Old Korea." In *Bonded Labour and Debt in the Indian Ocean World.* Edited by Gwyn Campbell and Alessandro Stanziani, 165–172. London: Pickering & Chatto, 2013.

K'o-ch'eng, Cheng. "Chen Ch'eng-kung's Maritime Expansion and Early Ch'ing Coastal Prohibition." In *Development and Decline of Fukien Province in the 17th and 18th Centuries.* Edited by Eduard B. Vermeer, translated by Burchard Mansvelt Beck, 217–244. Leiden: Brill, 1990.

Kueh, Joshua Eng Sin. "The Manila Chinese: Community, Trade and Empire, c. 1570–c. 1770." PhD diss., Georgetown University, 2014.

Laarhoven, Ruurdje. *Triumph of Moro Diplomacy: The Maguindanao Sultanate in the 17th Century.* Quezon City: New Day, 1989.

Laarhoven, Ruurdje, and Elizabeth Pino Wittermans. "From Blockade to Trade: Early Dutch Relations with Manila, 1600–1750." *Philippine Studies* 33, no. 4 (1985): 485–504.

Lamana, Gonzalo. *Domination without Dominance: Inca Spanish Encounters in Early Colonial Peru.* Durham, NC: Duke University Press, 2008.

Lambrecht, F. "The Hudhud of Dinulawan and Bugan at Gonhadan." *Saint Louis Quarterly* 5, (1967): 527–571.

Landa Jocano, F. "Conversion and the Patterning of Christian Experience in Malitbog, Central Panay, Philippines." *Philippine Sociological Review* 13, no. 2 (1965): 96–119.

Landa Jocano, F. "Filipino Catholicism: A Case Study in Religious Change." *Asian Studies* 5, no. 1 (1967): 42–64.

Landa Jocano, F. "The Sulod: A Mountain People in Central Panay, Philippines." *Philippine Studies* 6, no. 4 (1958): 401–436.

Landa Jocano, F. *Sulod Society: A Study in the Kinship System and Social Organization of a Mountain People of Central Panay.* Quezon City: University of the Philippines Press, 1968.

Larkin, John A. *The Pampangans: Colonial Society in a Philippine Province.* Berkeley: University of California Press, 1972.

Laufer, Berthold. *The Relations of the Chinese to the Philippine Islands.* Smithsonian Miscellaneous Collections, Vol. 50. Washington: Smithsonian Institution, 1908.

Leibsohn, Dana. "*Dentro y fuera de los muros*: Manila, Ethnicity, and Colonial Cartography." *Ethnohistory* 61, no. 2 (2014): 229–251.

Lieban, Richard W. *Cebuano Sorcery: Malign Magic in the Philippines*. Berkeley: University of California Press, 1967.

Lieberman, Victor. "Some Comparative Thoughts on Premodern Southeast Asian Warfare." *Journal of the Economic and Social History of the Orient* 46, no. 2 (2003): 215–225.

Lieberman, Victor. *Strange Parallels: Southeast Asia in Global Context, c. 800–1830*. Vol. 2, *Mainland Mirrors: Europe, Japan, China, South Asia, and the Islands*. Cambridge: Cambridge University Press, 2009.

Lockard, Craig A. "'The Sea Common to All': Maritime Frontiers, Port Cities, and Chinese Traders in the Southeast Asian Age of Commerce, ca. 1400–1750." *Journal of World History* 21, no. 2 (2010): 219–247.

Lu, Cheng-heng. "Between Bureaucrats and Bandits: The Rise of Zheng Zhilong and His Organization, the Zheng Ministry (Zheng Bu)." In *Sea Rovers, Silver, and Samurai: Maritime East Asia in Global History, 1550–1700*. Edited by Tonio Andrade and Xing Hang, 132–155. Honolulu: University of Hawai'i Press, 2016.

Lynch, Francis X. "Some Notes on a Brief Field Survey of the Hill People of Mt. Iriga, Camarines Sur, Philippines." *Primitive Man* 21, nos. 3–4 (1948): 65–73.

Macdonald, Charles. "Cleansing the Earth: The *Pangarris* Ceremony in Kulbi-Kanipaqan, Southern Palawan." *Philippine Studies* 45 (1997): 408–422.

Macdonald, Charles J. H. "Folk Catholicism and Pre-Spanish Religions in the Philippines." *Philippine Studies* 52, no. 1 (2004): 78–93.

Macdonald, Charles. "Invoking the Spirits in Palawan: Ethnography and Pragmatics." In *Sociolinguistics Today: International Perspectives*. Edited by Kingsley Bolton and Helen Kwok, 244–260. London: Routledge, 1992.

MacKay, Joseph. "Pirate Nations: Maritime Pirates as Escape Societies in Late Imperial China." *Social Science History* 37, no. 4 (2013): 551–573.

Majul, Cesar Adib. *Muslims in the Philippines*. Quezon City: University of the Philippines Press, 1973.

Mallari, Francisco. "Muslim Raids in Bicol, 1580–1792." *Philippine Studies* 34, no. 3 (1986): 257–286.

Mallari, Francisco A. "The Remontados of Isarog." *Kinaadman* 5 (1983): 103–117.

Mallari, Julieta C. "King Sinukwan Mythology and the Kapampangan Psyche." *Coolabah* 3 (2009): 227–234.

Malumbres, Fr. Julian, O. P. *Historia de Cagayan*. Manila: Tip. Linotype de Santo Tomás, 1918.

Manchado López, Marta María. "Cristianización y persistencia cultural en Filipinas: El caso de la provincia de la Laguna de Bay en la segunda mitad del siglo XVII." In *Filipinas y el Pacífico: Nueva miradas, nuevas reflexiones*. Edited by Salvador Bernabéu Albert, Carmen Mena García, and Emilio José Luque Azcona, 421–440. Sevilla: Editorial Universidad de Sevilla, 2016.

Manchado López, Marta María. "Los Zambales filipinos en la segunda mitad del siglo XVII: Evangelización, idolatría y sincretismo." In *Un mar de islas, un mar de gentes: población y diversidad en las islas Filipinas*. Edited by Marta María Manchado López and Miguel Luque Talaván, 145–174. Córdoba: Servicios de Publicaciones Universidad de Córdoba, 2014.

Martin, Marlon, Stephen Acabado, and Raymond Aquino Macapagal. "Hongan di Pa'ge: The Sacredness and Realism of Terraced Landscape in Ifugao Culture, Philippines." In *Indigenous Perspectives on Sacred Natural Sites: Culture, Governance and Conservation*. Edited by Jonathan Liljeblad and Bas Verschuuren, 167–179. London: Routledge, 2018.

Martínez-Valverde, Carlos. "Sobre la guerra contra moros, en filipinas, en el siglo XVI y en el XVII: expediciones de Don Sebastián Hurtado de Corcuera a Mindanao y Jolo." *Revista de Historia Militar* 29, no. 59 (1985): 9–56.

Matsui, Yoko. "The Debt-Servitude of Prostitutes in Japan during the Edo Period, 1600–1868." In *Bonded Labour and Debt in the Indian Ocean World*. Edited by Gwyn Campbell and Alessandro Stanziani, 173–186. London: Pickering & Chatto, 2013.

Matthew, Laura E., and Michel R. Oudijk, eds. *Indian Conquistadors: Indigenous Allies in the Conquest of Mesoamerica*. Norman: University of Oklahoma Press, 2007.

Mawson, Stephanie. "Convicts or *Conquistadores*? Spanish Soldiers in the Seventeenth-Century Pacific." *Past & Present* 232 (2016): 87–125.

Mawson, Stephanie. "Escaping Empire: Philippine Mountains and Indigenous Histories of Resistance." *American Historical Review* (forthcoming).

Mawson, Stephanie. "Philippine *Indios* in the Service of Empire: Indigenous Soldiers and Contingent Loyalty, 1600–1700." *Ethnohistory* 62, no. 2 (2016): 381–413.

Mawson, Stephanie. "Rebellion and Mutiny in the Mariana Islands, 1680–1690." *Journal of Pacific History* 50, no. 2 (2015): 128–148.

Mawson, Stephanie. "Slavery, Conflict, and Empire in the Seventeenth Century Philippines." In *Slavery and Bonded Labor in Asia, 1250–1900*. Edited by Richard B. Allen, 256–283. Leiden: Brill, 2022.

Mawson, Stephanie. "Unruly Plebeians and the *Forzado* System: Convict Transportation between New Spain and the Philippines during the Seventeenth Century." *Revista de Indias* 73, no. 259 (2013): 693–730.

McCarthy, Charles J. "Slaughter of Sangleys in 1639." *Philippine Studies* 18, no. 3 (1970): 659–667.

McCarthy, William J. "The Yards at Cavite: Shipbuilding in the Early Colonial Philippines." *International Journal of Maritime History* 7, no. 2 (1995): 149–162.

McCoy, Alfred. "Baylan, Animist Religion and Philippine Peasant Ideology." *Philippine Quarterly of Culture and Society* 10 (1982): 141–194.

McEnroe, Sean F. "Sites of Diplomacy, Violence, and Refuge: Topography and Negotiation in the Mountains of New Spain." *Americas* 69, no. 2 (2012): 179–202.

McKay, Deirdre. "Rethinking Locality in Ifugao: Tribes, Domains and Colonial Histories." *Philippine Studies* 53, no. 1 (2005): 459–490.

Mesquida Oliver, Juan. "La población de Manila y las capellanías de misas de los Españoles: Libro de registros, 1642–1672." *Revista de Indias* 70, no. 249 (2010): 469–500.

Metcalf, Alida C. *Go-Betweens and the Colonization of Brazil, 1500–1600*. Austin: University of Texas Press, 2005.

Miranda, José. "La función económica del encomendero en los orígenes del régimen colonial, Nueva España (1525–1531)." *Anales del Instituto Nacional de Antropología e Historia*, Sexta época (1939–1966), 2 (1946): 421–462.

Mojares, Resil B. *Waiting for Mariang Makiling: Essays in Philippine Cultural History.* Quezon City: Ateneo de Manila University Press, 2002

Montero y Vidal, José. *Historia de la piratería malayo-mahometana en Mindanao, Jolo y Borneo.* Madrid: M. Tello, 1888.

Mukherjee, Rila. "Mobility in the Bay of Bengal World: Medieval Raiders, Traders, States and the Slaves." *Indian Historical Review* 36, no. 1 (2009): 109–129.

Mumford, Jeremy Ravi. *Vertical Empire: The General Resettlement of Indians in the Colonial Andes.* Durham, NC: Duke University Press, 2012.

Mungello, D. E. *The Great Encounter of China and the West, 1500–1800.* Plymouth, UK: Rowman & Littlefield, 2009.

Neira, Eladio. *Conversion Methodology in the Philippines (1565–1665).* Manila: University of Santo Tomas, 1966.

Nesvig, Martin Austin. *Promiscuous Power: An Unorthodox History of New Spain.* Austin: University of Texas Press, 2018.

Newson, Linda. *Conquest and Pestilence in the Early Spanish Philippines.* Honolulu: University of Hawai'i Press, 2009.

Non, Domingo M. "Moro Piracy during the Spanish Period and Its Impact." *Southeast Asian Studies* 30, no. 4 (1993): 401–419.

Ollé, Manel. *La impresa de China: de la armada invencible al galeón de Manila.* Barcelona: Acantilado, 2002.

Ollé Rodríguez, Manel. "Manila in the Zheng Clan Maritime Networks." *Review of Culture* 29 (2009): 91–103.

Ollé, Manel. "La proyección de Fujian en Manila: los sangleyes del parián y el comercio de la Nao de China." In *Un océano de seda y plata: el universo económico del Galeón de Manila.* Edited by Salvador Bernabéu Albert and Carlos Martínez Shaw, 155–178. Sevilla: Consejo Superior de Investigaciones Científicas, 2013.

Oracion, Timoteo S. "The Magahats of Southern Negros, Philippines: Problems and Prospects." *Philippine Quarterly of Culture and Society* 2, nos. 1–2 (1974): 38–46.

Oropeza Keresey, Déborah. "La esclavitud asiática en el virreinato de la Nueva España, 1565–1673." *Historia Mexicana* 61, no. 1 (2011): 5–57.

Ortelli, Sara. "Entre desiertos y serranías: Población, espacio no controlado y fronteras permeables en el Septentrión novohispano tardocolonial." *Manuscrits. Revista d'Història Moderna* 32 (2014): 85–107.

O'Shaughnessy, Thomas J. "Philippine Islam and the Society of Jesus." *Philippine Studies* 4, no. 2 (1956): 215–239.

Otley Beyer, H. *Population of the Philippine Islands in 1916.* Manila: Philippine Education, 1917.

Oudijk, Michel R., and Matthew Restall. "Mesoamerican Conquistadors in the Sixteenth Century." In *Indian Conquistadors: Indigenous Allies in the Conquest of Mesoamerica.* Edited by Laura E. Matthew and Michel R. Oudijk, 28–64. Norman: University of Oklahoma Press, 2007.

Owen, Norman G. *Prosperity without Progress: Manila Hemp and Material Life in the Colonial Philippines.* Berkeley: University of California Press, 1984.

Palanco, Fernando. "Resistencia y rebelión indígena en Filipinas durante los primeros cien años de soberanía española (1565–1665)." In *España y el Pacífico:*

Legazpi. Vol. 2. Edited by Leoncio Cabrero, 71–98. Madrid: Sociedad Estatal de Conmemoraciones Culturales, 2004.

Panich, Lee M. "Archaeologies of Persistence: Reconsidering the Legacies of Colonialism in Native North America." *American Antiquity* 78, no. 1 (2013): 105–122.

Paredes, Oona. *A Mountain of Difference: The Lumad in Early Colonial Mindanao.* Ithaca, NY: Cornell Southeast Asia Program Publications, 2013.

Peckham, Robert. *Empires of Panic: Epidemics and Colonial Anxieties.* Hong Kong: Hong Kong University Press, 2015.

Pérez Morales, Edgardo. "La naturaleza como percepción cultural: Montes y selvas en el Nuevo Reino de Granada, siglo XVIII." *Fronteras de la Historia* 11 (2006): 57–85.

Phelan, John Leddy. "Free versus Compulsory Labor: Mexico and the Philippines 1540–1648." *Comparative Studies in Society and History* 1, no. 2 (1959): 189–201.

Phelan, John Leddy. *The Hispanization of the Philippines: Spanish Aims and Filipino Responses, 1565–1700.* Madison: University of Wisconsin Press, 1967.

Pin-Tsun, Chang. "Maritime Trade and Local Economy in Late Ming Fukien." In *Development and Decline of Fukien Province in the 17th and 18th Centuries.* Edited by Eduard B. Vermeer, 63–82. Leiden: Brill, 1990.

Prado, Fabricio. "The Fringes of Empires: Recent Scholarship on Colonial Frontiers and Borderlands in Latin America." *History Compass* 10, no. 4 (2012): 318–333.

Prieto Lucena, Ana María. *Filipinas durante el gobierno de Manrique de Lara, 1653–1663.* Sevilla: Escuela de Estudios Hispano-Americanos de Sevilla, 1984.

Ptak, Roderich, and Hu Baozhu. "Between Global and Regional Aspirations: China's Maritime Frontier and the Fujianese in the Early Seventeenth Century." *Journal of Asian History* 47, no. 2 (2013): 197–217.

Radding, Cynthia. "Colonial Spaces in the Fragmented Communities of Northern New Spain." In *Contested Spaces of Early America.* Edited by Juliana Barr and Edward Countryman, 115–141. Philadelphia: University of Pennsylvania Press, 2014.

Radding, Cynthia. *Wandering Peoples: Colonialism, Ethnic Spaces, and Ecological Frontiers in Northwestern Mexico, 1700–1850.* Durham, NC: Duke University Press, 1997.

Rafael, Vicente L. *Contracting Colonialism: Translation and Christian Conversion in Tagalog Society Under Early Spanish Rule.* Ithaca, NY: Cornell University Press, 1988.

Reed, Robert R. *Colonial Manila: The Context of Hispanic Urbanism and Process of Morphogenesis.* Berkeley: University of California Press, 1978.

Reid, Anthony. "'Closed' and 'Open' Slave Systems in Pre-Colonial Southeast Asia." In *Slavery, Bondage and Dependency in Southeast Asia.* Edited by Anthony Reid, 156–181. St. Lucia: University of Queensland Press, 1983.

Reid, Anthony. "Introduction: Slavery and Bondage in Southeast Asian History." In *Slavery, Bondage and Dependency in Southeast Asia.* Edited by Anthony Reid, 1–43. St. Lucia: University of Queensland Press, 1983.

Reid, Anthony. *Slavery, Bondage and Dependency in Southeast Asia.* St. Lucia: University of Queensland Press, 1983.

Reid, Anthony. *Southeast Asia in the Age of Commerce, 1450–1680*. Vol. 2, *Expansion and Crisis*. New Haven, CT: Yale University Press, 1993.

Ren-Chuan, Lin. "Fukien's Private Sea Trade in the 16th and 17th Centuries." In *Development and Decline of Fukien Province in the 17th and 18th Centuries*. Edited by E. B. Vermeer, translated by Barend ter Haar, 163–216. Leiden: E. J. Brill, 1990.

Reséndez, Andrés. "An Early Abolitionist Crusade." *Ethnohistory* 64, no.1 (2017): 19–40.

Restall, Matthew. *Seven Myths of the Spanish Conquest*. Oxford: Oxford University Press, 2021.

Reyes, Ramon C. "Religious Experiences in the Philippines: From Mythos through Lagos to Kairos." *Philippine Studies* 33, no. 2 (1985): 203–221.

Reyes, Raquel A. G. "Flaunting It: How the Galleon Trade Made Manila, circa 1571–1800." *Early American Studies: An Interdisciplinary Journal* 15, no. 4 (2017): 683–713.

Reyes, Raquel A. G. "Sodomy in Seventeenth-Century Manila: The Luck of a Mandarin from Taiwan." In *Sexual Diversity in Asia, c. 600–1950*. Edited by Raquel A. G. Reyes and William G. Clarence-Smith, 127–140. New York: Routledge, 2012.

Rocher Salas, Adriana. "La Montaña: Espacio de Rebelión, Fe y Conquista." *Estudios de Historia Novohispana* 50 (2014): 45–76.

Rodriguez, Felice Noelle. "Juan de Salcedo Joins the Native Form of Warfare." *Journal of the Economic and Social History of the Orient* 46, no. 2 (2003): 143–164.

Rodríguez, Leandro. "El 'Tornaviaje': motivaciones de la ida y vuelta desde Nueva España a Filipinas y viceversa." In *Caminería Hispánica: Actas del III Congreso Internacional de Caminería Hispánica, Celebrado en Morelia (Michoacán), México, Julio 1996*. Edited by Manuel Criado de Val, 315–326. Guadalajara, Spain: Aache Ediciones, 1996.

Rood, Steven. "Summary Report on a Research Programme: Issues on Cordillera Autonomy." *Sojourn: Journal of Social Issues in Southeast Asia* 7, no. 2 (1992): 305–325.

Roque, Ricardo. *Headhunting and Colonialism: Anthropology and the Circulation of Human Skulls in the Portuguese Empire, 1870–1930*. New York: Palgrave Macmillan, 2010.

Rosaldo, Michelle Zimbalist. *Knowledge and Passion: Ilongot Notions of Self and Social Life*. Cambridge: Cambridge University Press, 1980.

Rosaldo, Renato. *Ilongot Headhunting, 1883–1974: A Study in Society and History*. Stanford, CA: Stanford University Press, 1980.

Saleeby, Najeeb M. *History of Sulu*. Manila: Bureau of Public Printing, 1908.

Saleeby, Najeeb M. *Studies in Moro History, Law, and Religion*. Manila: Bureau of Public Printing, 1905.

Salgado, Pedro V. *Cagayan Valley and the Eastern Cordillera, 1581–1898*. Quezon City: Rex Commercial, 2002.

Sánchez Fuertes, Cayetano. "La Iglesia y sus relaciones con los Filipinos en los siglos XVI y XVII." In *España y el Pacífico: Legazpi*. Vol. 2. Edited by Leoncio Cabrero, 319–357. Madrid: Sociedad Estatal de Conmemoraciones Culturales, 2004.

Sánchez Gómez, Luis Ángel. "Las élites nativas y la construcción colonial de Filipinas (1565–1789)." In *España y el Pacífico: Legazpi*. Vol. 2. Edited by Leoncio Cabrero, 37–70. Madrid: Sociedad Estatal de Conmemoraciones Culturales, S.A., 2004.

Santamaria, Alberto, O. P. "The Chinese Parian (El Parian de los Sangleyes)." In *The Chinese in the Philippines, 1570–1770*. Edited by Alfonso Felix Jr., 67–118. Manila: Solidaridad, 1966.

Santiago, Luciano P. R. "The Filipino Indio Encomenderos (ca. 1620–1711)." *Philippine Quarterly of Culture and Society* 18, no. 3 (1990): 162–184.

Santiago, Luciano P. R. "The Houses of Lakandula, Matandá and Solimán (1571–1898): Genealogy and Group Identity." *Philippine Quarterly of Culture and Society* 18, no. 1 (1990): 39–73.

Saunders, Graham. *A History of Brunei*. Kuala Lumpur: Oxford University Press, 1994.

Schaffer, Simon, Lissa Roberts, Kapil Raj, and James Delbourgo, eds. *The Brokered World: Go-Betweens and Global Intelligence, 1770–1820*. Sagamore Beach, MA: Science History Publications, 2009.

Scheans, Daniel J. "A Remontado Legend from Ilocos Norte." *Philippine Studies* 15, no. 3 (1967): 496–497.

Schneider, Tsim D. "Placing Refuge and the Archaeology of Indigenous Hinterlands in Colonial California." *American Antiquity* 80, no. 4 (2015): 695–713.

Schottenhammer, Angela. "Slaves and Forms of Slavery in Late Imperial China (Seventeenth to Early Twentieth Centuries)." *Slavery & Abolition* 24, no. 2 (2003): 143–154.

Schreurs, Peter. *Caraga Antigua, 1521–1910: The Hispanization and Christianization of Agusan, Surigao and East Davao*. Cebu City: University of San Carlos, 1989.

Schumacher, John N., S. J. *Growth and Decline: Essays on Philippine Church History*. Quezon City: Ateneo de Manila University Press, 2009.

Schumacher, John N. "Syncretism in Philippine Catholicism: Its Historical Causes." *Philippine Studies* 32 (1984): 251–272.

Schurz, William Lytle. *The Manila Galleon: The Romantic History of the Spanish Galleons Trading between Manila and Acapulco*. New York: E. P. Dutton, 1959.

Scott, James C. *The Art of Not Being Governed: An Anarchist History of Upland Southeast Asia*. New Haven, CT: Yale University Press, 2009.

Scott, William Henry. *Barangay: Sixteenth-Century Philippine Culture and Society*. Quezon City: Ateneo de Manila University Press, 1994.

Scott, William Henry. "Class Structure in the Unhispanized Philippines." *Philippine Studies* 72, no. 2 (1797): 137–159.

Scott, William Henry. *Cracks in the Parchment Curtain and Other Essays in Philippine History*. Quezon City: New Day, 1982.

Scott, William Henry. *The Discovery of the Igorots: Spanish Contacts with the Pagans of Northern Luzon*. Quezon City: New Day, 1974.

Scott, William Henry. "An Historian Looks into the Philippine Kaleidoscope." *Philippine Studies* 24, no. 2 (1976): 220–227.

Scott, William Henry. "The Igorot: An Integrated Cultural Minority." *Philippine Sociological Review* 20, no. 4 (1972): 356–360.

Scott, William Henry. "Igorot Responses to Spanish Aims: 1576–1896." *Philippine Studies* 18, no. 4 (1970): 695–717.

Scott, William Henry. *Looking for the Prehispanic Filipino and Other Essays in Philippine History*. Quezon City: New Day, 1992.

Scott, William Henry. "*Oripun* and *Alipin* in the Sixteenth Century Philippines." In *Slavery, Bondage and Dependency in Southeast Asia*. Edited by Anthony Reid, 138–155. St. Lucia: University of Queensland Press, 1983.

Scott, William Henry. *Prehispanic Source Materials for the Study of Philippine History*. Quezon City: New Day, 1984.

Scott, William Henry. *A Sagada Reader*. Quezon City: New Day, 1988.

Scott, William Henry. *Slavery in the Spanish Philippines*. Manila: De la Salle University Press, 1991.

Scott, William Henry. "The Word Igorot." *Philippine Studies* 10, no. 2 (1962): 234–248.

Seijas, Tatiana. *Asian Slaves in Colonial Mexico: From Chinos to Indios*. Cambridge: Cambridge University Press, 2014.

Seijas, Tatiana. "The Portuguese Slave Trade to Spanish Manila: 1580–1640." *Itinerario* 31, no. 1 (2008): 19–38.

Sherman, William L. *Forced Native Labor in Sixteenth-Century Central America*. Lincoln: University of Nebraska Press, 1979.

Simpson, Thomas. *The Frontier in British India: Space, Science, and Power in the Nineteenth Century*. Cambridge: Cambridge University Press, 2021.

Stern, Steve J. *Peru's Indian Peoples and the Challenge of Spanish Conquest: Huamanga to 1640*. Madison: University of Wisconsin Press, 1982.

St. John, Rachel. "Imperial Spaces in Pekka Hämäläinen's 'The Comanche Empire.'" *History and Theory* 52, no. 1 (2013): 75–80.

Stoler, Ann Laura. *Along the Archival Grain: Epistemic Anxieties and Colonial Common Sense*. Princeton, NJ: Princeton University Press, 2010.

Stoler, Anne Laura, and Frederick Cooper. "Between Metropole and Colony: Rethinking a Research Agenda." In *Tensions of Empire: Colonial Cultures in a Bourgeois World*. Edited by Frederick Cooper and Ann Laura Stoler, 1–56. Berkeley: University of California Press, 1997.

Tortorici, Zeb. *Sins Against Nature: Sex and Archives in Colonial New Spain*. Durham, NC: Duke University Press, 2018.

Tremml, Birgit M. "The Global and the Local: Problematic Dynamics of the Triangular Trade in Early Modern Manila." *Journal of World History* 23, no. 3 (2012): 555–586.

Tremml-Werner, Birgit. *Spain, China, and Japan in Manila, 1571–1644: Local Comparisons and Global Connections*. Amsterdam: Amsterdam University Press, 2015.

Van den Muijzenberg, Otto. "A Short History of Social Connections between the Philippines and the Netherlands." *Philippine Studies* 51, no. 3 (2003): 339–374.

Van Deusen, Nancy E. *Global Indios: The Indigenous Struggle for Justice in Sixteenth-Century Spain*. Durham, NC: Duke University Press, 2015.

Villiers, John. "Manila and Maluku: Trade and Warfare in the Eastern Archipelago, 1580–1640." *Philippines Studies* 34, no. 2 (1986): 146–161.

Wagner, Kim A. "'Treading Upon Fires': The 'Mutiny'-Motif and Colonial Anxieties in British India." *Past & Present* 218, no. 1 (2013): 159–197.

Warren, James Francis. "The Balangingi Samal: The Global Economy, Maritime Raiding and Diasporic Identities in the Nineteenth-Century Philippines." *Asian Ethnicity* 4, no. 1 (2003): 7–29.

Warren, James Francis. *Iranun and Balangingi: Globalization, Maritime Raiding and the Birth of Ethnicity*. Singapore: Singapore University Press, 2002.

Warren, James. "The Iranun and Balangingi Slaving Voyage: Middle Passages in the Sulu Zone." In *Many Middle Passages: Forced Migration and the Making of the Modern World*. Edited by Emma Christopher, Cassandra Pybus, and Marcus Rediker, 52–71. Berkeley: University of California Press, 2007.

Warren, James Francis. *The Sulu Zone: The World Capitalist Economy and the Historical Imagination*. Amsterdam: VU University Press, 1998.

Weber, David J. *Bárbaros: Spaniards and Their Savages in the Age of Enlightenment*. New Haven, CT: Yale University Press, 2005.

White, Richard. *The Middle Ground: Indians, Empires, and Republics in the Great Lakes Region, 1650–1815*. Cambridge: Cambridge University Press, 1991.

Williams, Caroline A. "Opening New Frontiers in Colonial Spanish American History: New Perspectives on Indigenous-Spanish Interactions on the Margins of Empire." *History Compass* 6, no. 4 (2008): 1121–1139.

Wills, John E. Jr. "Maritime Europe and the Ming." In *China and Maritime Europe, 1500–1800: Trade, Settlement, Diplomacy, and Missions*. Edited by John E. Wills Jr., 24–77. Cambridge: Cambridge University Press, 2012.

Woods, Damon L. "Out of the Silence, the Men of Naujan Speak: Tagalog Texts from the Seventeenth Century." *Philippine Studies* 63, no. 3 (2015): 303–340.

Yang, Shu-Yuan. "Headhunting, Christianity, and History among the Bugkalot (Ilongot) of Northern Luzon, Philippines." *Philippine Studies* 59, no. 2 (2011): 155–186.

Yannakakis, Yanna. *The Art of Being In-Between: Native Intermediaries, Indian Identity, and Local Rule in Colonial Oaxaca*. Durham, NC: Duke University Press, 2008.

Yuste López, Carmen. *El comercio de la Nueva España con Filipinas, 1590–1785*. México: Departamento de Investigaciones Históricas, 1984.

Zafra, Nicolas. *The Colonization of the Philippines and the Beginnings of the Spanish City of Manila*. Manila: National Historical Commission, 1974.

Index

Locators in *italics* refer to tables and illustrations. Locators in the form 211n58 refer to note 58 on page 211. As the geography of the Philippines is central to this book, place names have been more extensively indexed than usual and smaller locations within the Philippines have their province or region included in their heading.